THE WONDER OF THE NILE

The confluence of two great rivers brought the desert sands to life – thus providing the backdrop to Egypt's rich history

Egypt only exists thanks to a bit of geographical nonsense. The line of least resistance for water escaping from two African lakes 1,600km (1,000 miles) apart, one of them actually straddling the equator, was not a quick dive into the Indian Ocean and Red Sea that lay close at hand. Instead, one went off as if looking to join the Congo River for its immense journey west to the Atlantic. The other went roughly south for hundreds of kilometres before that, too, proved to be a feint. Between them, the two rivers logged some 5,600km (3,500 miles) of idle wandering through Ethiopia and Uganda before combining their forces in Sudan's capital, Khartoum, for a 3,200km (2,000-mile) mercy mission through what would otherwise have been one of the most barren places on earth.

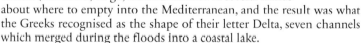

The Nile not only survived but at the hottest and driest time of every year conjured up a tidal wave of flood water. The sheer volume of silt which the flood brought defied comprehension. Moreover, it was silt of great fertility, capable of turning a vast tract of desert into an agricultural paradise. In southern (Upper) Egypt, the miracle was confined to a narrow ribbon along the banks but, with only 160km (100 miles) to go, the river seemed in several minds about where to empty into the Mediterranean, and the result was what the Greeks recognised as the shape of their letter Delta, seven channels which merged during the floods into a coastal lake.

The decision taken by the river to follow a leisurely trans-continental route is the major contributing factor in the development of Egypt as a tourism destination. Without the Nile, this great African nation would not possess the numerous wonders for which it is known. The Pyramids and all that followed were built on the unique combination of effortless subsistence, efficient communications and transport. Prevailing winds blew vessels up the Nile towards Aswan, the current brought them down. The engineers who constructed the Pyramids did not have the wheel; as long as they stayed close to the river, they didn't need it. ❑

PRECEDING PAGES: feluccas on the Nile at Aswan; relief at the temple of Bayt Al Wali, at Kalabsha; camels are still the favoured beast of burden.
LEFT: bread-making in a traditional oven for a restaurant in Giza.
ABOVE: a cruise ship on Lake Nasser; river life.

THE NILE FROM SOURCE TO DELTA

The Nile is the world's longest river, stretching 6,695km (4,160 miles) from source to sea, acting as a lifeline for millions of people along its journey

The Nile is probably the world's most important river in terms of human dependence. Over 100 million people rely on the Nile for food, water and employment in four countries of Africa: Ethiopia, Uganda, Sudan and Egypt.

In reality two rivers in one, the Nile has two tributaries, the Blue Nile and the White Nile. Fed by numerous other streams, they cross Africa from Ethiopia and Uganda to meet at the Sudanese capital of Khartoum. From here, the river continues north to the Mediterranean coast, passing by celebrated cities past and present, including Aswan, Luxor (Thebes), Cairo and Alexandria.

The Blue Nile

Of the two major tributaries that make up the Nile, the Blue Nile is by far the more integral of the two. Despite being shorter in length than the White Nile at only 1,450km (900 miles), the Blue Nile contributes over 80 percent of the total volume of water that ends up in the world's longest river.

> *Almost 95 percent of the Egyptian population lives within 20km (12 miles) of the Nile. Current estimates predict that the number of people in Egypt will rise to 121 million by 2050.*

A product of the Ethiopian Highlands, the Blue Nile emerges out of Lake Tana to embark on its journey to Khartoum in Sudan. The river's strength is reliant on the seasonal rains.

LEFT: a sphinx of Rameses II at the temple of Wadi Al Sebua. **RIGHT:** locals cross Lake Nasser.

Before the construction of a lowhead dam, the size of the lake could vary by as much as 500 sq km (200 sq miles). Today, the dam regulates the water as it flows out of the lake and into the river before heading 30km (19 miles) south to the famous Tis Abbai (Blue Nile) Falls and a hydroelectric generating station.

A popular tourist destination, Lake Tana is home to numerous sites of cultural significance to the Ethiopian Orthodox Church. For further details, *see the Blue Nile feature on page 144*.

Leaving Lake Tana

After plummeting over the falls, the Nile continues on its course through a deep canyon running southeast before looping in a semicircle around the Choke Mountains until it reaches the Sudanese border and the plains of Sennar. It is during this stretch of the river's course that it is fed by numerous tributaries, including the Bashilo, the Jamma and – the largest of them all – the Didessa, which meets the Blue Nile after flowing down from the Kaffa hills.

The river passes through the Blue Nile State of Sudan at this point, a region known for its fertile woodland savannah and significant rainfall. Civil war in the Sudan heavily affected this part of the nation, displacing many of the long-term residents. Thousands remain in refugee camps on both sides of the border awaiting repatriation. Travel here is not recommended due to the danger of land mines throughout the state.

The Blue Nile finally meets the White Nile at Khartoum, the first large city the Nile passes through on its journey to the Mediterranean. Khartoum today has a population of just over 1 million and is enjoying economic prosperity thanks to Sudan's oil revenues.

The White Nile

The White Nile begins its journey to Khartoum north out of the waters of Lake Victoria at the city of Jinja in Uganda. A century ago, Jinja was a minor fishing village with a long history as a trading centre. Today, the city is the second-busiest commercial centre in Uganda. A scruffy little town, it boasts a population of just over 80,000, the bulk of whom work on the hydro-electric projects or survive by fishing.

Rock steady

In the local language, Jinja means "rock", so called as this is one of the few places where the Nile could easily be crossed using the smooth,

ABOVE: view of the Blue Nile (on right) flowing into the While Nile at Khartoum, Sudan. **ABOVE RIGHT:** egret on Elephantine Island. **RIGHT:** the Nile Delta from space.

THE SENNAR DAM

The Aswan High Dam may be the most famous of the dams built on the Nile, but it is not the only one. The Sennar Dam, completed in 1925, was Sudan's first attempt to harness the power of the river. While it is overshadowed in terms of energy output by the Roseires Dam a few kilometres away, it remains integral to Sudan's infrastructure development.

Its purpose was to create a reservoir in support of a scheme designed to transform the triangle of land between the confluence of the Blue and White Niles into viable agricultural land. The plan worked and to this very day continues to bring water to remote farms using a series of canals and ditches.

flat rocks scattered like stepping stones across its width and along the riverbanks. In their day, the rocks acted as a natural barrier to help regulate the flow of water and were ideal launching pads for ferries and river crossings.

The first attempt to build a dam across the Nile was in 1011, when the Fatimid caliph summoned his engineer, Ibn Al Haytham. Realising the job was impossible, he feigned madness to escape the caliph's anger.

In 1954, the completion of the Nalubaale Hydroelectric Power Station (or Owen Falls Dam as it was then known) resulted in the submergence of the flat rocks that gave Jinja its name. It is at this point that the White Nile's journey officially begins.

To the northwest the river flows until it reaches Lake Kyoga in the centre of Uganda. Underdeveloped as a tourist centre, Lake Kyoga boasts ample birdlife, primate and hippopotamus viewing opportunities and a large population of Nile crocodiles.

For better and more guaranteed wildlife, go further along the river to Murchison Falls National Park, the largest national park in Uganda *(see page 161)*.

Into the swamp

North and west the river continues where it passes into Sudan. After crossing rapids and entering a large plain, the White Nile reaches the Sudd, a vast swamp that ranges in size drastically depending on the volume of rains each season. Over 400 different species of migrating birds visit the Sudd every year, drawn here by the fact the area is one of the few to offer fresh water supplies. When the water finally emerges from the Sudd, it flows towards Khartoum, where it meets the Blue Nile to embark on the last stage of its journey.

From Khartoum to Cairo

After the Nile flows north out of Khartoum, it loops back on itself and north again in an "S" shape until it reaches the heart of Nubia – an arid region that has seen human civilisation

SAVING THE SEDIMENT

The completion of the Aswan Dam in 1970 has been both a blessing and a curse for the Egyptian people. No longer prone to the annual floods that would inundate the nation and threaten riverbank dwellers every year, the Nile is now a tamed beast.

Unfortunately, the erection of the dam now means that the nutrient-rich sediment that acted as a natural fertiliser no longer reaches farmers living downstream, as the dam prevents it from passing through. Farmers living north of the dam now have to rely on artificial fertiliser, which is not only more expensive, but also more environmentally damaging over the long term.

Sediment loss is particularly critical in the region of the Delta where the lack of sediment is creating challenges with erosion and land shrinkage. Homes that were once on the Mediterranean coast are now completely submerged as the land is lapped away by the tide with no sediment arriving to replenish the lost soil. With no barrier against the sea, the river is facing increased salinity, causing major damage to soil quality.

dating as far back as the Neolithic period. This area was once home to the Nubian Kingdom *(see page 140)*, a civilisation that stretched from the First Cataract (the rapids near Aswan) down to the Sixth Cataract (between Khartoum and Meroe in Sudan).

> *There are 34 million inhabitants living in the Delta, a region approximately 25,000 sq km (9,600 sq miles) in size, making it one of the most densely populated agricultural zones in the world.*

to numerous transplanted Nubians moved here by the government to repay them for lost lands. (For information on Lake Nasser and Nubia, *see page 137.*)

Ever north the river continues after leaving Aswan, passing Luxor and the industrial towns of Middle Egypt until it reaches the Egyptian capital of Cairo. A look at a satellite image of Egypt reveals a tiny strip of green slicing through the impenetrable desert over the course of this phase of its journey. This is where canals and irrigation channels have been cut away from the river, drawing water for farming – and returning waste, chemicals and sewage.

The Aswan High Dam ripped the heart out of the Nubian people when it was completed, as the resulting reservoir flooded the bulk of the traditional Nubian homeland. Now known as Lake Nasser, the reservoir is the world's largest man-made lake, stretching 550km (342 miles) in length and 35km (22 miles) wide at its broadest point.

The waters leave Lake Nasser at the Aswan High Dam, located a few kilometres south of the city of Aswan. A popular market town, Aswan was strategically important as a frontier base that guarded the Egyptian heartland against attacks by Nubian warriors to the south during the days of the Ancient Egyptian empire. Today, Aswan is a tourist destination and home

The Delta

North of Cairo, the Nile spreads out into numerous channels as it drains into the Mediterranean Sea. Stretching from Alexandria in the west to Port Said in the east, the Nile covers 240km (150 miles) of coastline. Two main distributaries lead the Nile to the coast, referred to by the names of the ports near which they exit into the Mediterranean: Damietta and Rosetta. It is estimated that at current rates of erosion, the Delta will have completely disappeared by the year 2500. ❑

Above: heading towards Amadah Temple, Lake Nasser. **Right:** in its middle reaches, the White Nile meanders through the Sudd, the world's largest marshland.

DECISIVE DATES

EARLY DYNASTIC PERIOD

3100–2649 BC
1st–2nd dynasties. Memphis founded as capital of Egypt. Rulers buried at Saqqarah.

OLD KINGDOM

2649–2134 BC
3rd–6th dynasties. Construction of Djoser Complex, Pyramids at Dahshur, Giza and Abu Rawash and Sun-Temples at Abu Sir and Saqqarah.

FIRST INTERMEDIATE PERIOD

2134–2040 BC
7th–10th dynasties. Collapse of central government.

MIDDLE KINGDOM

2040–1640 BC
11th–13th dynasties. Reunification by Theban rulers. Pyramids at Dahshur, Al-Lisht, Mazghunah, South Saqqarah and Hawarah built.

SECOND INTERMEDIATE PERIOD

1640–1532 BC
14th–17th dynasties. Country divided. Asiatics ("Hyksos") rule in Delta.

NEW KINGDOM

1550–1070 BC
18th–20th dynasties. Egypt reunified under Theban kings. Famous pharaohs from the period include Akhenaten (1353–35), Tutankhamun (1333–23) and Rameses II.

THIRD INTERMEDIATE PERIOD

1070–712 BC
21st–24th dynasties. Egypt divided among several rulers.

LATE PERIOD

712–332 BC
Slow decline under a series of foreign rulers.

PTOLEMAIC EMPIRE

332–30 BC
Alexander the Great conquers Egypt. Ptolemy I rules as governor after Alexander's death in 323 BC, then after 304 BC as first king of dynasty that ends with Cleopatra VII.

ROMAN PERIOD

30 BC–AD 324
Rule from Rome. Spread of Christianity from 251 onwards.

BYZANTINE PERIOD

324–642
Rule from Constantinople (Byzantium).

324–619
Christianity made state religion, 379. Coptic (Egyptian) Church separates from Catholic Church, 451.

619–29
Third Persian occupation.

629–39
Re-establishment of Byzantine rule.

ARAB EMPIRE

642–868
Arab conquest (639–42) under Amr Ibn Al As. Rule by governors on behalf of caliph.

TULUNID EMPIRE

878–905
Ahmed Ibn Tulun, Turkish governor, declares independence, founds Al Qatai.

ABBASID INTERIM

905–935
Reassertion of power from Baghdad.

FATIMID EMPIRE

969–1171
Cairo's first golden age. Al Azhar mosque built (970–2).

996–1021
Reign of Al Hakim, "The Mad Caliph". Mosque of Al Hakim completed.

1168
Frankish invasion.

AYYUBID EMPIRE

1171–1250
Saladin (Salah Ad Din) and his successors conduct campaigns against Franks and other invaders.

BAHRI MAMLUK EMPIRE

1250–1382
Era of expansion and prosperity. Some 100 monuments remain as evidence.

1260–79
Reign of Baybars Al Bunduqdari. Extension of empire from Sudan to Anatolia.

1279–90
Reign of Qalawun.

1293–1340
Three reigns of An Nasir Muhammad Ibn Qalawun. Architectural splendour in Cairo.

1340–82
Reigns of heirs of An Nasir Muhammad. Pillage and destruction of Alexandria by Franks, 1365.

BURJI MAMLUK EMPIRE

1382–1517
Continuation of massive building programmes under the rule of 23 sultans.

OTTOMAN PERIOD

1517–1914
Ottoman rule through 106 governors (1517–1798). French invasion and occupation (1798–1805).

FAR LEFT TOP: Step Pyramid at Saqqarah. ABOVE: the Russian Baltic fleet passes through the Suez Canal on its way east to fight in the Russo-Japanese War, 1904. RIGHT: Egypt captain Ahmed Hassan and his goalkeeper celebrate winning the African Cup of Nations, 2010.

1854–63
Suez Canal concession granted. Cairo–Alexandria rail link, Nile steamship service opens river to mass tourism.

1863–79
Suez Canal opened (1869).

1882
British Occupation.

1892–1914
Construction of monuments including Egyptian Museum and Rifai Mosque.

POST-1914

1914–17
British Protectorate declared, martial law instituted.

1917–22
Revolution of 1919.

1922–36
Constitutional monarchy established.

1936–52
During World War II Egypt is neutral, but reoccupied by Britain.

1952–53
July Revolution deposes King Faruq in favour of his son, then declares Egypt a republic. Gamal Abdel Nasser becomes leader.

1956
Nationalisation of Suez Canal.

1967
Six Day War against Israel.

1970
Anwar Sadat succeeds Nasser as president.

1973
The October War against Israel.

1974–7
Open Door Policy, political liberalisation.

1979
Camp David accords lead to peace treaty with Israel.

1981
President Anwar Sadat assassinated. Hosni Mubarak becomes president.

1996–8
Escalation of Islamic terrorism, 58 tourists killed in Luxor.

2005
President Mubarak amends constitution to permit the first free presidential elections.

2007
Political parties prohibited from using religion as a basis for activity or policy.

2009
Global recession hits Egypt. Inbound tourism numbers drop by around 5 percent.

2010
President Mubarak renews emergency laws for a further two years. Egypt become the first football team to win the Africa Cup three times in a row.

FROM THE PALAEOLITHIC TO THE PTOLEMIES

The Nile has always been a potent symbol of Nature's cycle of life, death and rebirth. Its vast length gave rise to some of the world's first great civilisations, whose own epic rise and fall is attested to in remains of breathtaking beauty

Glance down at the Nile from the air and you will receive a stark lesson in the evolution of human communities. Were it not for the Nile, Egypt as such would not exist. A green strip borders the river; the rest is desert. Egypt is a land of unusual geographic isolation, with well defined boundaries. To the east and west are vast deserts. To the north is the Mediterranean Sea. To the south there was, before the construction of the High Dam at Aswan, a formidable barrier of igneous rock, beyond which lay the barren lands of Kush and Nubia, and beyond them the scattered kingdoms of Ethiopia. Within these recognisable boundaries, however, was a land divided: Upper Egypt extended from Aswan to a point just south of modern Cairo and was largely barren, apart from a narrow strip of land flanking the river; the Delta, or Lower Egypt, spread from the point where the Nile fanned into a fertile triangle some 200km (125 miles) before reaching the Mediterranean Sea. Linking Upper and Lower Egypt was the vital artery, the River Nile.

> *Since rainfall in Egypt is almost nil, the people depended on the river for their crops; and it was ultimately on the fertility of the soil that ancient Egyptian civilisation was based.*

Before the Nile was harnessed by technology, the annual flood, a result of the monsoon rains on the Ethiopian tableland, spilled into the flood plain, leaving a thick layer of alluvial soil.

LEFT: fishermen on the Nile at Luxor. **RIGHT:** lush flowers en route to the Temple of Philae.

Early Egypt

The lower Nile Valley was first inhabited by hunters who tracked game across northern Africa and eastern Sudan, later joined by nomadic tribes of Asiatic origin who filtered into Egypt in sporadic migrations across the Sinai Peninsula and the Red Sea. Late Palaeolithic settlements (*c.*12000–8000 BC) reveal that both these newcomers and the indigenous inhabitants had a hunting-and-gathering economy. Their lives became bound to the ebb and flow of the annual flood: as the water rose each year in July, they were obliged to draw back from the banks, and by August, when the waters swept across the lowlands, they took to the highlands and hunted antelope, hartebeest, wild ass and gazelle, with lances, bows and arrows. In the first half of October the river attained its highest level, and thereafter began to subside, leaving lagoons and streams that became natural reservoirs for fish.

A variety of plants grew in the fertile deposit of silt. During this season of plenty, hunting activity was at a minimum. From January to March seasonal pools dried out and fishing was limited, but in the swampy areas near the river there were turtles, rodents and clams. At low Nile, from April to June, game scattered, food became scarce and hunting was pursued once more. Despite their diverse origins, therefore, there was a natural tendency for the people to group together during the "season of abundance" when there was plenty of food to eat and then to split up into smaller groups during the low-flood season or during periods of drought.

Agriculture was introduced into the lower Nile Valley in about 5000 BC. Once grain could be cultivated and stored, people were assured of a regular food supply, an important factor in the movement away from primitive society and towards civilisation. Agriculture freed up time and economic resources, which resulted in population increase and craft specialisation. Polished stone axes, well-made knives and a variety of pottery vessels were produced, as well as ivory combs and slate palettes, on which paint for body decoration was prepared.

Slowly, assimilation took place. Some villages may have merged as their boundaries expanded, or small groups of people may have gravitated towards larger ones and started to trade with them. The affairs of the various communities became tied to major settlements, which undoubtedly represented the richest and most powerful. This tendency towards political unity occurred in both Upper and Lower Egypt. In Upper Egypt, the chief settlement was Nekhen, where the leader wore a conical White Crown and took the sedge plant as his emblem. In the

Resurrection Myth

People observed that the gifts of their naturally irrigated valley depended on a dual force. The life-giving rays of the sun that caused a crop to grow could also cause it to shrivel and die, while the river that invigorated the soil could destroy whatever lay in its path or bring famine. The two phenomena also shared in a pattern of death and rebirth: the sun "died" in the west each evening and was "reborn" in the east the following morning. Resurrection myths of this kind were central to the beliefs and customs of most societies throughout the ancient world, and among the people of the Nile Valley this belief would have been intensified by the annual flooding of the river.

Delta or Lower Egypt, the capital was Buto; the leader wore the characteristic Red Crown and adopted the bee as his symbol.

Beyond Aswan

While the might of pharaonic Egypt emerged in this area of famed agricultural productivity, it was a very different story upstream of Aswan, the location of the First Cataract (rapids) of the Nile. Here the valley is far less hospitable, with only isolated pockets of arable land along the riverbanks and on the islands.

Nonetheless, centres of food production emerged around Khartoum during the Neolithic era (3800–3400 BC) and across the vast area of Sudan known as Kush. With six cataracts between central Sudan and southern Egypt, the Nile was never an ideal waterway for communications, and its winding course made the valley a lengthy and impractical land route. North–south traffic was often obliged to leave the river for considerable stretches, turning whole areas into backwaters. However, Kush was rich in minerals, and these, plus its gold deposits and the desire to monopolise Nile traffic, were eventually to attract the attention of their powerful northern neighbours. Over the centuries Egypt and Kush were to clash time and again, with the Kushites even taking over as pharaohs in the 8th century BC *(see page 36)*.

LEFT: Roman mosaic depicting the flooding of the Nile, at Palestrina, near Rome. **ABOVE:** pyramids in the Meroe desert, north of Khartoum, part of the Kush Kingdom.

Ethiopia and Eritrea

At Khartoum in Sudan the great river divides into the White Nile and Blue Nile, a source of vexation to the would-be discoverers of the source of the Nile *(see page 78)*. The lands to the south and east beyond Kush and Nubia, in present-day Ethiopia and Eritrea, were referred to by the earliest traders as Punt and Yam, and there is evidence that some trade was conducted both on overland routes and via the Blue Nile and the River Atbara, a tributary of the Nile between the Fifth and Sixth cataracts, between the Egyptians and the people of these mysterious lands. Reliefs at Thebes record one such visit during the reign of Queen Hatshepsut in *c.*1495 BC, in which the trading part brought back myrrh, ivory, gold and other precious goods.

The Egyptian Old Kingdom

Unification of Upper and Lower Egypts has been ascribed to Narmer (Menes), around 3100 BC, who set up his capital at Memphis, at the apex of the Delta. He stands at the beginning of Egypt's ancient history, which was divided by Manetho, an Egyptian historian (*c.*280 BC), into

30 royal dynasties starting at Menes and ending with Alexander the Great.

The dynasties were subsequently combined and grouped into three main periods: the Old Kingdom or Pyramid Age, the Middle Kingdom and the New Kingdom. Although further divided by modern historians, these periods remain the basis of ancient Egyptian chronology.

The Old Kingdom, from the 3rd to the 6th dynasties (2686–2181 BC), is considered by many historians as the high-water mark of achievement. A series of vigorous and able monarchs established a highly organised, centralised government. These kings ruled during a period of great refinement, which saw rising productivity in all fields. Cattle and raw materials, including gold and copper, were taken in donkey caravans from Sudan and Nubia. Sinai was exploited for mineral wealth and a fleet of ships sailed to Byblos (on the coast of Lebanon) to import cedar wood.

The Pyramids

There are nearly 100 pyramids of different shapes and sizes along a 60km (100-mile) stretch of the Nile, but it is the trio of large pyramids on the Giza Plateau near Cairo that fill the imagination even of those who will never see them. The

Heavenly Creatures

The River Nile had its own roster of gods, principally the hippopotamus and the crocodile. Egyptians who worked or travelled on the Nile hoped that if they prayed to Sobek, the crocodile god, he would protect them from being attacked by crocodiles.

Towns along the river adopted their own particular favourites from lesser echelons. These creatures were given temples where, soothed by hymn-singing, they slithered or wriggled about with rings in their ears (if they had ears) and jewelled bracelets round their legs (if they had legs).

At the end of their pampered lives they were put to rest in a private cemetery. Local loyalties could lead to conflict; war was declared between neighbouring towns and villages over the status of a particular beast. Sacred in one, in the other it was blasphemously caught and eaten. The Hyksos invaders of about 1600 BC offended Egyptians with gratuitous jibes at the holy hippopotamus, but in Thebes, where the beasts in question were pampered in an artificial lake, there were paintings and sculpture which also showed how the hippo was hunted. It was crept up on, lassoed and played out on a line. Hunters then rushed up to get in their shots with javelins attached to lines. The instinct of this enraged pincushion was to find deep water, whereupon a tug-of-war commenced. The hippo would be hauled into a boat, break free, and the process would be repeated until the animal was exhausted.

Great Pyramids of Giza, on the western bank of the Nile southwest of Cairo, have secured undying fame for Khufu (Cheops), Khafra (Chephren) and Menkaura (Mycerinus).

The inspiration for the first pyramid was in the mud-brick *mastabas* of Saqqarah. Originally large but unremarkable oblong slabs, these developed into monumental buildings, still made out of mud-brick. The evolution of the straight-sided pyramid had to overcome a number of early examples of "back to the drawing board", and the dissatisfaction of King Snofru may explain why three pyramids are attributed to him.

According to the historian Herodotus, Cheops even steered his daughter into prostitution to raise money for his immortal monument, the Great Pyramid at Giza.

The preoccupation with pyramid design in his household came to fruition in his son, known to him as Khufu but to posterity by his Greek name, Cheops. The effort that went into this pyramid was immense. Herodotus describes shifts of 100,000 men taking 10 years just to build the enormous causeway, 18 metres (60ft) wide, from the water's edge to the plateau. Pyramids were built within easy reach of the Nile to simplify the last leg of the journey that brought blocks of granite, some weighing as much as 70 tonnes each, 800km (500 miles) down the river from Aswan – a feat achieved on reed barges. However, to be too close to the river would have exposed the site to annual flooding, so they were kept at a respectful distance and serviced by a canal.

The end of the Old Kingdom

In the Old Kingdom the power of the pharaoh was supreme and he took an active part in all affairs of state, which ranged from determining the height of the Nile during the annual inundation, to recruiting a labour force from the provinces, to leading mining and exploratory expeditions. Naturally, such responsibility was too much for one person and he therefore delegated power to the provincial lords, who were often members of the royal family. The provincial nobility became wealthier, began to exert power, and the result was an inevitable weakening of centralised authority. At the end of the 6th Dynasty some of the provinces shook themselves free from the central government and established independence. The monarchy collapsed. The Old Kingdom came to an end.

The Middle Kingdom

The First Intermediate Period which followed, between the 7th and 10th dynasties, saw anarchy, bloodshed and a restructuring of society.

The provincial lords who had gained power and prestige under the great monarchs began to reflect on the traditional beliefs of their forefathers. It was a time of soul-searching, and great contempt was voiced for the law and order of the past.

A powerful family of provincial lords from Herakleopolis Magna (Middle Egypt) achieved prominence in the 9th and 10th dynasties and restored order. In Upper Egypt, meanwhile, in the Theban area (near Luxor), a confederation had gathered around the strong Intef and Mentuhotep family, who extended their authority northwards until there was a clash with the family from Herakleopolis. A civil war resulted in triumph for the Thebans, and gave rise to

LEFT: the Great Pyramids of Giza. **RIGHT:** detail of a relief of Sobek, in the outer hypostyle hall of the joint Temple of Sobek and Haroeris at Kom Ombo.

Egypt's Middle Kingdom, which covers the 11th and 12th dynasties (*c.*2040–1782 BC).

Amenemhat I, whose rule heralded a revival in architecture and the arts, established the 12th Dynasty, one of the most peaceful and prosperous eras known to Egypt. Political stability was soon reflected in material prosperity. Building operations were undertaken throughout the whole country. Amenemhat III constructed his tomb at Hawarah (in Al Fayyum) with a funerary monument later described by classical writers as "The Labyrinth" and declared by Herodotus to be more wonderful than the Pyramids of Giza. Goldsmiths, jewellers and sculptors

perfected their skills, as Egyptian political and cultural influence extended to Nubia and Kush in the south, around the eastern Mediterranean to Libya, Palestine, Syria and even to Crete, the Aegean Islands and the mainland of Greece.

At the end of the 12th Dynasty the provincial rulers once again rose against the crown. During this period of instability the Hyksos, who are believed to have come from the direction of Syria, swept across northern Sinai to the apex of the Delta, from where they surged southwards. The humiliation of foreign occupation came to an end when Ahmose, father of the New Kingdom (18th–20th dynasties, 1570–1070 BC) started a war of liberation and finally expelled the hated invaders from the land.

This first unhappy exposure to foreign domination left a lasting mark on the Egyptian character. The seemingly inviolable land of Egypt had proved vulnerable, and now had to be protected from invasion. To do so meant not only to rid the country of enemies, but to pursue them into western Asia. Out of the desire for national security was born the spirit of military expansion characteristic of the New Kingdom.

The New Kingdom

The New Kingdom (1570–1070 BC) was the period of empire. The military conquests of Thutmose III, in no fewer than 17 campaigns, resulted in the establishment of Egyptian power throughout Syria and northern Mesopotamia, as well as in Nubia and Libya. Great wealth from conquered nations and vassal states poured into Thebes (Luxor), most of which was bestowed upon the god Amun who, with the aid of an influential priesthood, was established as Amun-Ra, "King of Gods". Thebes flourished, and some of Egypt's most extravagant monuments were built.

The 18th Dynasty, though, was a period of transition. Old values were passing and new ones emerging. The spirit of the age was based on wealth and power. But grave discontent, especially among the upper classes, was apparent in criticism of the national god Amun and the materialism of the priests who promoted his cult.

Akhenaten's revolution

It was in this atmosphere that Amenhotep IV (Akhenaten) grew up. He was the pharaoh who would revolt against the priests and order temple reliefs to be defaced, shrines to be destroyed and the image of the god Amun to be erased. Akhenaten transferred the royal residence to Al Amarnah, in Middle Egypt, and promoted the worship of one god, the Aten, the life-giving sun. The city was called Akhetaten ("Horizon of Aten"), the first ever city to be designed and built from scratch, for which barges brought granite down from Aswan and timber up from the Mediterranean. It included palaces, temples, a grid of streets broad enough to allow four carriages abreast and – a major innovation much imitated since – a working-class neighbourhood of neat, identical little houses.

ABOVE LEFT: bust of Queen Nefertiti from the Amarnah period (*c.*1350 BC). **RIGHT:** statuette of Akhenaten and Nerfertiti. **FAR RIGHT:** statue of Akhenaten from Karnak.

Its location, about halfway between Cairo and Luxor where the uncompromising sands of the Eastern Desert reached all the way to the river, puzzled archaeologists. When the Nile flooded, the water broke across the opposite bank; the city side was forever high, dry and barely fit for human habitation. This bewildering apparent hiatus in Egyptian history is one of archaeology's great tales *(see box below)*.

Unfortunately, the ideal needs of a religious community and the practical requirements of governing an extensive empire were to prove incompatible demands. After the deaths of Akhenaten and his half-brother Smenkhkara, the boy-king Tutankhamun came to the throne. Tutankhamun abandoned Al Amarnah and returned to Memphis and Thebes. The priests of Amun were able to make a spectacular return to power.

Empire-builders

Horemheb, the general who seized the throne at the end of the 18th Dynasty, was an excellent administrator. He re-established a strong government and started a programme of restoration, which continued into the 19th Dynasty, when the pharaohs channelled their energies into reorganising Akhenaten's rule. Sety I, builder of a famous mortuary temple at Abydos,

THE FIRST INDIVIDUAL IN HISTORY

When a peasant woman discovered some rotting wooden chests filled with small clay tablets at an abandoned archaeological site known as Tall Al Amarnah, experts in Cairo were not unduly excited. The site itself, in a high, dry location halfway between Cairo and Luxor, was a mystery: Prussian archaeologists had uncovered the remains of a sizeable city but it gave every indication of having been deliberately and comprehensively razed. Every pictorial or written reference to the notables who controlled the city had been obliterated.

The tablets – now known as the Amarnah Letters – uncovered by the woman were inscribed in an incomprehensible form of cuneiform. Initially dismissed as the work of a forger, they had in fact been written to the king of the mysterious city by the subject kings of Nineveh, Babylon, Canaan and Mitanni during the 18th Dynasty when Egypt was at the zenith of its imperial power. But who was he, and what was he doing in Amarnah rather than in Thebes?

The letters unlocked the world's best-kept secret. The king concerned was Amenhotep IV (afterwards Akhenaten) who, like some of Stalin's rivals, had been simply purged from the pages of history. In his case, though, the illusion lasted more than 3,000 years. As a picture of the facts emerged, the reprieved Amenhotep IV was given a tumultuous welcome by the academics. Some scholars drew parallels with Jesus Christ, others opted for the Prophet Muhammad. "The first individual in history," declared another.

fought battles against the Libyans, Syrians and Hittites. Rameses II, hero of a war against the Hittites, with whom he signed a famous peace treaty, was also celebrated as a builder of great monuments, including the famous temples at Abu Simbel; and Rameses III (1182–1151 BC) not only conquered the Libyans, but successfully protected his country from the "People of the Sea". However, Rameses III was the last of the great pharaohs. The priests of Amun, who controlled enormous wealth, eventually overthrew the 20th Dynasty. In theory the country remained united, but anarchy flourished and occupation by foreign powers ensued.

Centuries of foreign rule

In 945 BC Sheshonk, who was from a family of Libyan descent, but had become completely Egyptianised, took over the leadership. His Libyan followers were probably descendants of mercenary troops who had earlier been granted land in return for military service. The Libyan monarchs proceeded to conduct themselves as pharaohs, and their rule lasted for two centuries.

Then came a period which brought the Egyptians into contact with the Nilotic peoples of the south, from lands which the pharaohs had considered troublesome but subjugated – and ironically it was this very notion of being a subject people

RAMESES II

All the representations of Rameses II – and they far outnumber those of any other pharaoh – are of squared shoulders, a head held high and an expression of immense self-satisfaction. He ruled, initially as co-regent, for 67 years, lived for 90 or so, waged 20 wars, oppressed the Israelites (it was he from whom Moses fled), maintained an active harem of more than 200 women, and had more than 100 sons and about 60 daughters.

His fame as a builder is associated not with the New World he sought to establish in the Delta but with the "Old" he strained to leave. He was only a contributor to the Temple of Karnak, and tried to magnify his work by usurping the hypostyle hall, which was actually begun by Rameses I and completed by Rameses II's father, Sety I. Similarly, he was only one of a number of contributors to the Temple of Luxor, but he assumed pride of place with the front pylons and four colossal statues, two standing and two seated. The obelisk that is now in the Place de la Concorde in Paris was one of a pair that originally stood near the statues.

Despite his excessive self-glorification, Rameses could, however, justly claim all the credit for temples in Nubia, in particular for his masterpiece at Abu Simbel which also celebrates the victory at Qadesh. Four colossal statues of the seated king guard the entrance to a 54-metre (180ft) hall cut out of solid rock.

that fuelled their presence in Egypt. In 748 BC a military leader, Piankhy, from the region of Kush (northern Sudan), marched northwards. Because his people had absorbed Egyptian culture during a long period of Egyptian rule he did not view himself as a conqueror, but as a champion freeing Egypt from barbarism.

The Egyptians did not regard the Kushites as liberators, and it was only after a military clash at Memphis, when the foreign invaders surged over the ramparts, that they surrendered.

liberated the country from Assyrian occupation. He immediately turned his attention to reuniting Egypt and establishing order.

Egypt's revival came to an end when the Persian King Cambyses occupied the land in 525 BC and turned it into a Persian province. The new rulers, like the Libyans and the Kushites before them, at first showed respect for the religion and customs of the country in an effort to gain support. But the Egyptians were not deceived, and as soon as an opportunity arose they routed their invaders. Unfortunately, they maintained independence for only about 60 years before another Persian army invaded.

Like the Libyans before them, the Kushites established themselves as pharaohs, restored temples and were sympathetic to local customs.

The Assyrians, who were reputedly the most ruthless of ancient peoples, conquered Egypt in 667 and 663 BC. With a disciplined, well-trained army they moved southwards from province to province, assuring the local population of a speedy liberation from oppressive rule.

During these centuries of foreign rule Egypt had one short respite. This was the Saite Period, which ensued after an Egyptian named Psamtek

LEFT: sound and light show at the Grand Temple of Rameses II, Abu Simbel. **ABOVE:** illustration of Alexander the Great's army overawed by the Sphinx.

Alexander

When Alexander the Great marched on Egypt in 332 BC, he and his army were welcomed by the Egyptians as liberators. The Egyptians had no reason to fear that this would mark the end of their status as an independent nation. He first made his way to densely populated Memphis, the ancient capital, where he made an offering at the Temple of Ptah, then lost no time in travelling to Siwah Oasis to consult the famous oracle of Amun-Ra *(see page 188)*.

When he emerged from the sanctuary he announced that the sacred statue had recognised him, and the priests of Amun greeted him as the son of the god. Before he left Egypt, Alexander laid down the basic plans for its government. In the important provinces (nomes in Greek) he appointed local governors from among Egyptian nobles; he made provision for the collection of taxes and laid out the plans for his great city and seaport, Alexandria, so situated as to facilitate the flow of Egypt's surplus resources to Greece and to intercept all trade with Africa and Asia.

When Alexander died from a fever at Babylon, his conquests fell to lesser heirs. Egypt was held by a general named Ptolemy, who took over leadership as King Ptolemy I. During the three centuries of Ptolemaic rule that followed, Egypt became the seat of a brilliant empire once more.

Egypt under the Ptolemies

Ptolemy I did not continue Alexander's practice of founding independent cities. With the exception of Ptolemais, on the western bank of the Nile in Middle Egypt, and the old Greek city of Naucratis in the Delta, only Alexandria represented a traditional Greek city-state. It became capital in place of Memphis and was soon to become the major seat of learning in the Mediterranean world, replacing Athens as the centre of culture. Ptolemy II commissioned Egyptians to translate their literature into Greek; and a priest, Manetho, wrote the history of his country.

The Ptolemies regarded Egypt as their land and they consequently played a dual role in it, conducting themselves simultaneously as bearers of Greek culture and as guardians of Egyptian culture. Although they resided in Alexandria, as pharaohs they lavished revenues on local priesthoods for the upkeep of temples, or at least exempted them from taxes.

> *Bilingual Egyptians realised that if they transcribed their own language into the Greek alphabet, which was well known among the middle classes and was simpler to read, communication would be easier.*

Scribes introduced transliteration, adding seven extra letters from Egyptian to accommodate sounds for which there were no Greek letters, and created a new script, known as Coptic.

Greek also became the mother tongue of the Jews in Egypt, who constituted the second-largest foreign community. Many had been imported as soldiers, even before the arrival of the Ptolemies. When Palestine fell under the control of Ptolemy I in 301 BC, he brought back Jewish mercenaries, who joined the established communities.

The Ptolemies encouraged other foreigners to come to live in Egypt, including Syrians and Persians, as well as Greeks. There was a strong anti-Egyptian feeling among the sophisticated Greeks, who did not encourage Egyptians to become citizens of Alexandria and the Greek cities. Although they held Egyptian culture in reverence in many ways, they did not learn the Egyptian language or writing. Even the Greek masses, although they were fascinated by the "sacred mysteries" and "divine oracles" of the Land of Wonders, nevertheless held the Egyptians in contempt. There were reciprocal anti-Greek sentiments among the Egyptians, who had a strong sense of cultural superiority towards anyone who did not speak their language.

Towards the end of the 2nd century BC Egypt experienced economic problems and political unrest, along with a decline in foreign trade. Some territories outside Egypt were lost, and the prosperity of the kingdom waned. The court, rich in material wealth and lax in morals, became the scene of decadence and anarchy.

By the last century of Ptolemaic rule, the Egyptians had acquired a position that was somewhat closer in equality to the Greeks than they had endured under the earlier Ptolemies.

This era saw the emergence of a landed, wealthy Egyptian population, who were ardently nationalistic and had little respect for the settlers. It was from their ranks that the great spiritual leaders of Coptic Christianity were to arise.

Cleopatra and the end of Ptolemaic rule

Cleopatra VII, the most famous of the Ptolemies, came to the throne at the age of about 18, as co-regent with her even younger brother Ptolemy XII. They were at that time under the guardianship of the Roman Senate, and Romans interfered in the rivalry between them, which led Ptolemy to banish his 21-year-old sister from Egypt. Cleopatra sought refuge in Syria, with a view to raising an army and recovering the throne by force. When Julius Caesar arrived in Alexandria in 47 BC shortly after his crucial military victory over his rival Pompey in the Roman civil war, he took the side of the banished queen and set her on the throne. History has two popular versions of their first meeting. One has her being dumped at his feet in a sack as a trick to evade the pickets who surrounded the palace where Caesar was staying. The other has her choosing a seductive outfit and bursting in on him in the middle of the night. Either way, by morning Caesar was firmly on her side.

Caesar's stay with Cleopatra included nine months in a double-decker floating palace, after which Caesar decided that he had to return to Rome. He was not long gone when Cleopatra gave birth to a son, whom she named Caesarion.

A little over five years later, after Caesar's assassination, Cleopatra met Mark Antony at Tarsus. Their legendary love affair brought her three more children, but succeeded in alienating Antony from his supporters in Rome. His purported will, stating his wishes to be buried at Alexandria, angered many Romans, and gave Octavian (later known as Emperor Augustus) the excuse he was looking for to declare war on Antony. Octavian marched against him, defeating him at Actium and capturing Alexandria. Antony committed suicide and Cleopatra is recorded as having caused her own death with the bite of an asp. Caesarion, who had been co-regent since 43 BC, was murdered, and Octavian became sole ruler in 30 BC.

Egypt thenceforth was a province of the Roman empire, subject to the sole rule of the emperor in Rome, and to viceroys or prefects nominated by the emperor, who followed the example of the Ptolemies and represented themselves as successors of the ancient pharaohs. ❑

LEFT: Ptolemy's system, in which the earth is depicted at the centre of the cosmos, encircled by seven planets. **ABOVE:** Temple of Philae.

Pyramidology and Pyramidiocy

As feats of engineering, the Old Kingdom Pyramids have vexed the greatest scientific minds – and been the subject of outlandish theories

In about 1850 Pasha Abbas I, a discredited member of Egypt's last dynasty but nevertheless an indirect descendant of the pharaohs, described the Pyramids as "an ugly, useless pile of stones". He was unimpressed or possibly even unaware that the Greeks had ranked them among the Seven Wonders of the World. However, Abbas would not have found many in contemporary Europe who shared his contempt. Following the publication of the 24-volume *Description de L'Egypte* by Napoleon's *savants*, the Egyptian style in jewellery, clothing and furnishing was all the rage internationally.

"Pyramidologists" were pursuing all sorts of wonderful theories about the Pyramids, although those who pushed their fancy too far risked being demoted to "Pyramidiots". Some, wary of ridicule, remained perplexed and undecided. In London, John Taylor, editor of the *Observer* and a gifted astronomer and mathematician, had studied the Great Pyramid of Khufu (Cheops) and come to the astounding conclusion that its builders knew the earth was a sphere and had ascertained its circumference, of which the Pyramid was an imperishable record. Yet his profound faith in the literal truth of the Old Testament presented a problem. He believed that Adam had been created in exactly 4000 BC and that the Flood had occurred in 2400 BC. In marvelling at the sublime mathematics of pyramid design, he was quite ready to accept that the Great Pyramid had been built in 2100 BC. But how in just 300 years could the brains and labour required have recovered from mankind's watery grave?

From the fantastical...

The Pyramid had other peculiar properties too. Patent No. 91304 in Czechoslovakia was rushed through to protect the commercial possibilities of mysterious forces swirling around pyramid-shaped objects. The product in question was a cardboard contraption known as the "Cheops Pyramid Razor Blade Sharpener". British inventor Sir W. Siemens, a manufacturer of electrical appliances, took his guide up a pyramid to prove that a wine bottle wrapped in a moist newspaper and held above his head would emit a shower of sparks. When it did, the official witness let out a howl, hoisted his *gallabiya* and bolted.

The Curse of the Pharaohs and other demonic powers guarding the sanctity of the royal tombs *(see feature page 58)* do not seem to have bothered early Greek and Roman visitors; Strabo, who took a Nile cruise in 24 BC, described his party crawling down the descending passage of the Great Pyramid by the light of flaming torches. In the Middle Ages, however, the Arabs were put off by reports of an enormous naked woman whose lust no male intruder could decline or escape. If he survived at all, it would be as an insane wreck. It is conceivable that this insatiable woman was loosely based on the daughter whom Khufu, builder of the Great Pyramid, is reputed to have prostituted in order to defray building costs. She was installed in a special chamber and encouraged to charge each of her clients the cost of one block of finished limestone, 2½ million of which were needed before the Pyramid was finished.

...to the mathematical

In 1638 the astronomer John Greaves observed that the Pyramids were too well built simply to have been thrown together, so the architects must have drawn up plans with detailed measurements. What, he wondered, was the unit of measurement they used, and how had they arrived at it? Wriggling down the same descending passage that Strabo and his party had followed, Greaves measured anything that looked like a calculated length. Frequently recurring lengths would therefore be a unit or convenient multiples of a unit. His findings were published in *Pyramidographia*, in 1646; it caught the attention of Sir Isaac Newton, who used Greaves's figures to calculate what he called the "profane" or Memphis cubit, enabling him to interpret the geographical degree quoted in the classical authors and so move closer to his theory of gravitation.

The search for other examples of applied mathematics in the Pyramids then extended to *pi*, the ratio between the diameter and the circumference of a circle. This had traditionally been credited to Pythagoras, the Greek geometrician of *c.*500 BC. Modern computers have now calculated this incommensurate number to 10,000 decimal places, but it was only 1,100 years after Pythagoras that Hindu mathematician Arya-Bhata worked out the fourth decimal. Mathematicians were agog at what seemed like evidence that the pyramid-builders had reached at least the second decimal 2,000 years before Pythagoras.

Mystery and conjecture

Napoleon's *savants* cleared sand and rubbish which had all but buried most of Egypt's Pyramids in order to measure the external dimensions more accurately and unlock further mathematical sensations. Meanwhile the young general insisted on spending some time alone in the Great Pyramid's burial chamber. When he emerged, white in the face, he pointedly refused to answer questions and told his staff that the matter was never to be raised. He considered breaking his silence during his exile on St Helena, but held himself back and shook his head. "No," he remarked. "What's the use? You'd never believe me."

Conjecture about the hidden purpose of the Pyramids never ceases. Some of the discoveries are beyond dispute. Clearing the base of the Great Pyramid has established, for example, that the perimeter of the 5.4-hectare (13-acre) site is level to within a tolerance of 2cm (¾ inch). It has also confirmed that, like most pyramids, the axis is aligned on true north with an astonishing degree of accuracy. Such findings have led a new generation of pyramidologists to suggest that what were long thought to be access or ventilation passages into the centre of a pyramid were actually designed to time the moment of a star's transit across the sky. ❑

LEFT: Napoleon during his Egyptian campaign contemplating ancient artefacts, many of which ended up in Paris. **ABOVE:** John Greaves, English mathematician and astronomer, who made accurate measurements of the Pyramids.

Gods of Ancient Egypt

The ancient Egyptians explained the mysteries of nature and the world through myths concerning the origins and powers of their gods

The movement of the sun was one of the most significant forces in the ancients' world and, according to his myth, the sun-god Ra created himself from the primeval waters where everything was dark and chaotic. His eyes became the moon and the sun and, mating with his own shadow, he created Shu, god of the air, and Tefnut, goddess of mist. At this point, Ra wept and his tears fell as men and women. Shu and Tefnut then gave birth to Geb, god of the earth, and Nut, goddess of the sky, which completed the creation of the universe. Isis and Osiris, Seth and his sister-wife Nepthys were created through the union of Geb and Nut.

Rise and fall of the gods

Through the centuries, different gods gained importance as the capital moved from city to city. In Memphis, Ptah was considered the supreme god and creator of the universe. He was usually depicted as a bald man with a mummiform body and false beard. His consort Sekhmet, a woman with a lion's head, was goddess of war and represented the harmful powers of the sun. Imhotep, architect of the step pyramid at Saqqarah, was later deified as their son and the god of medicine (and equated with Asklepios by the Greeks). Amun was the supreme god of Thebes, depicted as a ram with curved horns. The life-bringing Nile was also personified as the god Hapy, while fertility was represented by Min, depicted with an erect phallus and celebrated in the important Feast of Min.

Left: Amun-Ra, a composite god of Ra, sun-god of Heliopolis, and Amun, god of the wind, became a national deity during the Middle Kingdom.

Above: in this painting, in the tomb of Horemheb in the Valley of the Kings, Osiris, god of the underworld and of resurrection, is depicted as a mummy with a false beard.

Below: Anubis, seen here in the tomb of Sennedjem, Deir Al Madinah, greeted the dead in the underworld and protected their bodies from decay. He was usually depicted as a jackal, or a man with a jackal's head.

THE MURDER OF OSIRIS

The myth of the murder of Osiris and his sister-wife's hunt for his body clearly illustrates the Egyptian belief in the afterlife.

Osiris was born a god but grew up as a man who became the king of Egypt. His brother Seth was so jealous of his popularity and success that he locked him in a coffin, which he threw into the Nile. Isis, mourning her husband's death, went looking for the coffin and eventually found it near Byblos (in modern Lebanon), where it had been surrounded by a tree.

Having recovered the body, Isis took the form of a bird (symbol of the spirit) to revive Osiris, but only managed to stir him long enough to impregnate herself with a son, Horus the Younger. While Isis was giving birth to her son, Seth was cutting Osiris's body into 14 pieces, which he scattered across Egypt. Isis later recovered all of them except his penis, which had been eaten by Nile fish. She reassembled the parts and made a mould of the missing organ, while Horus, having fought a battle with Seth, brought the eye of his father's murderer and placed it in Osiris's mouth, ensuring his eternal life.

ABOVE: one of the most important gods, falcon-headed god Horus, (seen here at Edfu) was a sun-god (he often has a sun-disk on his head), god of the sky, a protector of kings and a guide to the dead in the underworld. Every pharaoh was considered an incarnation of Horus.

ABOVE: on this relief on a statue in Luxor temple, the Nile god Hapy is shown as a plump male with breasts, representing the fecundity of the river.

BELOW: a relief of Seth, from a block in the temple of Karnak, depicted as a strange dog-type animal with huge ears.

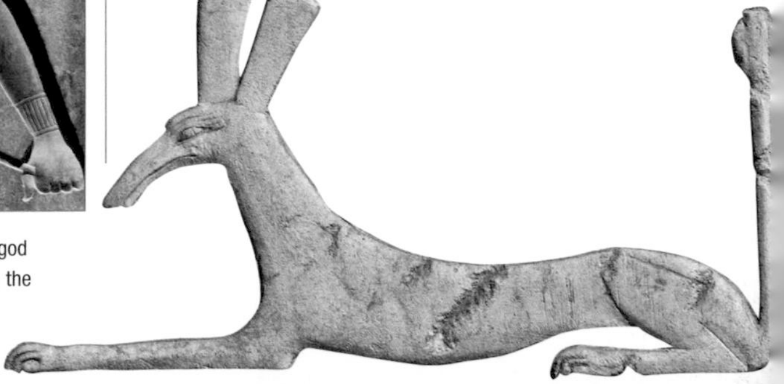

FROM PAX ROMANA TO THE RISE OF CHRISTIANITY

Rome's dominion was a troubled and violent time for Egyptians and Greeks, which saw brutal persecution of the early Christians. Once Christianity was established, dogmatic differences within the new religion led to fierce factional disputes – but the word was spreading down the Nile

The Roman occupation of Egypt, ostensibly a mere extension of Ptolemaic rule, was in fact markedly different. While a mutual hostility towards the Persians and a long history of commercial relations bound Egyptians and Greeks together, no such affinity existed between Egyptians and Romans. Alexander the Great had entered Egypt without striking a blow; Roman troops fought battles with Egyptians almost immediately. The Ptolemaic kings had lived in Egypt; the Roman emperors governed from Rome, and their prefects took over the position formerly held in the scheme of government by the kings.

The Romans regarded Egypt, like other parts of North Africa, as no more than a granary, supplying wheat to Rome, and as a pleasure-ground for the Roman upper classes.

Emperor Augustus aroused the ire of the Greeks when he abolished the Greek Senate in Alexandria and took administrative powers from Greek officials. Further, in response to an appeal by Herod, king of Judaea, he not only agreed to restore to him land that had been bestowed on Cleopatra, but agreed to grant self-government to the Hellenised Jews of Alexandria.

Fighting soon broke out, first between Greeks and Jews, then with the Romans when they tried to separate the two. The unrest that marks the beginning of the Christian era in Alexandria had already begun. Ships in the harbour were set on fire, the flames spread and the Mouseion Library was burned.

The Romans thenceforth stationed garrisons at Alexandria, which remained the capital; at Babylon (Old Cairo), which was the key to communications with Asia and with Lower Egypt; and at Syene (Aswan), which was Egypt's southern boundary. They controlled Egypt by force, and an enormous burden of taxation was placed on the people of the Nile Valley.

Egyptians who had enjoyed certain privileges under the later Ptolemies received no special consideration by the Romans, but had their problems compounded when Emperor Trajan declared that peasant farmers should be

LEFT: Cleopatra and Mark Antony as Osiris and Isis.
RIGHT: obverse of a Roman coin depicting Mark Antony.

recruited for the Roman army. Hadrian reduced rentals on imperial lands and exempted citizens of Greek cities and Greek settlers in the Fayyum from taxation, but the Egyptian rural population was assessed at a flat rate, without regard for income, age or capacity for work.

Although the Romans made an overt show of respect for Egyptian priesthoods by constructing new temples, temple lands elsewhere were placed under the control of the Roman government. Local priests were allotted only a small part of sacred property and their own material wealth was curbed. A Roman official held the title of "High Priest of Alexandria and all Egypt".

Early Christianity and its adversaries

Such were the conditions in Egypt during the 1st century of the Christian era, when the Apostle Mark preached in Alexandria. Remains from the period showing the diffusion of Christianity in Egypt are scant, but New Testament writings found in Bahnasa in Middle Egypt date from around AD 200, and a fragment of the gospel of St John, written in Coptic and found in Upper Egypt, can be dated even earlier. They testify to the spread of Christianity in Egypt within a century of St Mark's arrival.

The Catechetical School of Alexandria was the first important institution of religious learning in Christian antiquity. It was founded in 190 by Pantanaeus, a scholar who is believed to have come to Alexandria approximately 10 years earlier. He was succeeded by Clement (160–215) and then Origen (185–253), the theologian and writer who is considered as the greatest of the early Christian apologists. Both were highly critical of the Gnostic movement (from the Greek *gnosis* or "knowledge"), an obscure group who were hounded into silence, in the name of orthodox Christianity, from the 4th century onwards, and their writings burned.

Fortunately, however, a collection of their manuscripts was discovered in Naga' Hammadi in Upper Egypt in 1945, copied from original

THE NAGA' HAMMADI CODICES

The 12 Naga' Hammadi codices were collected by Egyptians and translated into Coptic, the Egyptian language of the time. They vary widely in content, presenting a spectrum of heritages that range from Egyptian folklore, Hermeticism, Greek philosophy and Persian mysticism to the Old and New Testaments. The codices include a "gospel of Thomas", a compilation of sayings attributed to Jesus; extracts from Plato's *Republic*; and apocrypha ("secret books") related to Zoroastrianism and Manichaeism. With such diversity, it is perhaps little wonder that the Gnostics came under attack from orthodox Christians, who eventually destroyed the majority of their writings.

writings that may date from the second half of the 1st century AD *(see box opposite)*.

A more formidable rival to Christianity was Neoplatonism. Coalescing in Alexandria during the 3rd century, this philosophical school revived the metaphysical and mystical side of Platonic doctrine, explaining the universe as a hierarchy rising from matter to soul, soul to reason and reason to God, conceived as pure being without matter or form. The first Neoplatonist, Ammonius Saccas, had been the teacher of Origen and was a lapsed Christian, while his successors, including Porphyry, were all pagans. Porphyry came to be regarded by the Christian bishops as their greatest enemy – they burned his books in public – but many Christians were students of Neoplatonism, and Neoplatonic ideas were co-opted into the teachings of the early Church.

Beginnings of monasticism

St Paul the Theban and St Anthony were two of Egypt's earliest and greatest spiritual leaders. Both lived lives of meditation and prayer at about this time; each, unknown to the other, had chosen a retreat in the Eastern Desert in a range of mountains near the Gulf of Suez. St Anthony, after visionary inspiration, sold his inheritance, gave his money to the poor, then retreated to the cliffs flanking the Nile Valley, later settling beneath a range of mountains known today as the South Qalala. These two men became regarded as having special powers and a special relationship with the divine, attracting other eremites who looked to them for guidance and spiritual instruction.

St Paul is believed to have retired to the desert at the age of 16 to escape the persecutions of the emperor Decius (249–51), who ordered Egyptians to participate in pagan worship.

LEFT: Roman birth house outside the Temple of Hathor at Dandarah. **ABOVE:** St Anthony of Egypt. **ABOVE RIGHT:** metope of two Roman legionaries, Alexandria.

A turning point

In 284 the Roman army elected Diocletian emperor, and his reforms mark a turning point in the history of Christianity. He divided Egypt into three major provinces, separated civic and military powers, then imposed new methods of tax assessment based on units of productivity. Under these reforms Egyptians were forced into public service and, to facilitate control, Latin was introduced as the official language.

Unification of the Roman empire was undoubtedly the reason for these reforms, but

Egyptians had had enough. They rebelled so violently that Diocletian decided that if they could not be subjugated, they should be eliminated. They were dismissed from government service, their property was confiscated and their houses levelled. Searches were made for Christian literature, and copies of the scriptures, when found, were burned. Though thousands of people died during the terrible persecutions of Diocletian, unknown numbers escaped to refuge in the deserts, taking their zeal for Christianity with them, to create new converts. One of them was St Pachom, who established no fewer than 11 monasteries in Upper Egypt.

Conversion and controversy

The famous revelation of the emperor Constantine in 312, which resulted in his conversion to Christianity, was followed by the Edict of Milan, which established Christianity as the favoured religion throughout the Roman empire. It was at last safe to admit to being a Christian in Egypt. Unfortunately, the theological disputes that had plagued the early Christian movement became even more fierce in the 4th and following centuries. The controversies centred on the attempt to define the Incarnation: if Jesus was both God and Man, had He two natures? Was He both human and divine?

The chief antagonists were the Arians, named after Arius, an elderly Alexandrian presbyter, and the Monophysites, led by Alexander, bishop of Alexandria. The former held that Jesus did not have the same nature as God the Father. The Monophysites regarded this doctrine as recognition of two gods and a reversion to polytheism. They believed that Father and Son were intrinsically of one nature, and that Jesus was therefore both divine and human.

The dispute reached such an impasse that Constantine felt impelled to define a dogma to unify Christian belief. The Council of Nicea was convened in Asia Minor in 325 for this purpose. Bishop Alexander officially led Egypt's delegation but his deacon, Athanasius, was his chief spokesman. It says a great deal for his eloquence, reasoning and persistence that the Nicene Creed, to the effect that Father and Son are of the same nature, was sanctioned and remains part of the Christian liturgy.

Byzantine period

Soon after the Council of Nicea, Constantine moved his capital to the ancient Greek town of Byzantium, which became Constantinople, and rapidly usurped Alexandria's reputation as a seat of learning, held since Ptolemaic times.

Under Theodosius I Christianity was formally declared the religion of the empire and the Arians were again declared heretics. The Monophysite bishops of Alexandria were reinstated but, as a result of the partition of the empire between the emperor Honorius of Rome and the emperor Arcadius of Constantinople, their power was limited. Egypt fell under the jurisdiction of the latter and the so-called Byzantine rule of Egypt began.

Theophilus was made patriarch of Alexandria and displayed tremendous zeal in destroying heathen temples. A wave of destruction swept over the land of Egypt. Tombs were ravaged, walls of ancient monuments scraped and statues toppled. In Alexandria the famous statue of Serapis was burned and the Serapeum destroyed, along with its library, which had replaced the Mouseion as a centre of learning. It was a folly of fanaticism in the name of orthodoxy not, ironically, so different from that which had earlier opposed Christianity.

LEFT: colossal head of Constantine in the Palazzo dei Conservatori, Rome. **RIGHT:** a Coptic cross engraved on a pillar at the Temple of Philae. **FAR RIGHT:** fragment of a Coptic textile showing the god of the Nile.

The Coptic Orthodox Church

Convened in 451, the Council of Chalcedon declared that Christ had two natures "concurring" in one person. When the Egyptians refused to endorse this revisionist doctrine, their patriarch was excommunicated. In the struggle that followed, several Egyptian leaders were killed, and Alexandria was pillaged by imperial troops. From then on, Egypt generally had two patriarchs, one representing the orthodoxy of Constantinople, the other upholding the "one person" beliefs of the majority of Egyptian Christians, embodied in the Coptic Orthodox Church, the national Church of Egypt.

Meanwhile, a Coptic Bible had been in circulation since the early 300s, and Egyptian missionaries had travelled south, spreading Christianity to Sudan, Ethiopia and Eritrea. The conversion of King Ezana of the Ethiopian kingdom of Aksum around 330 was a key moment – he declared Aksum officially Christian, as Ethiopia remains to this day. From the 500s, Christian kingdoms also flourished on the upper River Nile in Nubia, Sudan. The missionaries did not penetrate further south, however, and sub-Saharan Africa did not embrace Christianity until the Europeans reached those regions centuries later, during the great age of exploration.

Coptic Christians

The English word Copt, meaning "Egyptian Christian", is derived from the Arabic *qibt*, which is derived in turn from *Kyptaios*, the Coptic form of the Greek word *Aigyptios*. It also designates not only the last stages of the ancient Egyptian language and script, but also the distinctive art and architecture that developed everywhere in Egypt except Alexandria – which remained attached to cosmopolitan forms – during the country's Christian era. It is used, finally, to refer to most of modern Egypt's Christian minority, who officially constitute about 9 percent of the population and who continue to be identified with the same intense patriotism that distinguished their forebears.

The end of Byzantine rule

Under Justinian (528–65), the Copts were saved from persecution only by the interest of the empress Theodora, his wife. After her death, however, Justinian sent Alexandria a patriarch-prefect determinedly armed with both civil and religious powers.

Greeted by a mob, which stoned him when he attempted to speak in church, the new bishop retaliated with force by ordering the troops under his command to carry out a general slaughter. This act effectively quelled immediate resistance, but completed the alienation of the Copts, who henceforth simply ignored any ecclesiastical representatives sent from Constantinople. ❑

ABBASIDS, FATIMIDS AND MAMLUKS: THE SPREAD OF ISLAM

As Byzantium wilted, the Nile region found itself overrun by the newly united forces of Islam. During the centuries which followed, Egypt's fortunes followed those of successive Muslim empires, while the European presence proved ephemeral – for now

The Byzantine empire was already exhausted by its struggles against the Persian Sasanians when a new enemy appeared: the Arabs, spiritually and politically united by the Prophet Muhammad and led by his successors, the caliphs, came waging *jihad* (Holy War) against non-believers and hungry for booty.

Egypt was invaded in 639 by Amr Ibn Al 'ass, one of the ablest of the early Muslim generals, who defeated a Byzantine army near the ancient ruins of Heliopolis in 640, then besieged the fortress of Babylon, at the head of the Delta – where he founded Fustat, a garrison city for the control of the Nile Valley – and Alexandria itself. With the Byzantines unable to reinforce their army in Egypt and the native Copts hostile to Constantinople, the country fell easily.

At this point attempts were made to push further south and convert Sudan to Islam, but with little effect. The Arabs reached as far as Dongola beyond the Third Cataract of the Nile, but met with stiff resistance and, by comparison with Egypt, found little to interest them. A treaty was signed with the Nubians ensuring that trade across the frontier was not disrupted, and Arab influence asserted itself slowly and peacefully through commercial contact over the centuries. Egypt, meanwhile, was destined to become a major battleground on which the internal struggles of Muslim rule were fought.

The Abbasid caliphs

In 750 the Abbasid family seized control of the Islamic empire. Brought to power by a coalition of Arab and Iranian forces, the Abbasids established an international state, centred on Baghdad and drawing upon the services of all Muslims.

During the first 200 years of Muslim rule, Egypt was a mere pawn. Controlled by a series of military governors appointed by the caliphs in the east, most of the country's great agricultural wealth was channelled into the coffers of the central treasury, bringing Egypt to the verge of economic collapse in the early 9th century.

In order to hold their state together the caliphs in Baghdad began to employ Turkish slave armies to counterbalance their turbulent Arab and Iranian subjects. Far from being slaves in the Western sense of the word, these Turks were groomed as a ruling caste, loyal only to the

LEFT: Maqsurah, Mosque of Ibn Tuloan. **RIGHT:** Islamic glass cup from the Abbasid period, *c.*9th century.

Abbasids. The power of the Turkish generals became so great and the upkeep of their armies so expensive that the caliphs were compelled to distribute whole provinces to them in lieu of pay. In this manner Egypt became a private fief of the new Muslim military elite in 832.

Independence under Ibn Tuloan

The most famous Turkish governor was Ahmed Ibn Tuloan, posted to Egypt in 868. He gained total control of the provincial government, establishing the first autonomous Muslim state in Egypt and introducing a period of prosperity. However, his descendants failed to maintain his legacy, exhausting the state treasury and alienating the army, which left Egypt too weak to resist the re-establishment of direct Abbasid rule in 905.

For the next 30 years Egypt was again ruled by a series of oppressive and ineffectual provincial governors, appointed from Iraq. However, the growing threat of the Shi'a Fatimid Dynasty, centred in Tunisia, demanded a more effective form of government in the Nile Valley, and in 935 a new semi-autonomous state in Egypt was founded by Muhammad Ibn Tuglij. His main task was the creation of a strong Egyptian buffer state to prevent further Fatimid eastern expansion.

In 946 he was nominally succeeded by his young sons, but the real power was held by their regent, the Nubian eunuch Kafur. Kafur's strong rule held the state together, but on his death it fell when faced by a Fatimid invasion under General Jawhar in 969.

Fatimid Egypt

Jawhar's first action was to build a new royal enclosure to house the victorious Al Mu'izz and his Shi'a government. The new Fatimid capital was named Al Qahirah, "The Subduer", later corrupted by Italian merchants into Cairo.

The Fatimids gained control of Palestine and the holy cities of Mecca and Medina, but after reverses against the Byzantines in northern Syria they turned to trade, and Fatimid Egypt became fabulously wealthy. Plans for the conquest of the Abbasid empire were postponed indefinitely, and little effort was made to convert the Christian and Sunni Muslim native population to Shi'a Islam. As a minority sect in Egypt, unconcerned with proselytising, the Fatimids were extremely tolerant.

However, the third Fatimid caliph, Al Hakim (996–1021), was preoccupied with revitalising the spiritual mission of the Isma'ili movement and with the maintenance of his personal power. His fervour resulted in measures that were both extreme and brutal, and the Fatimid hierarchy eventually decided that he had to go. While he was riding his donkey alone in the

Muqattam hills at night, Al Hakim mysteriously disappeared, almost certainly murdered on the orders of his sister and the Fatimid elite, who now took over the reins of government.

Famine and threats

During the reign of Al Mustansir (1036–94) Fustat reached the peak of its prosperity, yet the Fatimid state rapidly began to decline. Unruly Turkish soldiers looted the Fatimid palaces on the pretext of arrears of pay, and Al Mustansir secretly called in Badr Al Jamali, the Fatimids' Armenian governor at Acre in Palestine, to restore order.

> *A series of seven low Niles between 1066 and 1072 plunged the country into chaos. Famine and plague spread throughout the Nile Valley, reducing the people of Fustat to cannibalism.*

A surprise attack on Al Qahirah in 1072 crushed all opposition and won Badr Al Jamali full dictatorial powers. He now had to face an impending invasion by the Seljuk Turks, and the enclosing walls of Al Qahirah were rebuilt, incorporating massive new gates, to withstand the expected siege. The sudden break-up of the Seljuk empire after 1092 saved the Fatimids from certain defeat, but left the Middle East crowded with petty Muslim states. Their lack of unity facilitated the victories of the First Crusade of 1099, launched in response to the Seljuk conquest of Jerusalem a few years earlier.

The rise of the Zangids of Mosul, who began absorbing their Muslim neighbours and preaching *jihad* in the first half of the 12th century, meant it was not long before the Christians were encircled and picked off one by one.

Saladin

The Fatimids tried to play one side against the other, but in 1169 were compelled to submit to the Zangid general Salah Addin (Saladin), who abolished the Fatimid caliphate in 1171, re-establishing Sunni Islam in Egypt. In theory Egypt was now a part of the Zangid empire, ruled by Nur Ad Din; in reality it was in the hands of Saladin.

LEFT: ablution fountain in the Mosque of Ahmad Ibn Tuloan, Cairo. **ABOVE RIGHT:** detail of an ivory inlay from a Fatimid piece of furniture, *c.*11th century.

The death of Nur Ad Din in 1174 and the break-up of his empire left Saladin undisputed master of Egypt. He spent the next 13 years conquering the divided Zangid principalities of Syria and placing them under the control of his family, the Ayyubids. With Egypt and Syria once again united, Saladin turned his attention to the crusaders, who were decisively defeated in 1187.

The capture of Jerusalem and Palestine established Saladin as a champion of Islam, but also triggered the Third Crusade. Led by Richard the Lionheart of England and Philippe II of France, the Christians retook Acre, but were unable to advance any further. The peace settle-

ment of 1192 recognised Saladin's gains, leaving the crusaders in possession of a small coastal strip of Palestine. Saladin died the following year a satisfied man.

The Ayyubid empire he had created was a federation of sovereign city-states, loosely held together by family solidarity. When the last major Ayyubid sultan, As Salih (1240–9), whose ruthless rise to power had alienated most of his relatives, found himself faced with the threat of a Mongol invasion from the east, he began building a Turkish slave army, loyal only to him, to defend the Ayyubid state – the Bahri Mamluks. They were put to the test in 1249, when the Sixth Crusade of St Louis IX of France invaded Egypt. During the course of hostilities As

Salih died; when his son Turan Shah witnessed the defeat of the French king by the Mamluks in 1250, he was alarmed by their power and began to replace them with his own men. The Mamluks, not to be ousted so easily, murdered Turan Shah and seized control of Egypt.

The Bahri Mamluks

The Mamluks proclaimed Shagar Ad Durr (As Salih's widow) as sultan. The Ayyubid princes of Syria, refusing to accept the loss of the richest province of their empire to a woman, prepared for war. Needing a man to lead her army, Shagar Ad Durr married the Mamluk commander Aybek, who ruled with her as sultan. The Ayyubids were defeated in 1250 and Aybek, encouraged by his victory, conquered Palestine.

The Mamluks had proved their military prowess against the crusaders and the Ayyubids, but were now called upon to face a far greater threat; the heathen Mongols, who in 1257 swept through Iraq into Syria, crushing all Muslim resistance. Undefeated in battle, the central Asian hordes seemed on the verge of extinguishing Muslim civilisation in the Middle East. Only the Mamluks remained to stop them, and at the battle of Ayn Jalut in 1260 they did, becoming the saviours of Islam.

Mamluk, a synonym for slave, means "possessed" in Arabic. There were two Egyptian Mamluk dynasties: the Bahri (1250–1382) were Mongols and Turks; they recruited the Burji (1382–1517), who were Circassians.

Under the sway of their first great sultans, Baybars Al Bunduqdari (1260–77) and then Qalawoan (1279–90), the Mamluks emerged as the foremost military power of their age. Kept in top fighting shape by the constant threat of the Mongols, now centred in Iran, the Mamluks recaptured Syria and expelled the last of the crusaders from the Palestinian coast.

The reign of An Nasir Muhammad

Qalawoan's son An Nasir Muhammad was made nominal sultan in 1293, at the age of nine. After ruling for a year he was deposed, but then reinstated in 1299. Raised in an atmosphere of intrigue and double-dealing, An Nasir emerged at the age of 25 as a ruthless and despotic sultan. Resolving to rule alone, he murdered the emirs of his father one by one, replacing them with his own men and thus inaugurating an era of peace. A period of trade and great prosperity ensued, the apex of Muslim civilisation in Egypt.

An Nasir's success in mastering the Mamluk system *(see box left)* brought about the beginning of its decline. So firmly did he grip the

The Mamluk System

The political system created by Baybars was based on a military slave oligarchy. Young Qipchaq Turks would be brought to Egypt as slaves, converted to Islam and given military training. On completion of their education they would be freed and enrolled in the private army of one of the great Mamluk emirs, of whom the most powerful would be chosen as the sultan.

The foundation of the system was the intense loyalty the individual Mamluk felt for his military house *(bayt)*. His political fortunes were linked to those of his emir. If his *bayt* was successful, the common Mamluk could expect to be promoted to the rank of emir and even to the sultanate.

Left: Saladin, sultan of Egypt. **Right:** early 14th-century mosque lamp bearing the name of Sultan An Nasir Muhammad, from the Al Nasir Mosque in Cairo. **Far Right:** Fatimid period plate showing seated figure holding drinking vessels, *c.*11th century.

reins of power that, on his death in 1340, none of the emirs was strong enough to replace him. He had filled the state's treasury but caused the Mamluks to neglect their military training.

The Circassian Mamluks

For 41 years after the death of An Nasir, 12 of his direct descendants ruled Egypt as nominal sultans. In 1382 the emir Barquq (1382–99) seized control and distributed all positions of power to his fellow Circassians. This second Mamluk dynasty maintained the same political system as their predecessors, but they had been brought to Egypt not as boys, but as young men. Instead

of being moulded by the rigours of a Mamluk education, they arrived in Cairo with clear ideas of how to manipulate the system to their own benefit. Ambitious, unruly and deficient in their military training, they were a terror to the inhabitants of Egypt, but poor soldiers.

Bred to be a cavalry elite, they despised gunpowder as unmanly. Their major rivals in the early 16th century, the Ottoman Turks, had no such snobbish qualms. When the two forces clashed at the battle of Marj Dabiq in 1517, the Mamluks were blown off the field by superior cannon fire. Following this victory, the Ottoman Sultan Selim the Grim conquered the Mamluk sultanate and Cairo became the provincial capital of a new Muslim empire centred in Istanbul.

Egypt as an Ottoman province

The Ottomans, engaged in continual warfare with Iran and the Christian West, could not spare the necessary men to uproot the Mamluks from Egypt, instead incorporating them into the Ottoman ruling elite and holding them in check with a provincial governor and a garrison of crack Ottoman troops, the Janissaries. In the 17th century, military defeats brought steady decline to the Ottoman empire, while rampant inflation upset the balance of power in Egypt. The office of governor was sold to the highest bidder, then resold at the first opportunity, to supply the central treasury with a steady flow of cash, and so

FUNJ AND FUR

It was during the Ottoman centuries in Egypt that powerful Muslim communities started to emerge in the south of Sudan. The Funj were a loose confederation of sultanates of shadowy origin in southern Nubia who thrived on the slave trade, supplanting remnants of a Christian kingdom there in the 16th century. Their capital at Sennar on the upper Blue Nile was an important city until its decline in the 19th century.

The Fur emerged west of the White Nile, establishing a sultanate in the 17th century which ruled here until 1916. They give their name to the troubled region of Darfur and remain a significant ethnic group in the area today.

the governors could never establish effective control over Egypt. The Janissaries became little more than armed shopkeepers and artisans.

The rise of Ali Bey Al Kabir (1760–72) saw the re-emergence of the Mamluks as an international power. He was on the verge of re-establishing the Mamluk empire when he was betrayed by his lieutenant Abu'l Dhahab, and Egypt was plunged into a devastating civil war which lasted until 1791. Although order was restored by the victory of Murad Bey and Ibrahim Bey, the economy of the country was in ruins. In this unsettled state, Egypt was invaded by the French under Napoleon Bonaparte.

Despite the propaganda churned out in Arabic by his printing press – the first in modern Egypt – his attempt to portray the Palestine debacle as a victory was not greeted with enthusiasm in Cairo. With communications to Paris cut by the marauding British and his own troops disillusioned, he concluded that his personal ambitions were unlikely to be served by lingering. Fourteen months after his arrival, Bonaparte slipped home, leaving General Kléber, his second-in-command, the news of his appointment as the new general-in-chief.

Although the French remained in Egypt two more years, they eventually succumbed. Kléber was assassinated in June 1800, and the task of negotiating with an Anglo-Ottoman force that landed in the Delta in 1801 was left to his successor. The French, now numbering only 5,000, were allowed to return home. In three years of occupation, they had not met any of their objectives. Britain still dominated the seas, the Ottomans had reinforced their hold on the Levant, and the Egyptians, though impressed by the power of European science and technology, rejected what little they had seen of the infidel's civilisation. ❑

The French expedition

On the morning of 21 July 1798, the combined musketry and artillery of 29,000 French troops smashed an onslaught of Mamluk cavalry in the battle of the Pyramids. However, within days the British had sunk the French fleet off Abu Qir and the Mamluks under Murad Bey had fallen back to Upper Egypt, from where they conducted a successful guerrilla war.

Hoping to regain momentum, Bonaparte embarked on a campaign in Palestine. After initial successes the French were brought to an abrupt halt at the fortress of Acre. Reinforced from the sea by a British fleet, the Turkish garrison managed to hold out for two months, while Bonaparte's army was depleted by disease.

Above: Napoleon at the battle of the Pyramids in 1798, telling his men that 40 centuries are watching them. **Right:** engraving of the dromedary regiment, created by Napoleon in 1799.

Grave Robbers and Curses

Through the years, the tombs of the pharaohs have been prone to desecration – despite ingenious defences and inscriptions

Pharaohs, priests and *felaheen* (peasants) were forever putting curses on people. Tomb curses could be startlingly detailed: before death, the culprit might suffer starvation, social ostracism, the death of his children and the violation of his wife before his eyes – and that was only the beginning. Superstition made these curses effective deterrents.

Hollywood's favourite curse, that of Tutankhamun, was another matter. It was reputed to have killed more than 20 people involved in the violation of Tutankhamun's tomb in 1922. The first was Lord Carnarvon, Howard Carter's patron and partner. In poor health for years, he had succumbed to pneumonia, but with popular interest running high, newspapers and magazines as well as the film industry made the most of the story. A peasant seen at the tomb-site was reported to have mumbled: "These people are looking for gold but they will find death." A deathbed repentance was put into Carnarvon's mouth and solemn significance attached to a power cut in his Cairo room 10 minutes before he expired.

It became virtually impossible for anyone connected with Carter's work to suffer any kind of misfortune without fingers pointing rigidly at the curse. The wording was quite specific: "Death will come on swift pinions to those who disturb the rest of the Pharaoh." It sounded authentic, but no one had actually seen any such inscription. The truth was that, while almost all the tombs did carry some curse or other, Tutankhamun's did not.

Tomb raiders: a history

The pharaohs themselves were often guilty of robbery, routinely emptying their predecessors' tombs of valuables, throwing out the coffin to make space for their own and even tampering with the cartouche to pretend they had built the tomb. The Pyramids were a maze of false passages and man-traps designed specifically to foil robbers, but these could hardly be concealed from the workforce: the solution was to murder them as soon as the job was done.

By the time of the 20th and 21st dynasties, the site of the Valley of the Kings was known and the situation had degenerated into a running battle between robbers and loyal necropolis guards. Unless they were well connected, justice was harsh for any robbers who were caught. Records show that a carpenter Tramun and his accomplices who confessed to taking "all the gold from the mummies of the God and the queen" were lashed until their palms and the soles of their feet turned to pulp and then executed.

The history of grave-robbing in Egypt reflects the changing value of antiques. Gold and jewels would appeal to any thief in any age, but it was when Egypt was drawn into the European orbit at the turn of the 19th century that the appeal of antiquities really picked up. Works by Napoleon's *savants* created a craze for anything Egyptian, and peasants became aware that there was cash to be made out of odds and ends in the sand which would previously have been ignored. Meanwhile foreign "collectors" raced to scoop up (or pull down) anything which could be sold to collections in Europe and America.

Above: illustration of Howard Carter and Lord Carnavaron in the tomb of Tutankhamun. **Right:** a worker carries part of a stone relief from a tomb discovered in Saqqarah in 2001 which dates from *c.*1350 BC.

The mystery of Al Qurnah

The appearance of some superb illustrated papyri on the European market in 1871 worried the Antiquities Service in Cairo. Suspecting that they had been removed from a tomb somewhere near Luxor, the Service despatched an agent, who was soon tipped off that he should call on the Abd Ar Rassul family in Al Qurnah, near the Ramesseum. Items for sale were produced, and the agent's suspicions were sufficient to have members of the family brought in for questioning. Muhammad, the head of the family, eventually led an Antiquities Service representative, the archaeologist Emile Brugsch, to a hole in a cliff above Hatshepsut's temple at Dair Al Bahari. Brugsch squeezed through and descended to a tiny passage which disappeared into the rock.

Chambers had been cut into the sides of the passage, and Brugsch gradually identified the contents in speechless disbelief. The names on the coffins defied an Egyptologist's imagination: Thutmose III, Rameses II, Amenhotep I, Sety I. The only explanation was that the coffins had been assembled here for safe-keeping by loyal subjects during an especially turbulent period when all royal tombs were threatened.

The objects found with the kings could have put the whole of Al Qurnah into the lap of luxury for the rest of time. As it was, Muhammad was rewarded with E£500 and the case against his family dropped. Brugsch arranged a guard of 300 men to see the find safely down to boats waiting on the Nile. The operation took two days and was enlivened by local women shrieking and tearing at their hair – it was unclear whether they were mourning the loss of the kings or the windfall.

Smuggling today

The Egyptian government has made it very clear that it is illegal to export any antiques without a valid licence issued by the Department of Antiquities. However, the trade in Egyptian items is so profitable that it now attracts arms and drug dealers, and the international art and antiques market is always quick to snap up anything Egyptian, as there seems to be an insatiable demand, even at very high prices.

It is often not even a matter of theft. The earth is so rich in ancient material that when local people build a house or work their land they are quite likely to stumble across some small ancient artefacts. When they take them to a local dealer they will get some cash, though this will be a fraction of the price eventually fetched on the Western market.

Another source is the Egyptian Museum itself. Much has been sold off or simply vanished from its basement over the years, but even when an inventory was compiled, artefacts continued to disappear. In 2005, three Old Kingdom statues went missing: it transpired that two men from the company doing the inventory had smuggled the statues out of the museum with construction debris. ❑

THROWING OFF THE YOKE: THE BIRTH PANGS OF MODERN EGYPT

Centuries of domination from the East gave way to persistent interference from the West. While such pressures may have put the brakes on Egypt's expansionist projects, they indirectly led to the modernisation of the country's infrastructure

Muhammad Ali Pasha, who is hailed as the founding father of modern Egypt, first entered the country as second-in-command of an Ottoman army sent to join the British in expelling the French. After the French and British troops left, the Ottoman troops stayed on to reassert the strength of the sultan's authority. Anarchy ensued, and in 1805 the people of Cairo turned to Muhammad Ali to restore order, naming him the new viceroy. After defeating a British force at Rosetta in 1807 and, most bloodily and boldly, arranging the massacre of 470 rebellious Mamluks in 1811, his authority in Egypt was absolute and his thoughts turned to expansion.

The Egyptian empire now rivalled the Ottoman in size, although Egypt itself was still nominally a part of the Ottoman empire and Muhammad Ali still only a pasha, the sultan's viceroy.

Muhammad Ali's military exploits

After placing western and central Arabia under Egyptian control in a campaign during the years 1811–18, Muhammad Ali sent an expedition under one of his sons up the Nile to gain control of Sudan's mineral resources and its active slave trade, which he saw as a possible source of military manpower. Campaigns in Greece led by his son Ibrahim followed in the 1820s, though they eventually led to intervention by the major European states Britain, France and Russia, and the sinking of the entire Egyptian fleet at Navarino in 1827.

Then in 1831, using a quarrel with a governor as a pretext, he sent Ibrahim into Syria with an army of peasant conscripts. At the end of 10 months all Syria had acknowledged Muhammad Ali as overlord. In 1832 Ibrahim pushed on into Anatolia, defeating the Ottomans at Konya. Before he could occupy Constantinople, however, Russia intervened and forced an agreement between the sultan and his unruly vassal, by which Egypt was formally accorded rule over Crete and Syria in return for an annual tribute.

In 1839 the sultan attempted to regain Syria by force, but was resoundingly defeated by Ibrahim, and his navy then deserted to Alexandria. This alarmed the European powers once again, and Muhammad Ali was forced to sign an agreement in 1841 which confirmed the sultan's suzerainty.

Modernising on all fronts

Deprived of his acquisitions abroad, the pasha turned his remaining energies back to the task of modernising Egypt. The benefits to his country were enormous. They include the comprehensive upgrading and extension of Egypt's irrigation system and the introduction of new crops such as rice, indigo and sugar cane, as well as the cultivation of long-time staple Egyptian cotton, which later became the country's principal export.

He nationalised all property, eliminated the iniquitous tax-farming system and created modern industries. Beginning with an industrial complex at Bulaq, the Nile port of Cairo – where the famous Bulaq Press, the most distinguished publisher in the Arab world, was set up – he built shipyards, foundries and armament factories. Textile mills, the basis of the European Industrial Revolution, soon followed.

In Alexandria Muhammad Ali established a Quarantine Commission, thus identifying the city once again as the country's main port of entry. And it was here that the pasha died in 1848, 80 years old, but predeceased by his son, the gallant Ibrahim, to whom he had given the viceregal throne 11 months before.

Muhammad Ali's successors

Abbas, the only son of Muhammad Ali's second son, Tussun, became viceroy and immediately rejected all his policies. While Muhammad Ali had been eager for Western agricultural and technical ideas, particularly those of the French, Abbas summarily expelled all the French advisors upon whom his grandfather had depended, closed all secular or European schools, and turned for support to religious leaders. Apart from the British railway completed after his murder in 1854, the sole positive relic of his six-year rule was that he left full coffers and no foreign debt.

Abbas was succeeded by his uncle Said, who favoured a return to his father's programmes. Open to European influences, Said is perhaps best known for his friendship with Ferdinand de Lesseps, to whom he granted a concession for the Suez Canal in 1854. In its original form this concession was one of the great swindles of all time, with terms extremely disadvantageous to Egypt, but Said managed to renegotiate more favourable terms – at the cost of an indemnity of more than E£3 million. To pay this sum he

LEFT: Muhammad Ali by Auguste Couder.
ABOVE: a lithograph of the Suez Canal made in 1839 by Louis Haghe (1806–85).

was forced to take Egypt's first foreign loan, thus not only setting a dangerous precedent, but planting a time bomb under Ismail, the third of Ibrahim's four sons, who became viceroy on Said's death in 1863.

Ismail the Magnificent (1863–79)

Under Ismail's rule the modernisation begun by Muhammad Ali moved forward with new dynamism. Reviving his grandfather's policy of independence from the sultan, in 1866 Ismail secured the throne for his own line and permission to maintain a standing army of 30,000, while pleasing Europe by summoning the first Chamber of Deputies. In 1867 he obtained the Persian title of *khedive* (sovereign), as well as the right to create institutions, issue regulations and conclude administrative agreements with foreign powers without consulting Constantinople.

When the Suez Canal opened in 1869, the sultan sent Ismail a decree forbidding him to undertake foreign loans without approval. The American Civil War had brought wealth to Egypt by raising the price of cotton, enriching the new class of landowners that Said and Ismail had created. This was not enough, however, even coupled with Egypt's tax revenues, to keep pace

ENCOUNTER AT FASHODA

In 1898, the wounds of Waterloo reopened. Britain wanted to rule an African corridor from the Cape to Cairo and France yearned for one that cut a swathe on the other axis between the Atlantic and Indian Ocean. The precise point where the two putative corridors met was a derelict, mud-brick Nile fort on the edge of an indescribably awful swamp, at a place called Fashoda in Sudan.

The race to occupy Fashoda began. On the British side was Horatio Herbert Kitchener, Sirdar of the Egyptian army. His opponent was Jean-Baptiste Marchand, a captain of marines and veteran of several "pacifications".

In the event, Marchand won the race, but Kitchener soon arrived. Marchand had possession of Fashoda and no intention of leaving. Kitchener, on the other hand, had the means to take it from him – five gunboats, 2,500 Sudanese troops, 100 Highlanders, not to mention machine-guns and artillery – but no wish to use them.

After initial awkwardness, the two men agreed that both sides would occupy the area. In the French officers' mess Kitchener listened with interest to the story of their hideous journey through the marsh, but he saved his bombshell for the moment of departure. The French government was in tatters, he said, ripped apart by the Dreyfus scandal. He did not believe they would have the time or the inclination to back up Marchand, and indeed the evacuation of the French troops soon followed.

with Ismail's ambitions. In the confusion of public and private exchequers, colossal debts had been run up, prompting alarm in Paris and London, where Ismail's independence was already regarded as a threat to the status quo.

Most of the debt was the result of swindles perpetrated by European adventurers, of which the largest was an inheritance from Said: the Suez Canal, built using the corvée, at Egyptian expense. In 1875, Ismail was forced to sell his shares in the canal company to Britain. An Anglo-French dual control set up to oversee his finances began creaming off three-quarters of the annual revenues of Egypt to pay European creditors. Ismail was forced to liquidate his personal estates and to accept British and French ministers in his cabinet. Eventually the Europeans lost patience altogether. Putting pressure on the sultan, they had Ismail deposed.

British intervention and rule

His son Tawfiq was no match for the adversaries who had defeated his father, but the army made a stand. British warships promptly bombarded Alexandria on 11 July 1882. Tawfiq abandoned his own government and put himself under their protection. Support for a provisional government also melted away. Near the end of August, 20,000 redcoats were landed on the supposedly sacrosanct banks of the new Suez Canal, and two weeks later the Egyptian army was crushed at Tall Al Kabir.

Thus came to an end 19th-century Egypt's experiments with modernisation. Evelyn Baring, who became Lord Cromer in 1891, first came to Egypt in 1879 as the British financial controller during the dual control of France and Britain but later returned in 1882 as the consul-general. The British government promised an early evacuation of its troops, but they lingered on and, since the British refused to formalise their presence, the British consul-general became the de facto ruler of Egypt.

Cromer's discouragement of both industrialisation and higher education fuelled Egyptian nationalism, which drew strength between 1890 and 1906 from the country's enormous prosperity, derived almost exclusively from cotton. His successor as consul-general, Sir Eldon Gorst, cultivated a friendship with the *khedive*, whom he permitted to wield increased power, and undertook several reforms. Egypt's first secular university was allowed to open in 1908 and the provincial councils were encouraged towards more autonomy. Unfortunately, Gorst's arrival coincided with a worldwide economic slump and his policies failed. In 1910 he was succeeded by Lord Kitchener.

Kitchener had served as commander-in-chief of the Egyptian army and knew Egypt well. He introduced regulations for censorship, school discipline and the suppression of conspiracy. Once again the *khedive* came under the consul-

LEFT: the Fashoda incident as seen by a French journal. **RIGHT:** a caricature from 1893 of the relationship between the *khedive* and the British occupying power.

TRANSFORMING AGRICULTURE

The most important achievements during British rule were the completion of the Delta Barrage in 1890 and the building of the first Aswan Dam in 1902. Begun under Muhammad Ali, the Delta Barrage made double and triple cropping possible in the Delta, while the Aswan Dam, coupled with barrages at Asyut (1903) and Esna (1906), extended the same system to Upper Egypt, reducing dependence on the annual flood. By the early 20th century, cotton had become the mainstay of the Egyptian economy. Other food crops continued to be grown, and Egypt was still able to feed its growing population without depending on imports.

general's strict authority, but in 1913 Kitchener introduced a new constitution that provided for a Legislative Assembly. It had met only once when World War I broke out.

The Protectorate (1914–22)

At the outbreak of the war, Britain severed Egypt's 400-year-old Ottoman connection, declaring it a protectorate. By the end of the war, the nationalist movement was stronger than ever, and was directed by the dynamic Saad Zaghlul, a lawyer who had been imprisoned briefly for participation in the 1882 resistance, but later appointed minister of education by Cromer. It was the declaration of the Protectorate which had prompted him to join the nationalists.

As soon as the armistice was signed, Zaghlul asked the British government to be allowed to present Egypt's case for independence, but was refused. This only hardened nationalist sentiment, leading to demonstrations in Cairo. Zaghlul and three other nationalists were exiled to Malta, provoking the successful uprising that Egyptians refer to as the Revolution of 1919 *(see box right)*. Lord Allenby was appointed to address the situation; he recalled Zaghlul from exile and allowed him to go to Paris with other members of the Wafd, as his followers had come to be called (*wafd* means "delegation" in Arabic). Zaghlul attended the conference, but on the same day that the Treaty of Versailles was signed Allenby issued a proclamation reaffirming the Protectorate.

In November 1919, a British government mission was sent to Egypt to produce a report recommending a constitution for the Protectorate. It concluded that, although Britain should maintain military forces in Egypt and control over foreign relations, the protection of foreign interests and Sudan, Egypt should be declared an independent country. But the report was not published until the end of 1921, and meanwhile Zaghlul was arrested and exiled again.

THE REVOLUTION OF 1919

The uprising known in Egypt as the Revolution of 1919, provoked by the exile to Malta of Zaghlul and three of his colleagues, was a short-lived but bloody affair. Violence in Cairo, the Delta and the Nile Valley, especially around Asyut, was accompanied by a general strike. Many upper-class women also came out onto the streets to demonstrate, led by Safia Zaghlul, wife of Saad.

Several hundred Cairo citizens were killed in confrontations with British and Australian troops. Forty British soldiers and civilians also died during the uprising, and railway and telegraph lines were destroyed.

For his part, Allenby had privately made conclusions similar to those of the mission. In February 1922, upon his return from a visit to England, he bore a proclamation that unilaterally ended the Protectorate, but reserved four areas of British control. Three weeks later,

Popular national sentiments were articulated by Saad Zaghlul, a brilliant young Egyptian politician, who said of the British: "I have no quarrel with them personally, but I want to see an independent Egypt."

Egypt's independence was officially declared, and Sultan Fuad – who had been chosen by the British – became King Fuad. A constitution based on that of Belgium was adopted in 1923.

Fuad as king (1922–36)

The Wafdists at first rejected this declaration of independence. When Zaghlul was finally allowed to return, however, they sought to participate in the forthcoming elections, which they won by an overwhelming majority. And so Zaghlul became Egypt's prime minister in early 1924.

LEFT: Cairo women exercising their new right to freedom of speech, May 1919. **ABOVE:** King Fuad. **ABOVE RIGHT:** the Prince of Wales and King Fuad.

Zaghlul gave up none of his demands connected with completing independence, which included the evacuation of all British troops and Egyptian sovereignty over Sudan. His hopes for their fulfilment were raised when a Labour government came to power in Britain. Less than a year after the Wafd's landslide victory, however, the assassination of Sir Lee Stack, the British commander-in-chief of the Egyptian army and governor-general of the Sudan, put an end to such optimism.

Allenby delivered an ultimatum to the Egyptian government, though it had clearly not been responsible for the murder, making puni-

tive demands. Badly shocked, Zaghlul accepted most of them, but refused withdrawal of Egyptian troops from Sudan, the right of Britain to protect foreign interests in Egypt and the suppression of political demonstrations. Defiance seemed impossible, however, and he could only resign, leaving it to a successor to accept all the British conditions.

King Fuad took the opportunity to dissolve the Wafdist parliament and rule by decree. Elections were held in March 1925 and the Wafd won by an overwhelming margin, so the king again dissolved parliament. A third set of elections in May 1926 also gave the Wafd a majority, but the British vetoed Zaghlul's reinstatement as prime minister. Already shattered by Stack's murder, Zaghlul's health deteriorated further, and he died a few months later.

For the next four years the struggle between the Wafd and King Fuad took the same pattern, with the Wafd winning general elections and the king dissolving the parliament to appoint his own ministers. In 1930, Fuad replaced the 1923 constitution with his own royally decreed one, which persisted until 1935, when combined nationalist, popular and British pressure forced him to restore the constitution of 1923.

Negotiations for an Anglo-Egyptian treaty concerning the status of Britain in Egypt and Sudan had long been under way. It was finally signed in August 1936 and became the basis of the two countries' relations for the next 18 years.

Fuad died in April 1936 and his son, Faruq, still a minor, succeeded him. The Wafd split, and a new party, the Saad Wafd, was formed. Extremist organisations also emerged, such as Misr Al Fatat, an ultra-nationalist pro-royalist group. Such groups joined Hassan Al Banna's Muslim Brotherhood, formed in 1928: their stated aim was to purify and revitalise Islam, but they also had political aspirations, and began to take an active part in politics in the late 1930s.

The Suez Crisis

The turning point in political orientation away from the West came in June 1956, after the US withdrew its financial backing for the High Dam at Aswan. Nasser nationalised the Suez Canal and announced that he would use the revenues from it to build the dam. This provoked the fury of France and Britain, whose nationals owned the Canal, and together with Israel they launched a tripartite attack on Egypt. The invasion was ended by the intervention of the US and the Soviet Union, which forced the three aggressors to withdraw. Nasser had won an important victory with very little effort and came to symbolise the defiance of imperialist domination.

World War II and its aftermath

When World War II broke out, in accordance with the terms of the treaty of 1936 Britain took control of all Egyptian military facilities, although Egypt itself remained officially neutral for most of the war. At the end of the war Egypt was in a precarious situation, and a new, fiercely nationalistic political force had appeared, the Free Officer movement in the army, led by Gamal Abdel Nasser.

The disastrous defeat of the Arabs in Palestine in 1948–9 fuelled the Muslim Brotherhood and increased the disaffection of the army with both the palace and the government. The Muslim Brotherhood and the Free Officers plotted to take power, and to this end the former carried out a series of terrorist operations, including the assassination of the prime minister, Noqrashy Pasha, in December 1948. Aware of the danger that the Muslim Brotherhood represented, the government retaliated with massive arrests of its members, and Al Banna himself was assassinated in February 1949.

In 1950 the Wafd was again elected to power. It instituted disastrous economic policies, but sought to hold onto popularity by releasing many members of the Brotherhood, abrogating the 1936 treaty and calling for the evacuation of British troops from the Canal Zone. Resistance to the British troops in the Canal area took the

form of guerrilla action with the tacit approval of the government. In January 1952 the British besieged and overran a post manned by Egyptian auxiliary police, who fought to the last man. Rioting broke out in Cairo, and on 26 January foreign shops, bars and nightclubs were burned and British landmarks such as Shepheard's Hotel and the Turf Club disappeared for ever.

The climax came in the night of 22 July, when the Free Officers took over key positions in a bloodless coup d'état engineered by Nasser and other members of his organisation. On the morning of 23 July, the people were informed that the army, commanded by General Naguib, had seized power. Disillusioned by their corrupt government and dissolute king, the Egyptians greeted the news with joy.

The Nasser era

The young officers moved quickly to consolidate their power. On 26 July, King Faruq was forced to abdicate, the constitution was repealed and all Egypt's political parties were suspended. In June 1953, the monarchy was formally ended and a republic declared. By May 1954 Nasser was prime minister and virtual dictator.

Nasser's first important public act as prime minister was the amicable negotiation of a new Anglo-Egyptian treaty that provided for the gradual evacuation of British troops from the Canal Zone, signed in October 1954 after six months of negotiations. Although his opponents grumbled that it was not favourable enough to Egypt, Nasser was generally hailed as the leader who finally ended foreign occupation in Egypt.

It was not until July 1961, five years after the Suez War *(see box opposite)*, that Nasser adopted a comprehensive programme of rapid industrialisation, to be financed in part by nationalisation of all manufacturing firms, financial institutions and public utilities. Created to

LEFT: construction of the Aswan Dam. **ABOVE:** President Nasser. **ABOVE RIGHT:** Nasser enjoys breakfast with fellow officers after ousting President Naguib.

further the new programme decreed that year, the Arab Socialist Union was to remain the only legal avenue for political activity open to the Egyptian people for more than a decade.

As Nasser built respect for Egypt abroad, he began to wave the banner of Arab unity. This led in 1958 to a union between Egypt and Syria, later joined by Yemen, called the United Arab Republic, but also to the Arab-Israeli War of June 1967, in which the Israelis wiped out the entire Egyptian air force on the ground, crossed the Suez Canal and were ready to march on Cairo. Only a ceasefire quickly worked out by the United States and the USSR prevented further disaster. Nasser resigned, only to resume his post the next day following mass demonstrations for his return, but he was a broken man presiding over a wrecked economy, and he died in 1970.

The Sadat era

Anwar Sadat, Nasser's vice-president, succeeded to the presidency. His boldest initiative was the launching of the Fourth Arab-Israeli War in October 1973, a qualified success which regained some of Egypt's lost pride and gave Sadat enough prestige to ignore Arab unity and seek a separate peace with Israel.

However, his economic policies, encouraging foreign investment and private enterprise, created high inflation and widened differences between the new rich and older salaried classes, as well as the poor. The high-handed style of his government, in an atmosphere of corruption and crony capitalism, alienated many. Overt opposition gathered around the new political parties, including a revived Wafd, while less public hostility crystallised in Islamic revivalism. The Muslim Brotherhood had regained most of its freedom of action, but there were other more radical groupings, one of which was responsible for Sadat's assassination on 6 October 1981 during a ceremony commemorating the crossing of the Suez Canal.

The Mubarak years

Vice-president Hosni Mubarak, a former air force commander, succeeded Sadat as president. He tried at first to promote more democratic government, and his greatest challenge came from the Islamic Group (Al Gama'a Al Islamiya), who aimed to turn Egypt into a fundamentalist Islamic state. Their attacks on tourist sites in the 1990s caused tourism to plummet, further increasing unemployment and discontent. The government reacted with a harsh crackdown, as it had to again a decade later, following further bomb attacks on tourist sites in 2004 and 2005.

Although Mubarak first tried to curtail the corruption of the Sadat years, it became a feature of his own regime, causing discontent among the masses. At the same time, the freeing of exchange rates, easing of import controls, creation of an Egyptian stock exchange and the repatriation of large sums privately invested abroad have helped the middle class.

In 2005 amid growing discontent, President Mubarak called for a constitutional amendment to introduce contested presidential elections. However, a few restrictions were retained to prevent serious opposition candidates from running, and in the election Mubarak won a landslide victory.

Despite Mubarak's tight grip on power in Egypt over the last three decades, a surprising number of ordinary Egyptians would vote for his son, Gamal, in presidential elections.

The challenges of today

In a similar vein, the Mubarak regime's human rights record remains under international scrutiny, in the wake of reports that it turns a blind eye to the continued use of torture and illegal detention by the Egyptian police.

LEFT: soldiers on tanks during the Arab-Israeli war of 1973. **ABOVE:** Essam Al Hadari celebrates Egypt getting through to the final of the Africa Cup.

Egypt enjoys good relations with its southern neighbour Sudan, though the continuing unrest in Darfur has contributed to an increase in the number of political and economic refugees seeking asylum in Egypt, already the most populous country in the Arab world. Egypt must contend with these problems against a background of parlous global economic conditions for which it has been ill prepared: the country is still a major recipient of US financial aid.

The Nile itself is under threat from the effects of climate change, with rising sea levels threatening to overwhelm the Delta, destroying farmland and disrupting the area's fragile ecosystem. Experts warn that if the trend continues the potential loss of agricultural produce could be catastrophic, turning an estimated 7 million people into "climate refugees".

Activists of all political persuasions are currently campaigning to prevent Mubarak's son, Gamal, from inheriting power. With the president's health deteriorating, there is much speculation about the direction Egypt will take in the post-Mubarak years.

Against these larger concerns, an unexpected source of hope and national pride has come in the form of the Egyptian national football team, which has just completed an unprecedented hat trick of consecutive triumphs in the Africa Cup of Nations, in 2006, 2008 and 2010. ❑

TAMING THE NILE

Control of the annual flood has always been the key to Egypt's prosperity. Before the construction of the Aswan Dam, the Nile's water level was a barometer for the state of the empire

Egyptian civilisation relied on a paradox: at the hottest, driest time of the year, in what would otherwise have been one of the least habitable places on earth, the Nile would break its banks with an ocean of water and rich silt.

All a farmer had to do was to wait for the flood to subside. Then he could scatter a few seeds, let his pigs trample them into the mud, and sit back to wait for the first of as many as three crops in a season. With subsistence more or less taking care of itself, the pharaohs had a pool of underemployed labour without which their unparalleled achievements along a 1,600km (1,000-mile) ribbon of riverbank would not have been conceivable. However, if the flood was too low, the amount of arable land could shrink disastrously; if too high, it washed away settlements that were supposedly on safe ground. Thus control of the Nile was a challenge to Egyptian ingenuity.

The first concerted effort to tame the river is credited to Menes, the first king of a united Upper and Lower Egypt who, in about 3000 BC, is said to have diverted the river in order to build the new capital, Memphis, on reclaimed land.

Early ingenuity

One example of early Nile engineering was that of a queen named Nitocris, who cunningly built an underground apartment with a secret channel leading to the river. This apparently allowed her to invite a group of guests to dinner only to pull the plug and drown the lot of them, on the grounds that they were suspected of murdering her brother.

The aquatic engineering feats of the Pyramid builders were inspired by rather more practical considerations. Enormous granite blocks were floated down the river from Aswan on reed barges. The Pyramids were generally built high above the flood plain, so special canals were dug to reduce the distance over which the blocks had to be dragged on sledges. A curious lapse in the technical precocity that produced the Pyramids was the failure to recognise the potential of the wheel, a concept already known to potters and shipwrights, for land transport.

PRECEDING PAGES: photo near the First Cataract at Aswan, *c.*1860. **LEFT:** Nile *dahabiyya*. **RIGHT:** fishing at dusk.

During the Middle Kingdom years especially *(see page 33)*, these works were carried out by prisoners of war, who supplemented local labour. According to Herodotus, Sesostris III put prisoners to work on a network of canals that served to increase the amount of arable land. His impatience with the enemy in Nubia to the south was such that he cleared a passage for ships through the First Cataract, enabling him to mount successful punitive raids.

King Amenemhat appreciated the extra crops that could be wrung out of the silt by efficient irrigation, so he initiated a bold programme of canals and reservoirs. The 32km (20-mile) dam wall he built across the oasis lake in Al Fayyum was still functioning a millennium later, when Herodotus wrote: "The water in this lake does not spring from the soil… It is conveyed through a channel from the Nile, and for six months flows into the lake, and for six months out again into the Nile." Herodotus was also impressed by a canal that joined the Nile and Red Sea, which reduced the fearsome overland journey to a comfortable four-day cruise. Some 120,000 labourers died for the project, Herodotus noted, but it was only completed by Darius, the Persian conqueror, not long before Herodotus' visit.

NILE NEWS

The entrance to the Khalig Canal in Cairo was opposite the Nilometer on the island of Roadah. Nilometers maintained at key points along the river from pharaonic times measured the rise of the water and, in particular, signalled the level (16 cubits) at which the farmers had to start paying tax on the land they worked.

The town crier, accompanied by a boy, would make his rounds with the latest news about the level. "Five digits today," he might cry, "and the Lord is bountiful!" To which the boy would respond with "Bless ye Muhammad!" The real excitement came when the government declared "Full Nile" as a prelude to cutting the dam and letting the water into the canal. With scores of small boys forming a procession, the town crier would improvise lines to stir the rich into producing a tip. The boys' chorus would proclaim: "Paradise is the abode of the generous." An unsympathetic response was likely to bring a quick change of tune: "Hell is the abode of the niggardly."

Innovation and neglect

The Romans, like the Persians and Greeks before them, improved the waterways of Egypt, and built a Red Sea canal that began near modern Cairo. At the time they considered but rejected the idea of a Suez canal because the Red Sea was thought to be 6 metres (30ft) higher than the Mediterranean (an objection put to de Lesseps when he resuscitated the plan in the 19th century). The Arabs continued this work: the Khalig Canal dissected the capital they built at Cairo.

The Mamluks neglected the waterways, but Napoleon, who arrived in 1798, wanted to clear the canals and repair the hydraulic machine that lifted water into a tower to supply the citadel. "The Mamluks never fixed anything," he said. Napoleon planned a series of dams along the Nile but, like a proposed Suez canal, they did not materialise before his enforced departure.

By 1833 Muhammad Ali, who rose from the French defeat to establish a new Egyptian dynasty, had been persuaded by the Frenchman Mougel Bey into adopting a scheme to regulate the water level over the Delta. The scheme faltered due to lack of funds but was revived by a British administration looking to rescue the ailing economy from Ali's heirs.

Sir Colin Scott-Moncrieff, the canal expert brought in from India to find another solution, noted wryly that Mougel Bey's project, idle for 50 years, still employed a large workforce which did nothing but draw their pay, "a duty which they performed with praiseworthy regularity".

A number of packing cases from England turned out to contain electric lighting. Henceforth, Scott-Moncrieff announced, the workers could look forward to labouring night and day. The dams were completed in 1891.

LEFT: building the Aswan Dam. **ABOVE:** the temple at Abu Simbel was relocated stone by stone to prevent it being flooded by the newly created Lake Nasser.

Aswan: achievements and controversies

The next major Nile project on the British agenda caused an outrage: a proposed dam at Aswan, the location of the First Cataract, would drown the island of Philae. Though the island was only 450 metres (1,500ft) long, it was the site of Egypt's finest Graeco-Roman works, notably the Temple of Isis. The height of the dam – which opened in 1902 – was lowered to answer these objections. Over the years its height was gradually increased.

The island was initially partially submerged for half of the year; later, all but the tip of the Temple of Isis remained under water. Tourists viewed the site from boats as if it were a coral reef. Ironically, the limestone monuments were impervious to water; with the added protection of a layer of mud, the immersion probably did them good, although it did erase some wall painting. The dam facilitated an increase in the number of acres under crops and, together with the higher yield produced by perennial irrigation generally, the increased revenue easily exceeded the cost.

In 1960 President Nasser decided that a High Dam should be constructed at Aswan. The apex of his dream for the future, it created the world's largest artificial lake, the 6,000-sq-km (2,300-sq-mile) Lake Nasser, which stretches into Sudan. An undertaking of pharaonic proportions, it was constructed by 30,000 Egyptians working day and night for 11 years under Soviet supervision after Britain and the US withdrew their support in protest at Nasser's nationalist politics. Its purpose was to protect Egypt from droughts or floods in Ethiopia and Sudan, as well as to provide water resources and cheap power needed by a rapidly growing population. The 280,000 hectares (700,000 acres) of land already cultivated could be harvested more than once a year, and more than 400,000 hectares (1 million acres) of desert land have been reclaimed for cultivation.

ABOVE: President Nasser in 1966. **RIGHT:** calm waters as a result of the High Dam at Aswan.

But the cost, potential and actual, was high. It would have sandwiched Philae in destructive currents between the new dam and the older British dam downstream. A Unesco rescue plan resulted in the nearby, higher island of Agiliqiyyah being blasted into a semblance of Philae, after which the monuments were dismantled block by block and reassembled on their new home.

Other areas fared less well in the building of the Aswan Dam. Lake Nasser wiped out Nubia; some 100,000 Nubians lost their land and most of their culture when they were resettled around Aswan and upriver.

The dam traps the silt that formerly enriched the fields, so farmers now rely on chemical fertilisers, which enter the food chain and exhaust the soil. The perennial irrigation has caused soil salinity requiring extra drainage systems, which in turn provide breeding grounds for mosquitoes and bilharzia-carrying snails. This salinity of the soil, rising water-tables and greater humidity also threaten the ancient monuments. The lack of silt deposits in the Delta area make the coastline more vulnerable to erosion.

The future

For all the unfortunate side effects, a tamed Nile has removed the uncertainties which, at least 7,000 years ago, began with questions of the river's source and durability.

In 2005, the Mubarak Pumping Station – the centrepiece of Egypt's ambitious Toshka Project – was opened. Seen as a solution to the debilitating overpopulation of the Nile Valley, the project aims to increase Egypt's inhabitable land from 5 to 25 per cent. The largest pumping station in the world, it will pump water from Lake Nasser to irrigate the Toshka area in southern Egypt. Sceptics question the wisdom of developing water-hungry agriculture in the hottest part of the country, and wonder if the project will benefit Egypt or foreign investors. In addition, the 10 countries sharing the Nile's resources have been disputing water reserves in the region for many years. When the Toshka Project is completed in 2020, the valley is projected to become home to more than 3 million residents and to increase Egypt's arable land area by 10 percent. ❑

The Search for the Source

The source of the Nile had been the subject of speculation since ancient times; finally it was discovered by two of the great Victorian explorers

In 1770 the Scotsman James Bruce stood in exultation on a mountain in Ethiopia: he believed he had discovered the source of the Nile. Unfortunately, he was in fact on the wrong branch of the wrong river: the Nile divides near Khartoum in the Sudan into the White Nile and Blue Nile, and Bruce's mistake was in thinking that the latter was the main river. In fact, at the confluence, the White has already flowed for some 3,200km (2,000 miles), the Blue for only about 800km (500 miles).

Classical accounts

Bruce had few references to work from. The richest source of material was still Herodotus, but the "Father of History" himself had had to rely on what contemporaries could tell him about the Nile. There were all sorts of theories, including the idea that it flowed backwards from the sea, but the one he found least plausible was ironically closest to the truth, that "the Nile flows from melted snow". How could that be, he asked, since it flowed from places which were even hotter than Egypt?

Other Greeks investigated, and the Roman emperor Nero sent an expedition upriver, but the hardest information was in a map produced by the geographer and astronomer Ptolemy in AD 150. Based on the work of the Syrian geographer Marinus of Tyre, the map showed the Nile rising from two great lakes in Central Africa which were fed by what he called the Mountains of the Moon.

Burton and Speke

After Bruce and others had failed, the search for the source fell to the Victorian explorers Richard Francis Burton, a formidable polymath of prodigious physical strength, and John Hanning Speke, six years his junior, elegant and temperate.This odd couple had met during an escapade in Aden while both were in the British Indian Army, and only later put their minds to finding the source of the Nile.

Starting in Zanzibar, they cut across Africa and after eight months drew up on the shores of Lake Tanganyika. Burton surmised that any river flowing north from the lake could well be the Nile. They found a river but it flowed into the lake, not out of it. Burton was not feeling well, so Speke went ahead to look into reports of a larger lake some three weeks to the north.

Speke found the lake but could not prove that it was the source, and so Burton stuck to the theory that the Nile sprang from the Mountains of the Moon, wherever they might be. Returning to the Indian Ocean, Burton had business to attend to in Zanzibar, so Speke took an earlier passage back to England, the agreement being (Burton claimed) that he would make no reference to their findings in Africa until Burton rejoined him.

However, Speke immediately told the Royal Geographical Society the sensational news that he had found the source. Money was made available so that he could lead another expedition to confirm his findings, and plans were well advanced when Burton returned. No one was terribly interested in his report on Lake Tanganyika or his objections to Speke's claim. His place on Speke's next expedition would be taken by another Indian Army officer, Captain James Grant.

Speke and Grant took a year over the journey inland from Zanzibar, spending a month with a convivial king who advised them that the country ahead was in a state of civil war, and that it would be

ABOVE: engraving of James Bruce, a Scottish explorer, discovering what he believes is the source of the Nile, *c.*1800. **RIGHT:** Lake Victoria.

necessary to receive permission to progress from a King Mutesa whose court was a six-week walk away. Grant had hurt his leg, so Speke went ahead alone to negotiate.

The search for Speke

Mutesa withheld permission to proceed for nearly five months, a delay which prompted Sir Roderick Murchison at the Royal Geographic Society in London to contact Samuel Baker, then big-game hunting in Sudan, to ask him to search for Speke and Grant.

In the meantime, Speke and Grant went off to investigate reports they had picked up at Mutesa's court of a large river flowing north from Lake Victoria. Grant could not keep up with the impatient pace of the march and agreed that Speke should again go ahead. On 21 July 1862, Speke discovered a broad river about 65km (40 miles) north of the lake. Marching upstream for a week, Speke was at last satisfied when he saw that the river made a spectacular exit from the lake, over what Speke named the Ripon Falls after an earlier president of the Royal Geographical Society.

Instead of going back the way they had come, Speke and Grant headed north. More than two years after their departure from Zanzibar, they heard welcoming rifle shots and the sound of a drum and fife band. On the strength of rumours of two white men in the vicinity, a column of Egyptian and Nubian soldiers in Turkish uniform had come out to greet them. Speke immediately sent a cable back to London: "Inform Sir Roderick Murchison that all is well, that we are in latitude 14° 30" upon the Nile, and that the Nile is settled."

At Gondokoro he ran into Baker and his wife preparing for their rescue mission. Speke said he had positively identified the source, but when he confided that there might be a second source, a large lake known locally as Luta Nzige, and gave Baker a map of their route, Baker immediately began to recruit a team of porters for the task.

Speke and Grant returned to a rapturous reception in England. Burton disputed Speke's discoveries, pointing out that Speke had not circumnavigated the lake to find out whether it was itself fed by a river, in which case the source of the Nile lay wherever that river originated; Burton was sure that there was another river, and that it flowed from his Mountains of the Moon.

Tragic news

The acrimony between Burton and Speke built up, but eventually they agreed to appear together at a meeting of the British Association for the Advancement of Science in Bath on 16 September 1864. Burton recorded what happened on the day: "Early in the forenoon fixed for what silly tongues called the 'Nile Duel' I found a large assembly in the rooms of Section E (Geography and Ethnography). A note was handed round in silence. Presently my friend Mr Findlay broke the tidings to me. Captain Speke had lost his life on the yesterday, at 4pm, whilst shooting over a cousin's grounds. He had been missed in the field

and his kinsman found him lying upon the earth, shot through the body close to the heart. He lived only a few minutes and his last words were a request not to be moved."

According to those present, Burton staggered visibly about the platform and sank into a chair "with his face working". He was heard to moan, "By God, he's killed himself!" He managed to pull himself together long enough to deliver a hastily substituted paper on Dahomey. On getting home, his wife said, "he wept long and bitterly". All she could make out was the same word repeated over and over again: "Jack."

Baker's progress

Deep in the heart of Africa, Baker and his wife did not hear of Speke's death. Conditions were worse than they feared. Not only was there a war swirling around them and rampant malaria, but they were suspected wherever they went of being slave traders, although matters improved when Baker started wearing a tweed suit. In African eyes he now resembled Speke, whom they trusted.

Mrs Baker's waist-length blonde hair was as mesmerising as her husband's tweed suit. Tribesmen brought their families to watch when she washed it, and it gave the trigger-happy King Mutesa ideas. The king had stubbornly refused to supply porters as long as he had reason to believe that Baker, who had already given him shotguns, beads, carpets and so forth, had more presents up his sleeve. One day, however, he appeared to have had a complete change of heart: Baker could have his team of porters and proceed if the king could have Mrs Baker. Baker drew his pistol and threatened to shoot the king there and then, while Mrs Baker "withered him with an outburst of furious indignation". The king dropped the idea, and a team of porters and a guide materialised the following day. Eventually, on 14 March 1864, Baker and his wife reached their goal, which he named Lake Albert, after Queen Victoria's consort.

It took them two months to return to King Mutesa. Their arrival produced a bizarre twist: the "king" was actually someone else; the man with designs on Mrs Baker was merely a stand-in who had been given the job as long as suspicion remained that the Bakers were slave traders bent on capturing the king.

The Bakers returned to Gondokoro after an absence of two years, but there was no one to meet them. They had long been presumed dead. A warmer welcome awaited them in Khartoum, but it was not until reaching Cairo that Baker was able to realise a dream that had haunted him for the past five years he had been in Africa: a decent glass of Allsopp's pale ale. Before even reaching England, he was awarded the Geographical Society's gold star and a knighthood soon followed. Officially he became Sir Samuel Baker; to the public, "Baker of the Nile".

Above: David Livingstone being carried to his African home in Tanzania to die. **Right:** Samuel Baker with his wife Florence. **Far Right:** Speke and Grant at the end of their expedition, met by Samuel and Florence Baker.

Dr Livingstone

The question now was whether lakes Albert and Victoria were in any way connected. On 22 May 1865, Sir Roderick Murchison announced that the Society had resolved to clear matters up once and for all. The man they had chosen for the job was 52-year-old David Livingstone, a former medical missionary who had explored the southern and central regions.

Livingstone started from Zanzibar and planned to travel through unexplored country below Lake Tanganyika, south of the usual caravan routes. After three years, most of his teeth had fallen out, he had contracted malaria, had lost all his medicines and nearly all of his men and animals, and had achieved next to nothing. After incredible hardships he had reached not the Nile but the Congo.

Meanwhile, Henry Morton Stanley, the English-born *New York Herald*'s man in Paris, had been assigned to cover the opening of the Suez Canal in 1869 and to write a piece on Nile cruises. After this and other commissions he was permitted to look for Livingstone. This he duly did, and, uttering the immortal words "Dr Livingstone, I presume?" arrived in the nick of time to rescue Livingstone.

Rather than turning back home, the two men went off to investigate a few of Livingstone's ideas concerning the source of the Nile. After a trek of some 960km (600 miles), Stanley started to feel the pressure of a deadline and went home. Livingstone had to wait several months for reinforcements which Stanley had promised, but was then on the go again, hoping to establish that the source of the Nile was a stream that ran into Lake Bangweolo. Eight months later, however, on 1 May 1873, Livingstone was dead.

On learning of Livingstone's death, Stanley resolved to settle the issue of the Nile source personally. Africa had never seen anything like the expedition he put together: 365 men, 8 tonnes of stores and a steel boat which came apart in sections. It was conducted like a military campaign; and any hint of African opposition was put down with force. The boat was lowered into the water as soon as they reached Lake Victoria. After a voyage of 1,600km (1,000 miles) lasting 57 days, Stanley had proof that the lake had only one outlet, Ripon Falls.

The riddle is solved

The argument was over and it remained only to award the garland to the solver of the great geographical secret. "Speke", Stanley wrote, "has now the full glory of having discovered the largest inland sea on the continent of Africa, also its principal affluent as well as its outlet. He also understood the geography of the countries we travelled through better than any of those who so persistently opposed his hypothesis..." Unfortunately for Speke himself, this recognition was posthumous. ❑

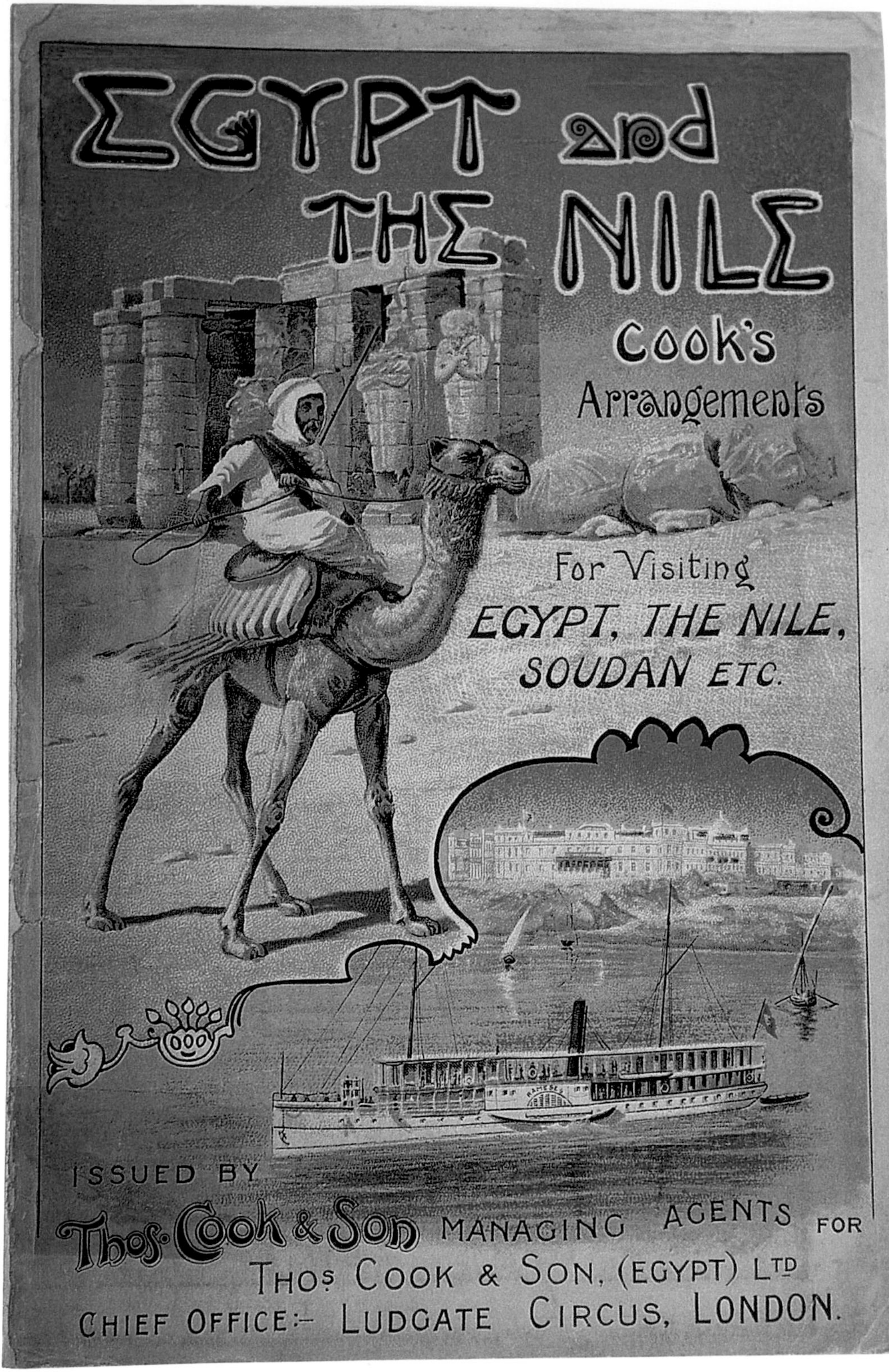
EGYPT and THE NILE
COOK'S
Arrangements
For Visiting
EGYPT, THE NILE,
SOUDAN ETC.
RAMESES
ISSUED BY
Thos. Cook & Son MANAGING AGENTS FOR
THOS. COOK & SON, (EGYPT) LTD
CHIEF OFFICE:- LUDGATE CIRCUS, LONDON.

THE HISTORY OF NILE CRUISING

Egypt is the Nile and the Nile is Egypt, so if you want to see more of the country than the Pyramids, it had best be from a boat

Thomas Cook, a printer from Leicester, England, and a member of the Temperance Society, went into tourism in the 1840s as a means of diverting people from drunken idleness. In 1869 the only viable way to see the sights of Egypt was by boat. It was only along the river that Egypt had ever been habitable. Everything was built along the river, and ordinary houses depended on bricks made out of Nile mud. The huge blocks of limestone and granite used to build the temples and pyramids could be easily transported by the river; on land, they had to be hauled over desert sand by vast armies of men.

The Great Pyramid of Khufu had in fact been in existence for more than 1,000 years before Egyptians were introduced to any refinements in land transport. The chariots of the invading Hyksos in about 1600 BC demonstrated the possibilities of the wheel, an invention that the Egyptians had taken only as far as the potter's wheel.

Ancient Egypt did not need the wheel to enjoy efficient transport and communications. These two elements, added to the agricultural windfall provided by the annual inundation, were the key to the creation in 3000 BC of a nation-state.

Early days

In those days, navigation on the Nile was efficient but not foolproof. Barges drifting down from Aswan with granite blocks for the Pyramids dragged a sizeable stone from the stern to keep them pointing in the right direction, and broad, upturned prows evolved to simplify dislodging after inevitable groundings on sandbanks. Sails, originally square but later "lateen", or triangular, under Arab influence, had to be disproportionately large or at least set high to catch wind passing above the shelter of high banks. A stiff breeze made them a handful.

Modern recreation

Thor Heyerdahl was a Norwegian adventurer whose *Kon-Tiki* expedition in the 1950s proved that primitive boat-building techniques could be used for oceanic crossings; he set out to show that the papyrus raft which was the starting point for Nile craft (the baby Moses is believed to have occupied a tiny version in the

LEFT: Thomas Cook pioneered the cruise business.
RIGHT: Thor Heyerdahl's *Ra II*, made of papyrus like the Nile's earliest boats.

bulrushes) could have been developed into an ocean-going vessel capable of reaching places as far away as Sri Lanka, a voyage mentioned in Pliny. Heyerdahl's first experiment in the Mediterranean failed when *Ra I* became water-logged, but in *Ra II* the next year, 1970, he was halfway across the Atlantic Ocean before the bindings came apart.

Early sails resembled Venetian blinds made of papyrus, but suitable materials were soon found and sails became works of art painted in rich colours and embroidered with the emblem of the king's soul.

Heyerdahl had copied the design from ancient drawings, collected papyrus reeds from Lake Tana (the Ethiopian source of the Blue Nile) and brought in craftsmen from Lake Chad to put the boat together by traditional means. The voyages were not totally successful, but he felt he had proved the point. Some experts argue that Heyerdahl set his sights unnecessarily high and that wood, more plentiful in ancient Egypt than at present, would have made up a significant content of craft, which nevertheless retained the old, "papyriform" shape.

A Boat Fit for Royalty

The royal solar boat is a marvellous sight. Discovered in 1954 and since determined to be from the period of Khufu's reign (4,800 years ago), it stands 44 metres (143ft) long and 6 metres (19½ft) wide, and would have had about 38cm (15 inches) of freeboard amidships, both prow and stern rising well clear of the water. The hull is made of boards stitched together with twisted hemp that shrank with water contact, thereby tightening the seams and making them watertight.

The captain occupied his own little "cabin" towards the bow, the greater part of the boat being given over to the opulent royal quarters and a long canopy. It is thought from the way the ropes have cut into the wood that the boat was actually used, but how and why is debatable. Six pairs of oars would not have provided much propulsion, so they might have been used for steering and the boat either towed or pulled along by ropes on land.

Housed in a museum that was specially built around the vessel close to where it was discovered on the south side of the Great Pyramid, the solar boat is well worth going to see. From the ramp that passes around the boat you can examine it from every angle. Be sure also to visit the boat pit, where it was buried, covered by limestone slabs, and the basement of the museum, which displays pictures of the boat's recovery. *(For more information, see page 238.)*

The early passenger boats on the Nile had a cabin that left enough room on either side for oarsmen. To judge from the amount of deck-scrubbing depicted in tomb paintings, a premium was put on cleanliness. The boats in common use were one-man papyrus canoes for fishing and fowling (the latter with a throwing stick resembling the boomerang but with the important difference that it did not come back) and "white-water" sport over the cataracts.

> *Ancient Euphrates river craft used hides stretched on wooden frames. They drifted down to Babylon before being dismantled, the pieces piled on the backs of donkeys brought along for the strenuous walk home.*

The solar boat

The royal boats were in a class of their own, symbolic of the boat which took the sun-god

Ra across the heavens, and hence the misleading term "solar boats" – nothing to do with solar energy. Smaller boats had been found with royal burials in the 19th century, but the best example was not found until 1954, when the Egyptologist Kamal Al Mallakh cleared away rubble on the south side of the Great Pyramid at Giza and found the entrance to what proved to be an airtight boat chamber. Prising it open, he was struck by a blast of hot air. "I closed my eyes and I smelt incense," he wrote, "I smelt time... I smelt centuries... I smelt history itself." For the first time in 4,800 years, sunlight broke the darkness of the pit and revealed first the tip of a steering oar and then the magnificent prow.

The sealing of the chamber had worked so well that the wood looked "fresh and new". The boat, however, was largely in kit form, 1,224 pieces of wood carefully stacked in 13 layers, together with rigging, baskets, matting and all the other accessories. What was singularly lacking, though, were instructions on how to put the thing together. It took several false starts and 10 years to work out the puzzle, and the solution may now be admired in the museum at the foot of the Great Pyramid (*see box opposite*).

LEFT: *Ra II*, a papyrus boat headed by Thor Heyerdahl, which sailed from Morocco to Barbados. **ABOVE:** solar boat of the pharaoh Khufu (Cheops), at Giza.

Medieval craft

By the Middle Ages there were said to be around 36,000 ships working the Nile. The Italian monk Frescobaldi reported that "there was such a great quantity of boats that all those that I have ever seen in the ports of Genoa, Venice and Ancona put together, not counting the double-decked

Behind the Scenes of the Cruise Business

Whether gin-and-tonic-fuelled getaway or authentic way to immerse yourself in local culture, there's more to a cruise than meets the eye

In the pleasantly cool hours of the evening, as you settle by the pool on the roof of your cruise ship with a glass of something mildly intoxicating in your hand, spare a moment to ponder the industry that is serving you. The pedigree of Nile cruising is as long as that of the temples on the river's banks. Egyptian pharaohs cruised up and down the river to survey their kingdom, and Cleopatra took Caesar for a magnificent river cruise as part of her seduction of the Roman general.

The more substantial Nile cruisers comprise around 50–80 cabins and a staff of 80 for a passenger complement of around 100. Only six or seven of the staff are actually ship's crew, usually distinguishable by their *galabiyas* (traditional dress). The captain is only in charge of the technical operation of the boat and has no jurisdiction over the passenger areas.

Each Nile cruiser has the equivalent of a hotel manager, who is the overall master of the boat. He will have moved into the cruise business from onshore hotel management, and it is to him that the captain answers. The two will have very different backgrounds – the hotel manager coming from urban middle management and the captain probably coming from an agricultural background.

Observant passengers may sometimes notice members of the crew conducting odd rituals, such as throwing bread or salt on to the water, or the hooting of the ship's horn for no apparent reason; as with any water-going people, the crews on the Nile boats are very superstitious, and pay homage at various shrines along the riverbank.

Beaching a Nile cruiser is a very embarrassing business, an occurrence that every captain dreads. Scraping the bottom is not infrequent, but just occasionally a boat gets so stuck – usually in the shallows near Edfu – that it has to apply to the Cairo Board of Navigation to have more water released into the river so that it can float free. In an incident like this the captain is unlikely to survive in his job unless he has a very good excuse.

Catering is a prime concern on a cruise ship, just as eating is a prime occupation. The bigger ships have a kitchen staff of around 15, who make all their own bread, cakes, pastries and so on, on the boat on a daily basis. Most of the meat and groceries are bought either in Luxor or Aswan, and are supplemented by fresh vegetables, fruit and cheese that are sometimes bought at the stops en route.

The crew on the passenger side work shift systems, and are paid a salary plus a bonus which depends on the bar takings and room occupancy rate. Every 45 days they usually get two weeks off. As a rule, they earn better money on cruise ships than they would in the equivalent quality of hotel onshore, and so such jobs are sought after. The work is varied and the scene – passengers and places – is always changing.

For the passengers, reclining with a cocktail on the top deck while watching the sun set brilliantly over the Nile, the combination of dry history, sumptuous self-indulgence, a delicious winter sun and an endless unrolling of landscape makes this the holiday of a lifetime. ❑

LEFT AND ABOVE: working on the cruise boats plying the Nile.

ships, would not come to one-third (their) number". Cairo was then one of the world's great commercial centres, with slaves, gold, ivory, and spices coming down the river to connect with traders operating across the Red Sea.

The Arab historian Abd Al Latif remarked on ships with "a wooden chamber over which

> Dahabiyyas, *beautifully crafted traditional sail-boats, are enjoying a revival in popularity, providing a quieter and more exclusive alternative to the larger Nile cruise vessels.*

Modern craft

The Egyptian nobility had always treated themselves to grand river craft; lesser beings travelled a lot more modestly. The modern cruise ship is in the tradition of the former, the ubiquitous felucca of the latter. It is still possible to hire a felucca, an Italian term applied loosely to any kind of pleasure boat, and explore the Nile independently, but to do so is to miss out on the grander scale of things.

Perhaps inspired by the example of Gustave Flaubert in 1850, the late William Golding tried an independent cruise and ended up writing a bad-tempered book *(Egyptian Journal)* about the

is elevated a dome with windows, and in the daytime furnished with shutters, and which give a view over the river in each direction. There is in this chamber a private cabinet and latrines, and they decorate it in various colours, with gilding, and the most beautiful varnish". In the end, of course, these beautiful designs had to yield to changing circumstances. The *dahabiyya* was replaced by the paddle-steamer, which in turn was replaced by the modern, diesel-powered cruise ship. Steel is more practical than wood, as wood was more practical than papyrus.

ABOVE: *Rameses I*, one of the first paddle-steamers on the Nile.

TAKING A CRUISE

The short cruise between Aswan and Luxor presently takes three days. On the way, the boat usually stops at Kom Ombo, Edfu and Esna. It would be a criminal waste to allow fewer than three days for the temples at Luxor (Thebes) and the attractions of the west bank (the Valley of the Kings, Queen Hatshepsut's Temple, etc). Government restrictions prevent cruise ships from going further north than Abydos and Dandarah, with the result that the great sites of Middle Egypt, such as Tall Al Amarnah and Bani Hasan, now see very few tourists; however, the cancellation of a number of land convoys across the country may mean that relaxation on the waterways could come next.

experience. His crew was forever jumping ship to look up relatives, and his skipper was argumentative about where they should moor for the night.

Flaubert and the photographer Maxime du Camp travelled as far as Wadi Halfa, although they were as interested in the brothels as in the ancient monuments. Flaubert was particularly taken by a certain Kuchuk Hanem: "a regal-looking creature… with slit nostrils, enormous eyes and magnificent knees; when she danced there were formidable folds of flesh on her stomach." Both men caught venereal diseases.

Thomas Cook, a militant abstainer, would not have approved. In his eyes, the secret of a good holiday was not to be found in bed. Nor did it involve haggling over prices. He charged his clients a lump sum for passage, accommodation, board and the services of a guide, and made no provision for alcoholic drinks.

Travellers' tales

Cook introduced the paddle-steamer, romantic in retrospect (with no small thanks to Agatha Christie's famous *Death on the Nile*) but at the time scorned by traditionalists who preferred the elegant *dahabiyya*. Napoleon commandeered *dahabiyyas* for his Nile expedition and named his flagship *L'Italie*.

THE GRAND OLD HOTELS ALONG THE NILE

Early tourists were obliged to sleep on their *dahabiyyas* because there were no hotels on the Nile south of Cairo, but that changed towards the end of the 19th century. The Winter Palace on the waterfront at Luxor was opened in 1905 and became almost as famous as any landmark in the city. In addition to hosting an unbroken stream of suitably qualified guests in the royal suite, the hotel was the headquarters for archaeologists exploring ancient Thebes (Luxor), and the ghosts of men like Howard Carter still hover in the bar.

The Old Cataract Hotel in Aswan has a glorious view from its eyrie on a granite bluff. It opened in 1899 and was immediately so popular that overflow guests had to be put up in tents. Its showpiece was and is the dining room. Its Mamluk-style ceiling rises in four sweeping arches to form a 22-metre (75ft) dome. The Old Cataract is currently under renovation and is set to re-emerge from its scaffolding in late 2010.

The most sadly missed of all Egypt's historic hotels is Shepheard's in Cairo, which had a ballroom modelled on the pillars of Karnak. A guest once wrote that "even the lavatories have something monumental about them… you feel as if you were sitting in the central chamber inside a pyramid."

The hotel was destroyed during riots in 1952; the present Shepheard's Hotel stands on a different site.

The 19th-century traveller and writer Amelia Edwards, whose *A Thousand Miles up the Nile* became a travel classic, did for the *dahabiyya* what *Death on the Nile* later did for the paddle-steamer. The redoubtable Miss Edwards joined a Miss Marianne Brocklehurst and her nephew Alfred of Cheshire for her voyage to Abu Simbel, the two parties travelling in separate boats. They made leisurely progress, pausing to collect innumerable objects and to allow Alfred to pursue his futile dream of bagging a crocodile. "Too clever for him," Miss Edwards remarked.

The cruise-ship deckchair is a fitting place in which to reflect on the fact that sailing is never easier than on the Nile. The prevailing wind blows a craft upstream, the current brings it back.

The two spinsters managed to acquire a mummy, but even stuffing it into a tight locker could not contain the terrible smell. Worried about being caught in illegal possession, they gave up after a week and tipped "the dear departed" over the side. At Abu Simbel, Miss Edwards cleaned the faces of the statues of Rameses II, "one of the handsomest men not only of his own day but of all history."

Thanks in part to the success of books such as *A Thousand Miles up the Nile*, Nile cruising caught the popular imagination, and soon hundreds of *dahabiyyas* were plying for trade on the Cairo waterfront. Miss Edwards ploughed back the royalties she received from her book into the Egypt Exploration Society and an Egyptology chair at University College, London.

Modern style

The steam engine and then the diesel forced the pace of change, but in the 1870s, just as Thomas Cook was getting his new business off the ground, something else was going on. Egypt was at last getting proper roads and feeling, for the first time, the full impact of the wheel. Nonetheless, a cruise remained the best way to see Egypt.

The present type of cruise ship was introduced in 1959. It is evident from their shape – like vast floating hotels – that today's cruise ships are made with the passenger in mind. They are not designed for rough weather or choppy seas (the Nile rarely experiences rough weather).

Cruising today

In 1975 there were only a couple of dozen boats on the river of the size and standard of today's cruisers. Today there are over 300 boats, most of them travelling between Luxor and Aswan or in Lake Nasser. Some cabins may be small bordering on claustrophobic, but in general the standards of accommodation, food and entertainment are good. Most boats have a small pool, and the bar staff cheerfully go without sleep for as long as passengers are likely to need their attention. Some of the better cruises employ a resident Egyptologist to hold lectures and answer questions.

With the exception of a few *dahabbiyas*, cruising is not as romantic as it used to be. Prices vary wildly depending on the quality of the cruise ship you book. At the top of the scale are the Oberoi-operated cruisers decorated with antiques, parquet flooring and wood panelling, while at the other end are the various boats booked in-resort by backpackers looking to go with the flow without having to spend an overflow of Egyptian pounds. Be sure to check out your selected ship before parting with any funds. ❑

LEFT: one of Thomas Cook's earliest tours of the Nile for tourists, in Victorian times. **RIGHT:** a gong signals dinner.

Nile Cruising

Once the ultimate in luxury, today a Nile river cruise is part of almost every package itinerary to Egypt. But if you choose carefully it is still the best way to enjoy the river

There are two major cruise routes along the Nile – one a classic journey and the other a more recent addition to the experience. The traditional cruise takes passengers between Aswan and Luxor, with trips sometimes extending as far as Abydos. More recently, cruises on Lake Nasser have become popular.

The large cruisers have fairly rigid itineraries, travelling between Aswan and Luxor and taking from three to six nights. Trips going south are usually longer than those heading north because they go against the flow of the current. On most cruises, meals and entertainment are included in the cost, in addition to stops at the most significant temples and sights along the route. Cruise ships vary in quality from little more than glorified (and ancient) ferries with simple rooms right up to five-star facilities boasting lavish interiors like the *Triton* or the liners operated by the Oberoi group.

The newest addition to cruising options in Egypt is the Lake Nasser cruise. There are currently six cruise lines operating on the world's largest man-made lake. Passengers will enjoy visiting Abu Simbel and a number of lakeside temples inaccessible by any other means.

Other cruising options include taking a felucca *(see right)*, or for the ultimate in splendour, chartering a *dahabbiyyah* – a private sailing boat inspired by the luxurious sailing vessels of the 19th century and only available to the super-rich.

Currently, cruises along the entire length of the Nile are not running due to security fears. The removal of the convoy system in large sections of Middle Egypt is giving hope to a reinstatement of itineraries from Aswan to Cairo, but nothing has been finalised to date.

For more on cruising, *see page 309.*

Above: one of the larger cruise ships which ply the Nile, seen here on the stretch between Luxor and Esna.

Below Left: you'll see this type of cruise ship lining the Corniche at Aswan.

Below: one of the best things about taking a cruise is that you get to observe everyday life on the river.

RIGHT: the captain on one of Thomas Cook's pioneering tourist tours in Victorian times.

BELOW: service with style on the top deck of the steam ship *Sudan* between Luxor and Aswan.

CHARTERING A FELUCCA

Sailing boats with large sails and a flat, shallow bottom have been plying these waters since the earliest days of the ancient empire. The shape you see today has little changed since the days of Rameses II, who reigned 3,000 years ago.

Feluccas are small sailing boats, which means fewer passengers (they usually carry between six and eight people) and a far more intimate – and quieter – experience than the bigger cruise ships provide. Because they do not need special mooring sites, they can stop at small islands and get nearer to the ancient temples.

Most felucca trips begin at Aswan, so they can take advantage of the strong northward current if the wind dies, and end south of Esna, where onward transport to Luxor can be arranged (at extra cost).The deck is covered in mattresses, and a canopy overhead in the day keeps the heat off. At night, the canopy becomes the "walls" of the boat to keep out the cold. Toilet facilities are basic.

Many of the felucca captains are Nubian, and you may have the added pleasure of visiting their village, or even dining with their family, along the way *(see also page 310)*.

BELOW: entertainment on the Mövenpick *Prince Abbas*, which cruises between the Aswan High Dam and Abu Simbel.

THE PEOPLE OF THE NILE

From its two sources and on to the Mediterranean, the Nile makes its mark on multiple nations, cultures and communities

When Allah created the nations, so Arab wisdom has it, he endowed each with two counterbalanced qualities: to the intelligence of the Syrians he thus added fatuousness; to Iraq he gave pride, but tempered it with hypocrisy; while for the desert Arabs he compensated hardship with good health. And Egypt he blessed with abundance at the cost of humility.

Egyptian humility takes many forms. One is a tragic sense of life, arising from a tragic view of history. While the West embraces the idea of progress as a solution to all man's ills, the Egyptians have an impulse to turn towards a utopian past, perhaps to a time when Muhammad's successors, the four Rightly Guided Caliphs, brought justice, prosperity and true belief to the land.

Naguib Mahfouz encapsulated the Egyptians' tragic sense of life when he wrote: "Life is wise to deceive us, for had it told us from the start what it had in store for us, we would refuse to be born."

Islam and popular piety

Any visitor to Egypt will be struck by the piety of its people. Humility is inherent in the very word Islam, the religion of nine-tenths of Egyptians and many tribal members in Uganda, Ethiopia and Sudan who dwell near the Nile. Islam (from the Arabic roots *salima*, to be safe,

aslama, to surrender, and *salaam*, peace) means "submission", whether it be to God, fate or the social system framed by the Qur'an.

Many Muslims do not go to the mosque or pray five times a day, but the majority consider themselves religious, believing in a supreme deity and the imminence of the Day of Judgement. The dawn-to-dusk fast during Ramadan is officially observed by the entire country, a sign of the pervasiveness of Islam. And many Egyptian tastes, habits and preferences are referred directly back to the Qur'an.

The Coptic Christians, too, conscious of being members of one of the earliest Christian sects, maintain a degree of devoutness that often

LEFT: an Egyptian boy stands beside the Colossi of Memnon, remains of the temple of Amenhotep III on the West Bank at Luxor. **RIGHT:** local Aswan man.

bewilders Westerners. Religious expressions of a kind that have almost vanished from European speech proliferate in everyday language. "God willing", "By God's permission", "Praise God" and "Our Lord prevails" are as common as the word "Goodbye" is in English.

An increase in extremism has resulted in a slight inflation in the number of skirmishes between Copts and Muslims throughout Egypt. In the workplace, however, you will often find employees of both religions working side by side convivially. This is in contrast to what occurs in other nations along the Nile's riverbanks, particularly to the south in Sudan.

Nation versus tribe

Translated from Arabic, the name Sudan means "Land of the Blacks". Despite this, years of civil war have pitted the northern "Arab" peoples against the southern "black Africans" who follow Christian or animist traditions. The people of the Sudan tend to have less allegiance to their nation, and more to local or regional tribes. The borders created when Sudan attained independence have a lot to do with this, as many tribes were divided by artificial map lines.

National policy is enforcing the use of Arabic in schools and government buildings in an attempt to unify the nation; however, it has merely caused more division as southerners feel their culture is being attacked.

THE POWER OF THE WORD

Many Westerners find perplexing the continuing dominance of Islam in what purports to be an age of reason. The important thing to recognise is that Muslims believe the Qur'an – literally, a "recitation" – is the Word of God as directly transmitted by the Prophet Muhammad. The power of the Word thus has a strength in Islam that is unmatched by the literature of any other "revealed" religion. For this reason translations of the Qur'an are considered vastly inferior, and all Muslims are urged to read the Qur'an in Arabic. For non-Arabic speakers, a 2008 translation by Tarif Khalidi (Penguin) is considered to be one of the best.

Despite the ever-present tension, and Sudan's status as one of the 25 poorest nations on the planet, the Sudanese people are very welcoming. Religious and cultural celebrations see entire villages come out to kill and roast a sheep.

Women in Sudan have much less freedom than their Egyptian counterparts, making the souq the one-stop-shop for gossip and conversation. Western clothing is common in the cities; however, you will note more frequent acceptance of the hijab or burqa in the countryside. In the rural south, you may even find villagers in farming communities adhering to ancient traditions by wearing nothing at all.

Facial scarring is an old custom of the Sudanese. While the tradition is dying out, it is still practised by some tribes. For men, patterns denote bravery, while for women the scars are supposed to accentuate beauty.

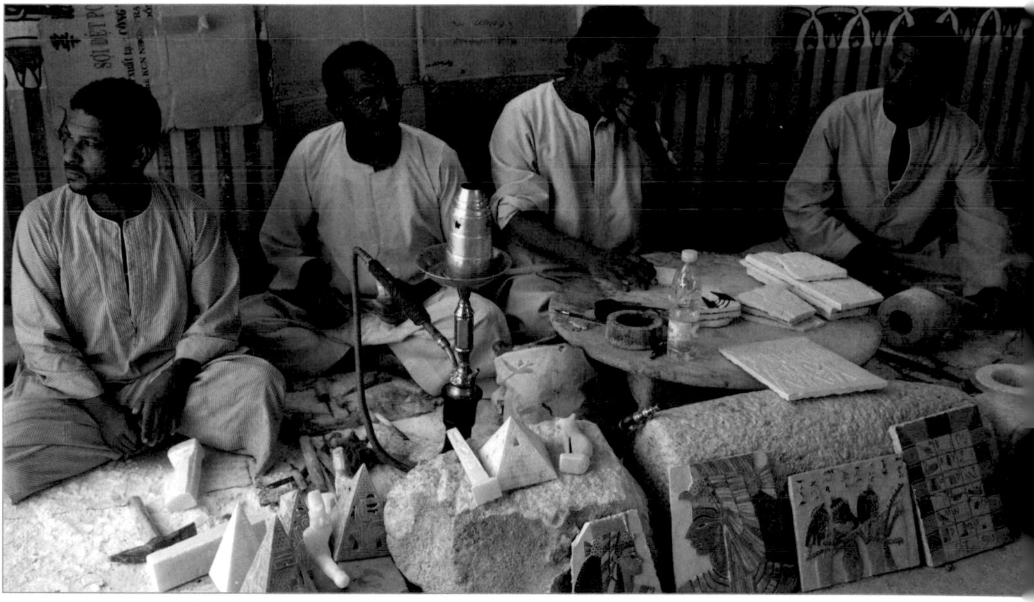

LEFT: life on the outskirts of Cairo. **ABOVE:** an alabaster factory open to tourists near Luxor.

A culture of deference and diversity

Tribal diversity is just as strong in Ethiopia and Uganda; however, Islam is the minority religion in both these nations. In Ethiopia, Christian ethnic groups live in the highlands (including the area around the source of the Blue Nile, Lake Tana), while Arabs stick to the lowlands. In Uganda, differentiation is made according to language kinships, with tribes based on the north and along the course of the Nile speaking Nilotic and Central Sudanic languages as opposed to the Bantu of the south.

Village life in both Uganda and Ethiopia focuses on the home, which is usually cylindrical in shape and made of wattle and daub. A thatched roof covers the structure, which, in Ethiopia, is held up by a central pole that takes on sacred significance. Cattle remain a symbol of prosperity and status, so if you want to see how economically strong a village is during your trip along the river, a headcount of horns would give a good initial idea.

Deference is the order of the day. In all villages along the Ethiopian branch of the Nile, it is not uncommon for adults to give up possessions, food and beds to family and friends – even if they are just a few years older. This is due to tradition, but also due to a desire for order in a land that only just emerged from years of civil war. In Uganda, deference is of female to male. While the mother rules the home, they are second-class citizens.

Pride and prejudice

In Ethiopia and southern Sudan tribal differentiation and deference is encouraged in order to ensure cultures stay alive. In Egypt, however, it is a different matter. Pride in Egypt and "the Egyptian way" is fervent, and doing anything "un-Egyptian" is frowned upon.

By inclination, habit and training Egyptians are tactful and diplomatic, sometimes to the point of obsequiousness. Forms of address are complex and varied, as befits a highly stratified and religious society. This diversity underlines the cohesiveness of the society rather than its disparateness: Egyptians see all men as equals, but allot to each a specific status and with it a given role.

Economic anxieties

As in many other developing countries, sharp disparities of wealth exist in all the nations along the Nile.

After years of economic restructuring, urban Egyptians generally are poorer than they were in 1958, and although life for rural people has improved they, too, are poorer today than in the early 1980s. In 2009 it was estimated that only 70 percent of the population was literate.

The primary condition of Egypt – too many people – doesn't help. The population pyramid looms menacingly on the horizon – it was estimated at just over 83 million in 2009, of which 26 million were under 14 years of age. Schools in Cairo already operate three shifts.

In Cairo, the housing shortage means that too many people are often cooped up in the same house, and there are some districts of the city where the average density is three to a room. With more than 25,000 people per square kilometre, Cairo is one of the most densely populated urban agglomerations in the world. Cairo has a similar population to Paris, but on a surface area nine times smaller.

Low pay and a general loathing for the bureaucracy has meant that government jobs have lost most of their prestige in Egypt. Increasingly one finds university graduates working as taxi drivers, plumbers, mechanics and the like. The money is better and tradesmen stand a likelier chance of saving in order to get married, though with inflation and the limited availability of decent apartments, many are obliged to scrimp for years before they can establish a household.

Despite the overpopulation and political doom and gloom, Egyptians are known for their humour. Political jokes are particularly sharp and irreverent. Historically, Egyptian mis-

ABOVE: schoolboys around town in Aswan.
RIGHT: Egyptian woman in a shop selling aromatherapy oils in Aswan.

INSTANT PRESTIGE

The ostentatious display of wealth in Egypt can, to Western eyes, seem vulgar. But the flaunting of riches only confirms that, in a society forced to count its pennies, money carries a special prestige. As a wealthy merchant, whose lifestyle is otherwise modest, commented, "Yes, I would rather have spent my money on something other than a Mercedes. But you wouldn't believe how much it saves me. I don't have to waste time – or money – proving myself. I get instant respect."

Likewise, extravagant weddings are also a symbol of prestige. Wealthy families will blow vast sums on a binge in a five-star hotel.

An old Arab adage serves to illustrate the pride in Egypt and all things Egyptian: "I and my brothers against my cousins, I and my cousins against my tribe, and I and my tribe against the world."

chievousness has its roots in the legacy of centuries of repressive government. Numerous are the stories that celebrate the victory, through a mix of cunning and trickery, of the poor *fellah* (peasant) over pashas or foreigners.

The mazes of matrimony

Marriage is deemed an absolute prerequisite for sex, as well as for full adulthood and respectability. Among women, whose freedom is still very much limited by rigid social norms, finding and keeping the right husband is the major focus of life. Since the 1920s substantial progress towards equality of the sexes has been made, but it is still the rule for a girl to remain in the care of her father until the day she is passed into the care of her husband.

Respect for parents and elders is so strongly ingrained that it is uncommon for even a male child to leave home before marriage. Things are gradually changing in Cairo and other major urban centres, but few urban males can afford to marry much before the age of 30. Despite Islam's flexibility on the subject – easy divorce and polygamy are both sanctioned – marriage is regarded as a binding agreement, made more absolute by economics. For this reason, couples are expected to work out every detail of their future life together before signing the marriage contract.

In the cities, political and business alliances are often reinforced through marriage. Because numerous children enlarge a family's potential for wealth and influence, and also because it is considered healthier for children to grow up with lots of siblings, the family planners have had a hard time bringing down the birth rates.

Life-support systems

Beyond the family, Egyptians have a strong attachment to their immediate community. Village solidarity is very strong. In the big towns the

WOMEN IN SOCIETY

Before the famous Egyptian feminist Hoda Shaarawi deliberately removed her veil in 1922, veils – which had no religious significance – were worn in public by all respectable middle- and upper-class women, Muslim, Jewish or Christian. By 1935, however, veils were a comparative rarity in Egypt, though they continued to be worn in countries like Syria and Jordan for 30 more years and have remained obligatory in the Arabian Peninsula to this day.

Nowadays in Egypt the full veil or *niqab*, leaving just the eyes uncovered, is worn by Bedu women, who are the inheritors of the urban fashions of a century ago, and also by younger middle-class urban women demonstrating deep Muslim piety. Women of Sudanese Arab tribes also choose to wear the veil – either because of a stronger adherence to tradition or because the influence of more permissive urban culture has been limited to date.

From the 1930s onwards, Egyptian women began to enter into businesses and professions. Thus by 1965, thanks in part to social changes effected in the course of the July Revolution, Egypt had a far higher proportion of professional women workers than in the US or in any European country outside Scandinavia. This remains the case only in the northern urban centres of Cairo and Alexandria, as conservative beliefs stay strong the further south you travel along the Nile. In Cairo, the veil is a rare sight except in the old Islamic part of the city.

hara (alley) is the main location of social bonding. An Egyptian's closest friends will be his or her next-door neighbours, and the people they see at the alley or street café, barber, corner shop and mosque. The main function of *hara* solidarity is to defend the interests of the community. The closer-knit the community, the more everyone can keep an eye on everyone else.

Regional loyalties persist strongly, too. Each major town and province has its acknowledged characteristic. Alexandrians are known chiefly for their toughness and willingness to fight, but also for their cosmopolitan outlook and business acumen. The farmers of Lower Egypt and the Delta are regarded as hard-working, thrifty and serious. Rashidis, from Rosetta, are supposed to be kind-hearted, while Dumyatis, from Dumyat at the Nile's eastern mouth, are said to be cunning. Cairenes, like New Yorkers or cockneys, are seen as slick, fast-talking and immoral. Simply being from the capital allows them to sneer at less sophisticated compatriots, a Cairene habit that their country cousins dislike.

The Saidi people of Upper Egypt are considered to be simple-minded and impulsive and will even joke about these traits themselves. On the positive side, Saidis are noted for their generosity, their courage, virility and sense of honour.

FOOTBALL FEVER

Cairo is the home of the two biggest football teams in Egypt, Al Ahly and Zamalek, whose success or failure is passionately followed throughout the autumn and winter season. Al Ahly (www.ahlyclub.com) is one of the biggest teams in Africa.

Originally formed by Englishman Mitchell Ince in 1907, Al Ahly soon became an Egyptian club for Egyptians, and has won the Egyptian League more times than any other team. Nicknamed "the Reds", Al Ahly is supported by the majority of football fans in the country – and not just because the translation of their team from the Arabic means "national".

Al Ahly's great rival is its fellow Cairo club, Zamalek (www.zamalek-sc.com), founded by a Belgian lawyer in 1911 and originally called Qasr Al Nil. After the 1952 Revolution it took the name Zamalek Sporting Club and was briefly managed in the mid-1980s by Dave Mackay, a former player with the north London club Tottenham Hotspur. They are nicknamed "the White Knights".

Of most pride to Egyptians is national success in the Africa Cup of Nations, when the best players from the league (and internationals) play against other nations of the continent. Egypt holds the record for winning the most cups, with seven titles to their name, including their latest in 2010.

This recent triumph made them the only nation to win the Africa Cup three times in a row.

The dark-skinned Nubians of the far south and Sudan, an ancient people with their own languages, are considered to be the most gentle and peaceful of Egyptians. Long isolated by the cataracts that made the Nile above Aswan impassable, Nubian life, relaxed and carefree, had a unique charm. Nubian villages are spotlessly clean, and both men and women are apt to be more enterprising than their Egyptian neighbours.

Compensations

The protective structure of society, based on the strength of family ties, allows Egyptian men and women to give free rein to their emotions. Families, neighbours and countrymen at large can all be relied on for compassion, commiseration or help. This solidarity makes Egypt one of the safest countries in the world. When someone shouts "Thief!" on the street, every shop empties as all and sundry help to chase the culprit, who is almost invariably caught and hauled off to the nearest police station by a gesticulating mob. Throughout Egypt, fewer murders are committed in a year than take place annually in any typical large city in America – a comparison reflecting the fact that Egyptian society allows fewer people to be marginalised.

Outside Egypt, this camaraderie is more limited as Ethiopia, Sudan and Uganda have experienced harsh civil war and dictatorships in the recent past. Additionally, these three nations are much less homogeneous than Egypt. In a village in Egypt, you are much more likely to know and/or be related to your neighbours.

In Sudan, Ethiopia and Uganda, your neighbours may not be of the same religion, let alone from the same tribe. As such, there is a more ingrained mentality that you have to watch your own back.

LEFT: football fans watch a qualifier match for the World Cup in Cairo. **ABOVE AND ABOVE RIGHT:** shopping malls are found on the outskirts of the cities.

Taking time out

Modern technology *(see page 110)* now provides the entertainment of the majority. These appurtenances of modern life have a powerful effect in a traditional society. Visiting shopping malls is also a popular pastime, particularly for the young, and mobile phones and Bluetooth have given them much more freedom than their parents ever had.

In spite of the changes, it will be a long time yet before the people of the banks of the Nile's various branches lose their special appeal. Sensitivity and kindness abound, despite economic hardship. The warmth of human relations brings a soft sweetness, even extended to visitors, that has always been part of the Nile's charm. ❑

Baraka

A Love of Food

Though not a bastion of haute cuisine, Egypt offers many tasty experiences, such as memorable mezes, great street food, succulent fruit and oriental pastries

In the Middle Ages, Egyptian cuisine enjoyed a high reputation all over the Islamic empire, but not many now travel to Egypt in search of a culinary experience. Those looking for the best of Middle Eastern cuisine will undoubtedly choose countries like Lebanon or Turkey. Nevertheless, Egyptians love to eat – and to share a meal – and will endlessly discuss the delight of the dishes served, simple as they may be. As in most Arab countries, the best food is found at home. Restaurants usually serve only the more common Egyptian dishes such as kebabs, meze and perhaps stuffed pigeon or *meloukhia* (a thick soup made of a deep-green leaf, similar to spinach). Over the past few years, trendy restaurants in Cairo have rediscovered typical Egyptian dishes, including *fatta* (a mix of rice, bread and garlic), often accompanied by water pipes.

Egyptian cuisine shows signs of a long history of occupation: the Persians, Greeks, Romans, Arabs and Ottomans have all left their mark. More recently, European influences have also been added.

Food for the pharaohs

The Egyptians' sense of hospitality and their love of food goes back a long way, according to the evidence of many well-preserved wall paintings and carvings in tombs and temples around the country, which depict large banquets and a wide variety of foods.

LEFT: a feast of flavours. **RIGHT:** hibiscus (*karkadeh* in Egyptian) is used to make a popular herbal tea.

Such images also provide proof that many of the dishes enjoyed in Egyptian households today were also on the menu in antiquity. *Meloukhia* soup, roast goose and salted dried fish (*fasieekh*) are examples.

A poor man's table

However elaborate the cuisine enjoyed by Egypt's former kings and sultans, the majority of today's *fellaheen* (peasants) are far too poor to make the most of gastronomic opportunities. As in other Arab countries, their diet consists mainly of locally grown vegetables, lentils and beans, with meat at weekends or on special occasions. With the huge influx of people from the countryside to towns and cities, this vegetable-based peasant cuisine has become common, and most middle-class families will elaborate on these basic recipes, adding more expensive ingredients when they can afford them.

A warm welcome

"Give your guest food to eat even though you are starving yourself" is one of the many proverbs insisting that hospitality is a duty and that all guests should be offered food and drink. Whatever their social standing, an Egyptian family will always serve guests several salads and a few vegetable and meat dishes. Guests will always be handed the best morsels of fish or the finest cut of meat.

Fuul above all

Fuul (fava or broad beans), stewed and eaten with bread, form Egypt's staple diet. Usually eaten for breakfast or as a sandwich between meals, *fuul* is eaten several times a day by those who can't afford any other food. Even in Cairo's most upmarket quarters, colourful carts can be found on street corners early in the morning, where they serve steaming *fuul* for breakfast.

Fava beans are also used in another of Egypt's favourite dishes, *taamiya* (deep-fried fava-bean balls, rather like falafels, which use chickpeas instead), which are often served with *fuul*. Another staple dish, usually sold as street food (which makes a delicious, inexpensive lunch), is *kushari*, a mixture of macaroni, lentils, rice and chickpeas, served with fried onions and topped with a generous dollop of hot tomato sauce. A familiar-sounding dish is *makarona* – pasta accompanied by a variety of sauces – which is also usually sold from a cart as street food.

Make a meal out of meze

Of all the dishes on offer in Egypt it is a table full of meze, dips and salads that best reflects the Egyptian and Middle Eastern character. Meze are served with drinks as a light snack or

FOOD ALONG THE NILE

While Egypt and Sudan have very similar tastes, Sudan is a much poorer nation. Almost all meals at home and in restaurants rely on local produce. Meat is a rarity, making food like kebabs a treat.

In Uganda, cooking is done by the women of the family; men and boys are forbidden to enter the kitchen after the age of 12. Staples include freshwater fish, *cassava* (manioc or tapioca) and *matoke* (made from bananas). Ethiopian staples are more grain-based, with a spongy, unleavened bread known as *injera* served at every meal. Stews are made from a variety of local vegetables including carrots, cabbage and peppers.

The evening air is often scented by the warm smell of roasting maize (corn on the cob), libb *(melon seeds) and* tirmis *(lupin seeds), sold from street carts, in little paper cones.*

as an appetiser before a meal. Egyptians love to sit and relax at home, on a terrace or in a café, chatting and laughing with friends and savouring a few salads and small dishes. These can be anything from a plate of hummus, pickled vegetables or elaborate *mahshi* (stuffed vegetables), to little meat pies. With such a variety of dishes, meze can easily turn out to be a pleasurable and leisurely meal on their own.

Celebrations

Meat has always been considered a food for the rich and aristocratic. Poorer Egyptians may only get a taste of meat one day of the year: Id Al Kebir, the 10th day of the last month of the Muslim calendar. In commemoration of Abraham's near-sacrifice of his son Ismail, rural families who can afford it will sacrifice a sheep or a lamb. The animal, which should be fat and young, is ritually slaughtered and roasted whole on a spit and usually some of its meat is distributed to the poor, according to the tenets of Islam. Sheep are also slaughtered to mark other important occasions such as death, birth or marriage.

Ramadan, the month of fasting from sunset to sunrise, is another occasion when more meat is consumed than usual. Families visit each other in the evenings and celebrate the end of another day of fasting with a rich display of foods and sweets.

Many Egyptian recipes won't stipulate what sort of meat is to be used, as traditionally there was only sheep or lamb, and occasionally camel, goat or gazelle. Islam prohibits pork, but beef and veal are now widely available in Egypt. Meat is usually grilled as kebab or kofta (minced lamb) or used in a stew. Offal – particularly liver, kidneys and testicles – is considered a delicacy.

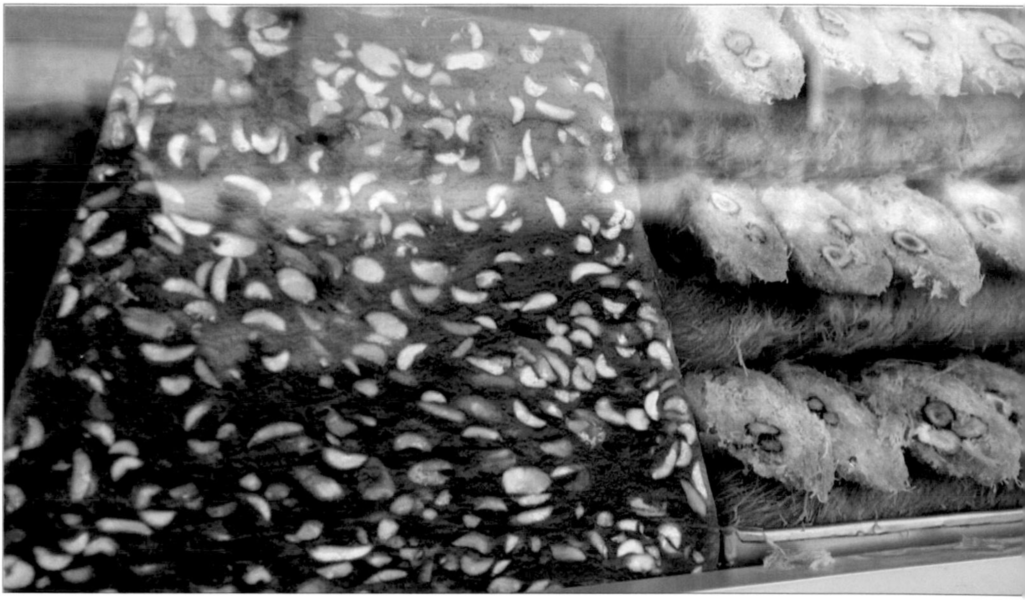

FAR LEFT: delivering bread to a restaurant. **LEFT:** a selection of dishes at the Hilton Luxor Resort. **ABOVE:** sweet treats along the Corniche, Alexandria.

Sweet as honey

The traditional end to a meal at home is a bowl of seasonal fruit, but Western-style ice cream and crème caramel will also be offered as a dessert in most restaurants. Even though they are not usually eaten as a dessert, there are some delicious Egyptian puddings, including *muhallabia*, a milk cream thickened by

Street vendors carry enormous glass containers from which they dispense drinks of laymun *(lemon),* tamar hindi *(tamarind) and* ersoos *(liquorice). The last concoction has given its name to the vendor, who is called an* erqsusi.

cornflour and ground rice, and *roz bi-laban*, a creamy rice pudding, both topped with chopped almonds and pistachio nuts. More elaborate is *umm ali*, a warm, comforting bread pudding with coconut, raisins, nuts and cream. According to some sources, *umm ali* was intro-

duced into Egypt by Miss O'Malley, the Irish mistress of the *khedive* Ismail.

Pastries are more likely to be served at parties and special, happy occasions such as weddings and births, than as a dessert. Baklava is the most famous oriental pastry, a filo wrapping stuffed with a mixture of nuts or almonds and covered with an orange-blossom syrup. More common are *basbousa*, a semolina cake of syrup and nuts, and the drier *kunafa*, angel hair filled with thick cream, ricotta cheese or chopped nuts and syrup.

Juicy drinks

Egyptians will tell you that "once you drink water from the Nile, you will always come back to Egypt". A nice sentiment, but Nile water is more likely to curse than bless; stick to mineral water or fresh juices. Brightly coloured juice bars with their picturesque pyramids of strawberries and oranges and baskets of mangoes attract thirsty customers. Freshly squeezed *asir* (juice) is excellent and very cheap. The most widely available juice is *asir laymun* (fresh lemon or lime), normally served sweetened unless you say otherwise.

Usually there will also be a choice of *asir burtuqan* (freshly squeezed winter or summer oranges), *moz* (banana), *gazar* (carrot) and *gawafa* (sweet guava). Depending on the season there could also be deep-red *asir ruman* (pomegranate juice), *farawla* (strawberry) and thick *manga* (mango). Some stalls also offer *asab* or *gasab*, the sweet juice pressed out of sugar-cane sticks.

Alcoholic pleasures

According to the Qur'an, Muslims should not drink alcohol and, with religious tensions rising, much of Egypt is becoming dry. But you can usually get alcohol in hotels and Western-style bars and restaurants, except during Ramadan, when no alcohol is served to Egyptians even if they are Copts. Many bars close for the month; others may ask to see a passport before they serve alcohol to foreigners.

Locally brewed Stella beer is quite enjoyable and reasonable value, while the more expensive Stella Export and Stella Premium are stronger, as is the better Sakkara.

The quality of the local wine has much improved since the Gianaclis Winery was privatised. Cru des Ptolémées is a white wine made from pinot blanc. Rubis d'Egypte is a rosé, while Omar Khayyam is a deep red from cabernet sauvignon grapes. Obélisque makes red and white wines from imported grapes. The more expensive Grand Marquis, red and white, is very palatable, and Egypt now has its own "champagne", Aida. Imported wines are much more expensive than local varieties.

Zibeeb, or arak, the Egyptian version of ouzo, is reliable, but local spirits with inspiring names such as Dry Din, Marcel Horse, Ricardo and Johnny Talker are best avoided. ❑

LEFT: Stella is brewed locally.
RIGHT: spices and all sorts of exotic goods are for sale at the souq in Aswan.

GAR
زهرة زرقاء
INDIGO
سمسم
SESO
AROS
سكران
HENBONE
True se

علاء الأسواني
عمارة يعقوبيان
مكتبة مدبولي
علاء الأسواني عمارة يعقوبيان مكتبة مدبولي

POPULAR CULTURE

Egypt has long been regarded as the hub of popular culture in the Arab world. From films to fiction and soaps to song, it has led the way

In *The One Thousand and One Nights*, Cairo is called "the mother of the world", a phrase that Egyptians nowadays tend to modify to "Mother of the Arab World". Although in politics that may no longer be true, Egypt can still claim to be in the forefront as far as popular culture is concerned: from Damascus to Casablanca, Egyptian films and television are screened, books by Egyptian writers are read, its singers are given radio airtime and, to a lesser extent, its theatre is respected.

The written word

The year 1988 was one of celebration for Egyptian writers, for that was when Naguib Mahfouz won the Nobel Prize for Literature. But even Mahfouz himself was astonished. Although a world-class writer, he was seen as a traditionalist – Dickens was a major influence – and the works cited by the Nobel committee were written more than a quarter of a century earlier.

The traditional storyteller has now become a rarity. Occasionally you can still see these masters of memory performing to a public who now – too late – appreciate an art that has all but disappeared.

Mahfouz (who died in 2006) and Taha Hussein (1889–1973) were the grand old men of Egyptian letters. Other central figures in the development of modern Egyptian literature are Tawfiq Al Hakim *(The Prison of Life)*, who defined Egyptian autobiographical writing (died 1987), and the Alexandrian-Greek poet C.P. Cavafy (1863–1933) *(Collected Poems)*, whose explorations of sexuality, memory and history have a universal appeal. They and their younger contemporaries – like Abdel Rahman Al Sharqawi *(Egyptian Earth)*, Sonallah Ibrahim *(Zaat)*, Ahdaf Soueif *(Aisha, In the Eye of the Sun)*, Gamal Al Ghitani *(Zayni Barakat)*, Nawal Al Saadawi *(Woman at Point Zero)*, Yusuf Idris (died 1991; *The Cheapest Nights)*, Ibrahim Abdel Meguid *(No One Sleeps in Alexandria)* and Bahaa Taher *(Love in Exile)* – created a tradition of modern storytelling, rich in folklore and heavy in allegory (a necessity given the censorship laws).

LEFT: Alaa Al Aswany, author of *The Yacoubian Building*. **RIGHT:** Adhaf Soueif, novelist and journalist.

In 2008, Bahaa Taher won the Booker Prize for Arab Fiction with *Sunset Oasis*, published in Cairo in 2007, which explores the themes of occupation and subjugation. Taher, now in his 70s, was an exile in Switzerland for 17 years before returning to Egypt in 1995.

Post-independence writers have taken different routes. The work of Edward Al Kharrat *(Girls of Alexandria)* and Yahya Taher Abdullah (died 1981; *The Mountain of Green Tea)* move away from Western literary traditions, but Ahdaf Soueif and Waguih Ghali (died 1969; *Beer in the Snooker Club)* write in English and have not been translated into Arabic. The 1990s saw the important new women writers Miral Al Tahawi *(The Tent)* and Somayya Ramadan *(Leaves of Narcissus)*. One of the biggest international successes in recent years is Alaa Al Aswany, who famously worked as a part-time dentist before turning to writing full-time. *The Yacoubian Building* (2002) follows the fictional relationships between the inhabitants of a downtown office-cum-apartment block (actually inspired by the real Yacoubian Building containing Al Aswany's dental surgery).

The novel, which is an engrossing metaphor for the ills of Egyptian society, touching several taboo subjects, was made into a star-studded film in 2006, directed by Marwan Hamid and with Adel Iman *(see page 109)* playing the lead role, and then a television series in 2007.

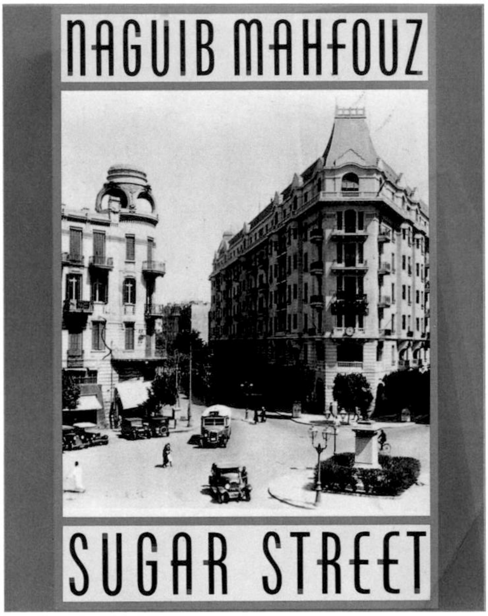

Worth Watching

One of the most important films to come out of Egypt was made by Shadi Abdelsalam. *The Night of Counting the Years* (1969) is unique among films about Egypt or directed by Egyptians. Telling the story of the discovery of the cache of royal mummies in the Theban hills in 1881, it is both political and topical, a brilliant allegory for the underlying tensions of the last years of President Nasser. Foreign experts, pashas from Cairo, dignified peasants and a good man who can do no right all have their roles to play in the film. Although spoken of as "the spearhead of the Egyptian cinema" Abdelsalam, who died in 1986, never produced another major film.

Cairo, cinema city

In 1927, Aziza Amir released the first Egyptian-made film, *Laila*. Much of Egypt's claim to cultural supremacy in the Arab world has been due to the phenomenal success of the film industry, which developed in the mid-20th century and peaked in the 1960s, when a new film was released almost every day. Subjects ranged from historical epics to back-alley melodramas, and one of the most popular film forms was the musical, whose plots were often copied from Hollywood.

> *So important was music in the development of Egyptian cinema that critic Samir Farid noted: "The Egyptian cinema only became talking in order to sing, without which it would be silent today."*

Singer Umm Kulthum *(see box, page 110)* dominated here as she dominated Cairo's concert halls. Her most successful partnership was with the actor Farid Al Atrash, who, like her, combined a talent for acting with an exceptional voice.

Salah Abou Seif made some of Egypt's most important post-revolution films, and won the Critics' Prize at the 1956 Cannes Film Festival with *La Sangsue*. Abou Seif directed the leading stars of his day, including the legendary belly dancer Tahiya Karioka, Hind Rostom, Omar Sharif and his wife Faten Hamama. Abu Seif's films very much reflected the mood of the time – political, questioning, fiercely pro-Arab and anti-royalist.

LEFT: the late Naguib Mahfouz and the jacket of *Sugar Street*, part of his Cairo Trilogy. **ABOVE:** Youssef Chahine, a radical influence on Egyptian film. **ABOVE RIGHT:** still from *The Yacoubian Building*, based on Alaa Al Aswany's novel and starring Adel Imam.

Youssef Chahine, who died in 2008, had been directing films since the 1940s and did more than anyone to bring credibility to Egyptian cinema. Chahine created a broad body of work, from the realism of the black-and-white *Cairo Station* to the more recent *The Emigrant*, an allegory about corruption, ignorance and injustice, set in ancient Egypt. Part of Chahine's success was due to his ability to convince European film bodies to provide money or facilities, which also guaranteed him an international audience. His work was recognised by a Lifetime Achievement Award at the 1997 Cannes Film Festival.

Few other Egyptian directors have achieved anything like Chahine's stature, with the exception perhaps of Yousri Nassallah, and the bulk of Egypt's output is low-grade melodrama and romantic comedy. Directors tread the fine line between titillating the audience and not offending the government's censors, who mostly succeed in keeping nudity, overt political criticism and religious slurs off their cinema screens.

Adel Imam is probably the most successful leading male actor currently at work in Egypt. Several of his films have tackled serious and topical subjects, most notable, perhaps, being *The Terrorist*, a comedy about an ordinary man getting himself into extraordinary difficulties in the bureaucratic nightmare of Cairo's

Interior Ministry building and being mistaken for a terrorist.

Released in 1994, when the government was struggling to control the activities of the fundamentalist groups, *The Terrorist* succeeded in making the public question why such people were driven to violent measures.

Rising costs, a lack of cinemas, failure to control video piracy and the spread of satellite TV have seen film production dwindle over the past 15 years, though the opening of a "Hollywood-on-the-Nile" with up-to-date film and TV production facilities 15km (9 miles) southwest of Cairo shows renewed confidence in the industry.

Umm Kulthum

In the 1960s, when nationalism ran high, Umm Kulthum, the singer with the trademark dark glasses, enjoyed the sort of pulling power now reserved for American TV soaps. Each month she performed a new song in her inimitable, passionate warble and, they say, the entire nation came to a standstill as people listened to the "Star of the East" on the radio. When she died in 1975, many Arab leaders attended her funeral.

Her songs and voice remain popular today, all over the Arab world. There is a museum in her honour, with photographs, personal possessions and other memorabilia on Roadah Island in Cairo *(see page 252)*.

Live on stage

Many stars of Egyptian cinema appear regularly on stage in Cairo. Most Egyptian theatre is comedy or melodrama – particularly popular during the long nights of Ramadan – and carried off by the status of stars like Adel Imam.

An alternative is provided by playwrights such as Muhammad Salmawy, although his work owes more to European than Egyptian tradition. Hassan Al Geretly's Al Warsha is one of the most convincing of Egypt's experimental theatre groups: its performances often mix storytelling with music and traditional shadow plays.

Television's revolution

It would be hard to overestimate the impact television has had on the lives of rural Egyptians. The promise Nasser and Sadat made to link every village in the country to the national electricity grid had an unforeseen effect and changed rural life for ever. With electricity came television and with television came late-night viewing, and that, in turn, put an end to farmers getting into their fields before dawn.

Now satellite TV is widespread, and this has had another effect. With the increased availability of a wide variety of foreign programming, Egypt's dominance has begun to wane. This was first noticed in 1997, when an Egyptian journalist working on the BBC's World Service reported that for the first time Egypt's famed Ramadan serial, the *Fawazeer* – a jamboree of song and dance and extravagant costumes that runs each night throughout the month of fasting – had lost ground to Syrian and Jordanian programmes broadcast by satellite.

The digital age

The possession of a television used to be the sign of how wealthy a person was in Egypt. Today it is the computer that is most desired by the privileged few. While the television is for entertainment, the computer can only be used by people with a minimum literacy level – already removing a significant proportion of the population from enjoying the device's usefulness.

Internet cafés are now widespread. And the lack of funds to buy a home computer means that young urbanites along the Nile rely on these centres to play video games, chat with mates, educate themselves or swap news. There are currently a number of programmes in operation across Africa to provide computer access to all, and Egypt is taking part in many of the projects. It remains to be seen what the long-term impact will be.

The sound of music

Evidence of Egypt's domination of the Arab cultural scene in the 1960s is provided by the music of the Egyptian singer Umm Kulthum *(see box opposite)*. Her contemporaries, including Muhammad Abdel Wahab, Abdel Halim Hafez and Farid Al Atrash, still have a large audience among the older generation. But, with over half of the 82-million population aged under 25, the biggest slice of Egypt's music market is taken by modern musicians.

Among the latest sounds to be heard is *shaabi* (people) music, developed by singer Ahmed Adawiya in the 1970s, mixing protest lyrics with a strong backbeat. After a decade and more of phenomenal sales, Adawiya began singing about God, relinquishing his place as king of *shaabi* to Hakim and to the hugely popular Shaaban Abdel-Rahim. In contrast, *al jeel* (the generation) music is a fusion of disco and local rhythms, its lyrics generally confined to enduring themes of love and nostalgia. Muhammad Foad and Hisham Abbas are two names to listen out for, but Amr Diab is the most popular.

The sound of Egypt that has reached the West is an eclectic mix of Arab, Egyptian, Turkish and Indian sounds, produced by musicians such as George Kazazian, Natacha Atlas and the popular Les Musiciens du Nil, a group of Upper Egyptian musicians led by the folk singer Metqal, himself a mix of Sudanese, Nubian and Egyptian influences.

Western music has marked a number of milestones in Egypt, including the inaugural production of Verdi's *Aida* in 1871 at the original Cairo Opera House. The *khedive* Ismail commissioned the opera house in 1869 to celebrate the completion of the Suez Canal. The intention was that it would become a home to all the arts – and it was for over a century until destroyed by fire in 1971.

Today's opera house was completed in 1988 using funds donated by the Japanese government, and is the home of choice for Egypt's biggest performers and many international visiting companies. A spectacular concert featuring a who's who of popular Egyptian comedians and TV stars lights up the opera house every New Year's Eve in the social event of the season.

LEFT: the much-loved Umm Kulthum.
ABOVE: Les Musicians du Nil whose music is appreciated on the World Music scene.

The visual arts

Because the Prophet Muhammad denounced "image-makers", visual art in Egypt cannot claim an ancient tradition. However, contacts with Western culture in the 19th century stimulated a debate, with the pro-independence nationalists being keen to promote a recognisable Egyptian style. In the early 20th century, the mufti of Egypt suggested the Prophet's comment should be seen in context, having been made in an age of idolatry, and Prince Yusuf Kamal founded the School of Fine Arts in Cairo.

Egyptian artists started by confronting their ancient traditions. As sculptor Mahmoud Mukhtar (1883–1934) said, "When I was a child, there had been no sculpture in my country for more than 700 years." The Neo-Pharaonists, as they were called, believed that a new Egyptian identity would emerge by examining the past. The work of Modernist artists like Mukhtar, Mahmoud Said and Muhammad Nagui reflected this.

The Atelier of Alexandria – founded by Muhammad Nagui, his sister Effat Nagui and her husband Saad Al Khadem, one of Egypt's most important folklorists – did much to further a purely Egyptian style in a European context. The contemporary art scene is now

ART AND CULTURE IN UGANDA, SUDAN AND ETHIOPIA

Years of civil war have taken their toll on the other nations that house the Nile, forcing many artists to self-support their efforts. In Uganda, grass-roots efforts are under way to revive cultural traditions; however, they are still in their infancy. Most performance is conducted at tribal gatherings as part of religious festivals.

Sudan boasts a strong literary tradition, especially in the Arab north. The most noted writer, Tayeb Salih, has had two novels translated into English: *The Wedding of Zein* and *Season of Migration to the North*. Poetry is another notable form of expression, often involving musical accompaniment. Woodcarving is also strong throughout Sudan, with specialists in the north and south evolving to adapt to local materials. The north of Sudan finds experts in the production of silver and bone carvings, while woodcarvers live in the south. In almost all cases, final products are in the form of functional pieces such as knife handles and traditional weapons.

Ethiopia's artistic traditions can trace their lineage back to early Christendom. Like in Sudan, woodcarving and sculpture are common; however, there is also a history of religious painting that uses scenes from the Bible as inspiration.

Early Christian music dates its rhythms and words back to the 6th century and is still sung in the Ge'ez language – the ancient language of the original Ethiopian Christians.

blossoming, with the opening of the Town House Gallery in Cairo and numerous others.

Belly dancing

As recently as 20 years ago, belly dancing was celebrated as an art form in Egypt, with its stars becoming some of the richest performers in the country. Those glory days are no longer, as the religious conservatism of the recent past has attacked practitioners and branded them as immoral and against the values of Islam.

Many of the five-star hotels offer a belly-dancing spectacular at a greatly inflated price. Dinner-cruise boats also often feature a floor show with a belly-dancing act.

Belly dancing is actually the offspring of three traditional dance forms: Baladi, Sharqi and Sha'abi. In the 19th century, Ottoman culture restricted dancing to the harem or brothel. Europeans were seduced by the idea of the exotic dancing maiden and the belly dance was born in a swirl of scarves, veils and silks.

Post-independence, Egyptians yearned to celebrate any form of culture that they could call indigenous, and a renaissance began. From the 1960s until the mid-1980s, proficient belly dancers became national treasures adored for their skill and beauty. Names like Samia Gamal, Naima Akef, Nagua Fouad and Fifi Abdou dominated television screens and gossip columns. Performers could demand thousands of pounds for their presence on stage.

Today, some of the best-known stars have given up their costumes in favour of traditional acting roles. You can still find performers plying their trade in dinner shows and cabaret bars in Cairo.

FAR LEFT: belly dancer. **LEFT:** *Egypt's Awakening* by Mahmoud Mukhtar. **ABOVE:** Sufi dancers spinning at the Citadel in Cairo.

Sufi spinning

Found in Egypt and Sudan, Sufi dancers (also known as whirling dervishes) are followers of a religious order founded in Turkey that incorporates physically active meditation into its rituals. Dancers abandon their sense of self while listening to music and enter a form of trance while they focus on Allah, spinning faster and faster as the ritual progresses.

While you will find dancing inspired by Sufism in many tourist shows, the one guaranteed location to find the real thing is in the Dervish Theatre at Wikala Al Ghoury *(see page 260)*. Travelling Sufi dancers can also be found at public celebrations in villages up and down the Nile. ❑

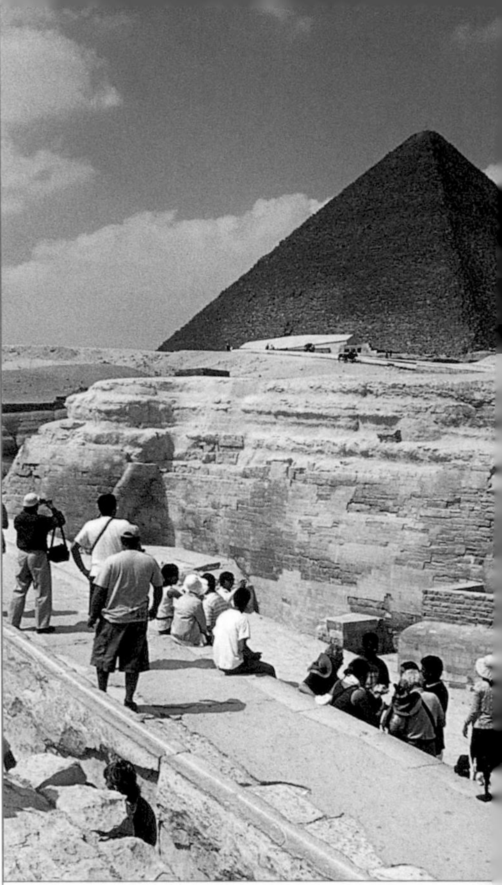

THE PYRAMIDS

The magnificent Pyramids of Giza, tombs of the ancient pharaohs, are the only survivors of the Seven Wonders of the World

The builders of the Pyramids were kings of the 3rd–6th dynasties of the Old Kingdom (2686–2181 BC) and of the Middle Kingdom (2040–1840 BC). About 100 structures have been identified. Their use is still debated, but most experts agree that they were the tombs of pharaohs. The evolution of burial sites from early *mastaba* ("bench" in Arabic) to step pyramid, on to the "true" pyramids, is a fascinating journey of spiritual ideals and "hit and miss" engineering. One theory for the pyramid shape is that it represents the *benben*, a triangular-shaped stone found in early temples, associated with the sun-god Ra and the creation of life. In hieroglyphics, the *benben* is represented as a pyramid shape.

Throughout this pyramid-building period, there were five major developments. The first was Djoser's Step Pyramid at Saqqarah, which had six steps and a burial chamber below ground. Half a century later this was copied by King Snofru, first king of the 4th Dynasty, who planned an eight-stepped pyramid covered in limestone blocks, known as the Maidum or "Collapsed" Pyramid. He also built the "Bent" Pyramid at Dahshur further north, then embarked on a third and final one, known as the Red Pyramid – the first "true" pyramid. Built with much shallower angles, this is a graceful construction, containing a single burial chamber above ground. Snofru's son Khufu learned from his father and embarked on the fifth version, which became the Great Pyramid at Giza.

In his book *The Pyramids of Egypt*, I.E.S. Edwards says that "the temptation to regard the true pyramid as a material representation of the sun's rays and consequently as a means whereby the dead king could ascend to heaven seems irresistible".

LEFT: the tiny entrance into the Red Pyramid at Dahshur leads to steep internal passageways with almost no air circulation inside.

BUILDING MATERIALS

The Pyramids that we see today would have looked very different when they were built. All the major Pyramids had coverings of highly polished stone at one time, but over the millennia these have been stripped away, leaving the rough surfaces of the limestone construction blocks, which each weigh around two tonnes. The best remaining examples of this covering are the "Dent" Pyramid at Dahshur and towards the top of the Khafra Pyramid at Giza. The most popular covering material was polished white limestone from the Tura quarry in the Muqattam hills, on the opposite side of the Nile overlooking Cairo.

Occasionally darker granite from Aswan was used, but because it was very hard and difficult to smooth – and because of the additional costs of transporting it along the Nile – the granite was laid in smaller bands. The best example of this is along the lower level of the Menkaura Pyramid at Giza. There is evidence that some pyramids also had a small granite cap *(pyramidion)*, often covered in electrum (gold, silver and copper mixture) to reflect the rays of the sun.

BOVE: the Sphinx, with a lion's body and a man's head, was carved ut of a natural outcrop of rock, left behind when the causeway to hafra's Pyramid was being built.

BOVE LEFT: the Step Pyramid of King Djoser was the vital link etween a *mastaba* tomb and the first "true" pyramid. The idea of is massive tomb being a "stairway to heaven" for the king's *ka* or irit can be clearly understood.

EFT: this tomb near the Great Pyramid of Khufu is pical of the smaller constructions built around the mb of the pharaoh. These are the burial ambers of important ministers and viziers or her members of the royal family.

ABOVE RIGHT: a fanciful image of a young Khufu, who grew up to build the Great Pyramid.

LEFT: the scale of the Pyramids at Giza can be seen when you compare the size of a person with just one building block.

BELOW: the Pyramids of Giza comprise one of the most famous silhouettes in the world. Contrary to popular opinion, they were built not by slaves but by teams of skilled labourers and local quarrymen.

THE NILE IN THE CINEMA

The river and its surrounding history have provided a rich source for some memorable epics of the screen. From murderous mummies to sweeping romance, the river and its iconic sites have hosted hundreds of film stars

There were films about the great past of Egypt in the earliest days of cinema. Mark Antony and Cleopatra were on the Italian screen before World War I; Helen Gardner played Cleopatra in 1911, Theda Bara played her in 1917. Of course, these were all silent films in black and white. It was when the talkies arrived, and colour, that the spectacular fictions of history held the day.

> *Biblical tales involving the conflict between Egypt and the Children of Israel was a popular subject when film-making first began.*

The stage led the way. In the restless gap between the wars, George Bernard Shaw looked with new eyes on the vagaries of history, but his own plays were guarded: he would not abandon them to the caprices of the screen. He was won over at last by the persuasive voice of Gabriel Pascal. Pascal came from Hungary, and he brought a mood of irony new to the British screen; he prevailed on Shaw to yield. *Pygmalion* became a film; so did *Major Barbara*, and in 1945 Pascal directed a version of *Caesar and Cleopatra*.

The lively cast was led by Vivien Leigh as the young Cleopatra; Claude Rains played Caesar; Stewart Granger was there, so was Basil Sydney, and Flora Robson appeared as Ftatateeta. In its day it was the most expensive film ever made in Britain. But it disappointed. If you wanted spectacle it was there, but only in fleeting moments.

The home of romance

The baldness of *Caesar and Cleopatra* as a piece of visual art was to allow irreverence into a story of classical history: theatre was used to it, but cinema, at any rate where Cleopatra was concerned, was the home of romance. In another way, too, the film was making changes. To an Anglo-Saxon audience, if not to Continental watchers, Egypt in close view rather than in the compressed vision of the silent screen was unfamiliar territory. Biblical influence and years of Old Testament teaching had impressed on the public an image of the Israelites crossing the Red Sea under Egyptian pursuit. The cinema, always searching for a good story (and where could it find better narrative material than in the Book of Genesis?) had repeatedly clutched the idea of a hostile Egypt.

Cecil B. de Mille made two versions of *The Ten Commandments*, the first in 1923; the second was to come more than 30 years later. Naturally, though, the theme of the enslaving Egyptians still held true. This time there was a new insistence on the background of history; there was emphasis as well on the part played by the Nile itself. The tale of the birth of Moses cannot exclude the presence of the river: the Pharaoh decrees that every newborn Hebrew boy must die, one mother wraps her child in bulrushes and entrusts his cradle to the water, and it is the Nile which carries him away to the rescuing hands of the Pharaoh's own daughter.

But tastes were shifting. There was Rome to be considered as well as Israel, and there was Egypt but the film was four years in the making. There were endless interruptions, including the illness of Elizabeth Taylor herself; and when at last the opening came the public, too, was starting to feel exhausted. History and two appalling wars had left audiences ready for another kind of spectacle, a spectacle with reality behind it.

There was something else. Archaeology, once the precinct of the learned, became popular. Discoveries in the Mediterranean made young people think of excavation; the Tutankhamun discoveries focused interest on Egypt; and fantasies, disguised as learning,

itself. In 1934 de Mille made a *Cleopatra* film with Claudette Colbert as the queen, but it made no lasting impression; another name would take over. In 1953 Joseph L. Mankiewicz made a version of Shakespeare's *Julius Caesar* with John Gielgud as Cassius and Marlon Brando as Mark Antony; in 1963 he wrote and directed the version of the Cleopatra story which is generally remembered today. It was fabulously expensive and had a dazzling cast, including Elizabeth Taylor and Richard Burton.

The spectacle was splendid – in particular Cleopatra's entry into Rome was admired –

LEFT: Cecil B. de Mille's 1923 *The Ten Commandments*.
ABOVE: de Mille's *Cleopatra*, with Claudette Colbert.

LIZ AS CLEO

In Joseph L. Mankiewicz's spectacular screen version of the Antony and Cleopatra story (made in 1963), Elizabeth Taylor appeared as the queen herself and Richard Burton, who was enjoying with her a relationship closer than publicly permitted on the screen, was Mark Antony.

But Miss Taylor, whose stunning physical beauty was sometimes allowed to overshadow her natural gifts as a player, was not at her best; personal preoccupations, perhaps, got in the way of a rendering of the great historical tragedy. In the end, it was Rex Harrison's portrayal of Julius Caesar that impressed the critical audience of the day.

occupied the cinemas. Not that they had ever quite vanished.

Thrills, chills and spills

The early years of the 1930s brought Germany's extraordinary horror-thrillers: *The Cabinet of Dr Caligari* came in 1920, but it had followers later on, before Hitler, and in America, too. In 1932 *The Mummy*, directed by Karl Freund, was one of the funerary leaders: other equally threatening mummies appeared in Britain, where in the 1970s Hammer horror films had a vogue. In these films there are reminders of the themes of the past. In 1956, for instance, Jean Simmons and Victor Mature appeared in *The Egyptian*; it told the story of a medical student and a military cadet who, centuries before Christ, accidentally save the life of a future pharaoh. But to touch a pharaoh was a criminal offence. Sooner or later ghosts would rise from the relics of history, the vengeful dead would threaten the incautious living.

The burial places of Egypt caught the imagination of the thriller-writer. Bram Stoker wrote *The Jewel of the Seven Stars*, a tale of a man unlucky enough to find the tomb of a murderous Egyptian queen: the spirit of the woman, dead for thousands of years, haunts him and takes possession of his daughter. The story has been used on the screen on two occasions: first in 1971 in *Blood from the Mummy's Tomb*, second in 1980 in *The Awakening*, which was directed by Mike Newell. Egyptian ghosts die hard, it seems, a theme that continues with the resurrection of High Priest Imhotep and his beloved Ankh-su-Namun in the 1999 hit *The Mummy*. Successful enough to spawn a number of sequels, it brought hieroglyphs back to Hollywood with a bang.

In both 1994's *Stargate* and the critically reviled yet popular *Transformers* sequel released in 2009, *Transformers: Revenge of the Fallen*, Egypt's beloved Pyramids acted as portals to other dimensions and hiding spots for ancient power sources. Less fantastical, although still fantasy, were the celluloid icons of James Bond and Indiana Jones who both made stops in Egypt; Indiana in his first outing, *Raiders of the Lost Ark*, and Bond in 1977's *The Spy Who Loved Me*. The Mosque of Ibn Tuloan, Pyramids, Gayer-Anderson Museum, Abu Simbel and – especially – Karnak Temple all feature highly throughout the British spy caper.

Novel interpretations

The background of contemporary Egypt is less familiar through the cinema than the images of remote history. But the Nile, lodestar of tourists, still haunts imaginations, still serves the novelist.

Now and then it is the Egypt of the comfortable traveller which we see on the screen – usually with murder thrown in. *Death on the Nile*, say the posters; the screen has recorded more than one multiple murder, including a case by Agatha Christie, that industrious chronicler of

> *It is natural that Egypt should be the frequent source of funereal fantasy films. After all, the country devoted the most urgent attention to the preservation of the body in its science of mummification.*

the geography of crime. There was a *Death on the Nile* in 1978, with the popular Peter Ustinov as Hercule Poirot; it was made in Britain, but with an international cast that included Bette Davis. Then in 1996 came the Academy Award-winning *The English Patient* featuring Ralph Fiennes, Kristin Scott Thomas and Juliette Binoche. Egypt's high costs as a filming location meant that the crew actually shot the famous scenes of rolling dunes in Tunisia, yet Egypt reaped the rewards, drawing numerous fans of the inspired cinematography.

Egypt's own story

Egypt has also contributed to the list of cinema directors. *The Night of Counting the Years* was an Egyptian film made by an Egyptian, Shadi Abdelsalam; it was produced by Italy's distinguished Roberto Rossellini; it won France's Georges Sadoul Prize in 1970. The narrative deals with fact; it begins in 1881, when the authorities in Cairo were surprised to find that valuable objects from the 21st Dynasty had been appearing on the black market. Archaeologists were sent to investigate, and it was found that a tribe had passed on from generation to generation the secret of a tomb they had discovered and were selling its contents in times of need. But then there was a disagreement; one of the sons of the family was horrified by what he regarded as sacrilege; and there was murder – a body was thrown into the Nile.

Cinema has also moved into another area of adventure: the Nile is still concerned, but not Egypt. In the 1850s two men set out on a dangerous expedition, hoping to find the source of the Nile. One of the two men was John Hanning Speke; the other, Richard Francis Burton, is better known as the author of an unexpurgated English version of *The Arabian Nights*.

The first expedition ended in disaster. But the explorers persevered; funds were raised; and the result was the discovery that the great lake named Victoria is now accepted as feeding the Nile. The tale is told in *Mountains of the Moon*, directed and part-written by Bob Rafelson in 1990.

LEFT: *The Cabinet of Dr Caligari.*
RIGHT: Brendan Fraser and Rachel Weisz in *The Mummy Returns*, 2001.

IMAX Spectacular

Released in 2005, the IMAX film *Mystery of the Nile* follows a team of explorers led by expedition leader Pasquale Scaturro and his partner Gordon Brown as they become the first in history to conquer the entire length of the Nile in a single descent.

During the 114 days it took to film, the team faced many tough challenges: dangerous rapids, deadly crocodiles and hippos, attacks from armed bandits, arrests by local militia, blinding sandstorms, malaria, and the relentless heat of the desert sun. The film relates the adventure but also offers insights into the cultures along the Nile, the monuments, the people and animals. ❑

WILDLIFE

The banks of the Nile may no longer be home to crocodiles north of the Aswan Dam, but they are the habitat of many other species. Birdlife is especially prolific during migration season

Despite the great cities that line its banks, and the growing number of dams that harness it, the Nile in many ways belongs to the flora and fauna that still proliferate along its shores and in its waters. The mild weather and rural expanse through which the river runs – unpolluted – offer a great habitat for wildlife.

In parts of Uganda and Sudan the variety of wildlife remains as it was centuries ago, but in Egypt this is not the case. In pre-pharaonic times Egypt was a savannah on which leopards, cheetahs and lions roamed freely. Herds of elephant, buffalo, oryx and gazelle fed on the wild grasses and drank from the river. In the Nile, crocodiles and hippopotamuses foraged from source to outlet. But with environmental changes and the growth of civilisation, by which man began to dominate the Nile Valley, local animals were pushed further and further south.

> *Hieroglyphic symbols included depictions of animals, birds, flowers and trees. Houses were decorated with paintings of flowers, and public buildings had pillars and colonnades in the form of papyrus and lotus plants.*

Animal gods

The ancient Egyptians seemed to like the natural world – many of their gods were associated with animals: Sobek, god of Al Fayyum and Kom Ombo, was linked to the crocodile; Anubis, god of the dead, with the jackal; Thoth, god of wisdom, with the ibis.

By the time of the New Kingdom many of the Nile's indigenous species – elephants, giraffes, monkeys – were disappearing from Egypt. The hippopotamus took longer to make its journey south. Hippos outlasted ancient Egypt and the Islamic medieval period and were quite a novelty for European travellers of the Middle Ages. Their vivid descriptions must have thrilled the people back home. Hippos still lived in the Delta in 1685, and a lone specimen was sighted in Aswan in 1816. By the 20th century, of the great creatures, only crocodiles remained in Egyptian waters. Now they too are gone. The

LEFT: homeward-bound birds.
RIGHT: life on the Nile.

construction of the Aswan Dam in the 1960s pushed the crocodile into Sudan, though a baby croc sometime gets churned through the dam's sluice gates.

The long migration

By contrast the country is still home to a tremendous variety of birds, whose numbers are swollen each winter as they are joined by additional species migrating to escape the winters of Europe and western Asia. Known as the Palaearctic-African Bird Migration, this massive movement begins in August and can last until early December. The birds take to the air following a variety of migratory paths that take them over the Maghreb, Egypt, Saudi Arabia, Iraq, Iran and parts of Russia. Some birds travel nearly 2,000km (1,240 miles) before they reach their journey's end south of the Sahara. They come in their thousands, but are often so exhausted by their journey that they are vulnerable to predators.

Birds of prey

Raptors (hawks, eagles and vultures) make their way south following land routes. These paths, sometimes known as flyways, begin in eastern Europe and Asia Minor. They follow the eastern shore of the Mediterranean, move south over Israel and Jordan and cross the Gulf of Aqaba to the east of Sinai. From Sinai the migrating birds cut west over the Red Sea gulfs to the Egyptian coast, turn south and head to Safaga. At Safaga they turn west again and soar over the Red Sea Mountains to Qena along the Nile. At Qena their journey continues south and, as they pass Luxor, Esna and Aswan, some birds settle, wintering on the Egyptian Nile. Others continue to lakes nearer the source and some go as far as South Africa.

The little green bee-eater is one of several species of bee-eater in Egypt but is the only one which is native to the country; its light-green feathers appear almost brown at a distance,

EGRETS AND IBIS

One of the most common residents of Egypt is the cattle egret. This graceful white bird can be seen in fields, along canals and at the river's edge foraging for food. A cattle egret sometimes perches on the back of a water buffalo to peck at ticks and other pests. Many people confuse the cattle egret and its cousin the common egret (the former has yellow legs and bill while the latter has black legs) with the sacred ibis. But the ibis, symbol of Thoth, the god of wisdom, and raised by the thousand as sacrificial birds (4 million mummified ibises were found in one king's tomb), no longer finds the habitat suitable in Egypt. It can still be found in Sudan.

but on closer viewing its delicate lime-green plumage can be seen. The ochre-bodied hoopoe is so spectacularly adorned that it cannot be mistaken at any distance. In addition to its orange and black crown, it has black and white striped wings.

Two of the most exciting birds to be seen along the Nile are the green bee-eater, seen perching on telephone wires, and the hoopoe, which has an orange and black feathery crown that opens like a fan when it's excited.

Purple plumage

Of the resident birds that enjoy the shores of the Nile, the most colourful and elusive is the purple gallinule, a stunning bird with blue, purple and green plumage and a red beak and legs. It is half the size of a duck but just as plump.

Another stunning bird about the same size as the purple gallinule is the spur-winged plover, which has black, white and brown feathers. According to legend it once helped the crocodile by cleaning its teeth. Both migrant and resident is the grey heron, a tall, elegant, shy bird that wades knee-deep along the river's banks.

The water birds arrive in winter. Migrants include the white pelican, white stork, spoonbill, greater flamingo, and numerous species of gull and duck. The sight of these birds flying over the Nile is a spectacular one: gulls follow boats, foraging for food, flocks of pelicans and storks fly high overhead, and the flamingo, graceful long neck outstretched and black striped wings flapping gracefully, flies at eye level past cruise boats.

Among the birds of prey that can be seen all year round are the kite, black-shouldered kite and kestrel. If your luck is in, you may see one of these birds hovering in the air as it hunts for field mice or insects. Talons at the ready, the legs come down, toes spread out. Then it plunges, disappearing into the grass. In a second the prey

Another garden resident is the Nile Valley sunbird. Once a year the male – resplendent in exotic iridescent purple-green plumage, yellow breast and long, slender tail feather – goes courting. Of African origin, this small bird is found in various habitats all along the Nile. The sunbird is most frequently seen in flower gardens, particularly when hovering around trumpet-like flowers as it pierces the corolla and sips the nectar. In winter the sunbird, along with other resident birds, shares the gardens with migrating wheatears, warblers and finches.

LEFT: a bee-eater and a flamingo.
ABOVE: green bee-eaters, the only species of bee-eater native to Egypt.

has been killed and it flies off to a safe place to eat its catch.

Ornithologists' delight

Crocodile Island in Luxor is a good year-round site for bird-watching. The Hotel Mövenpick Jolie Ville has made a special effort to cultivate and preserve the island's natural environment, and a variety of birds can be seen in winter and summer alike. Aswan is a nature-lover's paradise. Saloga Island, now a protected natural area, is one of the best spots for bird-watching.

Lake Qarun in Al Fayyum is a spectacular natural habitat. The saltwater lake is situated in a pastoral environment with desert along its northern shore and farmland to the south. Protected by newly enforced laws, water birds winter in this area in their tens of thousands, with Senegal thick-knees flying in particularly graceful formations. At the shore of the lake smaller birds, from sandpipers to spotted shanks and pips, flutter. At night thousands of gulls roost in backwaters; during the day, accompanied by coots, grebes and an impressive variety of ducks, they dot the shores. In recent winters flamingos have returned to the western shores of Lake Qarun. It is hoped that other species will follow.

DROUGHT CREATES DESERTION

If climate change experts are right, then the Nile and its wildlife will suffer as global temperatures rise. Already, riverside residents are claiming that the river is slowly ebbing and that fish stocks and birdlife are being affected by the shrinking of riverbeds. No water means no good nesting or spawning grounds – and the effect on both human and wildlife populations would be devastating, especially in more challenged locations such as Sudan.

Shooting game

Given its abundance of wildlife, it's no surprise that the Nile Valley became a destination of game hunters. The white hunter supplanted the intrepid explorer in the first half of the 20th century, when the wholesale slaughter of some of Africa's finest animals began.

But today's visitors come armed with nothing more lethal than binoculars and cameras. In recent times, local environmental agencies have prevented European hunters from shooting birds on illegal hunts in Egypt. ❑

ABOVE: hunting scenes such as this one, from the tomb of Nebamun (now in the British Museum) give us an idea of the wildlife around in Ancient Egypt.

Flourishing Flora

Unique species have developed along the riverbank, familiar with the Nile's moods and able to withstand the heat of the tropical sun

Most of Egypt's population lives in the Nile Valley, but few towns have been built on the rich soil near the river. A trip downriver runs through the heart of agricultural land. Along the river, between acacia and tamarisk trees, are fields of sugar cane, banana groves and palm trees.

There are several varieties of native acacia (mimosa) trees, all of which bloom with tiny yellow flowers. The largest, the Nile acacia, rises high above the river. The smallest is the sweet acacia – its flowers are the famous *cassie* flowers used in perfumes and cosmetics, and their fragrance fills the air when they bloom in the late autumn.

Sugar cane is not native to Egypt but was introduced by Muhammad Ali early in the 19th century. Cane fields exist all along the Nile – a government decree stipulates that all farmers must grow sugar cane. The cane is harvested in November and shipped on narrow-gauge railways to government-owned factories, also located along the Nile. The cane is processed from December to June, when the sweet smell of molasses fills the air. In addition to refined sugar, Egypt's only refinery produces molasses, alcohol, yeast and vinegar.

The banana is also an import, probably brought to Egypt in the Middle Ages. The plant has a short life, yielding its fruit for only three years, after which it must be destroyed and a new one planted.

The date palm is the country's most important and prolific tree. From Aswan to the Delta, in Sinai and the Western Desert, the palm provides farmers with food, shelter and income. A tree takes six or seven years to bear fruit; once mature it will produce for over 100 years. When it no longer bears fruit, the top can be transplanted to create another tree.

There are a variety of date trees in Egypt, each of which bears a different kind of date, which are categorised as dry, semi-dry or soft. Dry dates are crimson, crunchy and astringent. Orange-coloured dates are semi-sweet and can often be seen drying in the sun, thousands of them spread on the ground. Brown and black dates are usually soft and sweet.

Palm trees must be pollinated by hand each spring; the female can be pollinated for only two weeks a year. At harvest time (September) the farmer climbs the palm tree and picks each date by hand. By the end of November the harvest is over and the tree is carefully pruned of dead branches.

The giant fronds, which can be 7 metres (20ft) long, are weaved into baskets and mats. The leaf ribs are made into crates and furniture such as chairs, tables and beds. The residue is turned into sawdust.

South of the Aswan Dam, the flora of the region contrasts heavily. From the Sudanese-Egyptian border to the region of the Sudd swamp in the south, the topography is of the desert and savannah variety.

RIGHT: harvesting the date palm.

Palm dates can be found along the riverbanks, with vegetation getting more lush and tropical in the form of broad-leafed woodland as the river progresses towards the Uganda border.

In Ethiopia, the riverbank features sub-desert scrub progressing to woodland and wooded grassland as it moves away from Sudan. In the higher altitudes, closer to the source, the river cuts through highlands dotted with shrubs and evergreens.

In Uganda, population growth and civil war have done much to decimate large tracts of native flora, especially in the region around Lake Victoria. Dry acacia woodland and grassland are found near the Sudanese border, changing to papyrus and grassy swamp. As Lake Victoria approaches, wild vegetation is replaced by cultivated plots and farming. ❑

PLACES

A detailed guide to the Nile, with principal sites cross-referenced by number to the maps

Most Nile cruises travel the historically rich stretch of river between Aswan and Luxor, a basic cruise of 208km (130 miles) which takes three days to complete but which is sometimes supplemented with a trip further downriver to Abydos and Dandarah. It is no longer possible to take a cruise as far as Cairo (downriver, because the Nile flows due north), due to government regulations. Even before the restrictions were put in place, cruise boats never travelled north of the capital into the Delta, partly because of the difficulties of navigation but also because the ancient monuments have been washed away, and little remains worth seeing.

The riverbank varies from parched desert near Aswan to highly fertile agricultural land in Middle Egypt and the Delta. Because of the river's history of annual floods, most of Egypt's towns outside Cairo (with the notable exceptions of Luxor and Aswan) are situated on raised land on the edge of the floodplain. As a result, the impression that many cruise passengers get of Egypt is of a green and pleasant land occupied by farmers and fishermen, temples and tombs.

Luxor, a small provincial town, and Aswan, a market town and a gate to Africa, have retained a lot of their charm, despite the ever-expanding tourism industry. But Cairo, the Mother of the World, is where Western passengers are most likely to get a taste of modern Egypt. Cairo is a monument to Islamic architectural achievement in which almost 18 million Egyptians struggle to make a living; the history of Cairo begins where the temples and tombs of the Nile River leave off, and its history is still in the making.

Upriver, south of Aswan, the Nile disappears behind the dam into the Sudan and beyond, dividing into White and Blue Niles at Khartoum. Between them, these rivers complete another 5,600km (3,500 miles) through inaccessible territory into central Africa. For most travellers this has to be a journey of the mind. ❑

PRECEDING PAGES: a tourist boat visiting the Temple of Philae above the Aswan Dam; Temple of Amadah on Lake Nasser; getting around Elephantine Island. **LEFT:** the Temple of Horus at Edfu, in the Hypostyle Hall. **ABOVE:** mosque in Cairo; view beyond Lake Nasser.

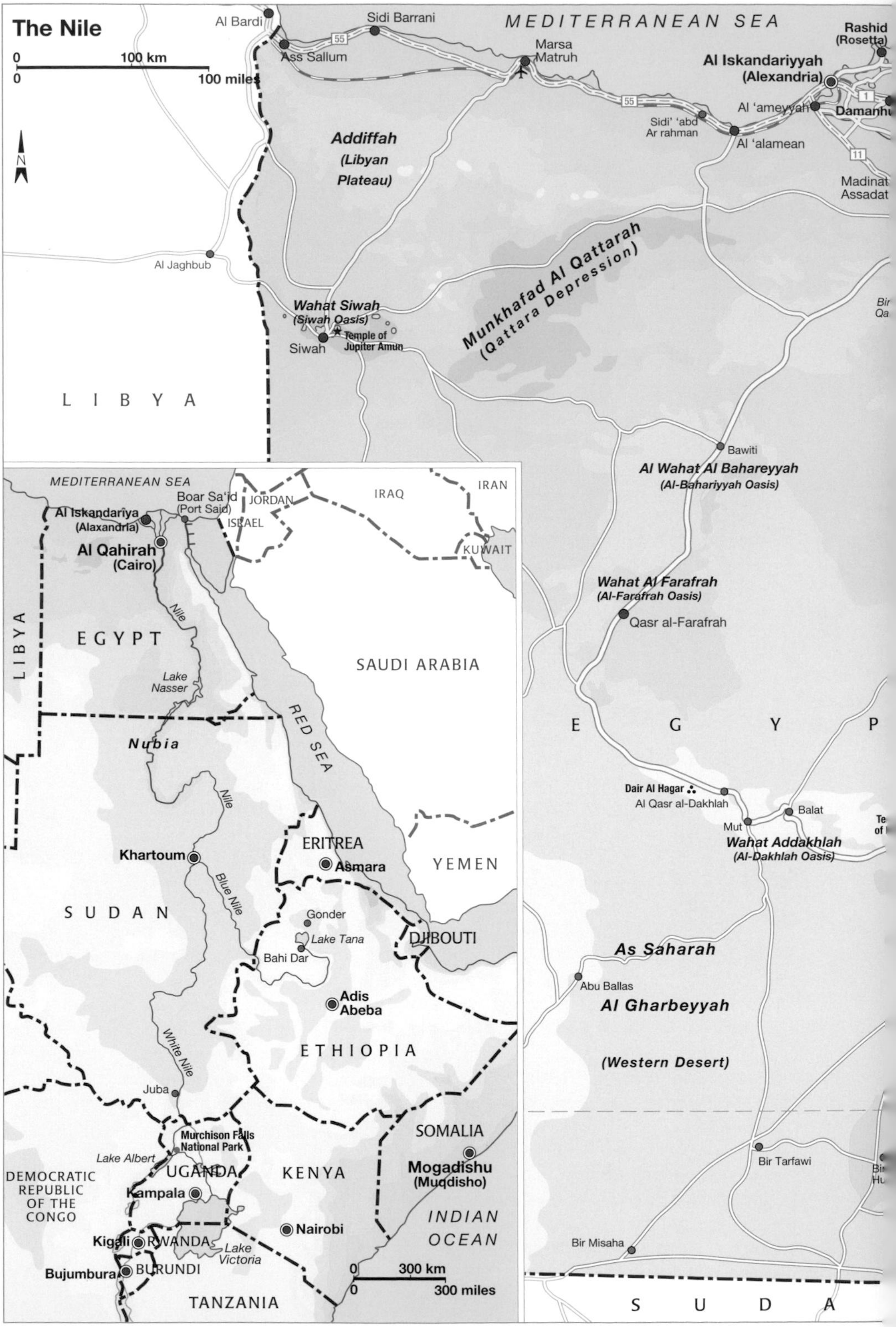
The Nile
0
100 km
0
100 miles
MEDITERRANEAN SEA
Al Bardi
Sidi Barrani
Ass Sallum
Marsa Matruh
Rashid (Rosetta)
Al Iskandariyyah (Alexandria)
Al 'ameyyah
Sidi' 'abd Ar rahman
Al 'alamean
Madinat Assadat
Addiffah (Libyan Plateau)
Munkhafad Al Qattarah (Qattara Depression)
Al Jaghbub
Wahat Siwah (Siwah Oasis)
Siwah
Temple of Jupiter Amun
LIBYA
Bawiti
Al Wahat Al Bahareyyah (Al-Bahariyyah Oasis)
Wahat Al Farafrah (Al-Farafrah Oasis)
Qasr al-Farafrah
EGYP
Dair Al Hagar
Al Qasr al-Dakhlah
Mut
Balat
Wahat Addakhlah (Al-Dakhlah Oasis)
As Saharah
Abu Ballas
Al Gharbeyyah
(Western Desert)
Bir Tarfawi
Bir Misaha
SUDA
MEDITERRANEAN SEA
Al Iskandariya (Alaxandria)
Boar Sa'id (Port Said)
Al Qahirah (Cairo)
JORDAN
ISRAEL
IRAQ
IRAN
KUWAIT
LIBYA
EGYPT
Nile
Lake Nasser
SAUDI ARABIA
RED SEA
Nubia
Nile
Khartoum
ERITREA
Asmara
YEMEN
SUDAN
Blue Nile
Gonder
Lake Tana
Bahi Dar
DJIBOUTI
Adis Abeba
ETHIOPIA
White Nile
Juba
Murchison Falls National Park
SOMALIA
Lake Albert
UGANDA
KENYA
Mogadishu (Muqdisho)
DEMOCRATIC REPUBLIC OF THE CONGO
Kampala
INDIAN OCEAN
Nairobi
Kigali
RWANDA
Lake Victoria
Bujumbura
BURUNDI
0
300 km
0
300 miles
TANZANIA

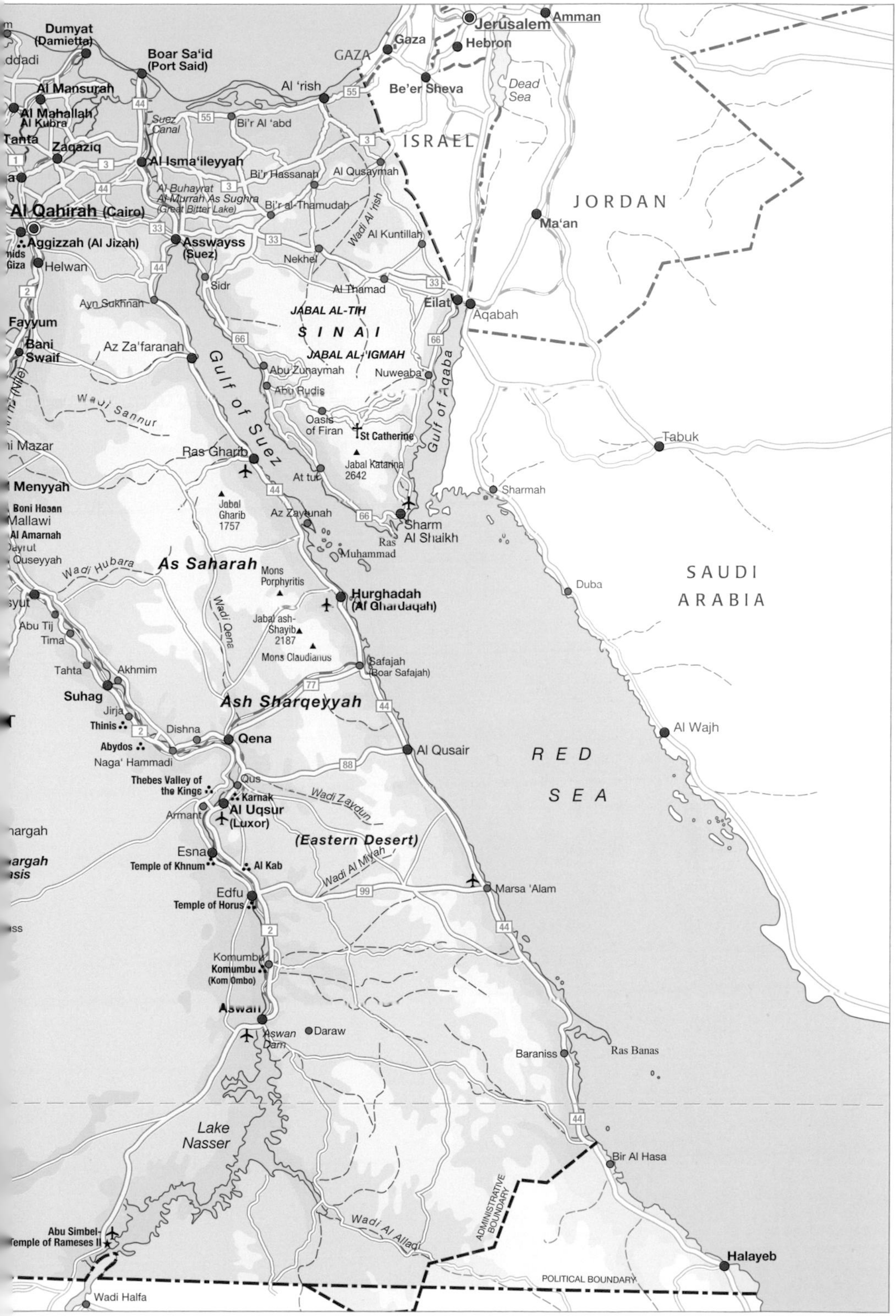
Dumyat (Damietta)
Boar Sa'id (Port Said)
Al Mansurah
Al Mahallah Al Kubra
Tanta
Zaqaziq
Al Isma'ileyyah
Al Qahirah (Cairo)
Aggizzah (Al Jizah)
Asswayss (Suez)
Helwan
Fayyum
Bani Swaif
Az Za'faranah
Ayn Sukhnah
Suez Canal
Al Buhayrat Al Murrah As Sughra (Great Bitter Lake)
Al 'rish
Bi'r Al 'abd
Bi'r Hassanah
Al Qusaymah
Bi'r al-Thamudah
Wadi Al 'rish
Al Kuntillah
Nekhel
Sidr
Al Thamad
GAZA
Gaza
Jerusalem
Amman
Hebron
Be'er Sheva
Dead Sea
ISRAEL
JORDAN
Ma'an
Eilat
Aqabah
JABAL AL-TIH
SINAI
JABAL AL-'IGMAH
Gulf of Suez
Gulf of Aqaba
Abu Zunaymah
Abu Rudis
Nuweaba'
Oasis of Firan
St Catherine
Jabal Katarina 2642
At tur
Ras Gharib
Jabal Gharib 1757
Az Zaytunah
Sharm Al Shaikh
Ras Muhammad
Sharmah
Tabuk
Duba
SAUDI ARABIA
Wadi Sannur
Menyyah
Boni Hasan
Mallawi
Al Amarnah
Dayrut
Quseyyah
Wadi Hubara
As Saharah
Mons Porphyritis
Wadi Qena
Hurghadah (Al Ghardaqah)
Jabal ash-Shayib 2187
Mons Claudianus
Safajah (Boar Safajah)
Asyut
Abu Tij
Tima
Tahta
Akhmim
Suhag
Jirja
Thinis
Abydos
Naga' Hammadi
Dishna
Qena
Ash Sharqeyyah
Al Qusair
Al Wajh
RED SEA
Qus
Thebes Valley of the Kings
Karnak
Armant
Al Uqsur (Luxor)
Wadi Zaydun
(Eastern Desert)
Esna
Temple of Khnum
Al Kab
Wadi Al Miyah
Marsa 'Alam
Edfu
Temple of Horus
Komumbu
Komumbu (Kom Ombo)
Aswan
Aswan Dam
Daraw
Baraniss
Ras Banas
Lake Nasser
Bir Al Hasa
ADMINISTRATIVE BOUNDARY
Wadi Al Allaqi
Abu Simbel-Temple of Rameses II
Halayeb
POLITICAL BOUNDARY
Wadi Halfa
55
44
3
1
33
2
66
77
88
99

NUBIA AND LAKE NASSER

Travellers in the know are turning to Lake Nasser, the reservoir created by the Aswan High Dam, for a cruise experience offering serenity and sunsets without the overcrowding of the Nile

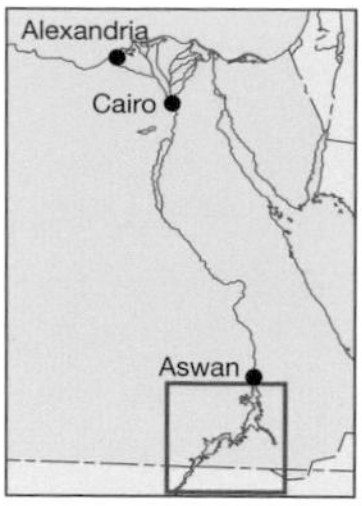

Main attractions
ABU SIMBEL
IBRIM PALACE
AMADAH
TEMPLE OF DERR
TOMB OF PENNUT
VALLEY OF THE LIONS
TEMPLE OF MUHARRAQAH
TEMPLE OF DAKKAH
TEMPLE OF KALABSHAH

In 1972, Nubia – an arid stretch of land of about 22,000 sq km (8,500 sq miles) between the Sudanese border and the Egyptian town of Aswan – disappeared under the largest artificial lake in the world, Lake Nasser. The Nile was tamed once and for all by the building of the High Dam, which created the vast lake, but the Nubians paid a high price. Though the world community rallied to save most of the ancient monuments, including the spectacular Sun Temple built by Rameses II at Abu Simbel and the impressive temple in Philae, by dismantling them block by block and transplanting them elsewhere on the shores of the lake, some 800,000 Nubians lost everything else. They lost their lands, much of their culture and their ancestral homes, as they were relocated, mainly to Aswan, Kom Ombo and to Kashem Al Girba in Sudan, but also to Cairo, Alexandria or abroad.

Nubian culture

Although Nubia was strategically important as a buffer zone to the ancients, historically the Egyptians have always looked down on the region as a vast barren area, and its loss was considered inconsequential. However, a growing realisation of the cultural value of what had been destroyed gathered momentum during the 1980s, and in the late 1990s a new Nubian Museum, backed by international interest and funds, opened its doors in Aswan *(see page 152)*. Dedicated to the memory of Nubia, it houses a collection of ancient Nubian artefacts and a section on lost traditions.

Travelling through Nubia

Independent travel through Nubia can be a challenge, as most of the temples and sights on the tourist radar are not visited as part of organised group tours. Roads to the temples have only just

LEFT: smoking a sheesha pipe, Nubian-style. **RIGHT:** cruise ship on Lake Nasser.

TIP

Nubian music is incredibly popular in Egyptian society, and Aswan is a great place to sample the beats. Many Nile-side restaurants feature nightly performances given by talented locals. There are also souq sellers who specialise in selling Nubian music CDs. When making a purchase, ask them if they know of any performances coming to town and they'll give you all the listings.

been completed, making the temples accessible by land. Unfortunately, the convoy system continues to be in place in this region *(see page 139)*, meaning you will either have to arrange for a private convoy with the police or independently charter a boat to see the more remote locations in the region – both very expensive options.

A better alternative is to join one of the cruises that now ply Lake Nasser's waters. Cruises traditionally begin in Aswan and head south for four days or start in Abu Simbel and head north for a three-day itinerary (*see page 309*).

Saving history

After it became clear that the creation of Lake Nasser would submerge all the Nubian monuments, Egypt and Sudan asked the world for help. The response was immediate. In the largest archaeological operation ever undertaken, 30 countries worked against time to save what they could, which in the end totalled 23 temples. The monuments were dismantled block by block and relocated elsewhere. Most found a new home on the shores of the lakes, while a few are now housed in museums around the world.

The biggest challenge for archaeologists was saving Nubia's most magnificent monument, the two temples of Abu Simbel which, unlike most of the other temples, were not freestanding but cut into the rock face. The temples were hand-sawed into more than 1,000 blocks and rebuilt on an artificial hill above the lake. The reconstruction was almost perfect: every year on 22 February and 22 October the dawn rays of the sun illuminate the inner sanctuary, to revive the cult statues, just one day later than the original plan.

Visiting Abu Simbel

The temples of **Abu Simbel** ❶ (daily winter 6am–5pm, summer 6am–6pm; charge for each temple) count among the highlights of Egypt's many ancient monuments. Rameses II built his temples of the sun-god Ra-Horakhty and his wife Nefertari to intimidate visitors from the south by flaunting Egypt's might and glory. It was known as "Hut Rameses Meryamun" (the Temple of Rameses beloved of Amun).

BELOW RIGHT: Nubian man.

The Nubian People

Despite their unfortunate plight in the modern world, the Nubians have managed to retain their distinct identity and are immensely proud to be Nubian. They rarely marry Egyptians, even when they live in Cairo or Alexandria, and as is discernible from the many Nubian boatmen in Aswan, they speak their own language, which is totally different from Egyptian Arabic.

Other elements of traditional Nubian culture survive in the villages on Elephantine Island and neighbouring islands – many women, for instance, still wear the Nubian-style dress of a black transparent gown over a brightly coloured dress. Wedding celebrations last over a week, and include performances by Nubian musicians.

Following the diaspora, the Nubians were much in demand in Cairo as doormen, cooks and servants, as they are known for their honesty and reliability. Some used their earnings to give their children a better education, with the result that many Nubians have entered tourism, commerce and even politics.

Ethnic Nubians are making their mark in Egyptian society, particularly in the arts. Probably the most famous person of Nubian descent was Anwar Al Sadat, the late president of Egypt and Nobel Prize-winner, whose mother was Nubian.

A good road leads from Aswan to Abu Simbel, but as the police still consider independent travel to be off-limits for foreigners in this corner of Egypt, the organised tour or private taxi are the only options, a journey that takes 3½–4 hours. This trip is one of the last in the country that requires you to travel in a convoy – a leftover rule from the days immediately following the 1997 massacre in Luxor when the police established new rules and regulations to help ensure the lucrative travel industry didn't collapse.

Organised tours have their advantages as they will include the entrance charge and the services of a guide, however, you may feel like you are a head of cattle being herded through the temples with very little time for self-exploration. Choose either the short tour, which takes you there and back, or the long tour, which includes stops at the High Dam and unfinished obelisk *(see page 157)* during your return.

Be warned: the long tour is a very extended day and should not be undertaken during the height of summer or if you have kids in tow.

There are also daily flights from Luxor and Aswan, but this option is a lot more expensive, and unless you plan to stay the night permits only a short time at the site, especially if your flight is delayed. If you do take the plane, choose a seat on the left-hand side of the aircraft for great aerial views of the temple. The convoy departs twice a day: between 3–4am and 10–11am. Return convoys depart about 90 minutes after you arrive. It is possible to travel to Abu Simbel in the early convoy and then return in the late convoy, but you will need to travel independently if you choose this option, as the organised tours are almost ruthless in their timings, with no flexibility if you want to stay longer.

Abu Simbel gets incredibly crowded – but only during the periods when the organised tours are on site. If you want to enjoy the temples in near-silence with no crowds, aim to spend the night in town *(see page 290)*. Not only will you be able to enjoy the sound and light show *(see page 141)*, you'll also be able to savour the sunrise in near-solitude. The shades of light and colour

Not all the temples found homes on the shores of Lake Nasser. Some were relocated abroad, including the Temple of Debod, which is now in Madrid, and the two Roman temples of Tafa which were sent to the Rijksmuseum in Leiden, Holland.

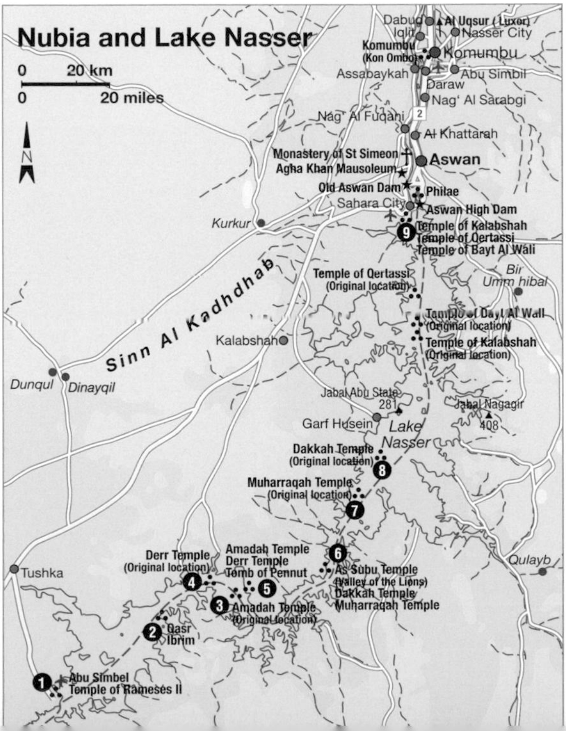

BELOW: moving Abu Simbel.

Nubia Old and New

As the gateway to Africa, Nubia and its riches have been prized since the dawn of ancient Egyptian civilisation

Look into the eyes of a Nubian and you will see great natural joy (which is in their character) and great pain. For very few Nubians in Egypt actually live in the land that they consider home. Scattered to the four winds, they dwell in cities and towns up and down the Nile, no longer able to visit the homes where grandparents – and even parents – were born and raised.

To understand the drama of the Nubian diaspora, formed following the flooding of the Nubian lands when the Aswan Dam was built, it is necessary to understand the importance of ancient Nubia. Known as Kush, the area stretched from south of the First Cataract well into the north of modern Sudan. The area protected Egypt's southern frontier and was an essential gateway for the Egyptian trade with Africa. Around 1550 BC, the Theban pharaohs turned their attention to conquering Kush. However, this was not an easy task, and it took them over a century to subdue Lower and Upper Nubia, and southern Nubia never fell under the Egyptian yoke. From the middle of the 18th Dynasty, Upper and Lower Nubia were ruled by a viceroy appointed by the Egyptian pharaoh, and a process of Egyptianisation ensued.

During the New Kingdom the Nubians worshipped a deity in ram form, which the Egyptians accepted as another form of their god Amun. From that point on the Nubians played a more important role in Egypt. They participated in the large religious festivals, such as the Opet festivals, and numerous Egyptian temples were built in Nubia. These temples are basically Egyptian in design and style, but also incorporate local Nubian elements and are often also dedicated to local gods. Most of the 25th Dynasty Kushite pharaohs were of Nubian descent, and some archaeologists even believe that Cleopatra was a Nubian woman from Wadi Halfa on the Sudanese border. *Kilu baba tarati*, the possible derivation of Cleopatra, is Nubian for "beautiful woman".

As Nubia was a largely barren land, it is not surprising that the Nile played a crucial role in the life of the Nubians. Their small riverside villages, each usually comprising one extended family, were supported by growing corn, melons and a few vegetables, fishing and cultivating date palms, which provided a nutritious source of food, fibre for ropes and wood for construction and furniture. They depended on the river spiritually, too. They would petition the water spirits when they needed a favour, and the river played an integral part in most of their celebrations. The imposing Egyptian-style temples were scattered between the villages, often flanked by the villagers' simple whitewashed shrines, dedicated to local saints. ❑

LEFT: copying text onto a slate in the village of Nyaro in Sudan. **ABOVE:** approach to the Temple of Wadi As Subu, Nubia, *c.*1845.

as the sun's rays dapple on the temple entrance are intoxicating.

Rameses II's temple

The facade of Rameses II's temple, flanked by four huge seated colossi of the pharaoh, each 21 metres (69ft) high and surrounded by other members of his family, is a spectacular sight. The rock-cut Hypostyle Hall is lined by eight large Osiride (with a crook and a flail) figures of Rameses which support the roof. The walls are decorated with superb reliefs depicting the king's military campaigns, including the battle of Qadesh against the Hittites, as well as wars against the Libyans and Nubians. The detail on the northern wall reliefs is extraordinary; filled with activity, they show more than 1,000 figures marching, fighting, riding or capturing enemies. The ceiling is adorned with flying vultures, with stars and the names and titles of the king over the side aisles.

Behind the Hypostyle Hall, a smaller pillared hall decorated with scenes of ritual offerings leads to the sanctuary carved 55 metres (180ft) deep into the rock. The rear niche contains damaged statues of Ptah, Amun-Ra, the deified Rameses and Ra-Horakhty the sun-god.

Outside the temple, on the way to the temple of Nefertari, a small door opens into the rock face. Here, inside the belly of the rock, is a section of the massive high-tech structure that supports the temple, a revealing insight into the mechanics of the rescue operation.

Temple of Queen Nefertari

The smaller **Temple of Queen Nefertari** was dedicated to the sun-god's wife, Hathor. Nefertari was the most beloved of the wives of Rameses II and throughout the temple, on pillars and walls, and even in the sanctuary, the names of the royal couple are linked in their shared dedication to the goddess. Testimony to Rameses' love for this wife is set down along with his titles: "Rameses, strong in *maat* (truth), beloved of Amun, made this divine abode for his royal wife, Nefertari, whom he loves." The facade is flanked by statues of Nefertari and Rameses II with their children standing between them. The Hypostyle Hall has Hathor-

TIP

A daily sound and light show is held at Abu Simbel every hour on the hour from 7–9pm in winter and 8–10pm in summer (www.soundandlight.com.eg).

BELOW: sound and light show at Abu Simbel.

Kiosk of Qertassi, on New Kalabshah Island, an excellent example of Egyptian art in Nubia.

headed columns and reliefs of the royal couple confronting the gods. A damaged cow-statue of Hathor adorns the sanctuary.

Further temples

Most of the other monuments on the lake, except for Philae and **Kalabshah**, have open access. Many of the temples now also have road access, but you will still have to take the convoy system if you plan on visiting *(see page 139)*.

Fifteen kilometres (9 miles) north of Abu Simbel, the imposing Roman site of **Ibrim Palace** (Qasr Ibrim) ❷ still stands in its original location, but it is now an island rather than a hilltop, as the rest of the settlement lies beneath the lake. Originally it was one of three massive peaks (the others lie below water), and it seems likely that the Romans, Saladin, the Ottoman sultans and Muhammad Ali all stationed troops here. Ongoing excavations on the site have revealed letters and legal documents, in Egyptian, Coptic, Greek and Old Nubian; the last has so far not been deciphered.

Further north on the lake is a group of three monuments. The small temple of **Amadah** ❸, built by Thutmose III, retains many of its painted reliefs, as well as some important historical inscriptions describing military campaigns. Rameses II built the rock-cut **Temple of Derr** ❹ in a similar style to that of Abu Simbel but without the colossi in the front. The third monument is the **Tomb of Pennut** ❺, the local 12th-century BC governor, which was moved here from Annoabah, 40km (25 miles) south.

On the western shore further north is another group of temples. The most complete is **Valley of the Lions** ❻ (Wadi As Subu), named after the avenue of sphinxes leading to a temple built by the viceroy of Kush for Rameses II. The court has 10 statues of the king carved into pillars. The front of the temple was built in sandstone, but the antechamber and sanctuary were carved into the rock. The central niche was decorated with reliefs of Rameses worshipping the gods Amun-Ra, Ra-Horakhty and his deified self, but those made way for depictions of the king making offerings to St Peter when the temple was later converted into a church.

BELOW RIGHT: carving on a temple, Lake Nasser.

Recreation on Lake Nasser

While a Nile cruise is all about temple-hopping and gin and tonics, Lake Nasser cruises and boat charters offer an altogether different experience. The sheer size of the lake and reduction in the number of boats that ply these waters translate into a more relaxing and traffic-free holiday.

Crocodiles, once visible up the entire length of the Nile, can now only be found south of the Aswan Dam. Bird-watching and crocodile-spotting are popular pastimes, with African skimmers, yellow-billed stork and African wagtails commonly spotted here. Miskaa Safari and Fishing is an Egyptian-run outfit that specialises in nature-packed tours of the lake for both groups and individuals (www.miskaa.com).

Fishing on Lake Nasser is increasingly popular, particularly to catch the giant Nile perch, one of the world's largest freshwater fish. In the days before the lake existed, the Nile deposited its rich silt along the valley to sustain the Nubian population. Today, that rich silt supports ample – and well-fed – fish stocks. Additionally, a comparative lack of industry along Lake Nasser's shores means that the pollution of the Nile has yet to affect the fragile environment, meaning you can eat what you catch.

Tour operators include UK-based operators African Angler (www.african-angler.co.uk) and Nile Perch Heaven (www.nileperchheaven.com), or the Egyptian outfit Lake Nasser Adventure (www.lakenasseradventure.com).

The neighbouring **Temple of Muharraqah** ❼ was built during Roman times, and dedicated to both Isis and Serapis. The **Temple of Dakkah** ❽, dedicated to Thoth, the god of wisdom, and built by the 3rd-century BC Nubian king Arganani, was expanded by the Ptolemies and Romans, but never finished; the pylon is undecorated, but the interior has some fine reliefs.

The temple of Philae also presented a serious challenge as the complex had to be moved to an alternative island. This temple is described in the chapter on Aswan, as it is a standard excursion from there *(see page 158)*.

Temple of Kalabshah

Closer to the High Dam is the less visited **Temple of Kalabshah** ❾ (daily 8am–4pm; charge), reached overland if the waters of the lake are low or by a boat hired from Aswan's boatyard. This is the largest freestanding temple of Lower Nubia, built during the reigns of the last Ptolemies and the Roman emperor Augustus. Dedicated to the Nubian god Horus-Mandulis and to Isis and Osiris, it is one of the finest examples of Egyptian architecture in Nubia, even though it was never completely finished. A granite entrance gate, now in the Egyptian Museum in Berlin, led to the pylon, followed by a colonnaded courtyard, a hypostyle hall and a sanctuary which was later used as a church. The pharaoh Amenhotep II (1450–1425 BC) is depicted in the reliefs as one of the founders of the temple, though most of the current structure was built under the Romans.

Nearby is the 1st-century BC Roman **Temple of Mandulis**, dedicated to the Nubian fertility god. Also used as a church in the Christian era, it has a great ramp leading up to the first pylon, followed by a court and hypostyle hall with floral columns. The emperor Augustus appears in front of the gods in the sanctuary. The smaller temple of the **House of the Governor** (Bayt Al Wali) was cut out of the rock by the viceroy of Kush in honour of Rameses II. Here again the victorious pharaoh is depicted in brightly coloured reliefs, leading campaigns in Nubia and Syria, and receiving tributes from his conquered enemies. ❑

TIP

Many cruise companies are now combining Lake Nasser itineraries with traditional Nile cruises. Trips begin in Abu Simbel and end in Luxor (or vice versa) with a change of ship in Aswan. Check with your selected cruise operator or travel agent to make a booking.

BELOW: working at the Temple of Kalabshah.

The Blue Nile

Together with the White Nile, the Blue Nile forms the headwaters of the river, running through Ethiopia and Sudan until it reaches Khartoum

The Blue Nile, one of the two strands of the Upper Nile *(see page 21)*, is almost biblical in its power, surging out of Lake Tana (1,788 metres/5,865ft) in the Ethiopian highlands to begin its journey towards Khartoum in Sudan. This tributary is so called because in times of flood, its waters turn extremely dark in colour, and in the Sudanese dialect, the word for black is the same as for blue.

As the source for over 80 percent of the waters that eventually flow into Egypt, it is by far the most important tributary, dependent on the seasonal rains that replenish it every year. Natives and visitors have been in awe of its beauty for centuries – so much so that many believe it to be the river that flowed out of the Garden of Eden as written about in the Old Testament. The following text describes the main places of interest along its path.

Gondar and Lake Tana

The most intriguing city in the vicinity of Lake Tana is Gondar, located on the Lesser Angereb, a river that flows into the northern reaches of the lake on the opposite side from the Nile's source. Gondar was once the rainy-season home to the Ethiopian royal family and was the capital of the nation from 1635 to 1856. Until the city of Gondar was founded, Ethiopia boasted no capital, as tradition dictated that the royal family encamped in a different area every season. Today it is a tourist destination, known for the wealth of unique architecture in its former Royal Enclosure *(Fasil Ghebbi)*, which is a Unesco World Heritage site.

Gondar is also the home of the Beta Israel. Known in Ethiopia as "*falasha*" (or outsiders), Beta Israel is the traditional name of the Jewish community of Ethiopia. Today, only 2,000 Beta Israel call Ethiopia home; however, it is estimated that there were at least 1 million as recently as the 17th century.

The roots of the Beta Israel are cloaked in mystery. Legend says that they are the descendants of Jews who arrived in Ethiopia with Menelik I, the rumoured son of King Solomon and the Queen of Sheba. In fact, some academics believe that Menelik may have removed the Ark of the Covenant from the Temple in Jerusalem and brought it to Ethiopia for safe-keeping. Another theory has it that the Beta Israel are the descendants of the lost tribe of Dan. Mention of this theory is made by the 9th-century Jewish scholar Eldad ha-Dani, the first time the term "Beta Israel" was ever referred to in a text.

For centuries, the Beta Israel called the area around Gondar and Lake Tana home – living side by side, but never completely integrating with the Ethiopian Christian majority.

In the mid-1970s, the first in a series of deadly famines hit Ethiopia, forcing the government to permit the exodus of the Jewish community. Three Israeli military-backed operations between 1985 and 1991 airlifted the vast majority of the Ethiopian Jews to the Holy Land, saving a community that was at risk of dying out.

Across Lake Tana are a number of islands housing early Ethiopian monasteries and churches, many with the remains of some of Ethiopia's earliest emperors. In terms of recreation, it is possible to enjoy sport fishing and arrange a tour of the islands for guided exploration. A recommended tour operator to consider for both adventurous and scenic tours of Lake Tana and the Blue Nile is Addis Ababa-based Nile River Safaris (tel: +261 209 552 347; www.nileriversafaris.com).

Bahir Dar and the Blue Nile Falls

A good base from which to travel around Lake Tana is Bahir Dar, the capital of the Amhara region, and widely considered to be the most beautiful city in Ethiopia. Known for its wide avenues and green spaces, it makes for a relaxing change of pace when compared to other African cities of comparable size.

Bahir Dar is the most popular jumping-off point for trips south to the Blue Nile Falls or *Tis Issat*, as they are known in the local Amharic language. Located 30km (18½ miles) downstream, they are one of the most popular tourist attractions in all Ethiopia. Before modern technology put in place regulation methods to control the flow of water out of Lake Tana and into the Blue Nile, the falls were known for their powerful flow during the rainy season, often expanding from a small trickle to a surge 45 metres (150ft) high and 400 metres (1,310ft) wide. The power of the surge is what gave the falls their Amharic name, which, when translated, means "smoking waters".

Between the falls and the Sudanese border, the Nile skirts around the mountain ranges of the Ethiopian highlands, fed by additional tributaries that emerge from the hills. The people who live along this stretch of the Blue Nile shift from being predominantly Christian in Ethiopia to predominantly Muslim as the river gets closer to the border. The vegetation also changes as the river drops in altitude from relatively lush tropical savannah to dry desert conditions. After crossing into Sudan, the river passes through a number of major dam projects before reaching Khartoum. Tourism is very limited in this part of the country due to the lengthy civil war that plagued Sudan for over 20 years, finally ending in 2005. For more information, *see pages 285 and 288*.

Khartoum

The Blue Nile finally meets the White Nile at Khartoum, capital of Sudan and the first large city the Nile passes through on its journey to the Mediterranean. Khartoum today has a population of just over 1 million people and is known for its economic prosperity, driven by Sudan's oil revenues. Highlights to visit include the Palace Museum and the National Museum of Sudan, with re-creations of two Egyptian temples relocated to Khartoum following the completion of the Aswan High Dam and subsequent flooding of the Nubia region.

Khartoum is very much geared towards business travel, specifically to those working in the oil trade. Tourists who don't have business in the city visit infrequently, although – despite the ongoing internal rebellions and strife – the city is safe to visit and walk around. As Sudan is a conservative country, women are advised to cover up as much as possible if they wish to avoid hassle. Petty theft does sometimes occur, especially in the open-air market at Omdurman, so keep valuables in the hotel safe and watch purchases and bags as you walk around. In order to get anywhere, you will have to take taxis, as there is no easily navigable transport system unless you speak Arabic. ❑

ABOVE LEFT: pied crows in Gondar, Ethiopia. **LEFT:** Lake Tana. **BELOW:** Ethiopian tribal woman.

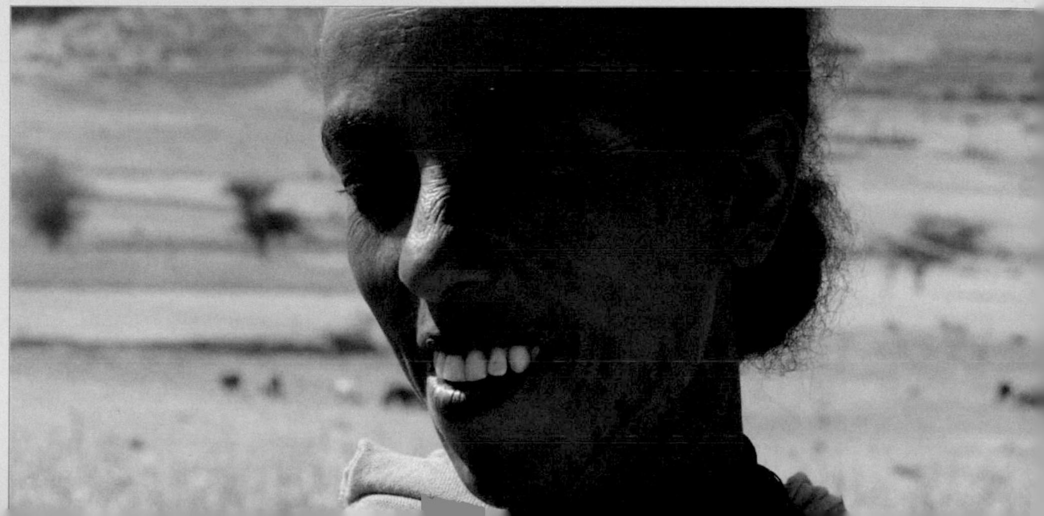

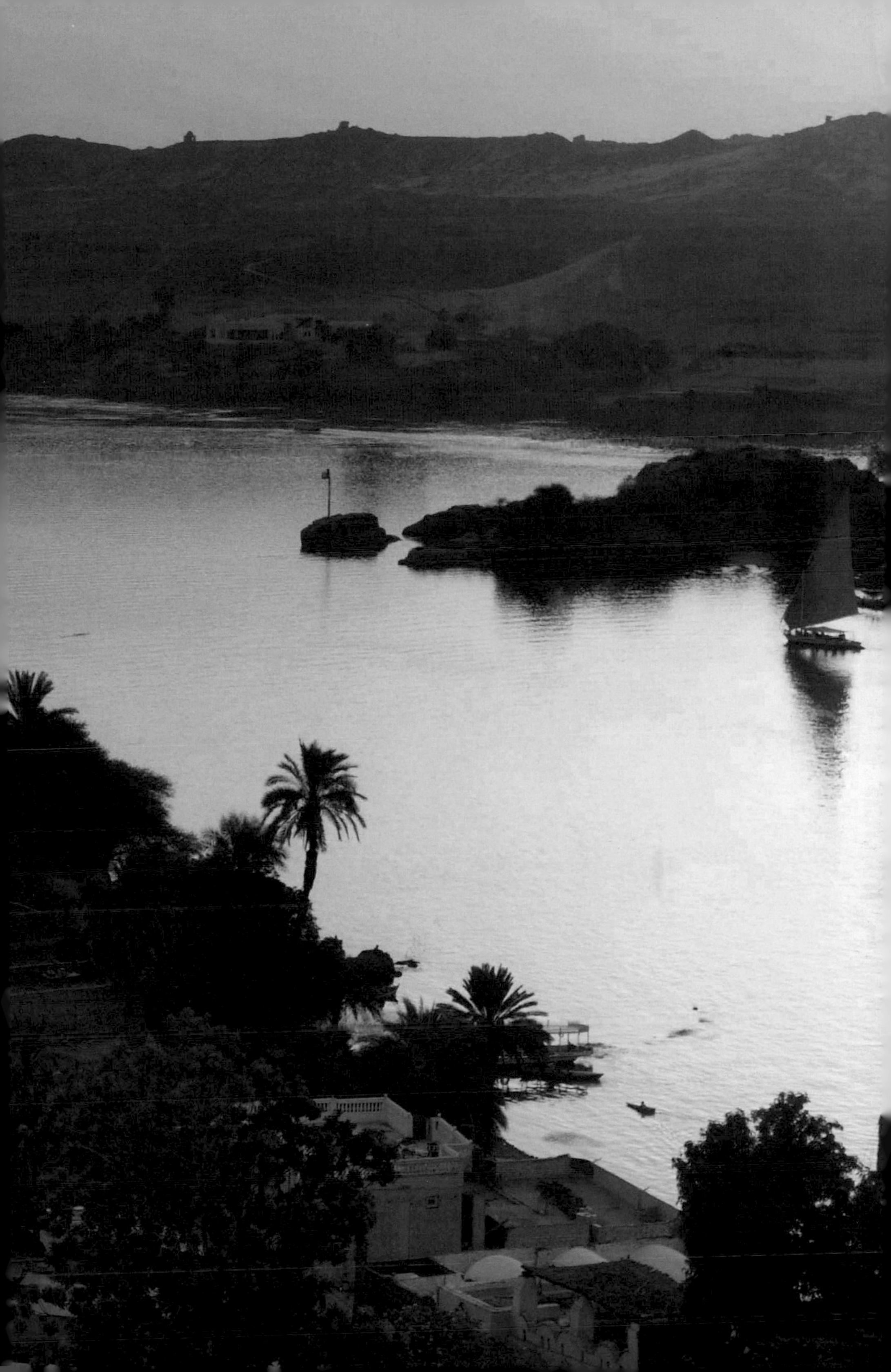

ASWAN

With its many palm-topped islands, lateen-sailed feluccas and perfect winter climate, Aswan is the ideal place to relax beside the Corniche or mess about in a boat

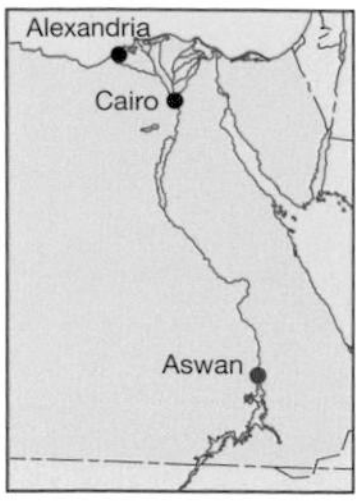

Main attractions
- OLD CATARACT HOTEL
- NUBIAN MUSEUM
- FATIMID CEMETERY
- ELEPHANTINE ISLAND
- KITCHENER'S ISLAND
- TOMBS OF THE NOBLES
- MONASTERY OF ST SIMEON
- UNFINISHED OBELISK
- ASWAN HIGH DAM
- TEMPLE OF ISIS AT PHILAE

In the eyes of many, **Aswan** is the most beautiful of Egypt's riverine cities. It became known for its healthy climate amongst 19th-century tourists, who came in winter to escape Europe's cold weather. Its warm winter temperatures and very dry air were considered especially beneficial for lung conditions; Lady Duff Gordon set a fashion when she travelled to Upper Egypt to seek a cure for tuberculosis in the mid-1800s. The late Aga Khan, and his wife the Begum, found such peace and beauty in Aswan that they not only built a villa on the west bank but also chose to be buried in a mausoleum on top of a hill overlooking the river they loved so much. It is said that the Aga Khan would bury himself neck-deep in warm sand as a cure for rheumatism. Summer temperatures can reach 48°C (118°F), but during winter it's a pleasant 22–25°C (72–77°F), although the nights can be seriously chilly.

Perfect setting

Situated 132 metres (400ft) above sea level, 900km (560 miles) south of Cairo, Aswan is effectively a border town, where Egypt ends and the rest of Africa begins. The governorate of Aswan covers approximately 850 sq km (340 sq miles), with a population of well over 1 million. Before the High Dam was built, only about 40,000 people lived in the town itself, but the industrialisation that ensued has swollen the population to around 256,000, which, together with the expansion of tourism, has transformed the town's character.

The first view many independent travellers have of the city is the train station, located in the north about two blocks east of the river. The tourist office is located immediately next to the station exit and is a good resource for information regarding organised excursions and budget hotels.

PRECEDING PAGES: view of Aswan. **LEFT:** boat boy securing a felucca at Aswan. **RIGHT:** Orthodox Coptic Cathedral, Aswan.

TIP

The Aswan souq is a good source for genuine Nubian and Bedouin arts and crafts, including daggers, hand-woven rugs, jewellery and baskets. If you want the best quality, you'll have to look inside each shop, as most of what you find on the street will be of a poorer standard, catering to the passing (and uninformed) tourist trade. The souq runs almost the entire length of the city, parallel to the river but approximately two blocks inland.

The Nile at Aswan, just north of the First Cataract, is thick with river vessels of all kinds and studded with islands of granite. **Elephantine Island** is the largest of these, with ancient monuments and a Nubian village; **Kitchener's Island** behind Elephantine hosts the botanical garden. On both banks, date palms grow down to the river's edge, but beyond them, the hinterland of Aswan is bleak, hot and arid.

Like Luxor, Aswan can sometimes seem overwhelmed by tourists and their interests, but in general it manages to shoulder the burden while preserving much of its unique character. The market streets are often filled with visitors from Sudan or tribes from the Eastern Desert, as well as with Europeans on package holidays. And compared to the hard-sell hawking performed by the shop owners in Luxor, it is a comparative delight. You will still get the patter and constant bellows of "One Egyptian pound" and "Where you from?" yelled your way as you pass – but in Aswan, a nod and polite "*No shoqhran*" will be enough to put a stop to any hassle.

A bridge was only recently built across the Nile (just north of Aswan), so the town has grown almost exclusively on the east bank behind the Corniche, the long riverside promenade. This street is usually lined with cruiseboats, feluccas and restaurants on the Nile side, and by travel offices and tourist shops on the land side. Several riverside restaurants offer Nubian folkloric entertainment.

Bridging two cultures

Aswan has been the link between the Egyptian and Nubian cultures for thousands of years. In antiquity Elephantine, the largest of the islands, situated immediately opposite Aswan *(see page 152)*, was known as Yebu or Elephant Land, because it was the trading post for ivory (although another theory for the island's name points to the shapes and textures of the rock formations).

The island commanded the First Cataract that formed a natural boundary to the south, and its noblemen bore the title "Guardians of the Southern Gate". During the Old Kingdom (2686–2181 BC), Egypt had a loose

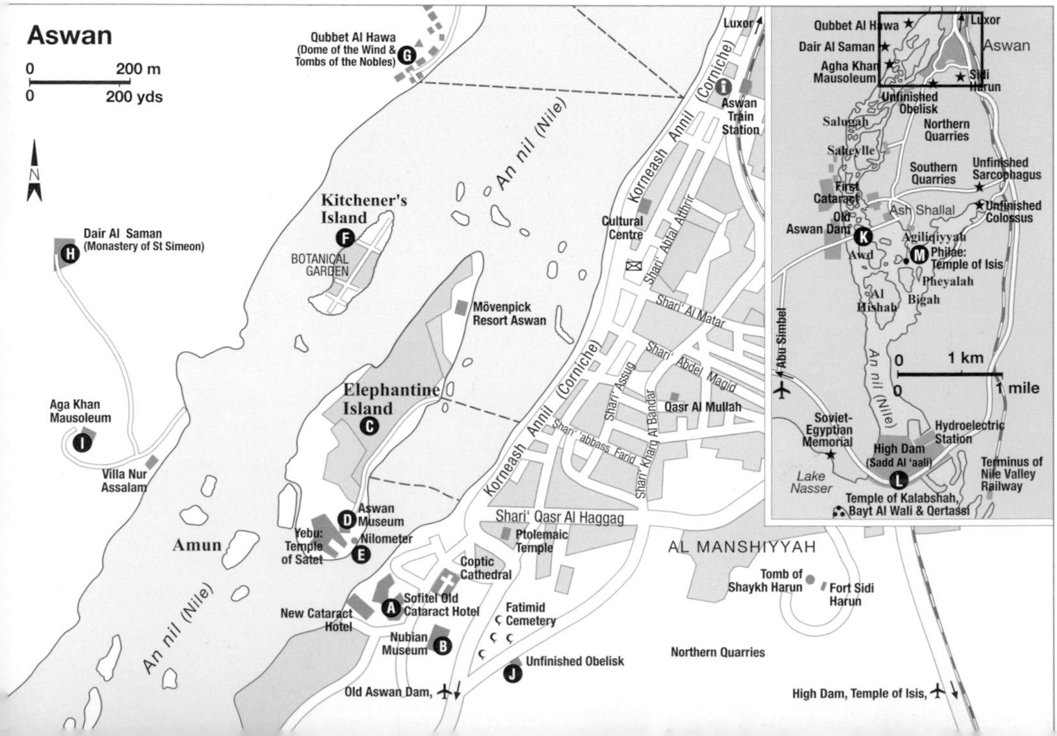

sovereignty over Nubia. The Nubians, moving with their herds of sheep and goats, relied on Egypt for grain and vegetable oil. Aware of the rich veins of gold-bearing quartz and iron ore in the seemingly impoverished land to the south, the Egyptians were only too happy to supply their needs.

The princes of Elephantine were a proud and independent breed who lived at a time when the pharaoh encouraged initiative and responsible action; a time when many Lower Egyptians travelled to Upper Egypt to find work, just as today Upper Egyptians travel to Cairo and the Delta. They held responsible positions that answered to central government, but they also controlled the caravan routes south. With the passing of the Old Kingdom, Aswan's time of glory ended.

Traders' town

Aswan's name stems from the ancient Egyptian word *swenet*, meaning "making business" or trade. Indeed, trade is the very essence of Aswan. Its market places are packed with Nubians, Egyptians and tribes from the surrounding deserts, especially the Bisharis of the Eastern Desert. They exchange their produce in the same way as they have for thousands of years.

In Egypt, Aswan is famous for its dry dates, *fuul sudani*, peanuts roasted in the hot sand, and *karkadeh*, dried hibiscus flowers that are used to make a refreshing drink. Colourful woven silk-cotton shawls, cotton tablecloths, African amulets and locally used spices such as red chilli pepper *(shatta)*, cumin *(qamoum)*, coriander *(qusbara)* and black pepper *(filfil aswad)* are also good buys. Bargaining here is a less aggressive process than it is in many Egyptian towns, and some products, notably the spices, are fixed-price.

The main sights

The finest relic from colonial times is the **Sofitel Old Cataract Hotel** (currently closed for renovation) **A**, at the southern end of the Corniche, with the interior of a fabulous Moorish palace. The hotel renovation was due to be completed in late 2010; however, this date has already been pushed back three times and at time of printing,

Aswan is a good place to buy spices and herbs. Look out for karkadeh *(dried hibiscus flowers), which are used to make a red tea, often served hot or cold to welcome visitors.*

BELOW LEFT: the Aswan Moon café.

Inspired by Nubia

Visitors to Aswan who spend time getting to know the local people may be lucky enough to get an invitation to a Nubian wedding in one of the Nubian villages on the islands south of the town. Such visitors are usually amazed and delighted by the harmony of these villages. While it is not essential to visit during a special occasion, only during a Nubian wedding will you witness the true character of Nubians and feel like you are immersing yourself in their culture rather than being "just another tourist". Visits can be organised through a tour company, but these are often sanitised versions of the real thing. Better still, ask your taxi driver and he may take you to his home village… for a price.

One of the most noticeable features is the architecture. Homes feature clean lines with decorative roofs. Many will be brightly painted with images of flowers or beautiful motifs. The internationally renowned Egyptian architect Hassan Fathy (1900–89) found his inspiration in vernacular Nubian architecture. Writing about his first visit to Elephantine Island in 1941 in his *Architecture for the Poor,* he said: "It was a new world for me, a whole village of spacious, lovely, clean and harmonious houses each more beautiful than the next. There was nothing else like it in Egypt." Fathy believed in adapting traditional materials, designs and techniques to create modern, attractive and economical solutions to housing the poor.

Nubian women like to decorate their hands and feet with henna patterns. Henna tattooists serving the tourist trade can be found along the Corniche and in the souq. However, you should avoid using black henna as it is very toxic and can cause damage to your skin.

it still looked nowhere near finished. Check in advance to see if the hotel is open by the time you are in Aswan. Tea on the hotel's terrace, overlooking the river and the ruins of Elephantine Island, is an institution. For a splurge you can stay in the huge suites of Agatha Christie or King Faruq.

A short walk south of the hotel is one of the most recent additions to Aswan's attractions, the **Nubia Museum** **B** (daily, winter 9am–1pm, 5–9pm, summer 10am–1pm, 6–10pm; charge). Partly funded by Unesco, the museum was belatedly established to commemorate the long history and rich heritage of the Nubians, much of which disappeared under the waters of Lake Nasser after the building of the High Dam. It is housed in a Nubian-style building and set in a well-tended garden dotted with sculpture, a typical Nubian house, some tombs of Nubian saints, including one of 77 *wali* (Muslim sheikhs), and caves with prehistoric rock paintings brought here from all over Nubia.

Exhibits, covering the area's history from prehistoric times up to the present, are well displayed and labelled in Arabic and English; a space is devoted to the international operation to rescue Nubia's monuments *(see page 138)*. The first section of the exhibition is devoted to archaeological finds such as jewellery, statues, sarcophagi and other objects, including, in the main exhibition hall, an impressive statue of Rameses II built by Setau, the viceroy of Kush. The second section illustrates Nubian culture and crafts in a series of tableaux.

There is a new annexe displaying recent finds from the site, and the old museum is being refurbished. Just behind the museum is the vast **Fatimid Cemetery** with domed mud-brick tombs, dating from the 9th century until the present day.

BELOW: view of the Old Cataract Hotel.

Elephantine Island

Most of Aswan's sights lie on the islands or on the west bank. A boatman or the public ferry will sail you across to **Elephantine Island** **C**. The island's small **museum** **D** (daily, winter 8am–4pm, summer 8am–5pm; charge) occupies a colonial-style building originally constructed as a resting place for the British engineers engaged on building the original Aswan Dam. The very dusty exhibits include Old and Middle Kingdom objects from local sites, treasures from the Heqaib Sanctuary, and sarcophagi containing mummies of a priest and priestess of Philae as well as a mummy of the sacred ram. However, many of the museum's best exhibits have been moved to the Nubia Museum *(see above)*. Descriptions are vague and there is very little explanation as to the significance of the finds, so if you are in a rush, then you can easily skip this collection. The museum has a pleasant, well-kept garden, and a path leads to the ruins of Yebu and two ancient Nilometers.

The **Nilometer** **E** of the Satet Temple may not be as striking as some, but it is still interesting. It consists of a stairway on the river's bank constructed of regular-shaped stones designed so that the water, rising and falling with the ebb and flow of the flood, could register maximum, minimum and average water levels. Be careful if exploring with children as there are steep, rubble-strewn paths and sudden drops into pits that can be dangerous if kids are running free. A text on a wall of the Temple of Horus at Edfu *(see page 170)* tells us that when the river rose to 24 cubits and three-and-a-half hands at Elephantine, there was sufficient water to supply the needs of the whole country.

The level of taxation was also governed by the level of the water, as a higher flood usually resulted in a better harvest. Plutarch, the Greek writer, recorded that the Nile once rose to a height of 28 cubits, or 14.7 metres (47ft). On the walls of the staircase are records in Demotic (fluid hieroglyphic hand) and Greek, showing different water levels. The other Nilometer is below the Khnum Temple terrace, and has stone stairs that lead down to the basin.

Yebu

The Old Town of Yebu, on the southern tip of Elephantine Island, is still being excavated. Among the monuments are a granite portal that once formed the entrance to a large temple, the foundations of a small temple built by Nektanebo II, the last native pharaoh, Julius Caesar and Trajan (AD 98–117), and blocks from the edifices of earlier temples. The most important piece of restoration is that of the elegant Temple of Satet, goddess of the Cataract region, wife of Khnum, who guarded the "new water" of the rising of the Nile.

On the other tip of the island is the concrete tower of the Mövenpick Hotel and several fast-growing Nubian villages set in lush gardens. While the tower is hideous, a bar on the 13th floor provides excellent, unimpeded views of the river and town. If you have the time, a walk from Yebu to the Mövenpick is recommended, as it takes you through a couple of interesting Nubian villages and offers good views of the west bank and the Aga Khan's Mausoleum. If you're on a felucca, you can ask your captain to sail to the hotel to wait for you to complete your stroll.

The abandoned, decaying building on the island to the north of the Mövenpick was intended as a resort,

Stalls on the streets of Aswan sell all sorts.

BELOW: home on Elephantine Island.

TIP

One of the most pleasurable things to do in Aswan is to hire a felucca in the late afternoon and either cruise among the islands opposite Aswan or sail down to the First Cataract and Saheylle Island. Your captain might serve mint tea on the way.

but the drop in tourism numbers caused by the 1997 Luxor massacre quickly shut down the project. and it is unknown what is going to happen to the structure in the future.

Kitchener's Island

Lord Kitchener, British consul of Egypt, was granted **Kitchener's Island** Ⓕ by the Egyptian government for his campaigns in Sudan. Kitchener was passionate about botany and imported and planted a large variety of rare African and Indian plants here. Kitchener's mark is also to be seen in graffiti relating to his Sudan campaigns on the walls of the Temple of Isis at Philae, on Agiliqiyyah Island near the Aswan Dam *(see page 158)*.

The whole island is open to the public as a fragrant **botanical garden** (daily 8am–sunset; charge) with an impressive collection of palm trees and other exotic plants. It makes a perfect escape from the heat and dust of the town. (If you arrive by felucca, your boatman will normally deposit you near the entrance to the botanical garden and then sail around to pick you up from the exit.) Be warned that weekends and holidays can see large groups of locals and children noisily running around the pathways – avoid during these times if a leisurely wander amongst the trees and flowers is what you're after.

Among the other islands are Amun Island, on which the Amoun Hotel occupies a former royal lodge, and, further south, Isis Island, which has a larger holiday resort owned by the Mubarak family and is popular with moneyed Egyptians.

Tombs of the Nobles

On the summit of a hill on the west bank opposite Aswan is the structure of the **Dome of the Wind** Ⓖ (Qubbet Al Hawa). This is not, as is popularly believed, the tomb of a sheikh, but one of several signal posts built in the 19th century, most of which bore the name of a saint or sheikh.

Nearby are the **Tombs of the Nobles** (daily, winter 7am–4pm, summer 7am–5pm; charge), the burial ground of the noblemen from Elephantine. The tombs were hewn out of rock about halfway up the hill, facing the river

BELOW: the granite boulders of Elephantine Island.

and approached by a narrow ledge. The group of Old Kingdom tombs is especially interesting because the door-jambs bear autobiographical texts written by ancient Egyptians who explored the African continent. A decree by Pharaoh Pepy I (*c.*2300 BC) refers several times to "the peaceful Nubians", and inscriptions in many of the tombs make reference to them.

One of these tombs (No. 34) belongs to a nobleman called Harkhuf who lived in the reign of the 6th Dynasty Pharaoh Merenra (*c.*2280 BC). Harkhuf styled himself a "caravan leader"; he went on many journeys southwards, perhaps as far as Sudan and beyond, and he recorded that "never had any companion or caravan-leader done it before". On each of his travels, Harkhuf brought back precious products: gold, ostrich feathers, animal skins, ivory, ebony, incense and gum.

On his fourth expedition, he brought back a "dancing pygmy" for his pharaoh, the young Pepy II, successor of Merenra, who acceded to the throne at the age of six. In his record of the event, Harkhuf states that he sent his messengers ahead of his convoy to inform His Majesty of his gift, to which Pepy wrote back, with enthusiasm, that the pygmy should be guarded so as not to let it fall overboard.

Another example of pioneering spirit and filial devotion can be found in the tombs of Mekhu and his son Sabni. A nobleman of Elephantine in the reign of Pepy II, *c.*2280 BC, Mekhu was attacked and killed by desert tribes while on an expedition in Lower Nubia. When his son Sabni received the news, he mustered a convoy of troops and marched southwards to recover the body.

The text on Sabni's tomb relates how he duly punished the tribe responsible for his father's death, recovered the body and started his journey home. Meanwhile the pharaoh, who had been informed by Sabni of his intention, had despatched a whole convoy of royal embalmers and mortuary priests along with the necessary oils and linens for the mummification of Mekhu. In an expression of gratitude, Sabni delivered the spoils of Mekhu's convoy to the pharaoh at Memphis.

A shady path in the botanical garden on Kitchener's Island, which is planted with flora from all around the world.

BELOW: Aswan fishermen.

Aswan is a good place for spotting wintering birds. Salugah Island, between Elephantine and Saheylle islands, is a protected reserve.

Monastery and mausoleum

Southwest of the Dome of the Wind, hidden in the flanks of the Western Desert, is the large and well-preserved **Monastery of St Simeon** ⓗ (Deir Al Saman; daily 7am–4pm; charge), dedicated to a local 5th-century saint. The present construction dates from the 7th century, and there is evidence of restoration in the 10th century, but the building is thought to have originated from much earlier times. The monastery was abandoned in the 13th century, either because of lack of water or the threat of marauding tribes. At over 6 metres (18ft) high, the enclosing wall is fortress-like. The view from the upper level, built over the northern wall, is one of the most picturesque of Egypt's desert scenes. The easiest way to reach the monastery is by felucca. The boats will dock at the landing pier and then it is either a 30-minute walk through the desert or a 10-minute camel trip. Each camel can take a maximum of two people and should cost around E£40 if you haggle well.

The **Mausoleum of the Aga Khan** ❶ and his wife the Begum (closed to the public), also in the Western Desert, is another famous landmark. Muhammad Shah Aga Khan, who was the spiritual leader of the Ismaili sect of Islam (he claimed direct descent from Fatima, the daughter of the Prophet Muhammad) liked to winter in Egypt, where he found relief from rheumatism. His tomb was built in the Fatimid style with a single dome. Its outer walls are of rose granite and the inner walls are of marble embellished with verses from the Qur'an.

Saheylle Island

South of the mausoleum is the island of **Saheylle**, a pleasant spot for a picnic, where you can also visit the Nubian village. The island is dominated by two hills in which over 250 inscriptions from the Middle Kingdom up to Ptolemaic times are carved into the granite rock. These inscriptions record expeditions further south or tell about their safe return. On top of the eastern hill is the Famine Stele, relating how a seven-year famine during the Old Kingdom was ended by building a temple for Khnum, the god

BELOW: the Monastery of St Simeon.

of the cataract. The summit commands great views over the First Cataract.

The unfinished obelisk

On the fringes of the Eastern Desert, in the southern perimeters of Aswan, lie the famous granite quarries, the main source of granite in ancient Egypt. The quarries were exploited throughout the ancient period right through to Graeco-Roman times. The 4th Dynasty pharaohs who built the Pyramids of Giza (2613–2494 BC) were among those who used stone from here. Nine great slabs of granite, 54 tonnes each, were extracted for the ceiling of the so-called King's Chamber of the Pyramid of Khufu (Cheops); red granite was chosen for the Temple of Khafra (Chephren), and black granite was quarried for the lower reaches of the outer casing of the Pyramid of Menkaura (Mycerinus).

The lofty obelisk of Queen Hatshepsut at Karnak, made of a single block of pink granite, was also quarried in Aswan and transported by river to Luxor. A further **unfinished obelisk** **J** is still lying in the quarry (daily, winter 7am–4pm, summer 7am–5pm) attached to the bedrock. There is no indication for whom it was intended but, had it been completed as originally planned, it would have weighed some 1,162 tonnes, and soared to a height of 42 metres (126ft). It seems to have been abandoned because of a crack in the stone.

The process by which the stone was extracted is deduced by examining the quarry. Holes are bored along a prescribed straight line, and balls of dolerite, one of the hardest types of stone, were attached to rammers and simultaneously struck with great force until the stone separated. These dolerite balls, some weighing up to 5.5kg (12lbs), have been found in their hundreds in the area.

The Aswan dams

South of the quarries is the **Old Aswan Dam** **K**. The first barrage across the Nile was built at the apex of the Delta north of Cairo in 1842. This was soon followed by others: at Assiut in Middle Egypt and at Esna and Aswan in Upper Egypt. The Aswan Dam was erected above the First Cataract between 1899 and 1902 when Egypt was still a British Protectorate. Its height was increased between 1908 to 1912 and again between 1929 and 1934.

With each successive heightening, the thwarted waters simply increased in volume, threatening ancient monuments and settlements alike. In the 1960s the **High Dam** **L** was built by President Nasser with the help of what was then the Soviet Union *(see page 76)*, necessitating the movement of many ancient monuments that would otherwise have been engulfed by Lake Nasser.

Both the High Dam and the unfinished obelisk are often included as part of an organised tour to Abu Simbel *(see page 138)*. If you are planning to visit, it will save both time and money to stop at all three locations in one day; however, it does make for a very long excursion.

The unfinished obelisk, with its fatal crack, still lies in its ancient quarry. The proximity of the quarry to the Nile made transporting such obelisks relatively easy.

BELOW: cataract below the Aswan High Dam.

TIP

Don't pay your boatman to Philae any money until your return journey is complete. This will ensure that he waits for you before going back to the pier on the mainland.

Excursion to Philae

Between the dams is one of the most important of the monuments that were moved after the building of the High Dam, the Ptolemaic **Temple of Isis** Ⓜ at **Philae** (daily, winter 7am–4pm, summer 7am–5pm; charge plus boat charge). The cult of Isis flourished here until well into the Christian era, and the temple was in use until around AD 550. Bigah Island, believed to be the burial place of the left leg of the god Osiris and the first tip of land to appear out of the primeval waters, was so sacred that only the priesthood had access to it, so it was on the neighbouring island of Philae that the popular cult of Isis developed.

The Temple of Isis was developed over more than 700 years by Ptolemaic and Roman rulers who wanted to identify with this Egyptian cult. Fantastic tales were told of the goddess's magical powers. When the evil god Seth chopped his brother Osiris' body into pieces, and scattered them all over Egypt, his beloved wife Isis, the Great Mother of All Gods, searched the land to find them and, using her knowledge of sacred formulae, pieced him back together. Her spells also saved her son Horus from a poisonous snake.

BELOW: Trajan's Kiosk, part of the Temple of Philae.

Rescuing the temple

After the first dam was built, the temple was under water for six months of the year, and the rest of the time visitors could sail amongst its ruins by boat, like the traveller Amelia Edwards. The creation of Lake Nasser following the building of the High Dam threatened to submerge the temple completely, so it was moved it to the nearby island of Agiliqiyyah, which was landscaped to resemble the original site.

The salvage contract to rescue the temple from the water was awarded to an Italian company, which started work with the construction of a coffer dam in 1977. The stone blocks (47,000 in number) were then cleaned and stored. Meanwhile, 450 tonnes of granite were blown off the top of Agiliqiyyah to accommodate the temples. Some of the granite was used to enlarge part of the island so as to resemble the shape of Philae.

The stones were transported and, in just 30 months, re-erected. Many of the blocks were replaced in the course of the reconstruction, so the result is rather pristine, but you can still see a water-level mark on the entrance pylons. The old island of Philae – a sandbank surrounded by the rusty remains of the coffer dam – is still visible from Agiliqiyyah.

Exploring Philae

Today the temple is approached by boat from the Shallal boatyard south of Aswan, where you can also buy tickets to the temple. The official price for boats is posted at the dockyard, but this only allows for a one-hour visit, so if you want to spend more time you should negotiate with your captain. He will ask for more *baksheesh* when you return, and you may have to clamber through boats piled five deep next to each other to get back onto dry land.

Boats usually land near the ancient quay and the Vestibule of Nectanebo I, the oldest structure on the island. Beyond lies a vast court, surrounded by elegant colonnades, in front of the massive **First Pylon** of the Temple of Isis. Taking the small door to the left, you can see the lovely carvings of Isis suckling her baby in the marshes in the 3rd-century BC **Birth House**, built by Ptolemy I; this is sometimes cited as the origin of the Christian image of the Virgin Mary suckling the infant Christ.

The larger gate, flanked by two granite lions, leads to the **Second Pylon** and **Hypostyle Hall**. Beyond is the Inner Sanctuary, but the granite shrines are now in European museums. Stairs lead to the upper floor and the **Osiris Room** (tip the guardian to obtain access), with reliefs depicting the story of Osiris and Isis.

A fascinating relief alluding to the source of the Nile can be seen in **Hadrian's Gateway**, just to the west of the Temple of Isis. It shows blocks of stone heaped one upon the other, with a vulture (representing Upper Egypt) and a hawk (representing Lower Egypt) standing on top of the stones. Beneath the rocks is a circular chamber that is outlined by the contours of a serpent within which Hapy, the Nile-god, crouches. He clasps a vessel in each hand, ready to pour the water towards Egypt and bring goodness to the land. Also here is a beautifully tender scene of Isis looking at a crocodile carrying her husband's body to Bigah.

Ancient graffitti

The monuments at Philae, particularly the grand **Trajan's Kiosk**, dating from about AD 100, are covered in graffiti from almost every era of history. A Greek inscription in the Osiris shrine above the sanctuary of the Temple of Isis reveals that even as late as AD 453 Isis was worshipped here by the Blemmys, tribes of the Eastern Desert, long after the edict of Theodosius had declared that pagan temples should be closed. The monuments of Philae, therefore, represent the last outpost of ancient Egyptian tradition on its native soil. ❑

"Seen from the level of a small boat," wrote Amelia Edwards of Philae in A Thousand Miles up the Nile *in 1873–4, "those sculptured towers rise higher and ever higher against the sky. They show no sign of ruin or of age. All look solid, stately, perfect."*

Below Left: image of Isis at the Temple of Philae.
Below: a pylon from the Temple of Philae.

Son et Lumière

Sound and light shows are available at almost every major temple in Egypt, combining kitsch music and lights with voiceovers conducted by actors with very plummy British accents.

If you want to give one a try, the show at Philae is generally acknowledged to be one of the better ones. Try to arrive about an hour before sunset so you can enjoy the natural view before sitting down to watch the man-made one. Performances are conducted in multiple languages, so it is best to check the schedule before arrival.

Private tour companies often book the entire show and Ramadan plays havoc with the timings, so check with the tourist office or call 097-230 5376 for the latest updates and availability.

The White Nile

Longer than the Blue Nile, the White Nile flows out of Africa's largest inland lake through some of the world's most war-torn regions

The White Nile begins its journey on the northern shores of Lake Victoria in Uganda – a fact that eluded European explorers until Henry Morton Stanley returned to the Ripon Falls *(see page 81)*. Named after the reigning British queen at the time of its discovery, Lake Victoria is Africa's largest lake and the world's third-largest freshwater lake in terms of size.

Lake Victoria relaxation

Three countries border onto Lake Victoria: Uganda, Tanzania and Kenya. All three nations have large ports on this inland body of water, with Kenya and Tanzania offering the most established resort-style accommodation and travel opportunities. The political instability of the 1970s and civil war in nearby Rwanda has meant that Uganda has had to play catch-up in its development of a viable tourist industry, with few offerings currently available catering to the upmarket traveller. Most accommodation on a Ugandan island or Lake Victoria adventure will be simple, unless you choose to base yourself in the lakeside town of Entebbe or the Ugandan capital, Kampala, where international-standard hotels are available. The capital is located approximately 86km (52 miles) away from the Nile's source near the town of Jinja.

Avid anglers speak of Lake Victoria in reverent tones. Nile perch fishing is exceptional, rivalling Egypt's Lake Nasser as a destination. The sport-fishing industry is still in its infancy in these waters, with few international operators offering Uganda as a holiday option. Bookings will need to be made through local operators, of which Uganda Safaris (www.safari-uganda.com) is recommended.

Adventure travel is a popular pastime in this part of Uganda. White-water rafting and kayaking safaris give an alternative method by which to see the heart of Africa, and can be suitable for novices through to the most intrepid. Operators also offer mountain-bike expeditions and guided camping trips through the lush countryside. Nile River Explorers has been in operation in the region since 1995 and is widely considered to be the best (and most safety-conscious). Go to www.raftafrica.com for more information or to make a secure online booking.

Gorilla-watching

Take a side-trip to the southwest of Uganda, where you will have the opportunity to view the elusive mountain gorilla. While the gorilla-viewing region is a bit of a trek from the river, it is one of the highlights of any visit to the country – and also one of the most expensive. The Ugandan government ensures that numbers are kept low (and coffers full) by charging mightily for the opportunity to come up close and personal with these fascinating and highly endangered creatures. Count on shelling out between £1,000–1,400 for a seven-day itinerary, excluding flights.

Gorillas are found in two highly protected regions; the Kibale Forest and Bwindi Impenetrable Forest. If you haven't arranged a tour before arriving in the country, operators can be contacted and booked in Kampala upon arrival; through them you can either join a scheduled tour or arrange a bespoke itinerary.

Murchison Falls National Park

Located in the north of Uganda is Murchison Falls National Park, the largest national park in Uganda. The White Nile cuts right through the middle of the park, named for a 7-metre (23ft) gap in the rocks through which the river flows on its way to Lake Albert.

Murchison Falls NP is the only location in Uganda where tourists can encounter all the members of the "Big Five" mammal species: buffalo, lion, leopard, rhino and elephant. Three-day safaris in the park are gaining in popularity as the hard work of animal breeders reintroduces animal populations to Uganda's protected wilderness.

During the years of civil war and the leadership of Idi Amin, the wildlife of the national park was decimated. It is only now that populations are rising to sustainable levels. Specific activity is being performed to ensure the survival of rhino in the region, with plans afoot to release at least 50 into the wild over the next two decades.

Be sure to bring a guide if planning a safari in Murchison Falls NP. Armed robberies are common, making independent trips a foolish idea. But don't let that dissuade you from visiting. Guides will know the simple precautions needed to avoid any unpleasant experiences.

Visiting Sudan

Due to the effects of the Sudanese Civil War, tourism in Sudan is virtually non-existent, especially in the south. The White Nile runs through the part of the nation that was most decimated by the years of conflict. The Sudanese Civil War was one of the longest and deadliest in history, lasting from 1983–2005 and killing an estimated 1.9 million people. While there were multiple root causes behind the conflict, the commonly accepted reason for the war was animosity between the southern, predominantly Christian and animist population and the Arab-controlled government.

Prior to independence, southern Sudan was governed independently from northern Sudan. However, pressure applied by the Arabs caused the British to integrate the two nations. The Arabs coveted the south, which boasted vast oil reserves and access to large amounts of fresh water, and laws were put in place to enforce government control over resources as soon as the British departed. Southerners, unwilling to give control over their native lands to the Arab elite, decided to fight back, and civil war ensued.

It is estimated that since 1983, the government has killed over 2 million civilians, with an additional 200,000 forced into slavery in the north. Over 4 million people have been displaced by the war, fleeing to other points in the country or to neighbouring nations. A peace agreement was finally brokered in 2005, giving autonomy to the south with the promise of a referendum on secession in 2011. Following the referendum, it is hoped that southern Sudan will be able to move forward in building an infrastructure for its population. The autonomous government is striving to develop tourism as the viable industry, focusing on ecotourism as a segment with the biggest growth potential. Currently, the only hotels that can be found in southern Sudan are in the regional capital, the city of Juba. ❑

FAR LEFT: Victoria Falls. **LEFT:** gorilla in Kibale Forest, Uganda. **ABOVE:** crocodile at Murchison Falls National Park. **RIGHT:** buffalo paddling in the Nile.

ASWAN TO LUXOR

The lush riverbanks between Aswan and Luxor are peppered with Ptolemaic temples, one or two of them right on the riverbank

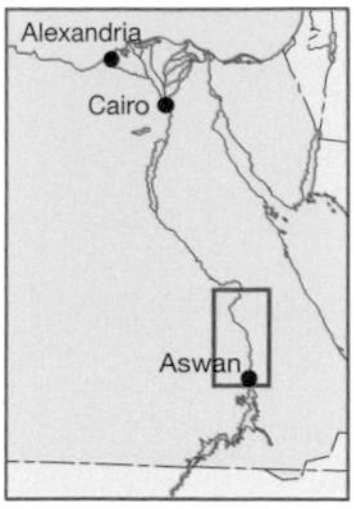

Main attractions
- DARAW
- KOM OMBO
- JABAL AS SILSILAH
- EDFU
- TEMPLE OF WADI 'ABBAD
- AL KAB
- KOM AL AHMAR
- ESNA

The river journey between Aswan and Luxor is a popular route for cruise boats, which usually spread the journey over three or four days. Village life along the Nile – particularly picturesque in this part of Upper Egypt – can be viewed from the comfort of a sun-lounger, and there are occasional stops to visit the Ptolemaic temples of **Kom Ombo**, **Edfu** and **Esna**, which are all well preserved and notable for their detailed reliefs. Such modern cruises have an ancient pedigree. Greeks, Macedonians, Carians and Persians visited Egypt for pleasure from as early as the 6th century BC. Then came Roman emperors and their ladies, many of whom also went river cruising. The fall of the Roman empire put a stop to tourism in the region for almost two millennia, until Thomas Cook revived the pastime to cater to moneyed Brits in the 19th century *(see page 83)*.

In recent years, the expansion in the size and number of Nile cruiseboats has detracted somewhat from the romance. Attempts to recover some of that magic have resulted in the introduction of a new type of cruise in 19th-century-style wooden *dahabiyyahs*, with three to five cabins. These boats take a week to cover the journey from Aswan to Luxor, with stops at some of the smaller temples not visited by the larger boats *(see page 310)*. Alternatively, if you want to really immerse yourself in river culture and don't mind making do with basic living standards, such as sleeping on deck, you might want to consider a trip by felucca in around five days (negotiate with the boat captains in Aswan; they will arrange the necessary permits and cook all the meals).

Travelling by land

The 1997 massacre of tourists at Luxor resulted in the creation of a system of convoys that forced tourists to travel

PRECEDING PAGES: temple at Kom Ombo.
LEFT: at Daraw camel market.
RIGHT: free-wheeling in Edfu.

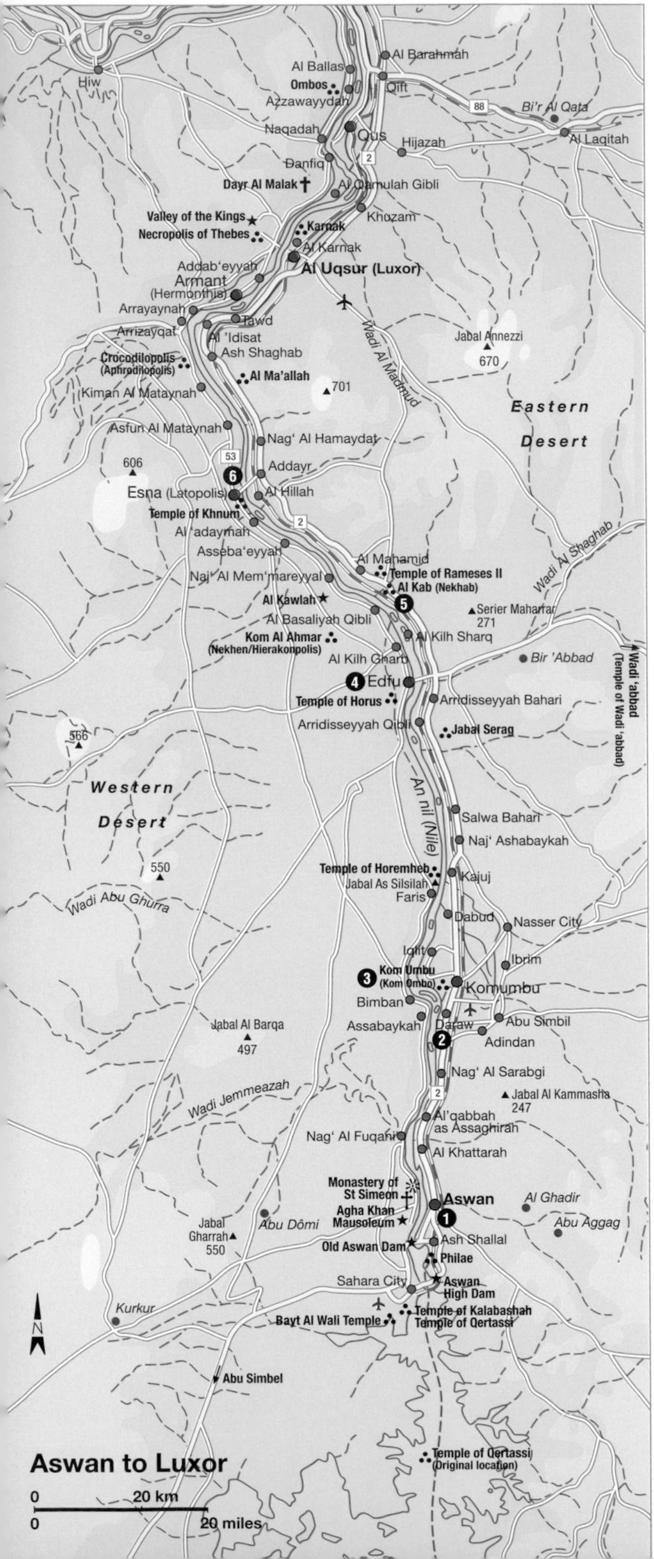

between Luxor and Aswan at two designated times per day, making leisurely visits to the major temples along the way a challenge. In 2009, this requirement was dropped and private taxis are once again an option *(see page 210)*.

South to north

The ancient Egyptians did not, as we do, orient themselves towards the north, but towards the south, the source of the flood, which was the bearer of life. In sailing from Aswan, you are therefore moving northwards from Egypt's "first" Upper Egyptian province, which extended from the cataract region to a mountain chain north of Kom Ombo known as **Jabal As Silsilah**. From there, the second to fourth provinces extended as far as Luxor. The nome capitals (chief towns of each province) acted as centres for local administration and housed the temples of the major deities of the region.

This is a fascinating part of Upper Egypt, where ancient monuments and early Christian settlements stand side by side with modern factories producing goods ranging from fertilisers to molasses. Though agriculture was probably introduced into the Nile Valley in about 5000 BC, a farmer today is probably almost as hard-working as his counterpart in ancient times. He rises with the sun and retires early (though electricity has brought television to many rural areas), transports produce by donkey, and draws water using a water wheel driven by buffaloes.

Leaving Aswan

As the river pushes north of **Aswan** ❶, it leaves behind the granite rocks that are characteristic of the area. The desert here comes virtually to the riverbank, tinted with red ochre from iron mines. After this arid beginning, the riverbanks become more fertile at the village of **Daraw** ❷, on the east bank of the Nile, where, if you are lucky, you may catch sight of a caravan of camels kicking up the dust or crossing the river on the ferry. Daraw is the end of the Darb Al Arba'in or the Forty Days Road, one of the most active trans-Saharan routes, running from Darfur and Kordofan in Sudan, through the Libyan Desert to Dongola, and then further along the Nile.

Camel market

The camels, which in Egypt are used as beasts of burden and for meat, are sold in Daraw's camel market (Souq Al Jemal; Tue, but also Sun and Mon Oct–Apr, 6.30am–2pm), where many are then transported by road to the Birqash camel market in northwest Cairo. The market attracts an increasing number of tourists, but it is still an exotic sight. It is best to visit it before 10.30am, when the Sudanese traders are at their liveliest.

Camels vary in price between about E£2,500 and E£5,000, depending on a number of factors, including age, sex, health and appearance. Strong, healthy females sell for the most, as they have the potential to reproduce. Only male camels are slaughtered for their meat. Factor spending about an hour at the market into your itinerary, as apart from the camels, there isn't a lot more to see in this workaday town.

A temple for crocodiles

The river now takes a curve to the west and, on the eastern bank, an imposing temple stands proud. It is the Ptolemaic temple of **Kom Ombo** ❸ (daily, Oct–May 7am–4pm, June–Sept 7am–5pm; charge), constructed on what must be one of the most picturesque locations in Egypt. Until recently it stood in splendid isolation, but a corniche road built about five years ago, with shops and internet cafés, now runs between the temple and the river. The temple, which was cleared by the Antiquities Department in 1873, is in an excellent state of preservation, despite some earthquake damage in 1992 and the fact that the river, which runs extremely fast at this point, has washed away parts of it. The new corniche enables vessels to moor immediately beneath the temple.

The ancient city of Ombos probably owed its foundation to the strategic importance of this site, on a hill *(kom)*

TIP

A Nubian from Daraw has opened the house of his grandfather, Hosh Al Kenzi, to visitors (next to Dar Rasul Mosque on Shari' Al Kunu; no set opening hours but should be open in daylight hours except during prayer times and Ramadan). Built in Nubian style out of mud-brick and palm-tree wood, it houses a collection of Nubian artefacts. The owner is happy to explain all about his culture and traditions in exchange for a little *baksheesh* (E£5–10).

BELOW LEFT: stylish visitor to Kom Ombo.

Ancient Beliefs

In a largely rainless country the sun was central to ancient Egyptian beliefs. The sun was seen to sail across the heavenly ocean in a barge each day, from the pink-speckled dawn to the fiery sunset. With the last rays of the day, it transferred to another barge that continued the voyage through the underworld, bringing light to its darkened spheres. During the sun's absence the northern stars, the ones that never set, were "the eternal ones", the place of the afterlife.

The ancient Egyptians saw their world as confined in something like a large box, with a narrow, oblong floor with Egypt as its centre. The river, arising from the eternal ocean in the south, flowed towards the eternal ocean (the Mediterranean) in the north. The sky was conceived like an iron ceiling sprinkled with suspended stars. The land was Geb the earth-god who, in the beginning, was locked in an embrace with Nut, the sky-goddess. Then Shu, representing the atmosphere, emerged from the primeval waters and separated the two by slipping between them and raising Nut aloft in his outstretched arms to her new abode. Geb and Nut were father and mother of four deities: Osiris, associated with the Nile and the fertile lands bordering it, Isis his wife, Seth, the god associated with the desert, and Nepthys his wife.

Detail in the sandstone temple at Kom Ombo.

commanding both the Nile and the trade routes from Nubia to the Nile Valley. Yet the town attained no great prosperity until Ptolemaic times (332–30 BC), when it became the capital of a separate province. Construction of the Great Temple of Kom Ombo began under Ptolemy V (*c.*205–80 BC), and was continued by Ptolemy VIII and XII (Neos Dionysos), but was finished under the Roman emperors Tiberius, Domitian, Geta, Caracalla and Macrinus.

The temple was not dedicated to a single deity, as was usual in ancient Egypt, but to two unrelated gods: Horus the Elder, or Harouris, and Sobek, the crocodile-god, a partnership that is particularly odd when you consider that reliefs at Edfu *(see page 170)*, a little to the north of Kom Ombo, depict the evil Seth in the guise of a crocodile being killed by Horus.

The reason for this may have been because the Ptolemies saw how many of Egypt's traditions were presented in dualistic terms (a double crown for the pharaoh, who was called "Lord of the Two Lands" – Upper and Lower Egypt), and saw nothing unusual in building this double temple to two hitherto unrelated deities. The gods are given equal billing in the temple and occupy symmetrical halves.

Temple interior

The temple is entered via a massive gateway built by Neos Dionysos, with, on the right, a small chapel of Hathor, which is now home to some mummified crocodiles found in a nearby cemetery. Hundreds of these mummified crocodiles were discovered in 1960 during the construction of the Aswan to Kom Ombo road, but the unpleasant smell became so overpowering that most of them had to be removed. It is thought that a crocodile was kept in the small square pool in the middle of the courtyard.

The temple complex was built on traditional lines with an entrance pylon, open court, hypostyle hall and sanctuary, but most of the first pylon, forecourt and birth house have slipped into the Nile. As it was dedicated to two gods, there is an invisible division down the middle of the temple: the right side is dedicated to Sobek, while the left side

BELOW: the camel market, Daraw.

is dedicated to Harouris. Two separate doorways lead past halls and antechambers to the twin sanctuaries where the sacred statues of the deities were kept. Two different sets of priests would have attended the sanctuaries.

The entrance of the temple leads into the **Hypostyle Hall**, which is noted for its grand columns with foliage capitals, and has walls decorated with fine reliefs of Neos Dionysos appearing in front of the gods. The **Second Hypostyle Hall** is older and shows well-preserved reliefs of Ptolemy V making the usual offerings. The sanctuaries are mostly ruined, but between the entrance doors is a superb relief of Ptolemy VI and his wife receiving a palm frond from both Sobek and Horus.

Between the two sanctuaries is a hidden corridor – now exposed – that was built into the thickness of the wall. This secret place could only be approached from a chamber situated immediately to the rear, where a portion of the floor could be raised to admit a priest to a passage below ground level. A priest whispering through the wall at the worshippers in the sanctuaries must have played an important part in the oracular power attributed to the two deities.

Behind the sanctuaries is a stairway leading up to the roof, which offers a good view over the complex and its surroundings. On the north wall of the corridor, look for a relief showing a display of what are taken to be surgical instruments. This is often upheld as evidence of the sophistication of medicine in Ancient Egypt. In fact, although medicine in Ancient Egypt was advanced for its time, there were great gaps in this knowledge. It was believed, for example, not only that the heart was connected to the stomach but also that it was the source of human intelligence. During the process of mummification, therefore, the brain was discarded.

Sandstone belt

North of Kom Ombo the range of hills known as the **Jabal As Silsilah** appears on the eastern bank, roughly halfway between Aswan and Luxor. This is the point at which the boat leaves the first province of Aswan, which belongs to the sandstone belt of Nubia, and enters

Right up until the end of the 19th century crocodiles infested this part of the Nile. In ancient Egypt crocodiles were worshipped in areas where the Nile was particularly dangerous, such as at Kom Ombo and in the cataract region south of Aswan.

BELOW: reliefs on the columns of Kom Ombo.

EAT

Almost all hotels in Egypt offer breakfast boxes for travellers planning early departures or temple-hopping. Usually filled with bread, cheese spread, butter, jam, juice and (sometimes) fruit, it's a convenient collection of snacks to abate hunger. Make sure to order it the evening before.

the limestone plateau of the rest of Egypt. The sandstone used at Thebes during the New Kingdom came from here. Prior to the New Kingdom most temples were built of mud-brick and quickly perished.

According to legend, the range was called Jabal As Silsilah ("Hills of the Chain") because the Nile was once closed against river traffic at this point by a great chain that stretched across it. The legend even points to two curiously shaped rocks that supposedly anchored the chain. In reality, the chain probably refers to the sandstone ridge that the Nile needed to break through in order to continue its journey north. Ancient rock-cut temples to Hapy, the god of the inundation, and Sobek, the crocodile-god, were built at this spot. The remains of these and the tombs can still be seen on the east and west banks, and they are well worth exploring. Ancient graffiti and stelae litter the sites.

Cruise ships cannot dock here, and organised tours don't include Jabal As Silsilah on any itinerary. Those travelling by felucca benefit hugely, as the remote location means that they often have the place to themselves when exploring. The **Temple of Horemheb** (daily winter 7am–4pm, summer 7am–5pm; charge) on the west bank technically has set hours, but can usually be opened up if your felucca arrives outside of these times simply by paying a little extra *baksheesh*.

Edfu and the Temple of Horus

The next stop is the provincial town of **Edfu** ❹. Its name is derived from the Coptic Atbo, which, in turn, derived from the ancient name Tbot. The Greeks, who gave the site great importance, knew it as Great Apollinopolis.

The focus of interest at Edfu is the **Temple of Horus** (daily, winter 7am–4pm, summer 7am–5pm; charge), on the west bank of the Nile (calèches or horse carts usually transfer visitors from the river to the site, and great numbers of these await the daily arrival of cruiseboats); if you are driving, cross the river just past the village of Arridisseyyah Bahari.

This cult temple was built over a period of 180 years during the Ptole-

BELOW: the temple at Kom Ombo. **BELOW RIGHT:** local boy.

maic era from 237–57 BC, yet it follows all the rules of classic pharaonic architecture. It is unquestionably the best-preserved temple in Egypt, not least because it was almost covered by sand until the 1860s, when the French Egyptologist Auguste Mariette undertook the massive task of excavating it.

A visit to the temple provides a clear picture of the layout and decoration of the archetypal Egyptian temple – an entrance pylon leading through to an open court with a 32-columned colonnade, a hypostyle hall and an inner sanctuary that would have contained a statue of the deity. The entrance is past the vast calèche park, shops and cafeteria, so start your visit at the **Pylon**, which is notable for its large carvings of Ptolemy XII (Neos Dionysus) slaying his enemies in front of Horus and Hathor.

Horus, to whom the temple was dedicated, was the falcon (hawk) god, known in one form as Horus of Behedet. He was foremost a sun-god (often depicted with the solar disk over his head) but also a protector of kings and a guide to the dead in the underworld. Edfu was a cult centre, since it was believed to be the spot where Horus fought with his uncle Seth for power over the world *(see page 43)*. Two large granite falcon statues of Horus stand at the entrance to the temple, while a majestic statue of Horus as a hawk guards the gateway into the hypostyle hall. The deity is represented in reliefs throughout the complex, either as a man with a falcon's head, or as a solar disk with outspread wings. Throughout the temple, inside and out, the walls, pylons, corridors, halls, antechambers, sanctuary and inner chambers are embellished with reliefs that are considered among the most beautiful in Egypt, despite being partially defaced by early Christians, who targeted faces and hands lest the images should come to life to haunt them.

The inner wall of the pylon, in the vast **Court of Offerings**, records the Festival of the Beautiful Meeting, when Horus joined his consort and sister Hathor at her temple in Dandarah. On the back walls of the first **Hypostyle Hall** are some superb reliefs illustrating the temple rituals. Off the hypostyle hall, a small room is known

A granite statue of Horus stands in the first courtyard of the temple at Edfu.

BELOW: pylon of the Temple of Horus, Edfu.

All pharaohs were believed to be the incarnation of the falcon-god Horus, a belief that was celebrated in the annual Festival of the Coronation, during which a falcon was taken from the sacred birdcage and crowned in the central court. The falcon was then kept inside the temple for a year, as a symbol of the divinity of the reigning pharaoh.

as the **House of the Morning**; it was here that the pharaoh would purify himself before performing temple rituals. Horus' statue was kept in the **Sanctuary**, in a shrine of syenite granite. Around three sides of the sanctuary, separated from it by an ambulatory, is a series of shrines reserved for certain rites or dedicated to other deities, all adorned with reliefs and showing traces of their original colour. One of them contains a copy of the god's sacred barge.

Note also (in the east ambulatory) a Nilometer, used for measuring the height of the annual inundation and setting taxes for the year, and, in front of the temple, a "birth house", or *mammisi*, a feature of all Ptolemaic temples in which the birth of a particular god occurred. There are also birth houses in the Ptolemaic temples of Dandarah and Philae.

Pharaoh's festivities

One of the most interesting series of representations in the Temple of Horus relates to the New Year Festival. They show that each year the pharaoh, accompanied by priests bearing standards representing Egypt's ancient provinces, mounted the roof of the temple (the staircase still exists but is closed to tourists). The king was followed by a long procession of priests of a lower order, chanting and reciting hymns, some shaking sistrums (rattles), burning incense or carrying offerings. Priests of a higher order carried two caskets, bearing the statues of Hathor the cow-goddess and Horus the hawk-god, towards the roof.

More priests are shown following the procession. They burn incense to safeguard the sacred statues from evil spirits lurking in the temple. At the top of the staircase, priests with standards welcome the pharaoh, who heads the procession. The caskets are placed on the roof of the temple to be revitalised by the rays of the rising sun.

Also depicted on the inner side of the outer walls, on the left side facing the sanctuary, is the second part of the Horus legend, telling the story of the battles against his evil brother Seth, who is represented both as a hippopotamus and a crocodile.

Farming in Ancient Egypt

The annual flood was the source of remarkable fertility, but unless the waters of the inundation were retained for times of need, the fertility of the soil would last for only a few months. Without the farmer to create and mend water channels to carry the moisture to the outlying fields, the land would have yielded no more than the wild grain collected by the hunter-gathering communities of pre-dynastic times. The full exploitation of the Nile was only achieved through unremitting toil. The first season was the *akhet*, the inundation, which started with the rising waters in June and reached its height by July, the start of the New Year. Within a few weeks the water receded and the land was soon ready. This was the second season – the *perit* or "going forth" – beginning in mid-November. Although the farmer could simply cast the seed, reliefs show that he frequently turned the soil by means of a hoe or a plough.

The *shemu* (harvest), the third season, began in mid-March. Ceremonies were performed to mark the cutting of the first sheaf of grain and afterwards there were festivals of thanks. Because such festivals related to the reaffirmation of life, it was a time for merry-making and, right into the Persian period in the 6th century BC, it was also a time for the taking of marriage vows.

BELOW RIGHT: 19th-century model of Horus' sacred barge at the Temple of Horus, Edfu.

River scenes

As the Nile slips under the bridge at Edfu, it is interesting to note the different kinds of boats in the river. Many are the classical flat-bottomed feluccas, transporting produce – mostly pottery, grain, sugar cane and limestone – and sometimes tourists. Sailing northwards, feluccas have the flow of the Nile to power them, and southbound the prevailing north wind. As the flow is more powerful than the wind, it takes one day longer to travel south from Luxor to Aswan than it does to travel north from Aswan. The smaller boats belong to fishermen, who use long nets laid out in a semicircle.

It is also possible to see an elegant *dahabiyyah* sailing past in all its renovated splendour. A traditional Arab sailing vessel introduced in the 7th century after the Arab conquest of Egypt, these large sailing boats were described by the 19th-century British writer and traveller Amelia Edwards as the ultimate in luxury travel on the Nile. Still common in the 19th century, they provided the first Nile cruises for Westerners. Recently revived, they are the most luxurious way to cruise (for more on cruises, *see page 309*).

Ancient irrigation and cultivation

On the riverbanks you may catch sight of one of the old methods of pumping water that are still used today: the *shadouf*, a bucket and counterweight attached to the ends of a pile, operated by downward pressure to lift water from one level to another, dates back to pharaonic times; the Archimedean screw comprises a screw thread in a cylinder dipping into the water at an angle of not more than 30°; and the *saqiyah* consists of a chain of buckets passing over a vertical wheel dipping in the water, geared to a horizontal wheel turned by a blindfolded buffalo walking in circles. Of course, today there are also numerous electrical pumping devices of all shapes and sizes.

Crops cultivated on the riverside have remained largely unchanged since ancient times. They include vegetables, grains, lettuce, melons, cucumbers, onions, garlic and a sweet red carrot

A snake charmer in Edfu scans the street for passing custom.

BELOW: life on the river at Kom Ombo.

A felah *(peasant) tends his fields. The ancient gods that were worshipped in the Esna region were all associated with agriculture and fertility.*

BELOW: locals sell souvenirs to cruise-boat passengers while they wait at Esna.

that is particular to Egypt. During pharaonic times flax was the fibre used for weaving, but this became obsolete with the arrival of cotton in the 7th century.

Egyptian farmers have always taken great care of their livestock, which in a poor country is an extremely valuable asset: several tombs have depictions of young farmhands feeding animals, milking them and assisting them in giving birth to their young. Similar scenes are still enacted all along the Nile today. A farmer giving his charge a bath in a canal or on the banks of the river is a very common sight. Modern Egyptians still house their animals in the courtyards of their homes.

Wadi 'abbad

The temples between Aswan and Luxor attract huge numbers of visitors, but very rarely visited, and well worth seeing, is the **Temple of Wadi 'abbad**. It's located in the desert about 58km (35 miles) east of Edfu near the village of Radesseyyah. Built by Sety I (1318–1304 BC) to serve gold-miners and traders en route to the Red Sea, it occupies a spectacular site at the foot of sandstone cliffs and is partly cut into the rock. It has outstanding carved reliefs.

Warrior tombs

The ancient city of **Al Kab** ❺, on the Nile north of Edfu, is visited by a few of the new *dahabiyyah* cruiseboats. This ancient city, known as Nekheb, once ranked among the chief cities of Egypt, and even under the Ptolemies it was the capital of the third province. The site (daily 8am–6pm; charge), which lies on the eastern bank, has recently been restored and prepared for tourists. The tombs have been made accessible by stairways and the surrounding area enhanced with trees and gardens.

Al Kab was most prominent in around 1567 BC during the 18th Dynasty, when two of the city's young men were recruited to fight in the armies of Ahmose and Thutmose I. The two youths bore the same name as their pharaoh, Ahmose, who later became known as the "Father of the New Kingdom". The first was Ahmose son of Ebana, and the other

was Ahmose Pennekhbet. Their tombs, among the most interesting of Ancient Egypt, date from after the war of liberation from the Hyksos, a foreign power that occupied Egypt during the 2nd millennium BC. They consequently shed light on an extremely important period in ancient Egyptian history.

Ahmose Pennekhbet lived through the war of liberation from the Hyksos and the wars that followed. His tomb is a fascinating record of military activities and conquests. The hieroglyphs describe, in somewhat exaggerated prose, how he personally took prisoners, captured horses and chariots, and, on one occasion, killed the enemy because it was less trouble to do this than to take "living prisoners". As an aged warrior, he was appointed to the prestigious post of tutor to the eldest daughter of Queen Hatshepsut "while she was a child upon the breast".

Ahmose, son of Ebana, lived through a similar period of crisis, but his tomb is more significant for its biographical data than its artistic merit. He claimed he was a "soldier and sailor too" and was also a "warrior of the ruler". The inscriptions describe how he fought "more than what is true" during a campaign in Nubia, and "showed great bravery" in the pharaoh's wars in western Asia. He claimed, furthermore, that he was at the head of the troops under Thutmose I, and that his king "beheld my valour" and "presented me with gold in double measure" in recognition of his worth. In his old age, Ahmose was apparently content in his retirement, happily reminiscing about his war years and his honourable record.

Kom Al Ahmar

Opposite Al Kab, on the western bank, is **Kom Al Ahmar**, the ancient city of **Nekhen**, an important archaeological site, which can only be visited by felucca or *dahabiyyah*. The city was the pre-dynastic capital of Upper Egypt, and relics of the earliest kings of Egypt have been found here. These include some of the most famous treasures of the Egyptian Museum in Cairo, including the Palette of Narmer, the pharaoh traditionally known as Menes who unified Upper and Lower Egypt in 3100 BC and brought the whole of the Nile Valley under his domination. The Palette, which commemorates the unification, depicts Narmer about to smash the skull of his defeated enemy.

Esna and the barrage

The barrage at Esna was erected in 1908–9 to regulate irrigation as far as Qena, north of Luxor. Today it is a major stumbling block for the cruise industry. The lock is slow to operate, so boats must sometimes queue for hours here, and at times of low water the lock is closed altogether, as it drains too much water from the upper reaches of the river. An Italian-built hydroelectric barrage, known locally as the "Electricity Bridge", was built in the 1990s; it also has a lock that lets vessels through. A new lock is currently under construction.

Esna ❻ itself is a district capital and the largest town between Aswan and

TIP

Don't be surprised if your cruise ship or felucca finishes the journey at Esna and you are then coached to Luxor. This is simply to avoid the long wait at the Esna lock.

BELOW: relief at the Temple of Khnum, Esna.

It was in Esna that the writer Gustave Flaubert encountered the dancer Kuchuk Hanem. He described her as a "tall, splendid creature… when she bends, her flesh ripples into bronze ridges.

Luxor. Although some of the buildings hint at the prosperity of times long past, the town is rather uninspiring today. Were it not for the temple one would be hard-pressed to recognise this as one of the most important places in Upper Egypt in antiquity; it is also a far cry from the city of brothels and dancing girls described by the French writer Gustave Flaubert. There is, however, a small camel market in town on Saturday mornings, and some old houses around the temple have kept their beautiful *mashrabiyyah* screens. Near the entrance to the temple is an Ottoman-period *caravanserai* (inn).

Temple of Khnum

The Ptolemaic **Temple of Khnum** (daily, winter 7am–4pm, summer 7am–5pm; charge) was almost totally obscured by the modern town until relatively recently, and today it lies in a large depression well below the level of the modern buildings, five minutes' walk from the river. Khnum was a ram-headed creator god said to have moulded man on a potter's wheel, who also guarded the source of the Nile.

The temple was probably as large as the one in Edfu, but so far only the Roman hypostyle hall has been excavated. This exercise was begun by Muhammad Ali in 1842, not, it is recorded, for cultural reasons, but "in order to provide a safe underground magazine for gunpowder". Mariette completed the task later that century. Literally dozens of houses were removed from its precincts, and the lip of the depression is still crowded with the modern buildings.

The most noticeable part of the temple is the **Hypostyle Court**; its roof is still intact and supported by six rows of four columns, each with elaborately carved capitals. There are 16 different types for the 24 bud- and flower-columns. The walls and columns are decorated with reliefs, which may not be the finest in quality but are of considerable interest for their content. They carry scenes of the various Roman emperors depicted as Egyptian pharaohs sacrificing to the gods and carrying out ritual observances, underlining how keen the Romans were to show respect to the Egyptian

BELOW RIGHT: Temple of Khnum.

Defeating the Hyksos

The Hyksos, foreign invaders believed to have come from the region of Syria, conquered Egypt in around 1648 BC. They came with horses and chariots (hitherto unknown in Egypt), swept across the northern Sinai, fortified a stronghold at Tall Ad Dabah, south of Tanis in the north-eastern Delta, then moved towards the apex of the Delta, from where they surged southwards.

The humiliation of foreign occupation came to an end when the young warrior-king Kamose and, later, his brother Ahmose, regarded as the Father of the New Kingdom (18th–20th Dynasties, 1551–1085 BC), started a war of liberation and finally expelled the invaders from the land of Egypt.

This first unhappy exposure to foreign domination left a lasting mark on the Egyptian character. The seemingly inviolable land of Egypt had to be protected from invasion and to do so meant not only to rid the country of enemies, but to pursue them into western Asia.

Out of the desire for national security was born the spirit of military expansion characteristic of the New Kingdom. The later military conquests of Thutmose III, in no fewer than 17 campaigns, resulted in the establishment of Egyptian power throughout Syria and northern Mesopotamia, as well as in Nubia and Libya.

pantheon, even though they did not enjoy the affinity that the Ptolemies had with the Egyptians.

Among the most interesting is a relief near the bottom of the northern wall showing the emperor Commodus in the company of the hawk-headed Horus and the ram-headed Khnum drawing in a clap-net full of waterfowl and fish (the Nile perch was a recognised deity here), observed by the ibis-headed Thoth.

The ceiling has an astronomical calendar, which is second only to the one in Dandarah for detail and fine execution.

The temple is important because the Emperor Decius (AD 249–51) is the last Roman name to appear in a royal cartouche (an elliptical sign bearing the name of the pharaoh) in an Egyptian temple.

Environs of Luxor

The last stretch of the journey towards Luxor is uneventful. In the background lie the hills of the Western Desert, with a foreground of extensive palm-groves interrupted by the smoking chimneys of brick factories. The town of **Armant**, the ancient Hermonthis, on the western bank of the Nile can hardly be seen from the river, but two summits, known as Jabalain ("two mountains") can be spotted. On the higher of these is the tomb of a holy woman called Sheikha Musa.

Armant is the site of one of many sugar factories in Upper Egypt. This important crop was introduced to Egypt at the beginning of the 19th century by the *khedive* Ismail. In spring you will find this part of Upper Egypt a hive of activity as the valuable sugar-cane harvest gets under way. Trucks race around delivering the cut cane to the sugar factories, where the juice is pressed, and then convey it to the sugar refineries in the north.

Approaching Luxor, the Nile begins to get wider, and the hills recede to the west and to the east, curving away from the river's bank and leaving broad plains on either side. This was the site chosen for Thebes: few spots in Egypt are so ideally suited for the growth of a great city; few places in the world have bequeathed to us more numerous or mightier monuments. ❑

Whenever you are near the Nile in Egypt, look out for the pied kingfisher (Ceryle rudis). *It has a large head, long sharp beak, very short legs, a white breast with two black rings and a mottled crest and back.*

BELOW: locals in Esna.

Wildlife on the River Nile

Despite the ravages made on Egypt's wildlife over the past hundred years, many of the creatures that the ancients revered are still found today

Before the building of the Aswan dams, the Nile flooded each year and its silt-rich water covered the valley. When the water subsided, the first creature that was seen to move was the scarabaeus, the dung beetle. This beetle laid its eggs in dung or in the corpses of other beetles. Egyptians called it Kheper, and used it to represent the essence of existence, the god Khepri. Scarab beetles can still be seen rolling their balls of dung, but many of the other animals that lived on land whose re-emergence the scarabaeus celebrated have long since disappeared.

Survivors

Egyptians used many living creatures to represent their gods, but where now are the Nile crocodile, the African elephant, the lions and ibises, green monkeys and baboons? Long since hunted out of existence or forced off the land as buildings gobbled it up.

Amongst the survivors that were common to the ancient Egyptians and are still found in Egypt today are the magnificent birds like the short-toed eagle, the long-legged buzzard, the hoopoe and the Egyptian vulture (all were used as hieroglyphics).

The Egyptians domesticated many animals including the cat, ox and cow, which feature on many tomb and temple decorations. In the river, grey mullet, catfish and Bulti fish would have been as familiar to the ancients as they are to Egyptians living by the Nile today.

Finally, while the scarab beetle reminds us of the eternal cycle that ancient Egyptians believed in, the pesky fly, also seen in hieroglyphics, reminds us that then, as now, there were trials and tribulations.

Above and Right: the ibis was sacred to the highly regarded god Thoth, the scribe of the gods, who was believed to have introduced writing to Egypt. It was often mummified. Now extinct in Egypt, it is still found in parts of sub-Saharan Africa and in Iraq.

Above Right: the Egyptian cobra was sacred to the goddess Wadjyt. Egyptian cobras are still very common, and highly venomous. They often enter homes in search of food.

ABOVE: one of the great pleasures of wealthy Egyptians in antiquity was to go hunting in the papyrus marshes, particularly in the Delta. Egyptians hunted birds and other animals for sport, not to provide food, and scenes of hunting and fowling are frequently depicted in tomb paintings. The Tombs of the Nobles in Thebes have some of the best examples. This fine painting, from the tomb of Nebamun, can be seen in the British Museum in London.

Papyrus – The First Paper

The papyrus plant *(Cyperus papyrus)*, a relative of sedge grasses, used to grow abundantly in Egypt, particularly in the marshy Delta. In antiquity Egyptians put papyrus to a number of uses. They wove it into mats, plaited it for ropes, bundled it together to form light rafts – perfect for fishing in the marshes – and pressed and wove it into a suitable medium on which to write. The creation of this technique was largely responsible for the explosion of literacy in Ancient Egypt. Until then stone had been the main means of conveying the written word.

Making papyrus sheets was time-consuming and labour-intensive, so even in antiquity they were reserved for writing that was intended to last, for religious texts and important legal works. More ephemeral information was put down on slates or on pottery shards.

Because of its proliferation and importance, the papyrus was one of the symbols of Upper Egypt, and its form was recreated in the shapes of pillars in several hypostyle halls.

Papyrus continued to be used for important texts into the 10th century, but the manufacturing technique was lost soon after paper was imported from the East, and wasn't rediscovered until the 20th century, by which time papyrus had vanished from most of the country. Recently, there has been some replanting.

To see papyrus being made today, you can visit Dr Ragab's Papyrus Institute in Cairo, which also sells a wide range of high-quality copies of famous papyrus scenes.

LEFT AND RIGHT: the jackal was sacred to the gods Wepwawet and Auamutef (one of the four sons of Horus), but it was its connection with Anubis, god and protector of the dead and helper of Osiris, that earned the jackal such a prominent role in Tutankhamun's tomb. Anubis, with dog-like fidelity, was trusted with the protection of the mummy. Jackals are still found on the edge of the desert in Egypt, and as that is where Egyptians still bury their dead, the association between the jackal and Anubis continues. Egypt also has four species of fox, an animal closely related to the jackal.

LUXOR

Egypt was the leader of all nations during the Middle and New Kingdoms, with Thebes as its capital. Designed to awe and inspire, it was a city of grand dimensions and artistry. No other city could match its beauty

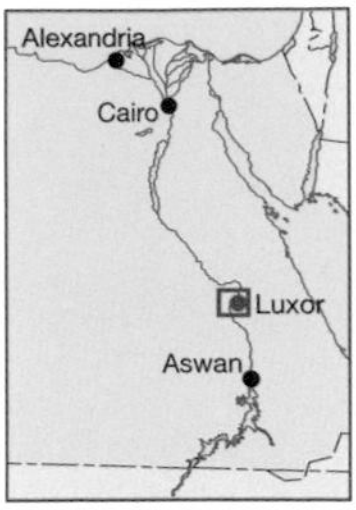

Luxor, ancient Thebes, is like a huge open-air museum spread over both sides of the Nile. On the east bank, the town side, are the **Temple of Luxor** and the **Temple of Amun-Ra at Karnak.** On the west bank, in the necropolis, or city of the dead, are the **Valley of the Kings**, the **Valley of the Queens**, hundreds of tombs of noblemen, and a semicircle of grand mortuary temples along the edge of the floodplain.

Lying 675km (420 miles) south of Cairo, Luxor (Al Uqsur) is often described by Egyptians as a "village", even though it has a population of nearly 200,000 and an international airport where charter flights bring in more than 2,000 tourists a day. Unlike Aswan, with twice the population yet no international flights, it conducts very little trade other than in staple foods and tourist services. Fundamentally it is a tourists' and farmers' town, and once you get past the barrage of pushy salesmen and calèche drivers (who actually do offer the best way of touring Luxor), it is a friendly place.

Tourists return

The city is only now just beginning to recover from the events of 1997, when 63 tourists were killed in a terrorist attack at the Temple of Hatshepsut. While the event itself was horrific, there were also dire consequences for Egypt's tourist industry; hotels went empty, cruise ships were banned from going north of the city and tourists were forced to go on convoys everywhere in the country, severely cramping any independent travel. Today, there seems to be a new energy – even if tourist numbers still haven't reached their pre-1997 levels.

From the river, the town is almost hidden by the forest of cruiseboats and other crafts which moor, often five

Main attractions
- TEMPLE OF LUXOR
- TEMPLE OF AMUN-RA AT KARNAK (KARNAK TEMPLE)
- COLOSSI OF MEMNON
- VALLEY OF THE KINGS
- DAIR AL MADINAH
- VALLEY OF THE QUEENS
- TEMPLE OF HATSHEPSUT
- RAMESSEUM
- MUMMIFICATION MUSEUM
- LUXOR MUSEUM

PRECEDING PAGES: the Hypostyle Hall in the Temple of Amun-Ra, Karnak. **LEFT:** alabaster workshop in Qurnah. **RIGHT:** spices and other goods for sale at Luxor's souq.

Luxor and Thebes
0 800 m
0 800 yds
Al Uqsur (Luxor)
An nil (Nile)
Necropolis of Thebes (Western Thebes)
Qena
Valley of the Kings
Esna, El-Nakhl
Esna
Badran Canal
Al Faddyah Canal
Shari' Almatar
Shari' Bahr Al Nil (Corniche)
Shari' Al Karnak
Temple of Montu
Ptolemaic Temple
Temple of Amun
Temple of Rameses II
Sacred Lake
Temple of Amenhotep II
Chapel of Osiris-Path
Hypostyle Hall
Temple of Rameses III
Temple of Khonsu
Karnak 2 (Temple of Amun-Ra)
Avenue of Sphinxes
Temple of Amenhotep III
Temple of Mut
Temple of Rameses III
Chicago House
Hospital
Shari' Mabad
Luxor Museum 3
Luxor City Council
Shari' Almoss
Shari' Salah Salim
Sh. Mustafa Kamel
Railway Station
Shari' Boat Sa'd
Shari' Al Mahattah
Abu Al haggag
Sh. M. Farid
Temple of Luxor 1
Avenue of Sphinxes
Mummification Museum 4
Ticket Office
Gezirat Sa'd
Algezirah
Al Bayyarat
At tarif
Howard Carter's House
Al-Qurna
Temple of Sety I 11
Al Qurnah Al Jadidah (New Village)
Tombs of the Nobles
Drah Abu Annaja
Temple of Rameses IV
Causeway of Hatshepsut
Al Asasif
Tombs of Late Period
Temple of Thutmose III
Temple of Amenophis II
Temple of Rameses II (Ramesseum) 12
Temple of Thutmose IV
Temple of Tawsert
Temple of Merenptah
Colossi of Memnon 5
Dair Al Bahari (Temple of Hatshepsut) 10
Temple of Mentuhotep
Tombs of the Nobles (Shaykh Abd Al Qurnah) 9
Shaykh Abd Al Qurnah
Ptolemaic Temple
Temple of Amenhotep, Son of Hapu
Temple of Thutmose II
Qurnet Mura'i
Tomb of the Royal Cache
Tomb & Temple of Mentuhotep Sa'ankhkara
Dair Al Madinah (Workers' Village) 7
Ticket Office
Temple of Ay & Horemheb
Madinat Habu 13
Temple of Rameses III
Temple of Thutmose III
Temple of Amun
Palace of Amenhotep III
Birkat Habu (Site of Lake of Amenhotep III)
Al Kom
Valley of the Kings (Biban Al Muluk) 6
Amenhotep III
Ai
page 197
Valley of the Queens (Wadi Al Malekat) 8
1 Nefertari
2 Amenherchopeshef
3 Teti
4 Khaemwaset

deep, along the east bank, many tied up alongside prestigious hotels. Two or three ferry services operate between the east and west bank (one of the most convenient operates from opposite Luxor Temple); taxis and buses take the road bridge south of town.

Inland from the corniche are the tourist souq, full of kitsch Egyptiana, and behind that the local souq for food and household goods, and the railway station.

THE EAST BANK

The two main monuments on Luxor's east bank are the Temple of Luxor near the centre of the city and the Temple of Amun-Ra at Karnak further north, which were originally linked by a 3km (1¾-mile) long processional avenue lined with sphinxes. Both state temples (as these two are) and mortuary temples (those on the west bank, *see page 193*) were generally decorated on the outside with battle reliefs, such as Rameses II's famous battle of Qadesh, in which the pharaoh is shown trampling the enemy beneath the wheels of his chariot and capturing the Hittite fortress (this battle is portrayed both on the entrance pylon of the Temple of Luxor and in the **Ramesseum** on Luxor's west bank).

Other popular topics are Sety I fighting against the Bedouin tribes of Libya, Palestine and Syria, as seen on the northern outer wall of the Hypostyle Hall at Karnak, and Rameses III in his naval battle against the "People of the Sea", who were probably Phoenicians, depicted on the northern, outer wall of the Temple of Rameses III at Madinat Habu.

The Temple of Luxor

The **Temple of Luxor** ❶ (daily, Oct–Apr 9am–9pm, May–Sept 9am–10pm; charge) was built by the 18th Dynasty pharaoh Amenhotep III, the great-grandson of the military genius Thutmose III, and expanded by the 19th Dynasty Rameses II. Most of the complex is well preserved, particularly the wall reliefs, as it was covered in sand and built over by the town until excavations started in 1885. The structure follows the classical pattern of pharaonic temples: the pavement progressively rises and the roof declines from the entrance to the inner sanctuary. Only the pharaoh, or the high priest in his stead, was permitted to enter the darkened inner sanctuary and behold the statue of the deity. Nowadays the temple lies in the heart of Luxor town, and every so often forms the setting for a production of Verdi's *Aida*.

The **Avenue of the Sphinxes** leads straight up to the entrance **pylon** Ⓐ, decorated with the reliefs of Rameses' victory in the battle of Qadesh. Fronting the pylon are two seated colossi of the pharaoh and a damaged standing colossus. Dog-headed baboons support a superb **obelisk**, the twin of which has adorned the Place de la Concorde in Paris since 1833. The pylon leads to the **Court of Rameses II** Ⓑ, surrounded by two rows of papyrus-bud columns.

To the left of the court, perched high up and easily missed at first, is the **Mosque of Abu Al haggag** Ⓒ, the

WHERE

Luxor opened a new and much-improved visitors' centre in 2009 immediately next to the train station. Head here for tour suggestions and hotel bookings if you have arrived without a reservation.

BELOW: the Court of Rameses II at Luxor.

The History of Luxor

Thebes was at the height of its power around 1550–1000 BC, when most of its greatest monuments were constructed

Thebes was of no particular significance for the first 2,000 years of ancient Egyptian history. It was only when the unlimited power enjoyed by the pharaohs was partly passed to their officials, and local governors sought to establish independence from central government, that political awareness developed in the region. This time was known as the First Intermediate Period (*c.*2181–2050 BC), and it was then that a powerful family of monarchs, whose capital was in nearby Armant, gained power and started to move northwards. Little by little they extended their authority, annexing local provinces until they came into conflict with the rulers of the north. Theban supremacy was recognised, Amun-Ra was introduced as the local deity and Thebes began to develop and prosper.

But the city achieved its prominent place in Egyptian history following the wars of liberation from the hated Hyksos occupation. Tribespeople from the region of Syria, the Hyksos ruled Egypt between about 1786 and 1567 BC, at which point an Egyptian prince called Sekenenre and his son Kamose rose against them. Kamose's brother Ahmose was able to establish the 18th Dynasty, marking the start of what is now known as the New Kingdom, with Thebes at its centre.

After ridding the country of foreign occupation, Thebes began to develop into the seat of a world power such as had never been seen before. Military conquests and territorial expansion went hand in hand with an artistic and architectural flowering of unparalleled grandeur. As a result of military victory, booty from conquered nations and tributes from the provinces of the then known powers poured into the gigantic storehouse of Thebes. The greater part of the wealth was bestowed upon Amun-Ra, who, with the aid of the influential priesthood, was established as "The King of Gods".

When Amun-Ra was dishonoured by Amenhotep IV (Akhenaten), who worshipped the life-giving rays of the full solar disk, the Aten, in place of the ascending sun Ra *(see page 34)*, Thebes was suddenly overshadowed by Akhenaten's new capital at Tall Al Amarnah. Reliefs were defaced, shrines destroyed and the image of Amun-Ra hacked away. But the god's dethronement was short-lived. Tutankhamun, on succeeding to the throne, restored Thebes as capital and started to repair the temples; Horemheb, Rameses I, Sety I and Rameses II continued the work of rebuilding and renovating the temples, to restore the reputation of Amun-Ra.

The dawn of Thebes' demise began during the reign of Rameses XI (*c.*1070 BC). A weak ruler, Rameses XI lost control of much of the southern half of the country, and many of the Theban tombs were desecrated or robbed during his reign. Four centuries later, in 663 BC, Ashurbanipal, king of the Assyrians, sacked Thebes and looted the Temple of Amun, marking the end of Thebes' role as the capital of the ancient world. The creation of the new capital, Memphis, and founding of Alexandria finally consigned Thebes to the history books and sand dunes.

The advent of Christianity brought systematic destruction to the ancient monuments. Later on the "pagan" statues were uprooted, sacred sanctuaries mutilated, and attempts made to topple obelisks and colossi to obliterate the visages of the "heathen gods". It wasn't until the 19th century that the pieces were slowly reassembled by modern archaeologists and Thebes was reborn as the tourist heart of the nation. ❑

LEFT: colourful hieroglyphs on the Temple of Amun-Ra.

patron saint of Luxor, who is buried on the site. Founded in the 12th century by the Sufi mystic Abu Al haggag, the mosque was built when the temple was almost completely covered in silt and sand. When excavations began on the temple and houses were cleared away, the local people refused to allow any disturbance of the mosque. Since then the picturesque mosque hangs about 13 metres (40ft) above ground level, with its foundations exposed.

On the western wall of the Court of Rameses II is a beautiful relief of a funeral procession led by 17 of Rameses II's 100 or so sons. A portal leads into the impressive **Colonnade of Amenhotep III** **D** (1402–1364 BC), of exquisite proportions and a fine example of the architecture of this period. The reliefs on its walls, dating from the time of Tutankhamun (1357–1348 BC), depict the great Opet festival that took place each year at the height of the flood.

Opet festival

During the festival the sacred statue of the god Amun-Ra was taken out of the sanctuary at Karnak and, amidst great pomp and ceremony, transported in a sacred barge to Luxor to be reunited with the statues of his consort Mut and their son Khonsu. It remained here for a few days of celebrations and festivities, before being returned to Karnak. The occasion offered the people of Thebes a rare opportunity to glimpse the statue of Amun-Ra, a chance repeated at the end of the year when a second festival was held in which Amun-Ra was carried across the Nile to visit the mortuary temples of the dead pharaohs *(see page 193)*.

Reliefs illustrating preparations for the Opet festival can be seen on the right-hand wall of the temple's colonnade (some of which was reconstructed in the 1970s), including a rehearsal by dancing girls. They show the procession beginning at the gate of Karnak Temple, shown complete with flagstaffs, from which white-robed priests bear the sacred barge of Amun-Ra down to the water's edge. An enthusiastic audience claps

The mosque of Luxor's patron saint, Abu Al haggag, perches on top of part of the Temple of Luxor. It is the focus for the biggest festival in Upper Egypt, when the town is strewn with flowers and feluccas are carried from the river to the mosque.

BELOW: statue at the Temple of Amun-Ra, Karnak.

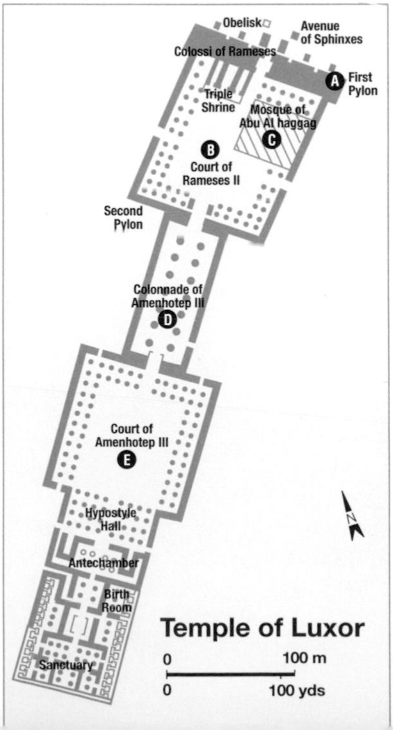

The Theban triad, or group of three gods, comprised Amun-Ra, usually portrayed as a ram-headed sun-god, his wife Mut and son Khonsu. Both temples in Luxor were built in their honour; Amun-Ra resided in the Temple of Karnak, while the Luxor temple was known as the "Harem of the South".

hands in unison, and it is accompanied upstream by celebrants along the shore; a sacrifice of slaughtered animals is followed by a group of acrobats, and finally offerings are made to the Theban triad *(see margin)* at the Temple of Luxor. On the opposite wall are scenes of the festival's return procession. The barges are floated downstream, and the final sacrifice and offerings of flowers are made to the deities at Karnak Temple.

An important discovery was made in the **Court of Amenhotep III** Ⓔ at the end of 1989. When the flagstones were being lifted to check on the tilt of the land and possible undermining of the temple's columns, archaeologists found a hidden cache containing, among other objects, life-size statues of various New Kingdom pharaohs. Many of these are displayed in the New Hall of the **Luxor Museum** *(see page 193)*.

Beyond this court are several chambers, some of which were adapted by the Romans into churches. Alexander the Great added the small end chapel, with reliefs of himself as a pharaoh.

Karnak

The great **Temple of Amun-Ra** at **Karnak** ❷ (daily, Oct–Apr 6am–5.30pm, May–Sept 6am–6.30pm, last tickets sold one hour before closing; charge) was the great god's chief sanctuary and is much larger and far more complex than the Temple of Luxor, or than any other monument in Egypt. The ancient Egyptians called it *Ipet-Isut* (the "most perfect of places").

It lies 2.5km (1½ miles) north of the town centre, a 20-minute walk along the Corniche or a pleasant ride by calèche (discuss the price with your driver beforehand and be clear about whether you want a one- or two-way trip; if you want your driver to return later, you should count on spending around 2½–3 hours at the temple).

This huge and splendid complex which actually contains many separate temples, covers 1,300 years of expansion and an area of 80 hectares (200 acres). Beneath its giant architraves and between bulky column and wall reliefs are records of its growth from a modest Middle Kingdom shrine to a magnificent temple of vast proportions. It

BELOW: view from the Winter Palace Hotel, which has now been demolished.

owes a column to one pharaoh, a pylon to another; an inspiration here, a whim there. But each has the sole purpose of honouring the god, Amun-Ra, who would then ensure the builder a long, powerful and glorious life.

Family rivalry was often the chief motivation behind new constructions. A reigning pharaoh would alter the royal cartouche of a former pharaoh and thereby take credit for the work of his predecessor (which may be why Rameses II seems to have been so prodigious in temple-building). To add to the confusion, some parts of the buildings were raised from dismantled shrines or the walls of other temples. In the case of Karnak, the matter was complicated further by the degradation of Amun-Ra, first at the hands of the rebel pharaoh Akhenaten *(see page 34)* and then by the early Christians.

The Precinct of Amun-Ra

The Temple of Karnak is unusually built on a north–south instead of an east–west axis. The largest and most important precinct is the Precinct of Amun-Ra, with the Precinct of Mut on the north side and the Precinct of Khonsu on the west, although these last are in a poor state of repair and rarely visited. The site of the car park and souvenir shops outside the temple complex was once a landing stage for a canal connecting the temple to the Nile; from here the builders' and the festival barges came and went, including the barges used in the Opet festival *(see page 187)*. The processional way of ram-headed sphinxes with sun-disks on their heads and statues of the pharaoh between their forepaws once led from the riverbank to the main entrance, while another row led all the way to the Temple of Luxor.

The two blocks of the massive entrance **pylon**, added by an Ethiopian king, are unadorned and unfinished. Note the mud-brick ramp (a large mass of rubble behind one of the entrance pylons) which was used during the construction of the pylon. It shows that the roughly shaped stones, heaved into position on ramps, were shaped after their erection, and that the polishing and decoration were performed from the top downwards as the mud-brick

After you've seen it in daylight, try to visit the Temple of Luxor at night (it's open until 9pm in winter and 10pm in summer). The shadows made by the floodlights help create an eerie atmosphere.

BELOW: massive columns in the Hypostyle Hall, Temple of Amun-Ra at Karnak.

Karnak's granite colossus attributed to Rameses II with one of his daughters at his feet. Rameses had some 60 daughters and actually married three of them.

ramps were removed layer by layer.

Behind lies the **Great Court** Ⓐ, a vast area of 8,919 sq metres (95,433 sq ft), built to enclose several older structures. It was the one part of the temple accessible to the general public. Within it are shrines, believed to have been used during the preparations of the Opet festival, another row of ram-headed sphinxes and a small, well-preserved **Temple of Rameses III** Ⓑ. Its court is lined with Osiride (with a crook and a flail) columns, and reliefs on the walls depict the annual festival. In front of the second pylon stands the granite colossus of Rameses II with one of his daughters.

Behind this pylon lies one of the highlights of Ancient Egypt, the **Great Hypostyle Hall** Ⓒ, covering an area of 4,983 sq metres (53,318 sq ft). To support the roof, 134 columns were arranged in 16 rows, with the double row of central columns higher than the others. They have smooth shafts and are 21 metres (67ft) high, topped with calyx capitals large enough, it is said, to accommodate 100 standing men. The columns are decorated with superb carvings of cult scenes. The overall effect is truly awe-inspiring. It was noted by the *savants* of Napoleon Bonaparte's expedition to Egypt in 1798 that the whole of the cathedral of Notre-Dame in Paris could comfortably be accommodated within its walls. At the time of Napoleon it was half-submerged in sand, and antique graffiti is clearly visible some distance up the columns.

Work on the Hypostyle Hall was started by Sety I and later finished by his son Rameses II; note the difference in decoration between the exquisite wall carvings from Sety I's era, in the left wing of the hall as well as on its outer walls, and the much cruder finish by Rameses II in the right wing.

Obelisks and courts

Beyond the Hypostyle Hall are the badly ruined third and fourth pylons, and further along, one of the two lofty **obelisks** Ⓓ erected by Queen Hatshepsut (1490–1468 BC) – the tip of the second lies near the Sacred Lake. Obelisks were characteristic monuments of the New Kingdom, intended

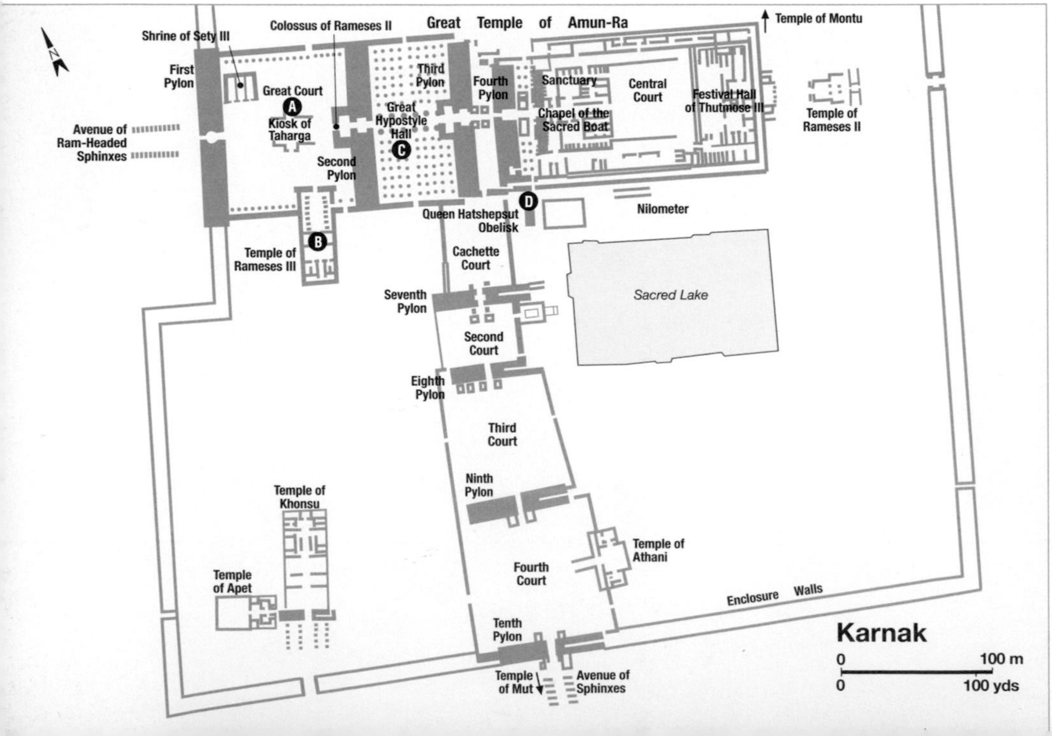

to represent the first ray of light that created the earth. This, the tallest obelisk in Egypt, was erected in the 16th year of the queen's glorious reign. It was carved from a single block of pink Aswan granite of the finest quality, and the apex was once covered with a mixture of gold and silver. It was made in seven months, and one cannot but marvel at the skills required to quarry and transport it – it weighs around 323 tonnes – downriver to Karnak and then erect it with perfect accuracy on a pedestal.

Behind the ruinous sixth pylon, in another court, are two granite pillars, one carved with lotus flowers, the other with papyrus flowers, representing Upper and Lower Egypt. At the end of the court is a **Chapel of the Sacred Boat** built by the brother of Alexander the Great. Further along lies the **Festival Hall of Thutmose III**, with fine reliefs.

Off the main axis near the Hypostyle Hall are the **Cachette Court**, where thousands of statues were discovered in 1903, the **Open-Air Museum** (extra charge) with more statues, and the **Sacred Lake**. The priests of Amun-Ra used the lake to purify themselves in holy water, piped through from the Nile in underground channels.

Unfortunately too few of the hewn rocks survived the years to allow for genuine restoration of the lake, but there is a pleasant cafeteria on its banks – a good place to ponder over the temple's history.

The top of a fallen obelisk at Hatshepsut at the Temple of Karnak.

Luxor's museums

On the riverbank about halfway between the temples of Luxor and Karnak is the **Luxor Museum** ❸ (daily, Oct–Apr 9am–3pm, 4–9pm, May–Sept 9am–3pm, 5–8pm, Ramadan 1–4pm; charge). This excellent museum was designed by one of Egypt's leading architects, the late Mahmoud Al Hakim, to display important finds from the temples and other local sites.

The selection, installation and illumination of the collection were done with the assistance of New York's Brooklyn Museum, and the difference between this designed environment and the warehouse approach of

BELOW LEFT: sphinx holding a statue of a pharaoh in its paws. **BELOW:** the god Amen-Ra, with Hatshepsut kneeling, seen on the obelisk above.

TIP

The Karnak sound and light show, which is one of the best in Egypt, is held three or four times a night. Performances are held in different languages, with English performed every night except Sunday (check the timetable at www.soundandlight.com.eg). To get to Karnak in the evening, hire a taxi. It is usual to ask your driver to wait while you watch. If you attend a performance in winter, be sure to wear warm clothing.

Cairo's Egyptian Museum is particularly marked. The museum offers the opportunity to examine in close-up the superb workmanship of the artists and craftsmen.

Highlights of Luxor Museum

Inside the museum, the first focal point is a magnificent cow-head of the sky-goddess Mehit Weret, covered in gold leaf, from Tutankhamun's tomb. Walking towards the rear of the main hall, you pass a seated statue of Amenhotep, the son of Hapu, who was so important in Ancient Egypt that he was accorded special prerogatives during his life and was finally deified thousands of years after his death. Also in the main gallery is a huge alabaster statue of Amenhotep III, seated beside, and under the protection of, Sobek, the crocodile-god. Found at the bottom of a water-filled shaft in a canal in Armant, south of Luxor, in 1967, this is one of the most important finds in the Thebes region in modern times. It is remarkable for the harmonious balance between two figures of markedly different scale. As Sobek presents the *ankh* (the key of life) to Amenhotep, the sweep of his arm draws attention to the handsome face of the king.

BELOW: unfinished statue of Amenhotep III in Luxor Museum.

Two royal mummies are housed in the museum: that of Ahmose I, founder of the 18th Dynasty, has been confirmed as authentic, while the other is thought to be Rameses I, founder of the 19th Dynasty. Displayed in darkened rooms without their wrappings, they make a gruesome sight (children may find them frightening).

Nearby is a statue of Thutmose III, one of the best preserved statues of this famous ruler to survive, and a masterpiece of Ancient Egyptian art.

Another major exhibit is a representation of Amenhotep II as an archer, from sections of a red granite stela found in the third pylon at Karnak (pylons are often hollow). Amenhotep is depicted driving arrows through a copper target tied to a pole whilst galloping at full speed in his chariot, thus demonstrating his athletic prowess.

Part of the famous "Akhenaten Wall", an 18-metre (54ft) wall, has been reconstructed on the upper floor of the museum from some 300 of the 6,000 blocks of Akhenaten's Sun Temple, extracted from Horemheb's ninth pylon at Karnak. These *talatat*, as the decorated and uniform sandstone blocks are called, were discovered by a team of French excavators restoring the pylon. They soon realised that the fill inside the pylon had not been deposited in a haphazard manner. Rather, the upper courses had been dismantled and placed in the lowest level with the middle courses on top, and the bottom courses higher up the pylon. This enabled the easy reconstruction of a wall that had been deliberately dismantled 33 centuries earlier. The heads of three of the colossal statues of Akhenaten from his demolished temple at Karnak are also on display in this area.

The museum also contains monuments from the early centuries of the Christian era and the Coptic period. Among the former objects is a headless limestone and marble statue of the Greek goddess Demeter, an unusual find to have made in Upper Egypt where the worship of foreign gods was not as prevalent as in other areas. There are also examples of so-called Roman portraits, which were painted on linen. One portrait of a man thought to be a Roman officer in a garrison at Luxor was found in a tomb that had been used for secondary burial in the 3rd century.

The **New Hall** displays 16 of the 22 statues found in Luxor Temple during excavations in 1989 *(see page 188)*.

Mummy Museum

More or less opposite Luxor Temple, on the river, is the **Mummification Museum** ❹ (daily, Oct–Apr 9am–9pm, May–Sept 9am–10pm, Ramadan 1–4pm; charge). As well as a small collection of mummies, the museum explains clearly the process of mummification and has a well-documented array of tools and materials used in the ancient art. It also throws light on some of the more essential grave goods that would be buried alongside the mummy *(see also page 196)*.

Along the river

The east bank's other attractions centre on the Corniche, where riverside cafés offer the chance to watch the sun go down over the west bank and feluccas offer cruises. You can also shop in the souq, which is at its liveliest in the early evening, when locals pour outdoors to enjoy the cool air, or have a drink on the terrace of the **Sofitel Old Winter Palace Hotel**, a splendid colonial-style hotel overlooking the Nile near the Temple of Luxor.

THE WEST BANK

To explore the tombs and mortuary temples of the west bank you should allow at least two days. Public ferries, leaving from the dock opposite the Temple of Luxor, take locals and tourists across in a matter of minutes, while buses and taxis must take the bridge 7km (4 miles) south of Luxor town.

The temples and tombs on the west bank are spread over a large area, so you will need transport to get around. Taxis are available for hire at the landing stage (ascertain current rates from the tourist office on the east

TIP

Currently severe restrictions on taking photos at tourist sights are in place; you are not allowed to take photos inside any of the tombs, or in most museums, or anywhere in the Valley of the Kings. *See page 317 for more information.*

BELOW: gilded wooden head of a cow from Tutankhamun's tomb, now in Luxor Museum.

The ancient Egyptians were expert embalmers. By 1500 BC, when mummification was at its peak, they had developed sophisticated recipes for preserving the body and had a detailed knowledge of the bacterial processes that caused decay. Among the products used to arrest decay were natron, beeswax, myrrh, pine resin and camphor oil.

bank before taking the ferry). If the weather is not too hot, then a bicycle is a pleasant way to get around; they can be hired from most of the larger hotels as well as rentals on the east bank (and can be taken on the ferry; make sure you pack plenty of water for the journey).

The central ticket office for all the monuments other than the Valley of the Kings and **Temple of Hatshepsut** is on the crossroads past the **Colossi of Memnon** *(see right)*. Be sure to make up your mind in advance which tombs or temples you wish to visit in a day (three or four are probably enough), because if you change your mind and want to see an extra monument it will mean coming all the way back to buy another ticket. The monuments are open daily from 9am–5pm in winter (Oct–Apr) and 6am–6pm in summer (May–Sept), but be aware that the less visited monuments sometimes close earlier, particularly in summer, and the ticket booth closes at 4pm daily throughout the year. Every monument and each group of tombs has a separate charge.

Crossing the floodplain

The necropolis starts where the floodplain ends, about 3km (2 miles) from the river. The area was not always as arid and lifeless as it seems today. Beside each mortuary temple there were once dwellings for the priests and stables for the sacrificial animals, as well as guardhouses and granaries, each with its own superintendent.

Surrounding or in front of each temple were lakes, groves and beautifully laid-out gardens, and beside the mortuary temples were large palaces where the pharaohs took up temporary residence to supervise the progress of their monuments. Such palaces have been excavated beside the mortuary temples of Sety I, the Ramesseum of Rameses II and the Temple of Rameses III.

The approach to the necropolis is marked by two massive, now sadly weathered statues known as the **Colossi of Memnon** ❺, 18 metres (54ft) high, just past which is the ticket office for the west-bank sites *(see left for information)*. The colossi are all that remain of what was once the largest mortuary temple, that of

BELOW: the Colossi of Memnon.

Amenhotep III. It was probably damaged from a high flood, and further devastated by Rameses II and his son Merenptah, who used the fallen blocks to build their own temples.

In ancient times, cracks and holes on the northern statue of the two colossi created a musical sound when the breeze blew through them at dawn. Early Greek and Roman travellers explained this in their mythology by claiming that when the Ethiopian hero Memnon fell at Troy, he reappeared at Thebes as a singing stone statue and each morning would greet his mother Aurora with a plaintive song. Aurora, on hearing the sound, shed tears in the form of morning dew on the cold stone of the statue. But the cracks on the statue were filled in during the reign of Septimius Severus in AD 193 and the sound ceased.

The Valley of the Kings

The most impressive tombs in the necropolis are those in the **Valley of the Kings** ❻, known locally as Biban Al Muluk. A road leads northwards from the ticket office, and then forks westwards past **Howard Carter's House**, the archaeologist's former mud-brick home which has opened as a **museum** (daily 9am–5pm, but opening times erratic due to lack of staff; free). The road continues up into the mountains where the tombs are hidden in a secluded valley.

The valley contains 63 tombs belonging to the pharaohs of the 18th, 19th and 20th dynasties (*c.*1567–1080 BC). Only nine of these are open to the public, on a rotation system. More may well be discovered, as a new tomb, KV5, the largest found so far and thought to contain 50 of Rameses II's 52 sons, was found in 1995 and is still being excavated *(see page 200)*.

The majestic Pyramids of the Old Kingdom were too conspicuous to be secure tombs for kings and their treasure. The later practice of building a monumental funerary temple in one place and discreetly burying the body in another was aimed at throwing grave robbers off the scent.

The tombs were laboriously hewn out of the bedrock and decorated with scenes of the journey of the sun-god through the underworld. The deceased

Modern alabaster souvenirs of Egyptian gods.

BELOW LEFT: gilded statue of the goddess Sekhmet, found in Tutankhamun's tomb.

Visiting the Tombs

The Valley of the Kings is one of the highlights of a visit to Egypt – as you'll see by all the tourists here. Already challenging enough to navigate due to the steep underground tunnels and cramped surroundings, they become even more so when you throw in the hundreds of tourists crammed inside each one. If you want to avoid the crowds, you'll need to wake up early. Aim to get there as soon as the site opens so you can be first in line.

The tombs were never intended to be visited – these are, after all, places of burial. Light levels are kept specifically low in order to safeguard the delicate paintings on the tomb walls. If you want to see detail, bring a torch with you. Not only will it help you navigate some of the trickier tunnels, it will also let you see the artistry and skill required to make these tombs so spectacular.

In summer, be sure to bring plenty of water and hop on the tourist train that takes visitors from the entrance to the tombs – otherwise you're looking at a 500-metre/yd walk in the searing heat. At E£1, it's a bargain.

Among the items placed in tombs would be a variety of amulets, which were often put on the mummy itself. The most popular of these were the scarab (dung beetle) representing rebirth, the eye of Horus to protect against the evil eye, the ankh, *the symbol of life, and the red* thet *(girdle of Isis), representing the blood of Isis that washed away sin.*

pharaoh, absorbed by the setting sun, travelled in the barge of the sun-god through the 12 hours of night, each hour separated from the other by gates guarded by serpents. The solar barge, safeguarded from the hazards of the underworld by protective deities and emblems, finally reached the Court of Osiris. Here the judge of the underworld, attended by Maat, goddess of truth and justice, and in the presence of 42 gods of the underworld, listened to the confession of the deceased and then watched over the weighing of the heart against the feather of truth. The ibis-headed Thoth, god of wisdom, recorded the verdict. If unfavourable, the deceased was consumed by a terrible animal or consigned to the fires. A favourable verdict gave access to everlasting life.

Some of the royal tombs (Rameses VI, for example) have burial chambers adorned with astrological signs. The decorations in others (such as Amenhotep II) were made to resemble papyrus texts pinned to the walls, while others again (Sety I) have wonderfully preserved painted reliefs.

Tutankhamun's tomb

The **Tomb of Tutankhamun**, the tomb all visitors to the west bank particularly want to see, is the smallest and, surprisingly, least impressive of the tombs in the Valley of the Kings; it is difficult to imagine how the pharaoh's fabulous treasures fitted into it. The mummy of Tutankhamun, which had been left inside the gilded coffin, has now been placed on display inside the first burial chamber of the tomb.

The tomb was discovered in 1922 by the British archaeologist Howard Carter, working for the English aristocrat Lord Carnarvon. It was estimated that some 200,000 tonnes of rubble were moved before Carter finally located the tomb immediately beneath that of Rameses VI, where workmen's huts had obscured its entrance.

Whatever had been expected or hoped for, there is no doubt that the tomb's actual contents surpassed their wildest dreams. When Carter first looked into the tomb and was asked by Carnarvon, who was standing behind him, "What do you see?" he replied: "Wonderful things!"

BELOW: the Tomb of Tutankhamun.

Tutankhamun was the only pharaoh to escape the grave robbers, who were so effective that the priests eventually removed 40 of the royal mummies for safe-keeping and reburied them in a cache near the Temple of Queen Hatshepsut, where they were finally discovered in 1899.

Other tombs

The **Tomb of Sety I** (indefinitely closed to the public) is a classical tomb that surpasses all others both in size and in the artistic execution of the sculptured walls. Every centimetre of wall space in its 100-metre (330ft) length is covered with paintings and reliefs executed by the finest craftsmen. The burial chamber (a long descent) contained a sarcophagus made out of a single piece of alabaster carved to a thickness of 5cm (2 inches) and with the exquisite reliefs filled in with blue paste.

Giovanni Belzoni, a former circus strongman who originally came to Egypt to market an irrigation pump he had designed in England, discovered Sety I's tomb in 1817. When Turkish officials in Egypt heard of the discovery they headed for Luxor bent on the delightful thought, no doubt, of acquiring priceless treasure. Down the corridors they went, ransacking every corner, only to find to their disappointment that the tomb contained no more than an empty sarcophagus. When Belzoni effected its transportation to England, the trustees of the British Museum considered his price too high, and the treasure was without a buyer until 1824. Sir John Soane paid £2,000 sterling for it, and it now sits in the museum that bears Soane's name in London.

The lengths to which the kings went to conceal their burial places and fool robbers is illustrated most graphically by the **Tomb of Thutmose III**, hidden in a crevice right at the back of the valley and with several twists, turns and traps in its construction.

Dair Al Madinah

After visiting the Tombs of the Kings it is interesting to see **Dair Al Madinah ❼**, the village, in use from the time of Thutmose I (1505–1493 BC), where the masons, carvers and painters of the royal tombs lived. The crafts-

> *...a gasp of wonderment escaped our lips, so gorgeous was the sight that met our eyes: a golden effigy of the young boy-king, of most magnificent workmanship.*
>
> Howard Carter

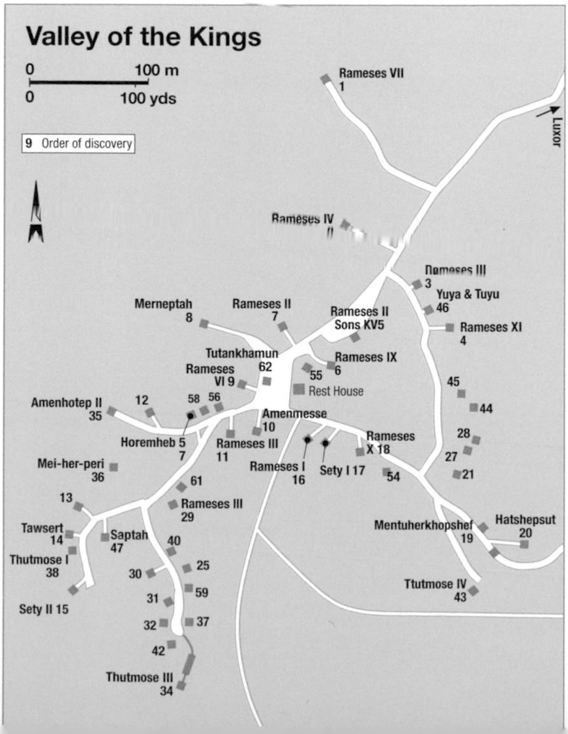

BELOW: cliff above the Valley of the Kings.

Discovering Tutankhamun

The boy-king was quickly forgotten by the ancient Egyptians, but the discovery of his tomb in 1922 made him the most famous pharaoh

The awesome sight which Howard Carter made out by candlelight when he opened up Tutankhamun's tomb in 1922 was all the more remarkable because, as royal tombs go, it probably was rather modest. The factor that had allowed it to go unplundered was the occupant's insignificance.

Carter had begun work in 1915 and, with little to show for it seven years later, his patron, Lord Carnarvon, was about to terminate his contract. But on arriving for work on 4 November 1922, Carter was immediately aware that something out of the ordinary had happened. While exploring the foundations of houses that had accommodated the workers on the tomb of Rameses VI, his diggers had come across a step cut into the rock. By the following afternoon they had exposed a flight of 16 steps and, at the bottom, a sealed door. The seal was merely that of a necropolis guard, not a royal one, but Carter dashed off a cable to Carnarvon and sportingly waited 17 days for him to arrive.

Together Carter and Carnarvon cleared the entrance and at the bottom of the door hit the jackpot. There, still intact, was the seal of Tutankhamun. Beyond the door lay a sloping passage full of rubble. About 9 metres (30ft) along the passage Carter found another door. "With trembling hands, I made a tiny breach in the upper left-hand corner... widening the hole a little, I inserted the candle and peered in. At first I could see nothing, the hot air escaping from the chamber, causing the candle flame to flicker, but presently, as my eyes grew accustomed to the light..."

To the men's astonishment the tomb was packed with an untidy mess of three gilded beds, two golden chariots, various chairs and stools, two black and gold life-size statues and a huge assortment of objects. That proved to be only the antechamber, and on 17 February 1923 began the exciting job of chipping away at the plaster to find what lay beyond – a massive golden shrine. Carter squeezed around it to find an open doorway which led to the treasury, watched over by a life-size statue of a guard dog. Here a box-like shrine provided the most exciting striptease ever performed. When a way was devised to open it up, it was found to contain another shrine only marginally smaller. It came apart like a Russian doll, four shrines in all.

It took a whole year to reach the fourth and final shrine, which produced a quartzite sarcophagus with a lid of pink granite. "The contents were covered with linen shrouds," Carter recalled, but inside was a coffin in the shape of the young boy-king.

The weight of the coffin was such that a hoist was needed to move it. It contained, in a repetition of the multi-layered shrine, a second coffin. On 17 October 1926, four years after the excavations had begun, this was opened, revealing what made the thing so heavy – a third and final coffin of solid gold, weighing nearly 110kg (300lbs). The mummy of the king was at last exposed: the now famous mask of gold with inlaid glass and lapis lazuli. The mask had protected the face well but the rest of the body was not as well preserved. ❑

LEFT: Howard Carter at work. **ABOVE:** gilded hawk.

men recorded their daily life on ostraca (pottery fragments) or papyrus, leaving archaeologists an invaluable record of their working practices and wages (in grain), not to mention all manner of notes relating to the details of their everyday activities, from laundry lists to letters. They worked eight hours a day for 10 days, and then came back to the village to work on their own tombs, which were inspired by those of the pharaohs.

With the rise of the Sea Peoples and the gradual collapse of the New Kingdom in the 12th century BC, the workmen of Dair Al Madinah lost their livelihoods. Unpaid by the pharaoh, they became desperate and ultimately plundered the very tombs they had built and adorned, including the tomb of the great Rameses II. They were the first grave robbers.

The village itself is closed to the public, but a few of the rock-cut tombs are well worth visiting, particularly the well-preserved tombs of Sennedjem and Inherkau. The former shows Sennedjem kneeling before Osiris while Anubis on one side prepares the mummy and on the other guides the dead.

Valley of the Queens

A road leaves from here to the **Valley of the Queens** ❽, containing the tombs of royal consorts and also of a number of sons of Rameses III who died young, possibly of smallpox during an epidemic. The most famous tomb is that of Nefertari, the favourite wife of Rameses II. Beautifully restored with help from the Getty Foundation, this tomb has exquisite low reliefs painted on a plaster base; it was opened to great acclaim in 1995 for the first time since its discovery in 1904. Sadly it has been closed since 2003.

One of the most appealing tombs in the Valley of the Queens, however, is that of Prince Amenhirkopshef. The tomb paintings portray the young prince being led by his father, Rameses III, through the mystical regions of the underworld. Rameses introduces the boy, one by one, to the various gods of the dead. The reliefs are of fine quality, in beautifully preserved colours.

Tombs of the Nobles

Just as the Royal Tombs in the Theban necropolis provide an insight into the realm of the dead and the pharaohs' vision of the afterlife, the 400 or so **Tombs of the Nobles** ❾ reveal aspects of the everyday life of important officials in the New Kingdom. Unlike the kings who wanted above all to conceal their tombs, the nobles were ostentatious and keen for their tombs to be seen.

The **Tomb of Rekhmira**, a vizier under Thutmose III and his son Amenhotep II, contains numerous painted scenes of jewellery-making, pottery manufacture and carpentry, as well as a court of law, in which tax evaders are brought to justice. Rekhmire was an outstanding official who was entrusted with so many duties that there was nothing, he claims in an inscription, "of which I am ignorant in heaven, on earth or in any part of

One way to visit the tombs and temples of Thebes is by donkey.

BELOW: metal workers depicted in the Tomb of Rekhmire.

TIP

To find out about the latest excavations in the Valley of the Kings, particularly for a progress report on the excavation of KV5, visit the website of the Theban Mapping Project: www.thebanmappingproject.com.

BELOW: statues of Hatshepsut at her temple at Dair Al Bahari.

the underworld." For many years this tomb was inhabited by a local peasant family, and the wall decorations suffered somewhat. Nevertheless, the tomb is a memorial to personal greatness and is, in the words of British Egyptologist James Breasted, "the most important private monument of the Empire".

The **Tomb of Ramose** is also historically and artistically noteworthy. Ramose was the vizier in the reign of Amenhotep III and his son, Amenhotep IV, later Akhenaten, leader of the rebel dynasty that promoted the worship of one god *(see page 34)*. Ramose's tomb provides a unique opportunity to see classical reliefs alongside the "realism" encouraged by Akhenaten. One scene, for example, depicts Ramose standing before his seated pharaoh, who is depicted in the stylised majesty of traditional royal representations; on the opposite wall Ramose stands beneath a balcony on which Akhenaten and his wife Nefertiti stand in an informal posture beneath the symbol of the Aten, a solar disk with rays ending in hands holding the symbols of life and prosperity.

The **Tomb of Nakht**, though small, ranks as one of the finest in the group. The reliefs are executed with infinite charm and are in a good state of repair. Nakht was a scribe of the granaries under Thutmose IV, and his tomb is beautifully decorated with reliefs of agricultural scenes including ploughing, digging and sowing, as well as stages of the harvest, especially measuring and winnowing the grain, reaping and pressing it into baskets. One of the most delightful scenes shows the nobleman on an outing with his family. He is depicted standing in a papyrus craft spearing fish and shooting fowl while his little daughter holds his leg to prevent him from falling into the water.

Female pharaoh

Just across the mountains from the Valley of the Kings is Dair Al Bahari, the **Temple of Hatshepsut** ⑩, one of the most spectacular mortuary temples in Egypt. The temple was built in terraces set against the steep cliffs, and it

was styled in ancient times as "Most Splendid of All". It was built by the queen's architect, Senemmut, who was also her political adviser and, according to graffiti of the time, her lover, though this may have stemmed from malicious gossip. Whatever the truth, he was granted the unique privilege of constructing his own tomb beneath the temple of his queen.

Queen Hatshepsut's famous voyage to Punt, on the Somali coast, is recorded in the carvings on one colonnade. This trading mission was the first time an Egyptian force had been so far for 5,000 years. It was a huge success and, as the carvings show, the army returned laden with ivory, baboons, leopard skins and, most precious of all, incense, an essential ingredient of temple rituals and said to embody the spirit of the deities. Reliefs on the southern colonnade depict the legend of her "divine birth" by the god Amun-Ra, who took on her father's appearance and made love to her mother.

This claim was made by the queen to help justify her position to the people. Queen Hatshepsut was of direct royal lineage to the Great Royal Wife of Thutmose I, while his other (male) children were from minor wives. Hatshepsut consequently married her half-brother Thutmose II, and when he died became regent for her young stepson. But she quickly declared herself pharaoh, and to underline her authority had herself depicted with a male body, a male kilt and a false ceremonial beard. She claimed, as one inscription records, that her father had appointed her as his successor. After her death her stepson and successor, Thutmose III, did his best to erase her image.

More mortuary temples

From Hatshepsut's temple you can clearly see the outline of two more mortuary temples: the **Mortuary Temple of Thutmose III**, long ago destroyed by a landslide, and the older **Temple of Nebhetepra Mentuhotep**, who was the first pharaoh to be buried in Thebes. In fact, there are around 30 such temples altogether, though many of them are in a poor state of repair, made worse by rising groundwater.

Near Howard Carter's House and

Following Hatshepsut's death, after 22 years on the throne, all records of her were erased by Thutmose III. She wasn't heard of again until 3,000 years later, when Howard Carter uncovered her tomb in 1903. Reading the name Hatshepsut, he was astonished to note the use of the female pronoun.

BELOW: burial chamber in the Tomb of Thutmose III.

Rameses II adored his chief wife, Nefertari, and her exquisitely decorated tomb was intended to be a testament of his love. He said of Nefertari, "Just by passing she has stolen away my heart." Rameses II lived until he was 93 years old. He had reigned for 67 years, longer than any other pharaoh. His mummy can still be seen in the Egyptian Museum in Cairo, with wisps of his red hair intact.

BELOW: statues of Rameses III in his temple at Madinat Habu. **BELOW RIGHT:** aerial view of Madinat Habu.

the villages of Al Qurnah and At tarif, is the little visited **Temple of Sety I** ⓫, the mortuary temple built by the mighty pharaoh Sety I, the father of Rameses II. It is in a ruinous state, but the carvings, although cruder than most carvings in Sety I's monuments, are still among the finest in Egypt. The columns in the Hypostyle Hall are decorated with superb reliefs of Sety and his ambitious son Rameses II. In the chapels and the sanctuary beyond are more interesting reliefs.

Ramesseum and Rameses III

Rameses II, that most active of builders, placed his mortuary temple, known as the **Ramesseum** ⓬, opposite the Tombs of the Nobles. Unlike the other still-standing monuments he built, his mortuary temple, which was especially meant to last for ever, collapsed because it was built on weak foundations. Although half in ruin, it is a magnificent monument and contains remains of a colossal figure of the pharaoh, the largest granite statue ever fashioned to such a high standard. Mathematicians who travelled to Egypt with Napoleon's army in 1798 made careful measurements of the chest, upper arm and foot. They calculated that the statue's total height must have been 17 metres (51ft), and its weight over 1,000 tonnes.

Rameses II did an extraordinary amount of building during his 67-year reign. He had his state sculptors depict him repeatedly, and there is hardly a pylon, hall or chamber in the temples of Egypt that does not bear his name. His favourite theme was his famous battle with the king of the Hittites, as depicted on the great pylon that forms the eastern entrance to the Ramesseum. Another series of reliefs concerns the festival of Min. The pharaoh was borne on a richly decorated carrying-chair, led by priests and soldiers, and followed by his sons and courtiers, to witness sacrifices and to watch the release of four birds which would carry the royal tidings to the corners of the earth.

Further back from the ticket office is **Madinat Habu** ⓭, the splendid Mortuary Temple of Rameses III, which, although built much later,

was modelled on the Ramesseum, the mortuary temple of his ancestor Rameses II. This huge temple is second only to Karnak in size, and it is one of the best preserved and easiest to understand of temple structures. It was built on an older structure, as legend has it that this was the first land that appeared from the Waters of Chaos. Centuries after it was built, the temple was surrounded by the town of Jeme, inhabited by a Coptic community.

The enclosure is entered from a gatehouse where stairs lead to Rameses III's pleasure apartments on the first floor, with beautiful carvings of dancers on the wall. To the right is a small temple built by Hatshepsut on the primeval hill. The gigantic pylons and walls of the temple are decorated with scenes of battles that were fought by Rameses III and inscriptions record a battle against the Sea People, who attacked Egypt early in the reign of Rameses III; it is thought to document the earliest known sea battle. The ultimate success of the Sea People, combined with the exhaustion of the Nubian goldmines, brought down the New Kingdom.

Festivals for pharaohs

Celebrations and festivals took place in the large First Court, which has an opening to the pharaoh's now ruinous palace to the left. Some of the colours of the fine reliefs are remarkably well preserved. The Second Court was later turned into a Coptic church, and the Copts carved many crosses on the walls. At the back are three sanctuaries dedicated to the triad of Mut, Khonsu and Amun. It is worth walking around the outer walls, which have some remarkable scenes of Rameses hunting and fishing, to get an idea of the splendour and grandeur of this temple. To the north is the outline of a sacred lake, and the temple is surrounded by a mud-brick enclosure.

A good way to end a day of sightseeing is to watch the sun go down behind this temple from one of the café terraces opposite the entrance.

The base of a column in the Temple of Rameses III at Madinat Habu.

BELOW LEFT: villager in Al Qurnah.

Living on the Tombs

Al Qurnah, the once picturesque village of ochre-coloured houses, where tour buses used to oblige you to stop to visit the alabaster workshops, sat right on top of the Theban necropolis.

Some 30 years ago, the world-renowned Egyptian architect Hassan Fathy built a model village for the community on the floodplain between the River Nile and the Colossi of Memnon. Although New Qurnah was designed with spacious homes, a mosque, schools, a healthcare centre and other facilities, the people of Al Qurnah were reluctant to settle there. They chose, instead, to remain where they were – on top of the tombs.

The reason, it is said, was because they were living on income derived from illegal pillage *(see page 59)*. However, the government has now demolished most of the houses above the tombs (not without controversy), and the local people have on the whole been rehoused nearby.

The inhabitants of Al Qurnah lived among the tombs for many generations, and their traditions and way of life were rooted in a strong sense of place. Al Qurnah Discovery (Sat–Thur 8am–4.30pm; free, but donations welcome; www.qurna.org) is a small centre near the Tomb of Sennofer, where you can learn more about the village's unique heritage.

A home in Al Qurnah is decorated with images of Mecca, denoting that the owner has completed the haj *(the pilgrimage to Mecca), which all Muslims with the necessary means are required to undertake at some point in their life.*

RIGHT: entrance into the Temple of Rameses III at Medinat Habu.

Endangered monuments

There are literally hundreds of tombs on the Theban necropolis, only a sampling of which are open to the public. Some have been "lost", that is to say, they were opened and partly recorded by early Egyptologists in the 19th and early 20th centuries, but have since become filled with sand, all signs of their presence obliterated. Locating them again, properly recording and documenting them is one of the chief tasks of Egyptologists today.

Luxor is today one of the most threatened archaeological sites in the world. The threat comes from three sources: contamination, desecration and abuse – environmental contamination from humidity and sub-soil water, plunder by grave robbers, and damage by tourists. The first is the most difficult to control, and although efforts to curb the environmental contamination have been made, it seems to be a losing battle. As the British Egyptologist Michael Jones observed, "You cannot save a monument; all you can really do, in the long run, is delay its rate of destruction." Measures to help prevent further damage – such as coaches not leaving their engines running near the tombs – are not always adhered to.

The deterioration of the reliefs on ancient monuments is even visible to the naked eye. The atmosphere – more humid as a result of water stored in Lake Nasser – and air pollution from factories are adversely affecting Egypt's ancient treasures. But worse still is the higher than average water-table since the construction of the High Dam, which results in salt-laden moisture creeping up the temple walls, leaving the reliefs pimpled, festered and spoiled, after which they quite literally flake off.

Plunder of tombs is another serious problem. So long as there have been tombs, there have been robbers *(see page 58)*, but the tragedy of modern-day plunder is that the antiquities are lost to the world of art and scholarship, as they usually make their way into private collections. The Egyptian government has clamped down on illicit digging and is working at many levels to curb or restore any damage, but with literally tens of thousands of monuments on both sides of the Nile, the task is enormous.

Meanwhile, epigraphers are hard at work, accurately documenting whatever they can.

Lightening the load

The damage caused by tourists is being attended to on many levels. In such places as the Valley of the Kings, tombs are opened on a rotating basis in order to spread the load and ease pressure on particularly popular tombs, tourists and tour leaders are expected to follow elementary ground rules (such as not touching the reliefs and paintings), and new access roads are being constructed.

One recurring suggestion is to keep tourists out of the most visited royal tombs altogether. Replicas of some of the tombs are now in the process of being made and will be exact copies using laser scans. The level of detail is extraordinary, capturing all the detail and colour of the original tombs. ❑

Theban Mapping Project

One of the most important archaeological projects being carried out is the production of the first detailed map of the necropolis since 1921. Known as the Theban Mapping Project (TMP, now based at the American Museum in Cairo; www.thebanmapping project.com), it is creating a detailed database on the Theban tombs, with plans and isometric drawings of each tomb and a system for monitoring deterioration. Its aim is to create a useful resource for professional archaeologists, but also to open up the fascinating subject of Ancient Egypt to the ordinary public, including schoolchildren.

The project uses state-of-the-art equipment and hot-air balloons for low-level photographs of the hidden valleys and mortuary temples. It has also been instrumental in introducing fibre-optic lighting in the tombs (safer and cooler than the old fluorescent lighting) and developing sophisticated methods of controlling temperature levels.

As well as working on the Theban necropolis, the organisation is embarking on another project to solve the problems caused by rising groundwater in the 30 or more mortuary temples along the edge of the valley floor. It is hoped that by working with the ministries of agriculture and irrigation, they can introduce new irrigation techniques that will halt further damage and allow restoration to take place.

LUXOR TO ABYDOS

Relaxation of travel restrictions means that the treasures of this region, including a superb Ptolemaic temple and the ancient cult city of Osiris, are once again within reach

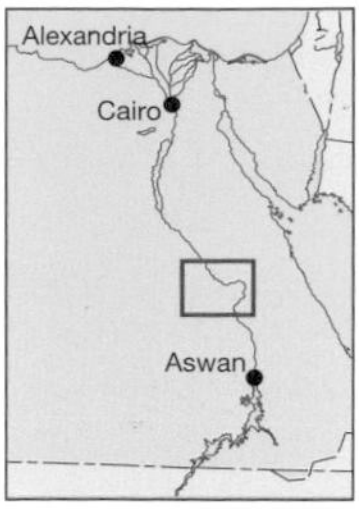

Main attractions
QENA
AL BALLAS
TEMPLE OF HATHOR AT DANDARAH
BASILICA OF ST PACHOMIUS
MONASTERY OF ST PALOMON
NAGA' HAMMADI
ABYDOS

Lush with crops and peppered with low, mud-built villages, the riverbanks north of Luxor are picturesque. After years of visitors having to use the dreaded convoy systems, the area has been opened up to free, independent travel, making exploration much less hassle-filled. You can now simply hire a taxi in Luxor and be on the move.

There are two main reasons for making the trip – the city of **Abydos**, which was of major importance from the time of the first dynasties (*c.*3100 BC), and the impressive **Ptolemaic Temple of Hathor at Dandarah**, which has a wealth of beautifully preserved reliefs and carvings.

To Dandarah

Leaving **Luxor** ❶ *(see page 183)*, the River Nile sweeps to the northeast, flowing smoothly past verdant fields and the town of **Qift** ❷ (ancient Coptos). With no ancient monuments, it is of no particular interest today, but it crops up again and again in the literature on Ancient Egypt, as the area was sacred to the licentious god Min, a guardian of the Eastern Desert.

The town was an important trading centre and the starting point of a caravan route from the Nile Valley to the Red Sea through the Wadi Al Hammamat. Today a tarmac road and railway connect this point of the Nile Valley to the Red Sea, following the route of ancient traders, who would have made their way from the port of Al Qusair on the coast, laden with goods from the Far East.

Just south of **Qena** ❸, the chief town of the province, situated about 20km (12 miles) north of Qift, is the village of **Al Ballas** on the west bank of the Nile, where the distinctive *ballas* pottery is made from the large clay

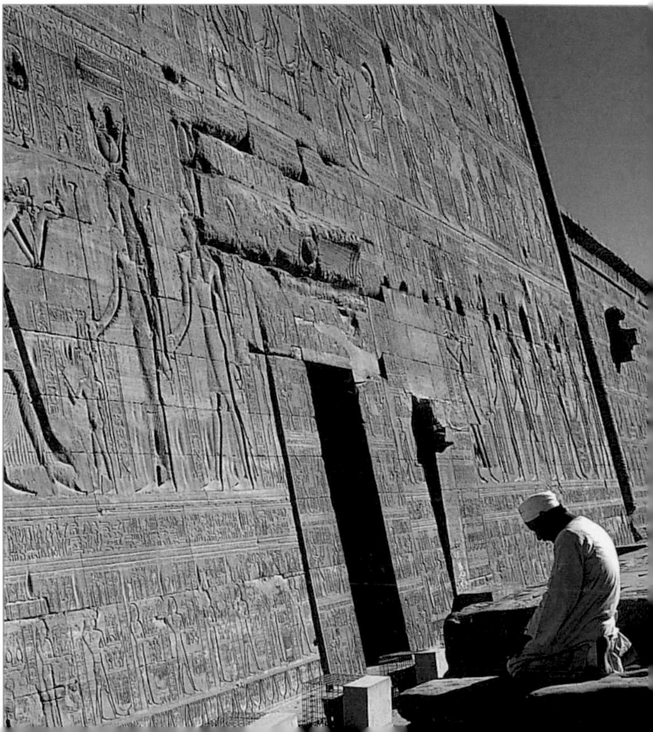

PRECEDING PAGES: drying dates near Luxor. **LEFT:** fresh fruit at Luxor souq. **RIGHT:** praying at the Temple of Hathor in Dandarah.

An early Egyptian Earth Mother, depicted as a cow, or as a woman with cow's ears or horns, Hathor (pronounced Hat-Hor and meaning "House of Horus") was the goddess of beauty, love and music. The Greeks identified her with Aphrodite, and she was also linked with Isis.

deposits in the region. If you are lucky, you may see pots lined along the banks awaiting shipment. These are the kind of pots that you see women carrying on their heads as they go to draw water from the Nile. You may also catch sight of a cargo boat laden with *ballas* being shipped northwards. In ancient times Qena, like Qift, was linked by a trade route to the Red Sea, but today it is of no particular significance.

At this point the river takes a great curve to the southwest before continuing its flow north. Within the curve is the first port of call, **Dandarah** ❹, famed for its great **Temple of Hathor** (Oct–Apr 7am–4pm, May–Sept 6am–5pm; entries stop one hour before closing; charge).

Although just a kilometre or so from the bank of the Nile, the temple is hidden by copious palm trees, and lies on the edge of the fertile plain with desert behind. Sacred to the cow-goddess Hathor, the temple was begun by Ptolemy IX (116–107 BC) and completed in the Roman era 250 years later. In dedicating a temple to Egypt's cow-goddess, the Ptolemaic kings were honouring one of Egypt's best-loved deities. Usually depicted as a cow, Hathor was sometimes portrayed as a female figure with the head of a cow, and there are representations of her in most Egyptian temples.

Temple of Hathor

The Temple of Hathor, like that of Horus at Edfu, is one of the best preserved and most lavishly decorated in Egypt, even though some of the chapels and chambers were used as homes by local people after it ceased to be a place of worship. Some residents even stayed right up until the early 20th century, surrounded by the rubble of the largely decaying outer walls.

Unlike most temples, it is not approached by a pylon and peristyle court but via the pillared facade of the **Hypostyle Hall**, where 24 Hathor-headed columns support a roof divided into seven registers and decorated with remarkable astrological scenes depicting the six signs of the Egyptian zodiac (the crab, the twins, the bull, the ram, the fishes and the water-carrier), the stars and the phases of the moon. The

BELOW RIGHT: Temple of Hathor.

Travel Restrictions Lifted

Following the rise of militant Islamic fundamentalism in the early 1990s, the Egyptian government clamped down on regional threats, resulting in the imprisonment of the leaders of the movements. One theory for the increase in terrorism is attributed to the area's predominantly rural employment base focusing largely on the sugar cane crop. As prices dropped, so did livelihoods, and with nowhere to turn for money, young men turned to revolution. Religious tensions between Muslims and Copts added fuel to the fire, prompting the armed forces and police to take action.

The massacre of 58 foreigners and four Egyptians at Queen Hatshepsut's Temple in Thebes in 1997 proved to be a turning point for the worse. Travel convoys became mandatory for tourists covering long distances. Checkpoints sprung up at regular intervals along the main roads and papers were needed at each stop. In 2009, the convoys finally disappeared, allowing freedom of movement as far as Abydos. Tourists can now negotiate independent travel with taxis at a time of their convenience. Leave early enough and you will arrive at the temples in the area long before any of the tour buses do.

Boats also make the trip as far as Dandarah. It's a relaxing journey, with fewer cruisers or feluccas accompanying you along the river past Luxor. Those wishing to visit Abydos can hire a taxi on arrival in Dandarah.

original colours have been revealed in their true glory following an ongoing cleaning and conservation project.

Hathor and Horus

Proceed through the smaller, inner temple, to the **Hall of the Company of Nine Gods**. A series of reliefs here link the traditions of Hathor of Dandarah with those of Horus of Edfu. Husband and wife, Horus and Hathor were deities of equal standing, and at both sites the triad consisted of Hathor, Horus and their son. Twice a year, on the occasion of the birthday of each deity, the "Festival of the Good Union" was celebrated. Reliefs on the walls of the staircase leading to the roof of the Temple of Hathor – approached from the antechamber to the rear of the second hypostyle hall, and affording an excellent view of desert and floodplain – describe the event.

The small chapel on the roof of the temple housed the sacred statue that would, at the start of the festival, be taken out of its shrine for the reunion. The vessel bearing the statue of Hathor would be carried upstream, while that of Horus would set off downstream, each in a splendid procession. Where the boats came together, they were encircled by a rope cast by other vessels, in a gesture of unity. Then the river craft would proceed to the appropriate temple to celebrate the reunion of husband and wife amidst joy, song and prayer. The mere mortals celebrated the union by copying the gods, or by getting drunk.

In the Ptolemaic period, Hathor was identified with the Greek goddess Aphrodite and began to enjoy immense popularity as "Mistress of music, dance and joy". However, some of the dignity of Hathor as the mother-goddess sacred to the Egyptians was lost when her temple became the "home of intoxication and place of enjoyment". Among the Roman emperors depicted in the temple are Augustus, Tiberius, Caligula, Claudius and Nero, who all played a role in the temple's construction.

The Temple of Hathor, one of the best-preserved ancient temples in Egypt.

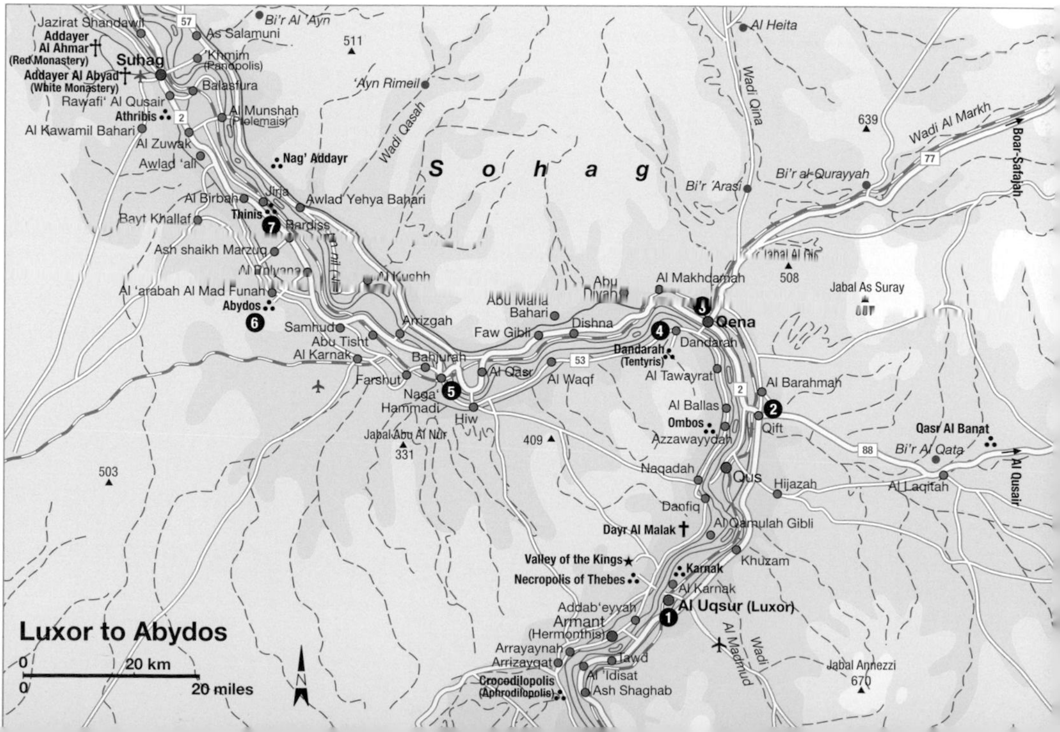

Entrance gateway at the Temple of Hathor.

While she might be associated with beauty, Hathor failed to seduce early Christians, who destroyed many of her depictions in the temple complex. All the faces atop each pillar have been subjected to vandalism as Christians tried to erase signs of the old religion.

In the precincts of the temple are two Roman-era "**birth houses**" containing scenes of the birth of Hor-sma-tawny, the son of Hathor and Horus. Nearby is a Christian **basilica**. It is one of the earliest Roman basilicas and may be the 4th-century Christian centre where 50,000 monks assembled to celebrate Easter, an event described by St Jerome as taking place somewhere in the neighbourhood of Dandarah.

Before departing, be sure to take a walk around the temple exterior for a view of one of the only depictions of Cleopatra VII. The famous female pharaoh is shown in relief on the rear exterior wall with Caesarion, her son by Julius Caesar, making offerings to Hathor. Cleopatra commissioned a great deal of work at the temple complex, continuing construction following the death of her father.

Christian sites

The river now continues its great sweep from east to west, so that the eastern bank of the Nile is to the north, and the western to the south. The tiny village of **Faw Gibli** to the north is the site of the **Basilica of St Pachomius**. Born in Thebes in AD 292 to pagan parents, Pachomius converted to Christianity as a young man, devoted to the ascetic Palamon *(see page 213)*. He went on to establish nine monasteries along the Nile and is considered to be the father of monasticism.

As the Nile continues north, the rugged cliffs of **Jabal At tarif** become visible. They often appear murky against the skyline, especially when the sun is overhead, but look closely and you will see that they are of immense height. This was the range of hills where the Gnostic codices, or books – as famous and as important as the Dead Sea Scrolls

BELOW: riding the sugar-cane train.

– were discovered in 1945. Now the 12 codices, known as the Naga' Hammadi Library *(see page 46)*, are housed in the Coptic Museum in Cairo.

The Hammadi codices

Accounts of the discovery differ. According to one, a huge boulder fell off a slope revealing a jar that was found by peasant farmers. In another account, two brothers chanced upon the jars while they were digging for fertiliser. It may be that the codices themselves were deliberately hidden when the Byzantine Church stamped out what it regarded as heretical Christian groups.

The 12 Hammadi codices were collected by Egyptians and translated into Coptic, the Egyptian language of the time. They vary widely in content, presenting a spectrum of heritages that range from Egyptian folklore, hereticism, Greek philosophy and Persian mysticism to the Old and New Testaments.

Christian sites in this part of Upper Egypt become more numerous from this point on, although few can be seen as you sail along the river. Within a great loop of the Nile at Al Qasr the land is extremely fertile and picturesque. Look out for the **Monastery of St Palomon**, the bell-tower and latticed walls of which can be seen rising above the surrounding agricultural land. St Palomon, or Anba Balamun in Arabic, was one of the earliest anchorites in Upper Egypt and was said to have died from excessive fasting. A *mawlid* or annual celebration is still observed in his honour.

Naga' Hammadi ❺ is a large and sprawling provincial town. Its population exploded in the 1960s when a large refinery and an aluminium factory were built here. A bridge crosses the Nile at this point, and cruiseboats, when sailing this far north *(see box, page 210)*, dock here, their passengers transferring to buses to visit the archaeological site of Abydos. Those who wish to venture even further north to see the many sites of Middle Egypt can hire a taxi from this point.

Abydos and the Osiris legend

Abydos ❻ (daily, Oct–Apr 7am–5pm, May–Sept 7am–6pm; charge) lies on the west bank of the Nile, 30km (18 miles) from Naga' Hammadi. Al Balyana is its nearest riverside town, and a broad plain leads to the village of Al 'arabah Al Mad Funah, which flanks the site.

Abydos was one of Egypt's most important cities. Not only was it associated with the kings of Ancient Egypt's founding dynasties, who came from nearby Thinis *(see page 216)*, but also with the great god Osiris *(see page 217)*. Ancient Egyptians aspired to make a pilgrimage to the revered city of Osiris at least once in a lifetime, just as today devout Muslims journey to Mecca, or Christians and Jews go on pilgrimages to Jerusalem. The ancients also aspired to be buried here. The temple was the cult centre of Osiris, Egypt's most beloved god, whose legend is depicted in the wall reliefs of many Egyptian temples. Osiris might have been an

TIP

Changes in the convoy guidelines mean that few tourists are aware of the ability to travel freely in the region. Go to Abydos early in the morning and you might have the entire temple complex to yourself.

BELOW: entrance to the Temple of Hathor.

Guardians share a simple meal below the temple walls at Abydos.

actual king of Egypt who was so loved by his people that his memory lingered on long after his death, passing from generation to generation.

The temples

Abydos reached its zenith during the New Kingdom (1567–1070 BC), when pharaohs left signs of their devotion in the great monuments they erected there. The most frequently visited of these are the temples of **Sety I** and Rameses II.

The former, begun by Sety I and completed by his son Rameses II, is considered one of the most beautiful in Egypt. Sety encouraged an artistic and architectural revival during his reign, and the temple is decorated with finely carved and coloured reliefs, in a good state of preservation.

Scenes on the eastern and northern walls of the hypostyle hall are particularly interesting in that they record the pharaoh's active participation in the planning of the temple. He is portrayed, in one scene, facing the goddess Seshat, the patron deity of records and archives, who is shown driving stakes into the earth to measure out the ground-plan. Behind her, Osiris watches over the activities being conducted on his behalf. Above is a scene of Sety, assisted by Horus, stretching out a measuring rope.

In each of the shrines of the temple seven scenes depict daily ceremonies that were performed by the priests. They include burning incense, perfuming and anointing the statue of the deity, adorning it with a crown and jewels, and then withdrawing backwards, while brushing away all footprints from the shrine before finally closing the door.

The reliefs display a naturalism unusual in the conservative canons of Egyptian art. The many representations of Sety, for example, may appear carbon copies of one another, but, on close scrutiny, they are found to differ. As the king looks into the face of an honoured deity, his expression is one of reverence. Before a goddess, there is a look of loving trust. Facing one of the great gods, he bends slightly at the waist to indicate awe.

Such emotional expression is rarely found in temples, as the pharaoh is gen-

BELOW: the Temple of Sety I.

Map on page 211

erally depicted larger than life, standing proudly erect and exalted. In the Temple of Sety, even the gods have human emotions: Osiris looks benevolent and majestic; Isis is gracious and tender; Horus is competent and direct.

List of Kings

To the rear of the temple is a wall covered with a record of Egypt's ancient rulers, known as the **List of Kings**. Containing the cartouches of 76 pharaohs, it has formed the basis of much of our understanding of pharaonic chronology. There are, however, notable omissions from the list: Queen Hatshepsut and Kings Amenhotep (Akhenaten) and Tutankhamun. Originally, the **Temple of Rameses II** (now in poor condition), northwest of the Temple of Sety I, also contained a list of kings; segments of this are now in the British Museum in London.

By the Graeco-Roman period, Abydos had come to be regarded as a place of healing. Sufferers from all over Egypt and, indeed, all over the Graeco-Roman world gathered in the corridors and halls of the temple of Sety to make humble pleas for health or fertility. Graffiti on the walls in hieratic (a late form of hieroglyphics), Greek, Phoenician and Aramaic attest to this.

Unfortunately, the Temple of Sety, like others throughout Egypt, is suffering from sub-soil water and air pollution. One of the most seriously threatened parts of the temple is a separate structure that lies behind the main temple, known as the **Osirion**. It is sunk into a depression and has variously been called a cenotaph and a mortuary temple. Most experts think it was built for Sety I, so that his body could rest here, in the company of Osiris, before being entombed in Thebes.

Sacred spot

There is a long-standing tradition of the sanctity of the area around the Osirion, and when the 13th Dynasty pharaoh Neferhotep (*c.*1786 BC) erected a boundary stele at Abydos, it stated that none should set foot in the sacred place. Up until the time of its restoration in the 1980s, the waters of the Osirion were regarded as advantageous to health. This recalls the hundreds of texts

Interior view of the Temple of Sety I, Abydos.

BELOW: an artist's impression.

Ancient rituals were revived last century at Abydos following the arrival of Umm Sety (mother of Sety), an Englishwoman by the name of Dorothy Eady who claimed she was the reincarnation of a virgin priestess. While some write her off as a lunatic, many finds at Abydos were only located through intervention from Eady based on her "memories".

connecting Osiris with Abydos, with water and with rebirth, in which this most beloved figure of ancient Egyptian tradition "sleeps in the midst of water".

Vestiges of powerful magic still cling to the spot. Local women, who blithely mix elements of paganism with Islamic or Christian beliefs, can sometimes be seen circling the pool of the Osirion. An English mystic, deeply versed in Egyptian history and religion, spent the last 25 years of her life living at Abydos, working daily in the temple and living in the nearby village of Qerbah. To the local people she was known as Umm Sety *(see margin)*.

The pollution and steep pathway down to the pool of Osirion should be enough to persuade you that a dip in the pool is ill-advised.

Oldest cemetery

Slightly to the north of Abydos is the site of ancient **Thinis** ❼, the home town of Narmer (Menes), the first pharaoh, who is credited with the unification of the two lands of Upper and Lower Egypt around 3100 BC. Narmer and his successors ruled from Memphis, the apex of the Delta, but they never forgot their ancestral home. Among the barren hills west of Abydos they constructed impressive cenotaphs where people could make offerings.

Generation after generation left offerings in pottery vessels, particularly at the cenotaph of the 1st Dynasty pharaoh Djer, which was considered to be the actual tomb of Osiris. Today the site has acquired the name **Um Al Gab**, or "mother of potsherds". It is not on the tourist trail, but for those with time to spare, this archaic cemetery, approached from a track leading westwards from the village of Qerbah, is worth seeing.

The huge funerary structures are believed to be the cenotaphs of Ancient Egypt's earliest kings, who were buried in similar graves on the Saqqarah Plateau. The huge outer walls of the tombs were decorated with recessed panelling, and surrounding them were two enclosure walls built of mud-brick. The subterranean chambers, hewn deep into the bedrock, contained funerary equipment such as tools, weapons and stone and copper vessels, as well as jewellery. Surrounding many of the tombs were subsidiary graves for the retainers of the deceased pharaoh, who, as and when they died, were buried in the vicinity of their monarch in order to serve him in the afterlife as dutifully as they had served him on earth.

Before leaving Abydos, it should be mentioned that, according to some of the mortuary texts, the "afterlife" lay in a gap in the mountains to the west of here. Indeed, the afterlife is depicted as a long mountainous valley with a river running through it; the banks are lined with wheatfields, fruit orchards and gardens of flowers. Here the deceased would enjoy hunting and fishing forever in the "Field of Reeds". ❑

LEFT: excavations in progress at Abydos.
ABOVE RIGHT: painting of Sety I before Horus from the Temple of Sety I at Abydos.
RIGHT: statues of Horus, Osiris and Isis, now housed in the Louvre.

Map on page 211

The Cult of Osiris

The Greek historian Plutarch in the 1st century AD was the first to record a coherent account of the Osiris legend

Plutarch described Osiris as the creator of law and agriculture, who, with his wife Isis at his side, ruled the world with justice. His brother Seth, however, was jealous and conspired against him. At a banquet, he tricked Osiris into entering a chest, which was then slammed closed, sealed and thrown into the Nile.

The broken-hearted Isis wandered far and wide in misery seeking the body of her beloved husband. Accompanied on her sad mission by the goddess Nepthys, she eventually found the body entangled in a tamarisk bush in the marshes of the Delta. She carefully hid it, but the vicious Seth, out boar-hunting, came across the body and cut it into 14 pieces, scattering them in all directions. The dismayed Isis searched out the pieces of her husband's body and at each spot where a part was found a monument was erected. Isis sought the help of the jackal-god Anubis – the god of embalming and greeter of the dead in the underworld – to prepare the body for burial. While he carried out her orders, Isis wept then prayed. She transformed herself into a bird (symbol of the spirit) to revive Osiris, but only managed to stir him long enough to impregnate herself with his heir.

In due course she bore a son, Horus, whom she raised in the marshes of the Delta until he was strong enough to avenge his father's death by slaying Seth. Horus then set out to seek his father and raise him from the dead. The risen Osiris, however, could no longer reign in the kingdom on earth and now became king of the underworld, while Horus took over his terrestrial throne.

Interpreting the legend

This widely known and most loved of ancient legends has been subject to many interpretations. One of the functions of mythology is to explain certain natural, social or political ideas, and the mythical Osiris (who was associated with settled community living and hence involved in agriculture and the annual rebirth of the land) falling victim to Seth (who was associated with the desert) is thought to represent the constant battle against the encroaching sands.

Seth's act of tearing the body of Osiris to pieces and scattering its parts up and down the Nile Valley may be interpreted as the concept of sowing grain, following which, with the necessary incantations (like those performed by Isis and Nepthys), or rural festivals, the stalks of grain would be reborn as Osiris was reborn. Thus Horus, son of gods related to the rebirth of the land, triumphed over the desert (Seth) and became the prototype of the pharaohs.

The myth of Osiris had become so well known by the Middle Kingdom (2134–1633 BC) that thousands of pilgrims came to Abydos to pay homage to their legendary ancestor. They would travel long distances to witness the ritualistic killing of Osiris by his brother Seth, followed by several days of mourning and lamentation in the manner of Isis. At a prescribed site a mock battle took place between Horus, son of Osiris and Isis, and Seth his father's murderer. The death of Osiris was duly avenged, Horus became king and life would go on. ❑

MIDDLE EGYPT

The broad floodplains of Middle Egypt now see very few tourists, in spite of the stunning Middle Kingdom tombs of Beni Hasan and the important site of Tall Al Amarnah, the power base of Akhenaten

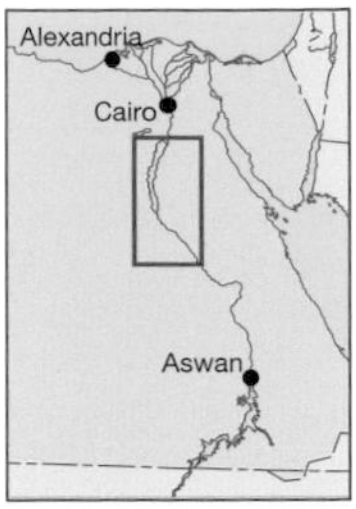

Main attractions
- TALL AL AMARNAH
- TUNAT AL JABAL
- AL ASHMUNEAN
- BENI HASAN

The term "Middle Egypt" describes the area between Abydos and Memphis. It is a long stretch, where the river is wide and flows a smooth course through verdant fields, with good paved roads on both sides of the river. The road on the east bank runs through the desert, while the west-bank route passes picturesque canals, cultivated fields, towns and villages. Despite the heavy traffic, the latter route is the more interesting one, especially for observing the rural scene; farmers can be seen at work at much closer quarters than is possible on a river cruise.

In ancient times, this central area was a distinct political entity, one of three. It was the Middle Kingdom pharaoh Senusret III (*c.* 1898 BC) who defined the first area, between Aswan and Abydos, as "the head" of Upper Egypt, the region from Abydos to Memphis as Upper Egypt (not Middle Egypt as it is called here) and the third region as the Delta.

Highlights of Middle Egypt

Although the archaeological sites of Middle Egypt are less well known than those of Upper Egypt, the region has four areas of special historic importance: **Tall Al Amarnah, Al Ashmunean, Tunat Al Jabal and Beni Hasan**. There are some tourist facilities at each of these – regular barge services across the river and vehicles for transport to the sites – and the local officials, guards and guides are refreshingly informative. However, because of terrorist incidents in the 1990s, travel between Al Menyyah and Luxor has been seriously restricted. There is a heavy police presence in the area and especially at the tourist sites. Convoys are no longer required, but you may get stopped and questioned during your journey through the region –

PRECEDING PAGES: flooded field prior to sowing the crop. **LEFT:** Coptic Christians prepare for Palm Sunday in Al Menyyah. **RIGHT:** domed tombs near Al Menyyah.

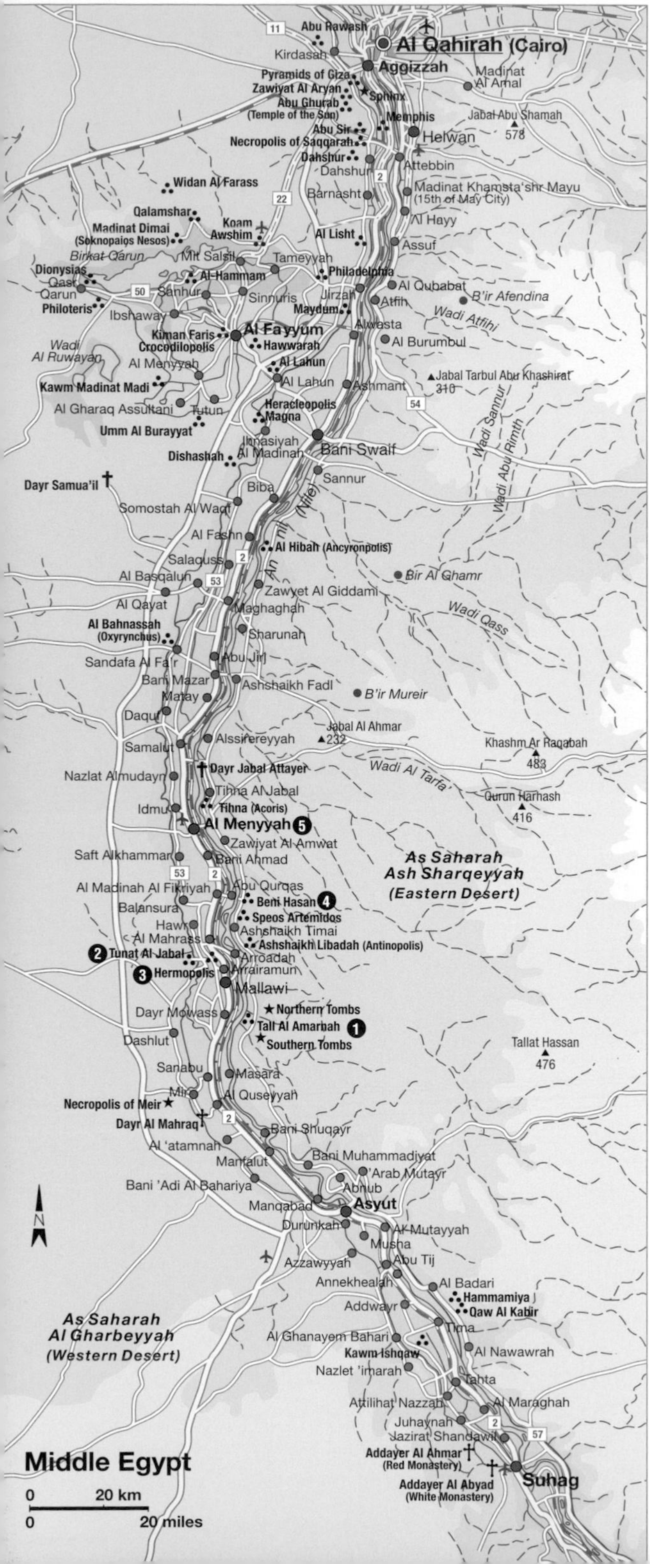

and the variety of independent travel methods is reduced. As Middle Egypt sees so few foreign tourists, you will stand out, so be prepared for increased requests for papers and *baksheesh* *(see also page 210)*.

Akhenaten's city

Tall Al Amarnah ❶ (daily 8am–5pm; charge), known today simply as Amarnah, lies on the east bank of the Nile, approximately 385km (240 miles) north of Luxor, opposite the modern town of Dayr Mowass (a ferry takes visitors over to the east bank). It was the site chosen by the Pharaoh Akhenaten (formerly Amenhotep IV) to found a city dedicated to the worship of a single god, the Aten (literally the sun's disk), rather than the whole pantheon of gods worshipped by his predecessors who had founded Thebes.

When Akhenaten revolted against the priests of Amun-Ra at Thebes, he chose to base his new capital on this expansive crescent-shaped plain over 4km (2½ miles) long and about 800 metres (½ mile) across. The site had no history of cult activity, no earlier settlement nor any existing priesthood. Akhenaten called it Akhet-Aten, the "Horizon of Aten".

City-planning

At first sight Tall Al Amarnah appears to be devoid of ancient structures, and it is difficult to visualise a bustling city here. The site is a far cry from the legendary "hundred-gated Thebes", and this is because the city was totally razed after Akhenaten died. Once the priests of Amun-Ra had been reinstated and Luxor restored as capital, all evidence of the religion of the Aten and the rule of "the heretic" were obliterated. All that was left of Akhenaten's unique city were a few walls and columns little more than waist high.

Yet it is from these ruins and from ground-plans that archaeologists have been able to get their clearest picture of city-planning in ancient Egypt. Elsewhere the palaces and dwelling-places built of sun-dried brick perished. The city of Akhet-Aten, however, was constructed on a plain above the level of the flood and was occupied for such a brief time (it was never re-inhabited) that it provides a unique opportunity to learn how an ancient city developed.

The site was designed with three main streets running parallel to the river. The central quarter, which spreads south from the modern village of At till to Al Hag Qandil, was the main residential area and also the site of the temple of the Aten. Some of the ruins of these can still be seen.

To the north and south were habitations for officials and priests. The side streets contained the houses of the middle classes and their servants; the working classes, especially those employed on the necropolis, lived in special compounds to the east of the plain. Their houses were built on parallel streets and were uniform in size, apart from one larger house to each compound which probably belonged to the community's supervisor.

Akhenaten took up residence at Akhet-Aten in the eighth year of his reign, about 1367 BC. He set up boundary stelae on the cliffs on both sides of the Nile, recording an oath in the name of his "father", the Aten, that neither he, his wife (the beautiful Queen Nefertiti) nor children would pass the limits he was setting, and that the land would remain sacred to the Aten for ever. This was not to be. Shortly after the 14th year of his reign, Queen Nefertiti, for unknown reasons, took up residence in her northern palace. Akhenaten appointed his half-brother Smenkhara as co-regent, and died shortly afterwards. The sacred city, which was still under construction, was destroyed.

Tomb scenes

Akhenaten's body was not found, but his **Tomb** is approached through a long narrow valley between the two mountain ranges to the east. The tomb, now accessible to the public, is worth mentioning because studies suggest that it was not a single tomb but a tomb complex; it may originally have been intended for the entire royal family. This would make it unique among royal tombs, because kings were usually

TIP

The towns and sights of Middle Egypt are still difficult to reach for most tourists. Visitors cannot take public buses, and taxis are prevented from going north of Abydos (if travelling from Luxor). The best way to reach the region is on one of the three approved trains that leave Luxor and Cairo each day. Ask at the tourist office or train station for daily schedules.

BELOW: tomb at Tall Al Amarnah.

Copts account for about one-fifth of the population of Middle Egypt. At one time their peaceful cohabitation with the Muslim majority was held up as a model of Egyptian tolerance, but tensions have risen over recent years and antagonism is rife.

buried alone to ensure their safety.

The tombs of the noblemen at Tall Al Amarnah, however, can be visited, and it is from these that we get an insight into life during the short rule of Akhenaten. Although many were badly damaged, not all the reliefs were destroyed, and the most important ones have been carefully restored.

The tombs were hewn out of the rock and are similar in plan to the tombs of the 18th Dynasty at Thebes, with a forecourt leading to a large columned hall. Among the northern group of tombs, one of the largest and best preserved belongs to a high priest of the Aten called **Meri-Ra** (No. 4). In one of the reliefs Akhenaten can be seen at a palace window casting forth golden ornaments to the owner of the tomb. In another he is depicted driving from his palace in a chariot, preceded by guards and followed by the queen, the princesses and escorts, some in chariots and some on foot. Priests await their arrival at the temple, where, after the necessary prayers the royal couple emerge and are greeted by other priests. They then proceed to inspect the storehouses, barns and other chambers, some of which are enclosed in a garden.

Similar scenes are found in the tombs of **Pentu** (No. 5), the royal physician, **Ahmose** (No. 3), the fan-bearer, and **Panehesi** (No. 6), chief servitor of the Aten. The scenes were decorated in the realism characteristic of what has become known as the "Amarnah period". Unlike traditional ancient Egyptian art, in which the pharaoh ruled as a god and was symbolically depicted as a giant at a temple entrance and in relief, Akhenaten was portrayed quite naturalistically. He is often shown as the same size as his people, as a mortal rather than as an aloof ruler, a family man who could delight in his daughters, eat a hearty meal and demonstrate tender affection.

Fragments of slabs carved in relief were found in many homes at Amarnah. They show figures of the royal family making offerings to the Aten, with a clear message: adore the one whom Akhenaten adores, and make offerings directly to the one to whom Akhenaten makes offerings.

BELOW RIGHT: in the tomb of Meri-Ra at Tall Al Amarnah.

Worship of the Sun-God

Akhenaten's introduction of the worship of one god, Aten (the disk of the sun), is frequently regarded as a form of monotheism, and in Akhenaten himself some scholars have seen metaphysical reasoning far ahead of his time. He has been variously described as a mystic and ascetic, and alternatively as a rebel and fanatic.

In fact, worship of the Aten was not so much a new realm of thought, since worship of the sun in one form or another was a constant thread throughout ancient Egyptian history. The novelty lay in the recognition of the unlimited power of the sun-god as the creator and preserver of all mankind. The celebrated hymn, which is inscribed in the tomb of one of his officials, has been ascribed to Akhenaten himself: "O living Aten… how manifold are thy works… thou sole god, like to whom there is no other. Thou didst create the earth after thy heart… even all men, herds and flocks, whatever is upon the earth, creatures that walk upon feet, which soar aloft flying with their wings…" (From a translation by Sir A. Gardiner in *Egypt of the Pharaohs*, Clarendon Press, Oxford.)

Ibis worship

A few kilometres to the north and on the opposite bank of the river is the town of **Mallawi**. Once the regional capital, it was usurped as the most prominent town in the area by Al Menyyah in 1824. Mallawi has a small **museum** (Sat–Thur 8am–3pm; charge), housing a collection of finds from the nearby sites of Tunat Al Jabal and Hermopolis.

Tunat Al Jabal ❷ (7am–4pm; charge), located a couple of kilometres to the northeast, is a unique archaeological site devoted to the mummified remains of the sacred ibis – also sacred to Thoth. This was the necropolis that the inhabitants of Hermopolis would visit. The ibis compound has been identified and near it is an extremely deep well fed by a waterwheel not unlike those that are still used for irrigation today. The ibis galleries themselves are long underground passages leading to the chambers where the mummified ibis and baboons were interred. Although most of the remains are now in the nearby museum in Mallawi, there are still plenty in situ.

There are several tombs at Tunat Al Jabal, one of which is well worth seeing. It is the **Tomb of Petosiris** (dating from around 300 BC), in which eight generations of high priests of Thoth at Hermopolis were buried. Although the facade is decorated with traditional Egyptian reliefs showing the deceased making offerings before the more important deities, the inside is covered in charming scenes displaying a particularly strong Greek influence in their workmanship. The scenes themselves are traditional – farming, hunting and fowling – but the farmers are portrayed with thick jowls, muscular legs and togas that are decidedly non-Egyptian. Not only do the men have curly hair, but the branches of the trees also curl, and so do the horns of the animals.

Behind the tomb spreads a large cemetery dating from late Ramesside times to the Roman period. It includes many house-tombs in which relatives of the dead could reside during festivals for the dead. The guardian will probably draw your attention to a small house-tomb which belongs to

Scene near Tunat Al Jabal.

BELOW: a marriage ceremony in Asyut.

Nefertiti lived up to her name, which meant "A beautiful woman has come", as the bust of her in the Egyptian Museum in Berlin (see page 34) *proves. When Amenhotep IV changed his name to Akhenaten "Horizon of Aten", Nefertiti changed hers to Nefernefruaten, or "Beautiful are the beauties of Aten".*

a girl called Isadora who drowned in the Nile in 120 BC. The mummy is surprisingly well preserved, with hair and teeth still visible.

Beak-headed Thoth

Hermopolis ❸, 10km (6 miles) north-east of Tunat Al Jabal, is known under its modern name of Al Ashmunean. A good road from Mallawi runs across the fertile floodplain towards the site, which, even in its ruined state, can be clearly seen in a picturesque palm-grove.

This was the site of the ancient Egyptian city of Khnumi, where Thoth, the beak-headed god of wisdom, was worshipped. Represented as an ibis or a baboon, Thoth was also viewed as the god of science and medicine, since it was Thoth that cured Horus' scorpion sting. To keep a record of the judgement of the dead, Thoth invented hieroglpyphics and became the scribe in the Hall of Judgement.

Of the original pharaonic site, however, little remains apart from two gigantic statues of baboons, sacred animals of Thoth, which were erected in front of the Temple of Thoth by Amenhotep III (1402–1364 BC). In the centre of the city is a low mound surmounted by red granite columns. Though originally thought to be an *agora* (market place), dating from Greek times, it is now known that it was a Christian basilica built of columns from an earlier temple erected by Ptolemy III (246–221 BC).

The Greeks identified Thoth with one of their own gods, Hermes, and under Greek rule the province experienced a revival.

Rock chambers

Beni Hasan ❹ (daily, Oct–Apr 7am–4pm, May–Sept 7am–5pm; charge) is located on the east bank of the Nile, 40km (25 miles) north of Tall Al Amarnah, opposite the modern town of Abu Qurqas; it's named after an Arab tribe that settled in the area in the 9th century. The site is famous for its Middle Kingdom tombs, dating from around 2000 BC. At one time Beni Hasan was seldom visited, as it was not easily accessible. The reliefs on the tombs were in poor condition, owing to the site's occupation by Christian hermits during the persecu-

BELOW: remains of a Christian basilica at Al Ashmunayn.

tions of Decius and Diocletian in the 2nd and 3rd centuries AD, and most of the wall paintings were blackened with soot from open fires and dulled by time and neglect.

But all that has changed. Access to the site is now easy, and the paintings have been superbly restored, some of the colours appearing as fresh as on the day they were painted.

The tombs comprise a long series of rock-hewn chambers about 200 metres (655ft) above the floodplain, extending for several kilometres along the face of the cliff. The most interesting group of 39 chambers, in the upper range, belong to noblemen who governed the province some 4,000 years ago. They have simple facades, some with elegant octagonal columns and others with 16-sided columns flanking the entrance doorways.

Inside, the main chambers have triple-vaulted ceilings, with two rows of rock-hewn pillars. The walls are adorned throughout with vivid scenes. The tomb belonging to the governor and commander-in-chief **Amenemhat** (tomb No. 4) includes a scene (near the centre of the left-hand wall) of a caravan of Semites arriving in Egypt with their herds; they are characterised by hook noses and multicoloured robes.

This representation dates from the time when Abraham, the "father of many nations", is believed to have lived (about 1900 BC). It was a period when food was scarce in the land of Canaan and "Abraham went down into Egypt to sojourn there, for the famine was grievous in the land" (Genesis 12:10). Egypt, by then, was a long-settled monarchy with Egyptian governors at the seaports on the Phoenician coast and, as is clear from this representation, willing to welcome strangers.

Another noteworthy scene painted in the same tomb, above the doorway leading into the inner shrine, shows Amenemhat hunting in the marshes. It shows the nobleman seated behind a hide made of reeds, from where he can observe hoopoes in a papyrus thicket. These, and other vivid scenes of men hunting, fishing and wrestling, and of women weaving, present a panorama of the everyday life of governors, courtiers and princes who lived in Upper Egypt during the Middle Kingdom.

The perfect base

Visitors keen to see the best of the region should, if circumstances permit, arrange overnight accommodation in **Al Menyyah** ❺ (Al-Minya), the principal town of the province, about 250km (155 miles) south of Cairo, which marks the divide between Upper and Lower Egypt. A good springboard for visiting the sites south of the city, it has the only choice of remotely international-standard hotels in the region – the best being the comfortable, yet tired, Nefertiti.

The town itself has some lovely early 20th-century buildings, and a popular souq crammed with stalls near the town centre. On the east bank is the impressive Zouhreyyet Al Mayteen, a very large Muslim and Christian cemetery with hundreds of mud domes. ❑

Statue of a baboon at Hermopolis. Baboons were sacred to Thoth, the god of wisdom. The annual Festival of Thoth, held when the Nile's flood waters began to rise each year, was one of the most important in the land.

BELOW: traffic in Al Menyyah.

MEMPHIS, SAQQARAH AND GIZA

This area close to modern Cairo was the power base of the Old Kingdom. Its capital was Memphis and its rulers were buried in the tombs and Pyramids of Saqqarah and Giza

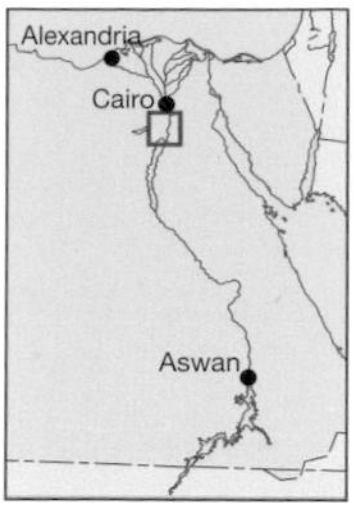

The Mediterranean Sea once reached at least to the foot of the Tal Al Muqattam that shelters modern Cairo to the east, and probably even as far south as ancient **Memphis**. In other words, the vast triangle of the Nile Delta that exists today was once a wide bay. This bay was gradually filled up by the ceaseless accumulation of alluvial deposits.

But it is not just the alluvial deposits that have made their mark on the geography of the region. Overpopulation is also affecting the ancient capital. The Giza Plateau has already been swallowed up by Cairo's growing suburbs, while Memphis and Saqqarah will be going the same way if population growth continues along its current trajectory.

The first capital

Memphis ❶, the first capital of Upper and Lower Egypt, was founded, according to legend, by King Menes, traditionally identified as the first king of the 1st Dynasty, who united Upper and Lower Egypt. The city stood at the apex of the Delta, and for 1,000 years it held the title of capital; even with the growth of other cities, it retained its importance as a religious and commercial centre right through to Graeco-Roman times. The necropolis of the ancient city was situated at nearby Saqqarah, though the Pyramids of the Memphite kings were built along the desert edge over a distance of about 30km (18 miles) from Abu Rawash to **Dahshur** *(see page 240)*. However, the most spectacular was the **Great Pyramid at Giza**, which ranked among the Seven Wonders of the Ancient World.

Memphis is situated on the west bank of the Nile some 25km (15 miles) south of Giza and almost opposite modern Cairo's suburb of Al Ma'adi. It was honoured by Egypt's most famous kings (some of whom built

Main attractions
- MEMPHIS
- STEP PYRAMID OF SAQQARAH
- IMHOTEP MUSEUM
- NOBLEMEN'S TOMBS
- PYRAMIDS OF GIZA
- MENA HOUSE OBEROI
- SOLAR BOAT MUSEUM
- THE SPHINX
- DAHSHUR

PRECEDING PAGES: the Great Pyramids of Giza. **LEFT:** date palms near Memphis. **RIGHT:** the Sphinx and the Pyramid of Khafra.

It was one of the names of Memphis, Hikaptah, "House of the ka *[spirit] of Ptah" that gave Egypt its name. This became Agyptos in Greek and hence "Egypt". The Arabic word for Egypt (Misr) is also the word for Cairo.*

palaces there), as the place where they were crowned. The city was lauded by classical writers in glowing terms, and was regarded as a place of pilgrimage or refuge. It was so great that any who sought control of Egypt knew that they first had to take Memphis.

Little remains of the ancient city today. Even the Temple of Ptah, one of the great gods of Ancient Egypt, is in ruin, and most of that ruin lies beneath and around the mound on which the modern village of **Mit Rahinah** stands. It is hard to imagine this derelict place as the former heart of one of the most important, heavily populated cities in Ancient Egypt.

Memphis is no more. It has suffered the ravages of war, fanaticism and time. Its monuments have been torn down, usurped, pillaged and used as quarry material. Whatever remained of the ancient city was buried beneath alluvial soil that started to build up in medieval times when the canals were neglected. Where once stood a mighty metropolis with a river port, factories and settlements, modern-day villagers cultivate date palms in the enriched earth.

Essential monuments

Because of the scanty remains, most visits to Memphis focus on the monuments in the **museum compound** (daily, Oct–Apr 8am–4pm, May–Sept 7.30am–5pm; charge), where the tourist buses park and where there is a café and shops selling imitation antiquities.

The main feature of the compound is a statue of Rameses II in a covered enclosure. Regarded as the finest statue of this pharaoh ever carved, it lies in a horizontal position and can only be viewed properly from the gallery. Part of the crown and the lower legs are missing, but the fine craftsmanship is apparent in the details of the king's mouth, with indentations at the corners, the muscular shoulders and the sturdy torso. The royal name, in an oblong cartouche, can be seen on the right shoulder, the breast and on the pharaoh's girdle.

There are two other objects of particular note in the museum compound – the **alabaster sphinx**, which is the largest statue ever found made of this stone (it weighs 80 tonnes and has been attributed to either Amenhotep I or

BELOW: alabaster sphinx at Memphis.

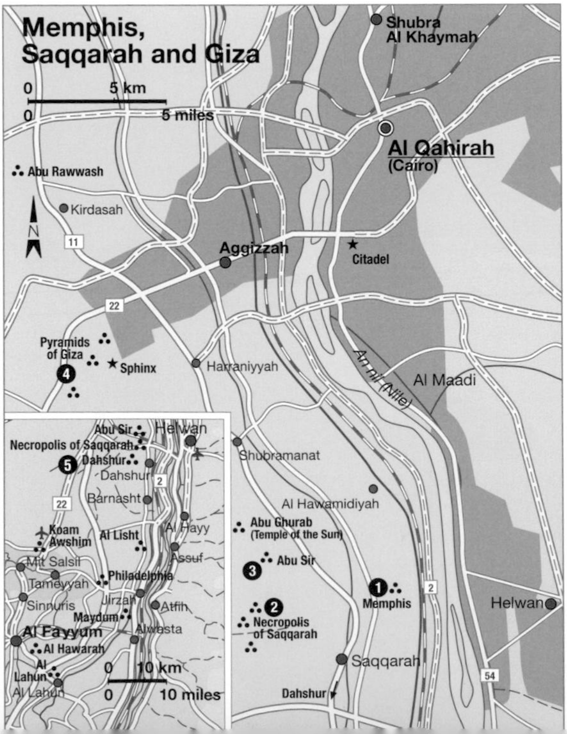

Thutmose I), and the **Stele of Apries**, a huge round-topped stone slab erected by the 26th Dynasty pharaoh, which bears an important historical text and figures of the gods Ptah and Sokar.

Despite its importance and occupation for thousands of years, less than 10 percent of the city of Memphis has ever been excavated. The Survey of Memphis is an Egypt Exploration Society project (www.ees.ac.uk) which is attempting to draw together all existing material (including those relics which are now in museums worldwide), excavate the site systematically and draw up a stratified map of ancient Memphis.

First Pyramids

To the southwest of Memphis on a very arid plateau is **Saqqarah** ❷ (daily 8am–4pm; charge), the ancient city's necropolis and one of the most important sites in Egypt. Its name is derived from Sokar, an agricultural god believed to dwell in the earth; the annual Festival of Sokar took place at the "White Wall of Memphis". Herds of draught animals would be driven round the walls of the ancient city, as if going round a threshing floor, in a ritual to awaken the soil. Because Sokar lived in the earth, he also came to be regarded as one of the gods of the dead, hence the adoption of his name for the whole necropolis.

Dominating the horizon of Saqqarah is the **Step Pyramid** Ⓐ, the central feature of a funerary complex built by Imhotep for Pharaoh Djoser, the first king of the 3rd Dynasty in 2686 BC. Djoser's reign marks the beginning of the Old Kingdom or "Pyramid Age", an era of great vision and invention.

Just behind the ticket office is the **Imhotep Museum** (daily 9am–4pm; charge), a new museum honouring the contributions made by the great architect Imhotep and filled with artefacts found at the site – many chronicling the ancient construction methods used to build the Pyramid at Saqqarah.

Until Saqqarah was built, no stone had ever been used for large-scale construction and there was no architectural tradition from which to draw. But Imhotep, a brilliant innovator, builder and "wise man", whose sayings were quoted for thousands of years,

TIP

A new complex, completed in 2008, now greets all visitors to the site. If you are taking a taxi, ask your driver to stop here so you can purchase entry tickets before driving up the hill, as there is no ticket office beyond. You may also want to use the facilities while you're here. Unlike most toilets in Egypt, which look like ancient monuments and smell like tombs, these are modern (and clean).

BELOW LEFT: entrance corridor to Djoser's pyramid complex at Saqqarah.

Visiting the Pyramids

You may think you've experienced crowds during your visit to the temples and museums of Egypt, but you haven't quite experienced anything until you visit the Pyramids of Giza. Included on every "must-see" checklist, the pyramids are at their busiest mid-morning when tour buses arrive, and on Thursdays and Fridays when visitors from cruise ships and day-trippers from the Sinai resorts descend.

If you want to go inside one of the Pyramids, you will need to plan ahead. Only 100 tickets are released at two distribution times each day; 8am and 1pm. To stand a chance, arrive at least an hour early and queue up. There is currently a lot of restoration work being performed on the Step Pyramid to ensure its survival. Check in advance to find out how close you can get to the structure on the day you plan to visit.

While it is possible to enjoy the experience of visiting the plateau on foot, horseback and camel adventures around the Pyramids can help you travel the large distances around the complex – and you're bound to be hassled into submission. If you can, try to book your tour before you reach the plateau at the stables near the Mena House Oberoi entrance, as it will reduce the price. Officially, a one-hour tour should cost E£35 and a short-tour E£20, but you will need to bargain. Experienced riders can even book a full-day tour from Giza to Saqqarah.

The Step Pyramid at Saqqarah, built by the ground-breaking architect Imhotep.

drew inspiration from contemporary buildings constructed of perishable materials: reeds, mud-brick and logs of wood. It is thanks to his genius that we can see today, sculpted in stone, how bundles of reeds were tied together with the heads fanning out to form the earliest capital; how logs were laid across parallel walls to form a roof; and how reed fences separated property. In short, the detail of Saqqarah mirrors the structures of the state capital of Memphis, which, as already mentioned, have almost disappeared.

The Step Pyramid, which rises in six unequal tiers, originally had one single step. This was the superstructure over the burial chamber. But during the long reign of Djoser the structure underwent no fewer than five alterations: the ground plan was successively enlarged, and the height was increased in stages until, superimposed on top of one another, the six steps of the terraced structure emerged in their final form. Imhotep's Step Pyramid is the forerunner of the true Pyramid, which reached its apogee in the three magnificent 4th Dynasty Pyramids at Giza *(see page 236)*. At the back of the Step Pyramid, don't miss seeing the *serdab*, a box with a life-size statue of Djoser staring towards the North Star in the hope of immortality.

The Pyramid Texts

Among the other structures on the Saqqarah Plateau are several 5th and 6th Dynasty Pyramids, which were built of poor-quality local limestone and fell to ruin when the outer casings were removed. Although unimpressive from the outside, they are of great interest and historical importance because many are inscribed with mortuary literature known as the Pyramid Texts. (The Giza Pyramids, incidentally, were not decorated at all.)

Long columns of inscribed hieroglyphics, the texts include hymns, prayers and rituals for the deceased pharaoh, as well as lists of offerings of food, drink and clothing for the afterlife. They are beautifully carved into the stone and filled with blue or green pigment. In the 5th Dynasty **Pyramid of Unas B**, for example, which was built about 2345 BC and situated out-

BELOW: statue of a nobleman, now in the Imhotep Museum, Saqqarah.

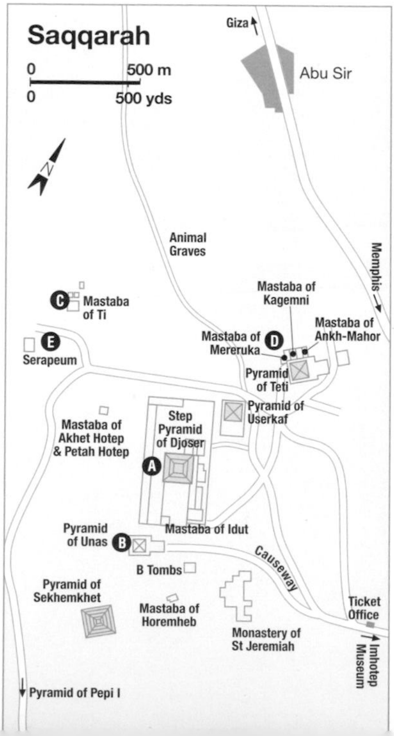

side the southwest corner of the Djoser Pyramid complex, the texts cover all the available space in the tomb chamber, apart from the walls behind and beside the empty sarcophagus, which are themselves painted to represent the facade of a building.

Near the boat pits of the Pyramid of Unas, you can visit several beautiful tombs, known as the **B Tombs** (extra charge). These include the tomb of the royal manicurists Niankhkhnum and Khnumhotep, the tomb of Neferherenptah, the chief of the royal hairdressers, and the Bird Tomb with a delightful bird-hunting scene.

The noblemen's tombs

It is from the **noblemen's tombs** (daily 8am–4pm; separate charge) dotted around the plateau, however, that we gain a real insight into everyday life in Ancient Egypt, especially from a group of tombs that date from the age of the Pyramid-builders. These are decorated with painted reliefs of everyday life, including agricultural activities, animal husbandry, hunting, various trades and industries, as well as family life.

The **Mastaba of Ti** C, a court dignitary, is one of the best preserved. It includes representations of the shipbuilding industry (in the offering chamber) which are particularly interesting, depicting every stage of the work from the unloading of the cedarwood – which was brought all the way across the Mediterranean from Byblos on the Phoenician coast in modern-day Lebanon – to the shaping of the hull, the sawing and the preparation of the planks of wood. Finally, the ship is shown in full sail.

Also in the offering chamber is a series of rural scenes, in one of which a grey cow gives birth with the help of a farmer, while, behind her, restive calves have their hind legs bound together or are tethered to pegs in the ground. Ti himself is charmingly depicted in the second corridor with his wife seated at his feet and being entertained by a flautist, two singers and two harpists.

The **Mastaba of Mereruka** D, the largest and finest of the Old Kingdom tombs at Saqqarah, is a family tomb, with chambers belonging to the nobleman himself, his wife and children,

SHOP

On the drive to Saqqarah, you may notice a number of carpet-making schools along the road towards the entrance. If you are travelling in a taxi, your driver may try to stop at one so you can see the weavers in action (and get a healthy cut of the sale if you buy anything). Be aware that if you enter any of the shops you will be subjected to a protracted and pressured sales pitch.

BELOW: entrance to the funerary complex of Djoser, Saqqarah.

Statue of an Apis bull with a sun-disk between its horns.

and it is decorated with scenes showing many different activities, such as the manufacture of jewellery from gold that is first weighed in a balance and registered by a scribe; pottery-making by workers who comment to each other on the excellence of one another's work; and life-size statues of the deceased being hauled to the tomb on sledges, found in the first chamber leading off the entrance chamber to the right.

The tombs of the Apis bulls

The **Serapeum** **E** (closed for restoration), is a vast sepulchre of rock-hewn galleries for the internment of the sacred Apis bull of Memphis. The tombs are hewn out of solid rock, and the flanking chambers contain mighty granite sarcophagi of an average weight of 65 tonnes each, and measuring some 4 metres (13ft) long by over 3 metres (9ft) high. Most of the lids are of solid granite.

When the discoverer of this sepulchre, the French archaeologist Mariette, first entered the galleries in 1851, he found that most of the sarcophagus lids had been pushed aside and the contents pillaged. Only one had been left intact because the robbers couldn't open it; Mariette succeeded where they had failed by using dynamite. Inside the sarcophagus he found a solid-gold statue of a bull that is now in the Louvre in Paris.

BELOW: the Great Pyramid.

Off the tourist trail

Most tourists to Cairo visit the Step Pyramid at Saqqarah and the Pyramid complexes in Giza, but there are many more buildings of note. In fact, between the beginning of the Pyramid Age in the 27th century BC and the end of the Middle Kingdom in the 18th century BC more than 80 Pyramids were built along the Nile between Giza and the oasis of Al Fayyum. For details of the Pyramids south of Saqqarah, *see page 240.*

On the road from Saqqarah to Giza, look for more Pyramids at **Abu Sir** **3**, including the **Pyramid of Neferirkara**, and the **Pyramid of Sahura**, around which the temple complexes have been relatively well preserved. A little further north is the Pyramid field of Zawiyat Al Aryan, with the **Unfinished Pyramid** made of granite blocks, and a Layer Pyramid, which was probably intended to be a Step Pyramid.

The Pyramids of Giza

The great **Pyramids of Giza** **4** (for the plateau: daily, Oct–Apr 8am–6pm, May–Sept 8am–4pm; for inside the Pyramids: 8am–4pm, 100 tickets distributed for Pyramid entry twice, a day at 8am and 1pm – *see box page 233*; separate charges for the Great Pyramid, the Solar Boat museum, Khafra's Pyramid and Menkaura's Pyramid) stand on a rocky plateau on the west bank of the Nile 25km (15 miles) north of Saqqarah, almost directly opposite Cairo. The Pyramids Road from Cairo is a dual carriageway that takes you to the foot of the desert plateau where the **Mena House Oberoi** hotel, escaping the fate of many other once-ancient hotels, greets guests daily.

It is not unusual for modern travellers to observe the Pyramids for the first time and say, "I thought they would be bigger." It is only when one has been on the plateau for several hours, looking at them in relation to people and the surrounding desert, that one starts to appreciate their incredible size. They are the most famous, intensely measured, studied and debated monuments in the world, and also, probably, the least understood. The geometrical accuracy and technical skill that went into their making is truly awe-inspiring.

The **Great Pyramid** Ⓐ, which was built in honour of the 4th Dynasty pharaoh Khufu (Cheops) in *c.*2600 BC, is the sole survivor of the Seven Wonders of the Ancient World. Originally 147 metres (480ft) high and covering an area of 5 hectares (13 acres), the Pyramid was constructed of some 2.3 million blocks of stone of an average weight of 2.5 tonnes (some weighed as much as 16 tonnes), which were brought into contact to tolerances as close as 0.05mm (one 500th of an inch). The sides of the Pyramid themselves were oriented almost exactly true north, south, east and west, with the four corners again at perfect right angles. The maximum error in alignment has been calculated as being a little over one-twelfth of a degree.

The outlines of the Pyramids were once smooth and covered with a limestone facing that was fitted and polished, nowhere betraying an entrance. Apart from some extractions during the First Intermediate Period (2181–2055 BC), the limestone facing encased the Pyramid until a 13th-century earthquake loosened some of the stones. The Arabs then removed the limestone for use in construction of some of the celebrated buildings of Islamic Cairo, including the Mosque and Madrassah of Sultan Hassan. The Pyramid of Khafra still retains some of the original limestone near its peak.

After the death of the reigning pharaoh, his mummified body would be brought by river to the valley temple, from there to be borne on the shoulders of white-robed priests to the mortuary temple, where rituals and prayers were carried out before the internment of the body. The valley and mortuary temples were linked by a covered causeway.

EAT

The Khan Al Khalili restaurant in the Mena House Oberoi hotel is a wonderful place for tea or lunch just before or at the end of your visit to the Pyramids of Giza.

Giza Mapping Project

The Giza Plateau Mapping Project is an in-depth archaeological study of the plateau, its geology and topography. The aim of the project is to provide the first complete and detailed map of every feature of the plateau. It will enable, among other things, the identification of different qualities of stone used to build the pyramids with the bedrock from which they came.

For example, while good quality limestone for its outer casing came from the Tura quarries on the eastern bank of the Nile, local limestone of mediocre quality was used for constructing the main body of the pyramids around a core of bedrock that was left intact. While work is ongoing, public access to data and the plateau model is not permitted but some information is available at http://oi.uchicago.edu/research/projects/giz/.

BELOW: you can take a camel tour round the Pyramids.

TIP

Entering the Great Pyramid is not for the claustrophobic, as the corridor is low and narrow, and usually crowded with tourists. If you want to go inside a Pyramid, go to Dahshur, where there are far fewer crowds, it's easier to get a ticket, and the entry charge is limited to a few pounds of *baksheesh*.

After entering the Pyramid, you follow a corridor leading upwards at a steep gradient to the first chamber, the Great Gallery. This room is 47 metres (154ft) long, and continues along the same gradient as it goes deeper into the Pyramid. Near the top, the chamber narrows as it leads into the King's Chamber, located 96m (315ft) directly below the Pyramid's apex.

The King's Chamber was the final resting place of the pharaoh Khufu (Cheops). The walls are lined with red granite, and his now-empty sarcophagus remains inside the room. Be aware that this room gets incredibly humid and very crowded *(see margin tip left)*. If you want to explore the chamber in detail, you may have to wait a while in uncomfortable surroundings before the room clears.

The Solar Boat

Behind the Pyramid is an ancient boat, known as the **Solar Boat** B (daily, Oct–Apr 9am–4pm, May–Sept 9am–5pm; charge), housed in a special museum. Discovered in a pit covered in limestone blocks and mortar near the Great Pyramid in 1954, it is regarded as one of the most important finds of the 20th century, although its exact purpose is a matter of debate. It was either the funerary boat of Khufu, which carried the pharaoh's body to Giza prior to embalming, or it was a solar boat, intended to carry the dead pharaoh across the sky from east to west to be united with the solar god Ra.

The boat was built of cedarwood imported from Lebanon, and the entire structure had been dismantled and laid in the pit. Reconstructed, it proved to be 43 metres (141ft) long and 8 metres (26ft) high. Although 4,500 years old it is still in excellent condition, with a massive curving hull which rises to elegant prow and stern posts. It had six pairs of long oars, two of which were larger than the others and used as rudders. The thick planks were "sewn" together by a system of ropes through holes that met in pairs on the inside. The expansion of the rope and wood in water ensured the boat would be watertight without the need for caulking.

Four other boat pits have been discovered. Three of these are empty, but an

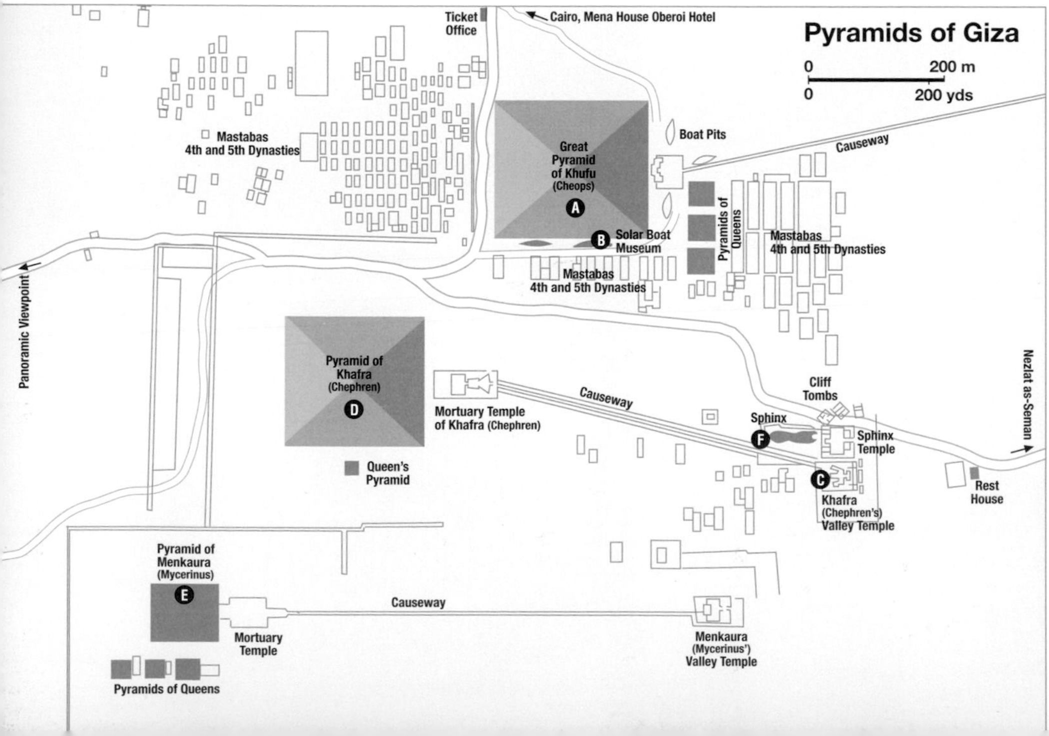

unexcavated boat is known to lie under the ground beside the boat museum. In time it, too, will be excavated, as there is evidence that the bedrock in which it lies is not hermetically sealed, and that the boat is, even now, deteriorating.

Pyramid of Khafra and the Sphinx

The **Valley Temple** Ⓒ, also known as the Granite Temple, is part of the funerary complex of Khafra (2558–2532 BC), Khufu's son. The **Pyramid of Khafra (Chephren)** Ⓓ appears taller than the Great Pyramid but is simply built on higher ground. The smaller **Pyramid of Menkaura (Mycerinus)** Ⓔ, illustrating that the pharaohs were getting weaker at that point, belonged to Khafra's successor. The Pyramid was sheathed in Aswan granite.

At the entrance to the Valley Temple stands the **Sphinx** Ⓕ, a recumbent lion with a human face – that of Khafra. Fashioned out of the bedrock of the Giza Plateau, it is 255 metres (840ft) long and some 20 metres (65ft) high at its head. Repeatedly covered in sand, the Sphinx has been the victim of rescue and conservation efforts since ancient times. Between its outstretched paws a red granite slab tells the story of the first attempt at conservation under the Pharaoh Thutmose IV of the 18th Dynasty. The text relates how the pharaoh was sleeping in its shadow one day, when the Sphinx appeared to him and instructed him to clear away the sand that was choking it. The Sphinx declared that if Thutmose hearkened to his words then he would be king and wear the crown of Upper and Lower Egypt – which, indeed, he did.

This inscription, which dates from *c.*1400 BC, is the first record of any excavation on the Giza Plateau, where wind-blown depressions are continually being filled with sand. The Sphinx itself was cleared of sand again in the Saitic period (600 BC), in the late Ptolemaic (Greek) period, and again in Roman times. In the modern era, Napoleon's team of *savants* cleared and measured the monument during the 1789 expedition to Egypt, and it has been successively cleared and restored by the Egyptian Antiquities Organisation. Unfortunately, despite all these

A human figure provides a sense of scale at the foot of the Great Pyramid.

BELOW: leading the way inside the Great Pyramid.

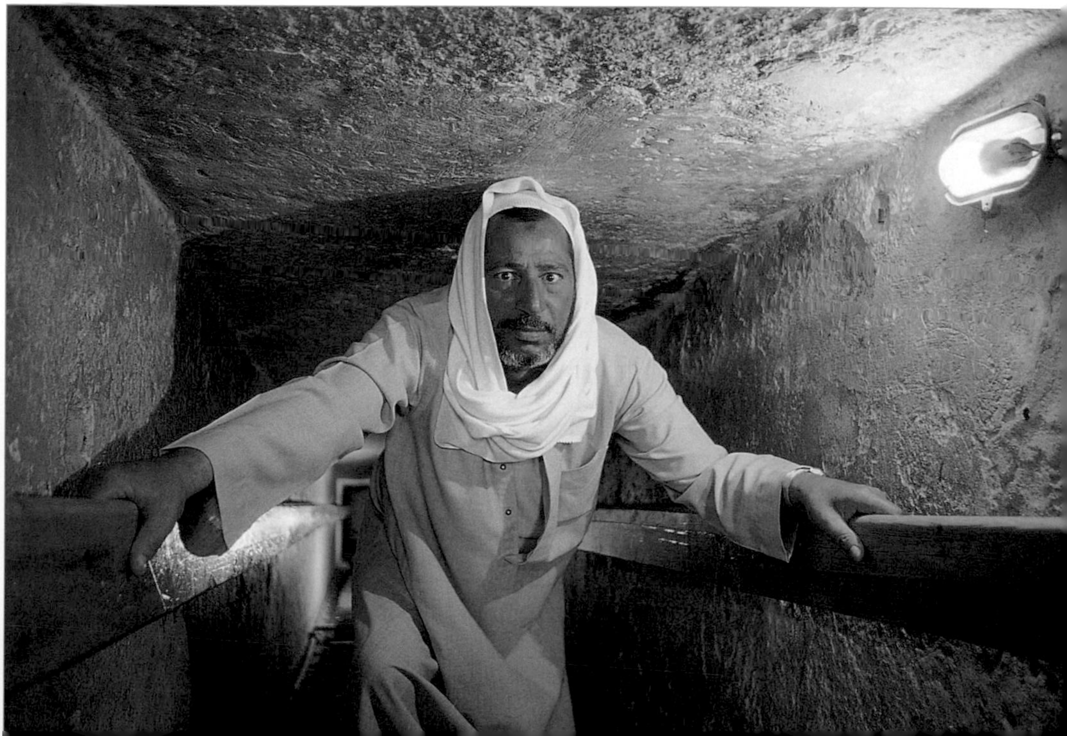

The classic Pyramid complex comprises the Pyramid for the pharaoh, a satellite Pyramid, thought to be for his queen, and a mortuary temple connected to a valley temple by a causeway. The entrance to a Pyramid was normally on the north side. The shape was inspired by the ben-ben *stone, the sacred symbol of the sun-god at Heliopolis.*

efforts, the Sphinx is suffering badly from age, environmental pollution and sub-soil water seepage. In addition, current restoration measures include replacing earlier, poor-quality repairs with "healthy stone".

In front of the Granite Temple and the Sphinx is the **Sphinx Theatre**, where a sound and light performance takes place every night, in a variety of languages (tel: +202 338 63 469 for more information, or *see page 305*).

Tourist development

Over the last few years much has been done to upgrade the Giza Plateau. Unesco and the Egyptian government have worked together to improve the management of visitors and facilities while preserving the monuments. The sights have been thoroughly cleaned, and mounted police have been introduced to regulate the horsemen and cameleers allowed on the plateau. A ventilation system was installed inside the Great Pyramid to reduce the temperature and humidity, and the interior of Khafra's Pyramid has been cleaned and restored.

Construction is under way of a new museum 3km (2 miles) south of the Giza Pyramids, which will mark the new entrance to the whole plateau. President Mubarak laid the foundation stone in 2000, but it is not yet clear when it will be finished. Current estimates predict that the new building may be ready by 2015.

When it opens, it is anticipated that Cairo's centre will lose a lot of its package tourists to Giza, especially as the latter has more space to offer developers looking to create resort-style properties. Unfortunately, more people equals more pollution; the sights of the Giza Plateau are already suffering the effects of mass tourism in the form of epic rubbish scattered on the sands. Additionally, the massive growth of the surrounding suburb has increased road traffic greatly, meaning more air pollution affecting the Pyramid exteriors.

Surprisingly, there are few good hotels to choose from in Giza at present – most tourists prefer to base themselves in downtown Cairo and make the trek to Giza as part of a day trip. This may soon change, though, as a new highway completed in 2009 now whisks people to and from Giza in half the time it used to take.

South of Saqqarah

A few kilometres south of Saqqarah is the impressive but rarely visited site of **Dahshur** ❺, comprising five Pyramids; this is essential viewing if you want to understand the history of Pyramid-building. On the east of the site are three Middle Kingdom Pyramids, built in the 19th–18th centuries BC, at the time of a Pyramid-building revival, including the **Black Pyramid** of Amenemhat III built in black mud-brick. More interesting, however, are the two Old Kingdom Pyramids, illustrating attempts at Pyramid-building by Snofru, the father of Khufu. The **Red Pyramid** was larger than Khafra's Pyramid in Giza, but more intriguing is Snofru's **Bent Pyramid**, which starts

BELOW: the boat of Khufu.

at an angle of 52° and then changes to a gentler 43°, either because the architect realised that the initial angle was impossible to sustain or because such a steep Pyramid would have put tremendous pressure upon the internal chambers.

The Bent Pyramid has the most intact casing of any Egyptian Pyramid, and is unusual in having two entrances – one on the north side, like most Pyramids, and the other on the west. On the south side of the Bent Pyramid is a smaller Pyramid, possibly for Snofru's wife, Heterpheres, which still retains some of its original limestone casing at its base.

About 50km (30 miles) south of Saqqarah is the spectacular **Pyramid of Maydum** (daily 8am–7pm; charge), another Step Pyramid that was supposed to be transformed into a Smooth Pyramid but, due to a design flaw, the outer layers collapsed into rubble. The main structure originally rose to a height of 93 metres (305ft). The surrounding tombs date from the 3rd and 4th Dynastics and include those of Prince Rahotep, the high priest of Heliopolis, and his wife Nofret, whose double sculpture in painted limestone is one of the most famous exhibits in the Egyptian Museum in Cairo.

About 16km (10 miles) southwest of the Pyramid of Maydum, at **Al Hawarah**, is the crumbling **Pyramid Complex of Amenemhat III** (daily 7am–5pm; charge), dating from the 18th century BC, towards the end of the Middle Kingdom. It has the remains of an intricate mortuary temple known as the Labyrinth, though its stone was extensively plundered during the Roman period and the remains are scant.

A few kilometres further south is the earlier 12th Dynasty **Pyramid of Al Lahun** (daily 7am–4pm; charge), the tomb of Senusret II (1897–1878 BC). Here, the Pyramid's architects diverged from the usual method of Pyramid building, employing limestone pillars on a rock base as the framework for a mud-brick structure that was then encased in stone.

Also in the Al Fayyum area are the even more dilapidated Pyramids of Al Lisht that belonged to the 20th-century BC Pharaoh Amenemhat I and his son Senusret I (1971–1928 BC). ❑

If you want to wake up with the Pyramids filling the view out of your window, then the Mena House Oberoi hotel, seen here, is the place to stay – particularly the Old Wing.

BELOW: the alabaster Sphinx at Memphis.

CAIRO

With a history spanning five millennia and a population of nearly 18 million people, Cairo is a diverse and fascinating metropolis and the hub of the Arab world

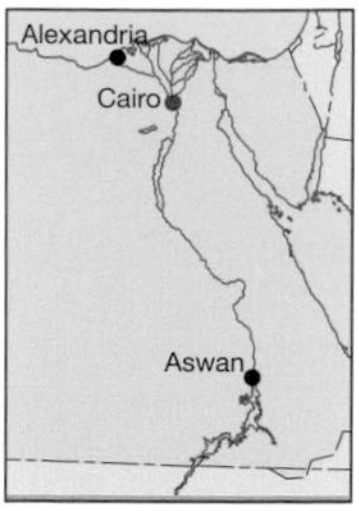

Larger than any other city in the Middle East or Africa, Cairo stretches ever further along the east bank of the Nile for more than 35km (20 miles), guarding the head of the Delta and marking the division between Upper and Lower Egypt. Across the river is Giza, technically a separate administrative district, but part of the same urban agglomeration. In the river between Cairo and Giza are two islands: Roadah, formed out of bedrock, which has been the site of human settlement since ancient times, and Gazirah, formed alluvially within the past six centuries, where the suburb of Zamalik has grown up since 1870 (for more on Cairo's history, *see page 249*).

Living in Cairo

With a headcount of approximately 18 million – there are more Cairenes than there are Scandinavians, Greeks, Dutch, Austrians or Hungarians – Cairo, Giza and the islands constitute the most populous urban area in the world between America and India. The city continues to grow with every passing day as the rural poor flood into the metropolis in search of a better life. A drive on the highways will pass endless crumbling tower blocks devastated by the effects of decades of chronic air pollution and shoddy construction. Rents in this city are extremely high. Many of the apartments are crammed with multiple families, and it is not always obvious what the difference is between a good neighbourhood and a bad one, as little investment is made into building exteriors, with the exception of the large five-star hotels.

Despite this, visitors are drawn to this chaotic city, with its boundless energy and extraordinary history. Even lifetime residents admit that much of the city is a mystery to them, as each neighbourhood has its own colourful characters

Main attractions
- EGYPTIAN MUSEUM
- COPTIC CAIRO
- UMM KULTHUM MUSEUM
- MOSQUE OF IBN TULOAN
- GAYER-ANDERSON MUSEUM
- THE CITADEL
- AL AZHAR PARK
- DARB AL AHMAR
- KHAN AL KHALILI BAZAAR
- CITIES OF THE DEAD

PRECEDING PAGES: Hoash Al Basha royal tombs, Cities of the Dead. **LEFT:** building housing the Nilometer. **RIGHT:** Meadan At tahrir.

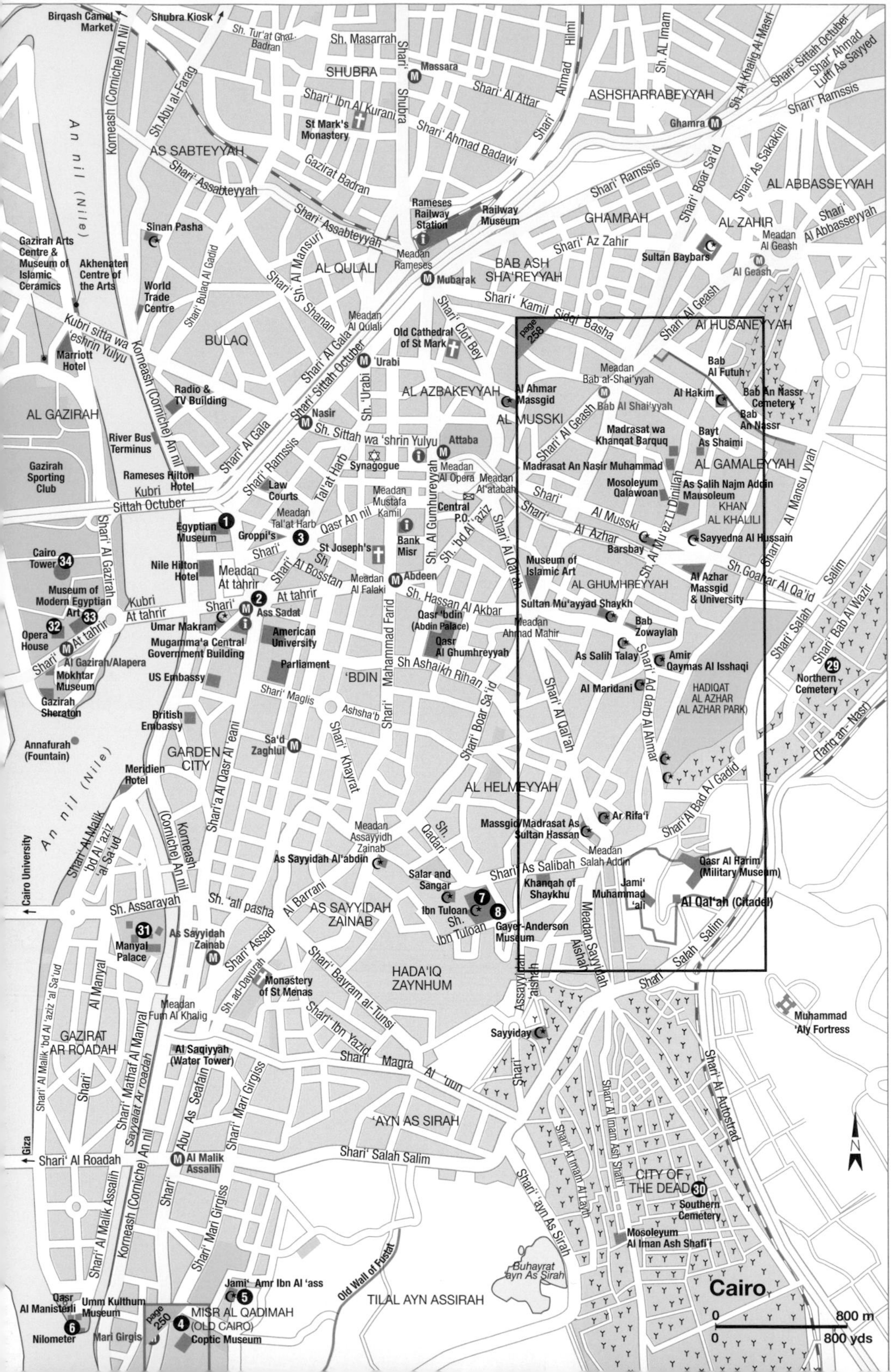

Birqash Camel Market
Shubra Kiosk
Sh. Tur'at Ghaz. Badran
Sh. Masarrah
SHUBRA
Massara
Shari' Shubra
Shari' Al Attar
Shari' Ahmad Hilmi
Sh. Al Imam
ASHSHARRABEYYAH
Sh. Al Khalig Al Masri
Shari' Sittah October
Shari' Ahmad Lutfi As Sayyed
Shari' Ramssis
Ghamra
Shari' Ibn Al Kurani
St Mark's Monastery
Shari' Ahmad Badawi
Korneash (Corniche) An Nil
Sh. Abu al-Farag
An nil (Nile)
AS SABTEYYAH
Shari' Assabteyyah
Gazirat Badran
Rameses Railway Station
Railway Museum
Meadan Rameses
GHAMRAH
Shari' Ramssis
Shari' Boar Sa'id
Shari' As Sakakini
AL ABBASSEYYAH
AL ZAHIR
Shari' Al Abbasseyyah
Meadan Al Geash
Al Geash
Shari' Az Zahir
Sultan Baybars
Sinan Pasha
Gazirah Arts Centre & Museum of Islamic Ceramics
Akhenaten Centre of the Arts
World Trade Centre
Shari' Bulaq Al Gadid
Sh. Al Mansuri
Shari' Shanan
AL QULALI
Mubarak
BAB ASH SHA'REYYAH
Shari' Kamil Sidqi Basha
Shari' Al Geash
Meadan Al Qulali
Shari' Clot Bey
Old Cathedral of St Mark
page 258
AL HUSANEYYAH
Kubri sitta wa 'eshrin Yulyu
Marriott Hotel
BULAQ
Shari' Al Gala
Shari' Sittah October
'Urabi
Sh. 'Urabi
AL AZBAKEYYAH
Al Ahmar Massgid
Meadan Bab al-Shai'yyah
Bab Al Shai'yyah
Bab Al Futuh
Al Hakim
Bab An Nassr Cemetery
Bab An Nassr
AL GAZIRAH
Radio & TV Building
Nasir
Sh. Sittah wa 'shrin Yulyu
AL MUSSKI
Shari' Al Geash
Madrasat wa Khanqat Barquq
Bayt As Shaimi
River Bus Terminus
Korneash (Corniche) An nil
Shari' Al Gala
Attaba
Synagogue
Meadan Al Opera
Meadan Al'atabah
Madrasat An Nasir Muhammad
AL GAMALEYYAH
Gazirah Sporting Club
Rameses Hilton Hotel
Shari' Ramssis
Law Courts
Tal'at Harb
Meadan Mustafa Kamil
Shari' Al Gumhureyyah
Central P.O.
Mosoleyum Qalawoon
As Salih Najm Addin Mausoleum
KHAN AL KHALILI
Kubri Sittah October
Egyptian Museum
Groppi's
Meadan Tal'at Harb
Qasr An nil
Bank Misr
Sh. 'bd Al 'aziz
Shari' Al Qal'ah
Al Musski
Al Azhar
Sh. Al Mu'ez Li Dinillah
Sayyedna Al Hussain
Shari' Al Mansuriyyah
Cairo Tower
Shari' Al Gazirah
Nile Hilton Hotel
Meadan At tahrir
Shari' Al Bosstan
St Joseph's
Meadan Al Falaki
Abdeen
Museum of Islamic Art
Barsbay
AL GHUMHREYYAH
Sh. Goahar Al Qa'id
Al Azhar Massgid & University
Salim
Museum of Modern Egyptian Art
Kubri At tahrir
At tahrir
Ass Sadat
Sh. Hassan Al Akbar
Qasr 'bdin (Abdin Palace)
Sultan Mu'ayyad Shaykh
Shari' Salah
Shari' Bab Al Wazir
Opera House
Umar Makram
Mugamma'a Central Government Building
American University
Qasr Al Ghumhreyyah
Meadan Ahmad Mahir
Bab Zowaylah
Shari' At tahrir
Al Gazirah/Alapera
Mokhtar Museum
Parliament
Sh Ashaikh Rihan
As Salih Talay
Amir Qaymas Al Isshaqi
Northern Cemetery
US Embassy
Shari' Maglis
'BDIN
Shari' Mahammad Farid
Al Maridani
Shari' Ad darb Al Ahmar
HADIQAT AL AZHAR (AL AZHAR PARK)
Gazirah Sheraton
Ashsha'b
British Embassy
Shari' Khayrat
Shari' Boar Sa'id
Shari' Al Qal'ah
(Tariq an-Nasr)
Annafurah (Fountain)
GARDEN CITY
Sa'd Zaghlul
Shari'a Al Qasr Al 'eani
Meridien Hotel
An nil (Nile)
AL HELMEYYAH
Shari' Al Bad Al Gadid
Ar Rifa'i
Cairo University
Shari' Al Malik 'bd Al 'aziz 'al Sa'ud
Korneash (Corniche) An nil
Meadan Assayyidh Zainab
Sh. Qadari
Massgid/Madrasat As Sultan Hassan
Meadan Salah Addin
As Sayyidah Al'abdin
Salar and Sangar
Shari' As Salibah
Khanqah of Shaykhu
Jami' Muhammad 'ali
Qasr Al Harim (Military Museum)
Al Qal'ah (Citadel)
Sh. Assarayah
Sh. 'ali pasha
Al Barrani
AS SAYYIDAH ZAINAB
Ibn Tuloan
Sh. Ibn Tuloan
Gayer-Anderson Museum
Meadan Sayyidah Aishah
Shari' Salah Salim
Manyal Palace
As Sayyidah Zainab
Shari' Assad
Sh. ad-Dayurah
Monastery of St Menas
Shari' Bayram al-Tunsi
HADA'IQ ZAYNHUM
Shari' Assayyidah 'aishah
Muhammad 'Aly Fortress
Al Manyal
Meadan Fum Al Khalig
Shari' Ibn Yazid
Sayyiday
GAZIRAT AR ROADAH
Shari' Mathal Al Manyal
Sayyalat Ar roadah
Al Saqiyyah (Water Tower)
Shari' Magra Al 'uun
Shari' Al Malik 'bd Al 'aziz 'al Sa'ud
Abu As Seafain
Shari' Mari Girgiss
Shari' Al Autostrad
Shari' Al Imam Ash Shafi'i
Shari' Al Imam Al Layth
'AYN AS SIRAH
Giza
Shari' Al Roadah
Al Malik Assalih
Shari' Salah Salim
N
CITY OF THE DEAD
Southern Cemetery
Shari' 'ayn As Sirah
Shari' Al Malik Assalih
Korneash (Corniche) An nil
Shari' Mari Girgiss
Mosoleyum Al Iman Ash Shafi'i
Buhayrat 'ayn As Sirah
Jami' Amr Ibn Al 'ass
Old Wall of Fustat
Cairo
Qasr Al Manisterli
Umm Kulthum Museum
page 250
MISR AL QADIMAH (OLD CAIRO)
TILAL AYN ASSIRAH
Nilometer
Mari Girgis
Coptic Museum
0
800 m
0
800 yds

and secrets ripe for exploration. It may seem chaotic, but it is precisely this chaos which draws the visitor in.

Downtown and the Egyptian Museum

Modern Cairo (or Misr as the locals refer to it), today's city's centre, contains few major historical attractions, though it does have some fine colonial-style architecture. At its heart is the **Egyptian Museum ❶** (9am–6.30pm, entry not permitted after 4.45pm, Ramadan 9am–4pm; charge, plus extra charge for the Mummy Room), founded by the great French Egyptologist Auguste Mariette (who is buried in a tomb in the museum's garden). The museum has a huge collection of ancient Egyptian artefacts on display, including the spectacular Tutankhamun exhibits. Its basement, until recently referred to as the largest unexcavated area in Egypt, is currently being cleared and catalogued, and a new museum, south of the Giza Pyramids, is being built which will ease the strain on the overstuffed Cairo building *(see page 240)*.

The best time to visit is either first thing in the morning as soon as the doors open (before the tour buses) or during the last two hours of the day when the tour parties have already departed. Independent guides can be found waiting near the entrance and will offer a two-hour tour for anything from E£50. Skill and knowledge levels vary greatly. Guides are useful if you have interest in specific eras of Egyptian history or simply want more information than that which is printed on the usually poor exhibit descriptions.

Displays on the ground floor are arranged chronologically, in a clockwise direction. Thus Pre-Dynastic and Old Kingdom exhibits are displayed to the left of the entrance, and Roman-period objects towards the right. Within the entrance lobby is a replica of the Rosetta Stone (the original is in the British Museum in London). Among the Old Kingdom highlights is a large black statue of Khafra, the builder of the second pyramid at Giza, seated on a lion throne. In Room 42 is the unusual wooden statue of Ka-Aper, known as Sheikh Al Beded, with rock-crystal and alabaster eyes, as well as a painted limestone seated scribe, with vivid inlaid eyes. In the next room is the magnificent double sculpture of Prince Rahotep and his wife Nofret, a symbol of marital bliss, as well as the venerated dwarf Seneb with his family.

The Narmer Palette in the first room marks the beginning of Egyptian art and history, recording the unification of Upper and Lower Egypt by King Menes (*c.*3000 BC).

Another important collection, in Room 3, dates from the Amarnah period of the rebel kingdom of Akhenaten *(see page 34)*. Carvings from Tall Al Amarnah illustrate the revolution in religion, politics and art. The pharaoh Akhenaten is depicted in a much more naturalistic manner than artistic convention previously allowed; he plays freely with his wife Nefertiti and their children.

A staircase leads up to the museum's biggest crowd-puller, the **treasures of**

A wooden statue of Senusret I in the Egyptian Museum.

BELOW: Menkaura between two goddesses in the Egyptian Museum.

KIDS

Parents visiting the Egyptian Museum with kids in tow should bear in mind that the sight of mummies can be frightening to children, and that noise has to be kept to a minimum in order to pay respect to the deceased. The children's museum in the basement will be more appealing, with exhibits of genuine antiquities, Lego models of Egyptian objects and scenes, and a hands-on activity centre.

BELOW: entrance to the Egyptian Museum.

Tutankhamun, the items discovered by Howard Carter in 1922 *(see page 198)*. Some 3,500 items were found by Carter, 1,700 of them on display here, including the pharaoh's jewellery and sarcophagus, games, clothes and furniture, many of them gold-plated and encrusted with jewels.

Many other galleries are also worth seeing. In Room 27 (upstairs), for instance, are models found in an 11th Dynasty tomb showing life as it was in 2000 BC. Room 4 has a marvellous display of ancient Egyptian jewellery, while a few of the famous **Fayyum Portraits**, faces painted on wooden panels placed over the mummy, are on display in Room 14. The beautifully displayed animal mummies on display in Rooms 53 and 54 give a fascinating insight into the ancient Egyptian animal cults.

The **Royal Mummy Room** (separate charge) house the remains of some of the most illustrious pharaohs and queens from *c*. 1650–950 BC. Many of the mummies here, including those of Ahmose I, Amenhotep I, Thutmose I, II and III, Sety I and Rameses II and III, were found in a cache near Dair Al Bahari, Thebes, in 1871 *(see page 59)*. With their hair and teeth visible, they are a gruesome but fascinating sight.

Recently a new children's museum has opened in the basement of the museum *(see margin, left)*.

Central Square

The museum faces the sprawling **Meadan At tahrir** ❷ ("Liberation Square"). Originally called Meadan Ismailiyyah, the square once boasted a statue of the "magnificent *khediv*" in its centre. After the 1952 revolution the square was renamed and the statue was hauled away, though its massive plinth was not dismantled for 25 years. Its site marks the approximate centre of modern Cairo, from which all distances in Egypt are measured.

Most of the streets, squares and parks of this area appear in the master plan for the city (modelled on Paris at that time), that the *khedive* Ismail's ministers developed between 1867 and 1873. The square has several of the city's most important landmarks: the **Mosque of Umar Makram**, used for the funerals of important Cairenes; the

Mugamma'a, a Soviet-style building devoted to Egypt's notorious bureaucracy; the **Nile Hilton**, the city's first modern luxury hotel (closed for renovation), and the **American University**, occupying a 19th-century palace, where children of the country's élite were educated; most of the students have moved elsewhere but the iconic building now houses a large bookstore, and you can enjoy a stroll and cultural performances on the pleasant campus.

Other renovation projects currently have much of the square covered in scaffolding and barriers. The Egyptian government is hoping to transform the area into a green and public showpiece – the ultimate goal being to de-clog the traffic and make the square more pedestrian-friendly.

Much more intimate than Meadan At tahrir, and for many the true heart of downtown Cairo, is **Meadan Tal'at Harb** ❸, still better known by its pre-revolution name of Meadan Sulieman Pasha. On the corner of this intersection stands the once legendary coffee house **Groppi**, a reminder of how elegant the area used to be.

The facades are crumbling along the two streets that radiate from here, Shari' Qasr An nil and Shari' Tal'at Harb, but it is still a pleasure to look up at the buildings as you walk along. The Opera on **Meaden Al operah** was burned down in 1971, and in its place, a much-needed car park was constructed. A new Opera House was later built on the island of Al Gazirah thanks to funding from the Japanese government. Although the Azbakeyyah Gardens have disappeared, the downtown area is still full of charm. Some of the 500 rooms of the **Abdin Palace** (Sat–Thur 9am–3pm; charge) are open to the public. Most of the exhibits on display are related to contemporary political history, including a room of gifts received on state visits, military medals and official portraits.

Coptic Cairo

The fortress of Babylon, the Mosque of Amr and the ruins of Al Fustat are all in the quarter called **Misr Al Qadimah** ❹, a district known as Mari Girgiss by Egyptians, and by Western visitors as **Old Cairo**, though it has no historical

A statue of Muhammad Ali on Meadan At tahrir. Muhammad Ali is known as the father of modern Egypt.

BELOW: Qibia Wall in the Mosque An nassir Muhammad.

Cairo Takes Shape

The city-site of Cairo has been settled since Neolithic times. Some 25km (15 miles) northeast of the Giza Pyramids, directly north of Memphis, was the temple-city of On, the Old Kingdom's greatest religious complex, centre of the cult of the sun-god Ra. At Giza the main road from Memphis to On crossed the Nile, using the island of Roadah as a stepping stone. The small settlement at the landing place opposite Roadah, on the east bank, was probably called Per-Hapi-n-On – "The Nile House of On" – and became known to Greek travellers as Babylon.

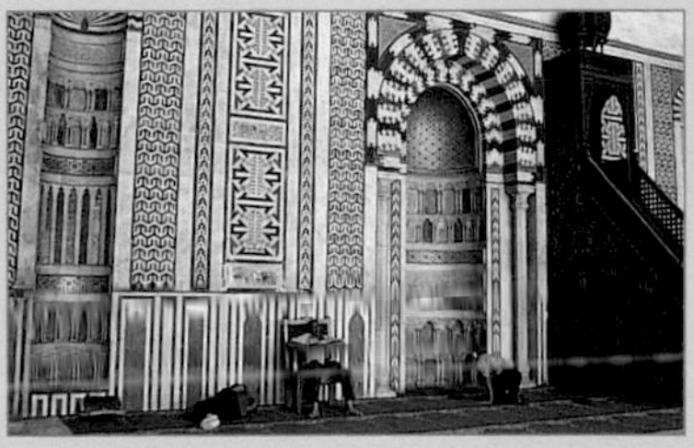

When Egypt became a Roman province in 30 BC, one of the three legions controlling the whole country was garrisoned in the fortress at Babylon (now Old Cairo). By the time of the Arab invasion in 639, the Delta, the country's richest region, remained impassable in any direction except north or south along one of the branches of the Nile, which also provided the only route between Upper Egypt and the Mediterranean. Babylon (as the embryonic Cairo was still called) controlled not only access to the Delta, but also access to Upper Egypt, and was thus a gateway to the entire country.

After a brief siege, Babylon fell to the Arabs under Amr Ibn Al As, who then founded the city of Al Fustat ("The Tent" or perhaps "The Earthworks"), where he settled his troops. The Fatimids, who arrived from Tunisia in the 10th century, built the royal enclosure called "Al Qahirah" north of Al Fustat, and it was this new area which was then mispronounced by Italian merchants as "Gran Cairo", a name which caught on throughout Europe.

Cairenes themselves do not call their city "Cairo". They call it "Misr", which means "metropolis", "capital", "that which is inhabited and civilised", but also means "Egypt". When Al Fustat became the capital of the country under the Arabs, it was called "Misr Fustat", and every succeeding settlement was simply absorbed into Misr.

The best way to get to the Coptic quarter of Old Cairo is by metro.

or topographical connection with Al Qahirah and offers only the dimmest foretaste of the city's true splendour, which is its medieval architecture. The easiest way to reach Old Cairo is by metro (the station is Mari Girgiss).

Useless for military purposes after the Arab conquest, the fortress of Babylon evolved into a Christian and Jewish enclave, and many churches were built within its walls. The metro stops by the modern Greek Orthodox Church of St George (Mari Girgiss), built on the remains of one of Trajan's two great circular towers. Originally created to flank the canal built to link the Red Sea and the Nile in the 6th century BC, the towers now frame the entrance to the garden of the **Coptic Museum** Ⓐ (daily 9am–5pm, Ramadan 9am–3pm; charge). The museum contains many items from the surrounding churches, but its pride is a fine collection of ancient manuscripts, including the earliest known copy of the Book of Psalms and the Naga' Hammadi codices, nearly 1,200 papyrus pages of Gnostic texts in Coptic, which were bound into books – the oldest leather-covered volumes known – and hidden in an Upper Egyptian cave in the 4th century *(see page 213)*. Also important are objects from the monastery of Apa Jeremiah at Saqqarah.

A portal in the south wall of the museum garden leads to the **Church of the Blessed Virgin Mary** Ⓑ (daily 7am–5pm; Mass Fri 8–11am, Sun 7–10am; donations welcomed), known as "Al Mu'allaqah" ("The Hanging"), built atop the bastions of another Roman gate. According to tradition, the church was built in the 7th century, but like the other churches in Old Cairo it has been repeatedly rebuilt, especially in recent times. Many items of furniture have been preserved, however, including a fine 11th-century marble *ambon* (pulpit) and a screen of ebony inlaid with ivory (12th- or 13th-century). The church also has a fine collection of icons.

A stairway near the museum's ticket office leads from the garden down to the stone-paved main street of the enclave. The **Church of St Sergius** Ⓒ (daily 8am–5pm) lies down the street to the right. Traditionally regarded as the oldest in Misr Al Qadimah, it is said to have

BELOW: the well-loved coffee house Groppi, in Meadan Tal'at Harb.

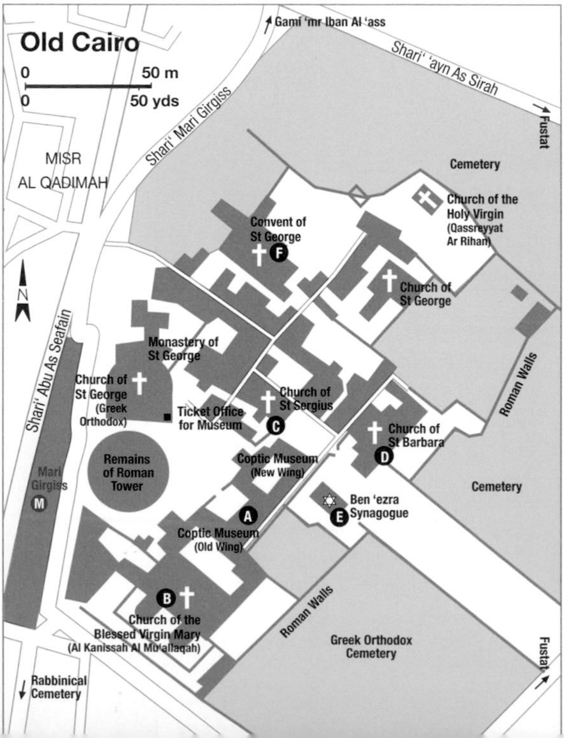

been built in the 5th or 6th century over a cave where the Holy Family stayed during their sojourn in Egypt. The **Church of St Barbara** Ⓓ (daily 8am–4pm) is further down the main alleyway, then to the left. Though continuously rebuilt, it has a fine inlaid iconostasis, one of the few surviving medieval icons of St Barbara, and an extraordinarily beautiful 13th-century icon of the Virgin with Child Enthroned.

A few steps away is the **Ben 'ezra Synagogue** Ⓔ (daily 9am–4pm), used as a church in the 8th and 9th centuries, closed under the fanatic Caliph Al Hakim (996–1021), then sold to the Sephardic community. From the 11th century onwards, it served as a *genizah*, a repository for discarded documents, which were discovered when it was rebuilt in the 19th century and have since provided a wealth of information. The spring next to the synagogue is supposedly where Mary collected water to wash Jesus, and also where the pharaoh's daughter found the baby Moses in the bulrushes.

The shortest route back to the main road outside the fortress returns past the Church of St Sergius, then curves round to the **Convent of St George** Ⓕ (daily during services), where modern believers wrap themselves in chains in remembrance of the persecution of St George. The convent incorporates a remarkable room with wooden doors 7 metres (23ft) high, thought to have originally formed part of a Fatimid (12th-century) house.

About 200 metres/yds north is the first mosque to be built in Africa, the **Mosque of Amr Ibn Al 'ass** ❺ (daily 8am–5pm), built in 641–2 by the Muslim conqueror of Egypt *(see page 51)*. It has been rebuilt several times, but the latest remodelling, finished in 1983, tried to recreate its original appearance.

The island of Roadah

Across a narrow branch of the Nile from Old Cairo onto the island of Roadah is the earliest Muslim structure still extant in the city: the Roadah **Nilometer** ❻ (daily 9am–5pm; charge), built in 861 by the governor of Egypt on the order of the Abbasid caliph. The building's conical dome is not part of the original Nilometer, but

Minarets in the moonlight.

BELOW: Egyptians love football.

Umm Kulthum

Born in the Delta region in 1904, Umm Kulthum moved to Cairo in 1920 and quickly became a favourite performer amongst the Egyptian people. But her star really shone in 1935 when she recorded her first song in a feature film. Her Thursday evening radio show was so popular that the streets would empty and businesses would shut in order to allow everyone the chance to hear their favourite daughter perform. From that moment on (with the exception of a period of ill-health from 1946–54) she was rarely out of the spotlight.

The regular monthly performances Umm Kulthum gave at the height of her career brought Cairo to a complete standstill, and her funeral in 1975 was attended by millions.

Some ancient Egyptian symbols were incorporated into Coptic iconography. The Coptic cross above is clearly derived from the ankh, *the ancient Egyptian symbol for life.*

a replica of the Ottoman-style dome that covered it in the 17th and 18th centuries. In the middle of a square, stone-lined shaft is the Nilometer itself, an octagonal column divided into cubits, which stands on a millstone at the bottom of the shaft. A stairway around the walls of the shaft leads past inlets at three levels: the level of the uppermost inlet is indicated by recesses outlined with what a Gothic architect would have recognised as "tiers-point" arches, but they were built three centuries before the earliest European example. Nilometers measured the height of the annual flood and thus the richness of the harvest, which would determine the level of taxes for that year.

The **Al Manisterli Palace**, next to the Nilometer, is the *salamlek* or reception kiosk of a palace complex built in the 1830s by the founder of a distinguished Cairene Turkish family. The palace was restored in the 1990s, and part of it is now an elegant venue for concerts, while another part houses the **Umm Kulthum Museum** (daily 10am–4pm; charge). The interesting small museum displays photographs, the signature sunglasses and good-luck scarves of Umm Kulthum, the most famous Arab singer of all time. A short film shows important episodes in her life, from when she started singing, disguised as a Bedouin boy, to her sell-out concerts *(see box, page 251)*.

Vanished quarter

Like all the rulers of Misr, the invading Abbasids of the 8th and 9th centuries built a new quarter to the city. Called "Al 'asskar", it was occupied by a succession of governors, the most famous of whom was Ahmed Ibn Tuloan, who declared his independence from the Baghdad caliphate in 872 by having the caliph's dedicatory inscription removed from the Nilometer. The autonomous state he established – the first in Egypt since 30 BC – soon became an empire.

He founded a regal new city north of both Al 'asskar and Al Fustat, naming it "Al Qatai" (The Wards), because of its division into separate districts defined by class and type of inhabitants. Al Qatai covered around 260 hectares

BELOW: inside the Gayer-Anderson Museum. **BELOW RIGHT:** relief in the Old Coptic Church.

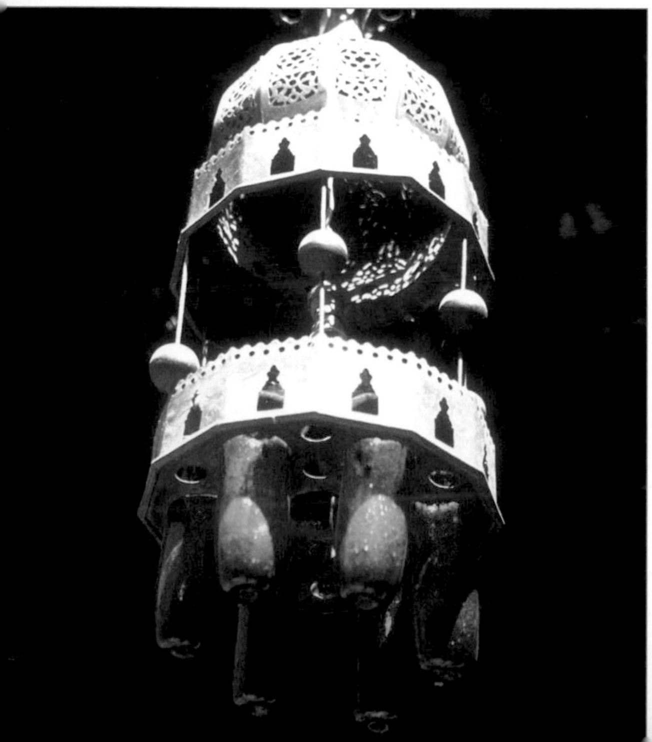

(640 acres) and contained palaces, government buildings, markets and even a hippodrome. At its centre was the congregational **Mosque of Ibn Tuloan** ❼ (daily 8am–5pm; free), designed to contain an army for Friday prayers. Erected between 876 and 879, it is one of the great masterpieces of Muslim architecture and all that remains to testify to the magnificence of the Al Qatai quarter. Echoing the architecture of Baghdad, it consists of a square enclosed by a massive flat-roofed arcade of baked brick, which is covered with fine plaster and surmounted by anthropomorphic cresting. In the centre of the mosque is a massive courtyard of nearly 2 hectares (5 acres) with an ablution fountain in the middle.

The arcading consists of elegant Syrian-style pointed arches, less elaborate than the arches of the Nilometer. The arcade is five rows deep on the eastern or Mecca-facing side, where several *mihrabs*, ornamental recesses, indicate the direction of prayer.

Also on this side is a wooden *minbar* – a structure like a staircase, which serves some of the same function that a pulpit fulfils in a church – the oldest (1296) still in use in Cairo and one of the finest. Carved stucco decoration is used throughout with wonderful inventiveness, and a band of sycamore wood carved with Qur'anic verses runs around the building's whole interior circumference – more than 2km (1¼ miles). The minaret was built in 1296 as a replacement for Ahmed Ibn Tuloan's original, which was modelled in turn on the minaret of the Great Mosque at Samarrah near Baghdad. The minaret has a unique spiral staircase on the exterior which is well worth climbing to enjoy the views over Islamic Cairo and beyond.

Built against one end of the mosque are the two old houses that compose the interesting **Gayer-Anderson Museum** ❽ (Sat–Thur 8.30am–4-.30pm, closed Fri noon–1pm; charge), also known as Bayt Al Kiretleyyah. The British major John Gayer-Anderson restored two beautiful 16th- and 17th-century houses, and filled them with his collection of Islamic objets d'art and paintings.

The interior of the Gayer-Anderson Museum. Each room is elaborately furnished in a different orientalist style. Visit the Chinese Room, the Turkish Room or the Persian Room.

BELOW: prayer hall of the Ibn Tuloan Mosque.

The Muhammad Ali Mosque is also known as the Alabaster Mosque because of the extensive use of alabaster from Beni Suef in Middle Egypt.

To the Citadel

Shari' As Salibah, running east of the Mosque of Ibn Tuloan, is lined with monuments, most of them restored after earthquake damage in the 1990s, including the Khanqat Sheikhu and Sabil kuttub Qayetbay. The street leads to Meaden Salah Addin, above which towers the **Citadel** ❾ (daily, Oct–Apr 8am–4pm, May–Sept 8am–5pm; charge), easily identifiable from the outline of the Ottoman-style Muhammad Ali Mosque, completed nearly 1,000 years later than the Ibn Tuloan. The entrance to the citadel is from Bab Algabal off the Shari' Salah Salim.

Both a fortress and a royal city, the Citadel continued the tradition among Cairo's rulers of building enclosures for themselves and their retainers. It was begun by Salah Ad Din Ibn Ayyub (1171–93), the founder of the Ayyubid Dynasty, the "Saladin" of the medieval Western chroniclers and Sir Walter Scott's novel *The Talisman*. The original walls and towers were erected between 1176 and 1183. Between 1200 and 1218 Salah Ad Din's round towers were encased in massive new constructions, and square keeps were planted around the perimeter. His nephew Al Kamil (1218–38) became the first sultan to live in the Citadel, which remained the seat of government for the next 650 years.

After the Bahri Mamluks overthrew the Ayyubids in 1250, their first great sultan, Baybars Al Bunduqdari (1260–77), divided the fortress into two enclosures linked by an inner gate, the **Bab Al Quallah**. During the various reigns of the Bahri Mamluk Sultan An Nasir Muhammad (1294–5, 1299–1309, 1310–41), most of the buildings in the Southern Enclosure were torn down and replaced by much grander structures. Standing next to the Bab Al Quallah is the **Mosque of An Nasir Muhammad** ❿, one of the finest arcaded mosques in Cairo, as well as the only Mamluk building in the Citadel to survive. Its inner court is a virtual museum of reused pharaonic and Roman-period columns, while its two minarets show Persian influence in their upper pavilions, which are covered in green tiles.

Under the rule of Muhammad Ali Pasha (1805–48), the outer walls of the Citadel were rebuilt to suit the needs of a modern army and the decaying medieval buildings in the interior were replaced by new palaces, barracks, military schools, armament factories, and his own colossal **Mosque of Muhammad Ali** ⓫ (also known as the Alabster Mosque). Alien to the architectural style and spirit of the rest of the city, this mosque was built between 1830 and 1848 and imitates the great religious structures of Istanbul, though the decoration is a hybrid of European, pharaonic and Islamic motifs. Its size, setting and ease of access, however, have made it a popular tourist site; and the Pasha himself is buried here under a marble cenotaph. The clock tower in the outer court was given to him in 1846 by Louis-Philippe, in belated exchange for the obelisk set up in the Place de la Concorde in Paris in 1833.

South of the mosque are the remains of Muhammad Ali's **Palace Al Gawha-**

BELOW: the Al Azhar Park.

rah, completed in 1814, with a refurbished audience hall and private apartments displaying furniture and curios that belonged to the Ali Dynasty.

The **National Police Museum**, near the mosque of An Nasir Muhammad, has a terrace that was built over the site of a Mamluk palace, commissioned by Muhammad Ali. It was originally intended as an artillery platform from which to bombard the city and thus offers a spectacular panorama of medieval Cairo's minarets and domes. On a rare clear day it is possible to see as far as the Pyramids of Giza and Saqqarah.

Dominating the Northern Enclosure is Muhammad Ali's **Al Harim Palace**, constructed in 1827 and now housing the **Egyptian Military Museum** (same opening hours as the Citadel). Especially attractive is the Summer Room, built around a cooling complex of marble fountains, basins and channels. Beyond the Al Harim Palace is a small **Carriage Museum**, containing eight carriages used by Muhammad Ali's family.

Tourists flock to the Citadel, believing it to be an important "must-do" sight in the city due to its sheer size and strategic location. While it was the seat of power for years, its architectural highlights pale in comparison to other structures in the city – and the ticket prices are high for what you get. If you have the time, it's worth a look but it's not a priority.

The Al Azhar Park

The 30-hectare (74-acre) **Al Azhar Park** (Thur–Tue 8am–11pm, Wed 8am–10pm; small charge), created by the Aga Khan Trust for Culture in the historic district of Cairo, is a wonderful addition to a city that has one of the lowest ratios of green space in the world. Part of the project was the excavation and restoration of the 12th-century Ayyubid wall, which had been entirely covered in rubbish that had been thrown over it for centuries (some 80,000 truckloads of rubbish were removed). Three large freshwater reservoirs for the city, each one 80 metres (260ft) in diameter and 14 metres (45ft) deep, were included, so the park has a wealth of water fountains and a lake. The park has also provided much-needed jobs and training for hundreds of people in

TIP

Most monuments in the Islamic part of Cairo are open from 9am–5pm daily. Some less visited monuments may open later or not at all, but a guardian can always be found nearby. Many mosques and museums close for Friday prayers from noon–2pm.

BELOW: inside the Muhammad Ali Mosque.

The Mummy Business

The rich and powerful of Ancient Egypt needed a body to house their soul in the afterlife – so they developed the art of embalming

The ancient Egyptians may have thought they were safe for eternity in their hidden stony tombs and sarcophagi, but very few mummies were allowed to remain in their original burial locations. Some were hacked to pieces by early tomb robbers in search of jewels; others were ground to dust in Europe in medieval times and sold as aphrodisiacs or remedies against abscesses, fractures, bruises, paralysis, migraine, epilepsy, coughs, sore throats and high blood pressure. Even though dealing in mummies was illegal, many wholesalers made a fortune in the trade. It was only heavy taxation that stopped the export business in the 17th century.

Mummification came about because of the ancient Egyptians' belief in life after death, for which they needed a body and soul. In a long procedure that took around 70 days in the case of a noble, the inner organs were removed, and the corpse was dried with natron and then embalmed to turn the papyrus-like skin into leather. In order to maintain its physical presence the body was often filled with mud, sawdust or sap and covered in hundreds of metres of sap-soaked bandages.

When mummification was at the peak of its popularity it was a massive industry, with embalmers working day and night shifts to wrap not only the "upper ten thousand" of society, but also holy bulls, ibises, crocodiles, pavians, cats, mice and scarabs.

A lot has been learned about the early Egyptians from mummification. X-rays of mummies have proved that illnesses such as rheumatism, arthritis, polio and even arteriosclerosis were well known in pharaonic days. Some mummies show death through heart attack or in pregnancy or childbirth (in one case a mummified foetus was discovered in the womb of its mummified mother).

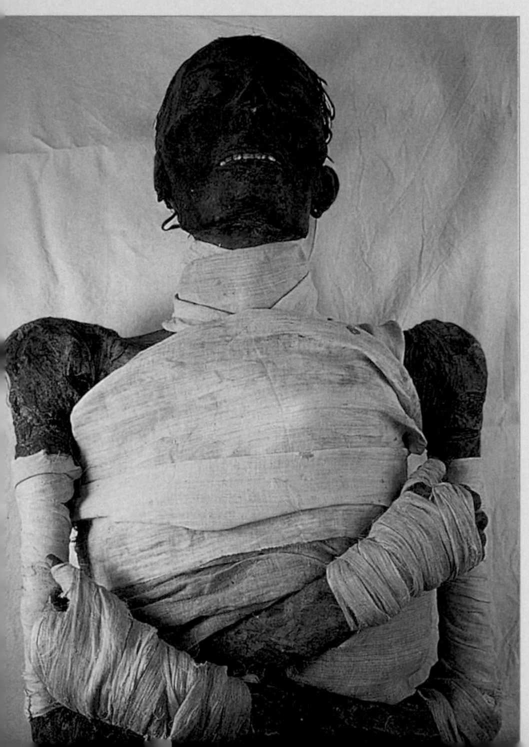

Cashing in on the mummy trade

In the 19th century, surgeons and anatomists found a new source of income by unwrapping mummies in front of audiences. A British anatomist, T.J. Pettigrew, began by staging shows in his own house, but soon moved to bigger venues. On 10 April 1834, a crowd of some 600 people gathered in his local town hall to witness the unwrapping of the "most interesting mummy ever discovered in Egypt". But the mummy proved to be a tough match. Neither hammer nor scissors nor knives succeeded in cutting through the thick protection. After three hours of cutting and sawing, Mr Pettigrew gave up and announced that "the result of the operation would be published some other time".

At the end of the 19th century, America also tried to turn the mummy trade to gold. A paper manufacturer called August Stanwood had the idea of making brown wrapping paper from the ancient bandages and shrouds. None of the American housewives ever knew that her vegetables and meat were wrapped in the remains of Egyptian mummies. However, a cholera epidemic traced back to Stanwood's paper mills marked the end of the trade. ❑

LEFT: the mummy of Thutmose IV in the Egyptian Museum. **ABOVE:** mummy of a boy, 2nd century AD.

the adjacent neighbourhood of Darb Al Ahmar. The park demonstrates how a neighbourhood can be revitalised by offering its inhabitants a serious stake in a local project. Outstanding views and pleasant restaurants attract local and foreign visitors alike.

Medieval Cairo

The glory of Cairo is its medieval architecture, plainly visible from the Al Azhar Park. Northwest is the 10th-century royal enclave of Al Qahirah, built by the Fatimid Dynasty. Here is the Islamic heart of the city, and certain etiquette should be followed in order to respect local customs. Women should wear modest clothing that covers their legs and arms and – if you are planning on entering any mosques – should also bring a headscarf to cover the head. Men should wear long trousers and should not wear vests. If you want to avoid endless tying and retying of footwear, a pair of slip-on shoes will also help if you want to go inside any religious centre.

The Red Alley

Between the Citadel and Al Qahirah lies the district developed as an aristocratic quarter in the 14th century by the relatives and retainers of the prolific Sultan An Nasir Muhammad. It is named **Darb Al Ahmar** (The Red Alley), after its major thoroughfare. On Meadan Salah Addin immediately below the Citadel, opposite the Bab Al azab, soar the walls of the **Mosque and Madrassah of Sultan Hassan** ⓬ (daily 8am–5pm, except during Friday prayers; free), the seventh son of An Nasir Muhammad.

The noblest and most outstanding example of Bahri Mamluk architecture, this mosque was begun in 1356 and not finished until seven years later. Sultan Hassan disappeared in 1361, presumably murdered, and therefore never saw it completed. In contrast with the congregational mosque of Ibn Tuloan, it combines four residential colleges (madrassahs) with a mausoleum. From the towering main entrance, with its canopy of stalactites, a bent passageway leads to the cruciform central court. Here four great arched recesses, or *iwans*, create sheltered spaces for instruction in each of the four schools of Islamic jurisprudence, the Hanafi, the Shafii, the Maliki and the Hanbali. Multi-storey living quarters for teachers and students are built into the corners of the court. From the domed tomb chamber behind it, six ground-level windows offer a splendid and unobstructed view up to the Citadel.

Across the street is the **Ar Rifa'i Mosque** ⓭ (daily 9am–4pm, except during prayers; free), begun in 1869, six centuries later than the Sultan Hassan Mosque, and completed in 1912. Because it was planned as a complement to its Mamluk neighbour in scale, fabric and architectural style, tourists frequently mistake it for an ancient monument. In it are interred the *khedive* Ismail, his mother, two of his daughters, three of his wives, four sons including Sultan Hussain Kamil and King Fuad, Fuad's son King Faruq, whose body was moved here from the

A nippy vehicle in Cairo's horrendously busy traffic.

BELOW: interior of the Mosque of Sultan Hassan.

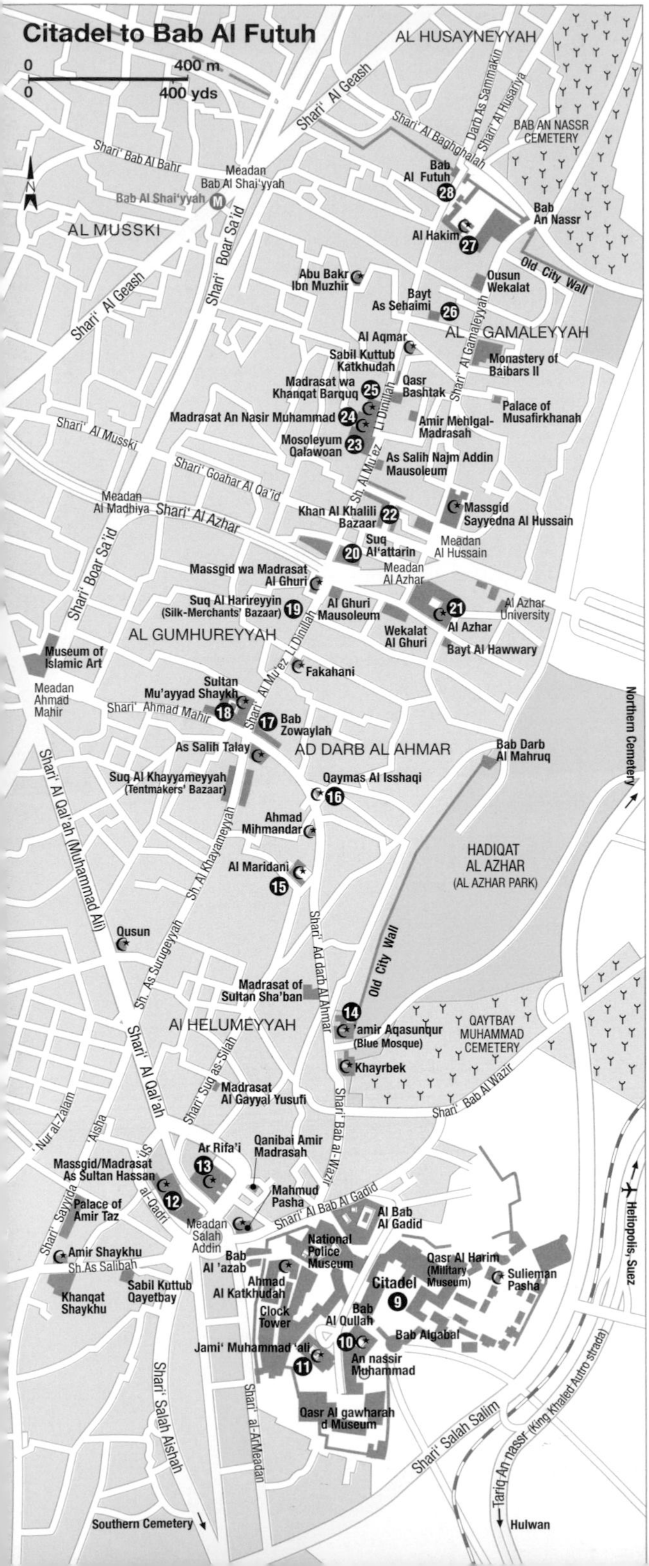

Southern Cemetery, and the last Shah of Iran, whose first wife was Faruq's sister. The roofed and carpeted interior is magnificently adorned with Mameluk-inspired motifs.

Running north

The Shari' Ad darb Al Ahmar runs from the Citadel to Bab Zowaylah, the southern gate of Al Qahirah, and is lined with medieval buildings, some of them undergoing restoration. Visitors are sometimes taken to see the **Mosque of 'amir Aqasunqur ⓮**(1347), also known as the "Blue Mosque", which contains the tomb of Kuchuk, the brother of Sultan Hassan, murdered in 1341 at the age of six. Over 300 years later (1652) it was half-heartedly renovated by an Ottoman officer, who had the walsls partially covered with Damascene tiles.

More notable is the nearby **Mosque of Al Maridani ⓯**, built in 1339 by a son-in-law of An Nasir Muhammad. Demarcated by a superb 14th-century wooden *mashrabiyyah* (a window which projects out like a balcony, enclosed in intricate wooden latticework to maintain privacy), its sanctuary contains a fine marble dado and a *mihrab* (a niche in the wall which denotes the direction of Mecca) decorated with coloured marble, mother-of-pearl and blue faïence.

Between these two mosques are the *mashrabiyyah* casements of an 18th-century townhouse called Bayt Ar Razzaz, constructed around a 15th-century core. As the Shari' Ad darb Al Ahmar curves westwards towards Bab Zowaylah, the exquisite **Mosque of Qaymas Al Isshaqi ⓰** (1481) appears on the right; it is notable for its carved stucco windows and coloured marble panelling.

Just outside Bab Zowaylah is the 14th-century **Souq Al Khayyameyyah** (Tentmakers' Bazaar), where you will see tentmakers sitting cross-legged on raised platforms in tiny shops on either side of the street, stitching away at the bright appliqué from which temporary pavilions are made.

A continuation of the Shari' Ad darb Al Ahmar, which here changes its name to **Shari' Ahmad Mahir**, heads past Bab Zowaylah west towards the **Museum of Islamic Art** (closed for restoration for many years, but the authorities say it will reopen in 2010/11), containing over 75,000 objects, many of them inscribed with the names of Cairo's princes, kings and caliphs. When it reopens, a visit is highly recommended as it has the best collection of Islamic art in the world.

Inside Al Qahirah

The beautiful gate of **Bab Zowaylah** ⓱ (daily 8.30am–5pm; charge), finished in 1092, marks the southern boundary of Al Qahirah, the walled royal enclosure founded by the Fatimids in 969. From the top of the gate are fine views of the area. Enclosing about 2 sq km (¾ sq mile), sections of its stone walls still stand, pierced by Bab Zowaylah in the south and two other fortified gates in the north, **Bab Al Futuh** (1087) and **Bab An Nassr** (1087). Except for the objects preserved in the Museum of Islamic Art, the Fatimids' considerable material wealth – including 120,000 manuscripts, the greatest library of the medieval world – was dispersed when they were overthrown by Salah Ad Din, who opened up their enclosure to ordinary citizens.

Inheriting the commercial role of Al Fustat, Al Qahirah became an international entrepôt specialising in eastern luxuries. *Wikalahs* – warehouses with lodgings – sprang up throughout the city, and many are still in use today. Three mosques from the Fatimid golden age survive within the Fatimids' royal enclosure, and a fourth – the **Mosque of As Salih Talay** (daily 9am–5pm; free), dating from 1160 – stands outside Bab Zowaylah.

Running in a straight line between Bab Zowaylah and Bab Al Futuh, thus bisecting Al Qahirah, is the **Qasabah** or High Street. A vital artery since medieval times, and changing names at several points along its course, it continues beyond both Bab Al Futuh and Bab Zowaylah, linking the entire Old City. The modern street called **Shari' Al Azhar**, built through the district in 1927, crosses the Qasabah at right

The Museum of Islamic Art contains many items from the Fatimid era (969–1171), a golden age for Cairo in terms of art and architecture.

BELOW: Bab Zowaylah.

TIP

The whirling dervishes of At Tannoura Egyptian Heritage Dance Troupe give performances at the Citadel's Sarayat Al Gabal Theatre at Wikala Al Ghouri (on Shari' Salah Salim) every Saturday and Wednesday at 8.30pm (tickets are free, but you need to arrive by 6.30pm to ensure you get a place).

angles and divides Al Qahirah into northern and southern zones.

Just inside Bab Zowaylah is the **Mosque of Sultan Mu'ayyad Sheikh** (18), built to fulfil a vow in 1412. To serve this last great courtyard mosque, the Burji Mamluk sultan erected two minarets (which can be climbed when you enter Bab Zowaylah and from which there are fabulous views), and built an adjoining bath complex of palatial scale. The interior is decorated in marble and stucco, ebony, mother-of-pearl and blue faïence; the doors came from the Mosque of Sultan Hassan.

Bargains and bazaars

Large sections of the Qasabah comprise bazaars and are named after their main trades or occupations. North of Bab Zowaylah the street offers all manner of household goods, from brass bedsteads to feather dusters. Just before Shari' Al Azhar is an area called the **Al Gumhureyyah**, named after Qansuh Al Ghuri, one of the last Mamluk sultans. In 1504 he built the mausoleum and madrassah that stand on opposite sides of the Qasabah here, with the **Souq Al Harireyyin** (19) (Silk-Merchants' Bazaar) occupying the basement of both buildings. Al Ghuri also built a *hammam* (bath), now restored, a *wikalah*, displaying traditional crafts (daily 8am–10pm; charge), and a palace, the remains of which are visible behind the mausoleum. The small Mosque and Madrassah of Al Ghuri has been beautifully restored: for a tip, it is usually possible to gain access to the minaret.

Part of the **Souq Al 'attarin** (20) (Herbalists' Bazaar) extends north of Shari' Al Azhar, which cuts through Al Qahirah at this point and can only be crossed by using the iron bridge or the tunnel. Slashing across the Qasabah, the street brings heavy traffic past the main entrance of the **Mosque of Al Azhar** (21) ("The Resplendent"), built in 970 and now the most famous seat of learning in the Muslim world. The mosque was transformed into a university in 988, making it possibly the oldest centre of higher education in the world. Little remains of the original structure due to constant expansion and rebuilding. Enter the mosque portion of the

BELOW: Bab Zowaylah street sign. **BELOW RIGHT:** gateway to the Khan Al Khalili Bazaar.

university through the Barber's Gate, where students traditionally had their hair cut. The gate opens up onto a Fatimid-era courtyard surrounded by minarets that boast great views of Islamic Cairo. While there is no charge for entrance, you will be asked for *baksheesh* to climb the minarets.

Khan Al Khalili

Opposite the university on the other side of Shari' Al Azhar, in the northern zone of Al Qahirah, is the popular shrine of **Sayyedna Al Hussain**, grandson of the Prophet, who was murdered in AD 680 (closed to non-Muslims). Between here and the Qasabah is the city's most famous tourist market, the labyrinthine **Khan Al Khalili Bazaar** **22**. Most people enjoy browsing through its welter of wares, though better quality and more variety are offered elsewhere in the city, and you will have to deal with the touts.

Khan Al Khalili has seen two major terrorist attacks over the past five years resulting in multiple deaths. A heightened police presence is now in effect in order to prevent any further incidents.

A highlight of a trip to the bazaar is a coffee at Fishawy's – believed to have been open every day, 24 hours a day for over 200 years (with the exception of Ramadan, when the café closes during the day like every other establishment in town). Despite the heavy tourist presence, Fishawy's remains a favourite with locals too. This is one of the few tourist traps in Cairo where you can mix and mingle with residents. It's also a popular place for sheesha smoking. Originally a male-only preserve, it is gaining favour with women too. If you decide to partake, order a pipe and choose your flavour of tobacco; it's usually apple-flavoured, but you can also get strawberry, peach or lemon.

If you are a fan of the work of Nobel Prize-winner Naguib Mahfouz, you may want to head southwest of the main market area to reach Midaq Alley, the real-life setting of the eponymous book. While the characters in the novel aren't real, you may be inspired to create your own story filled with the café owners, barbers, matchmakers and poets who populate the street in modern-day Cairo.

The minarets of the Mosque of Al Azhar, one of the oldest universities in the world.

BELOW: in the Khan Al Khalili Bazaar.

The recently renovated Darb Al Asfar, just off the Qasabah, forms part of the Bayt As Sehaimi restoration project, the aim of which is to document, restore and conserve historic Cairene architecture.

The stretch of the Qasabah running alongside Khan Al Khalili is the **Suq As Saghah** (Goldsmiths' Bazaar). Gold and silver are sold by weight, as are brass and copperware in the neighbouring **Suq An Nahhasin** (Coppersmiths' Bazaar), which has occupied the same place since the 14th century.

Between the palaces

Northwards the Qasabah widens out into the **Bayn Al Qasrayn**. The name means "Between the Two Palaces" and refers to two Fatimid palaces that once stood on this site. Dominating the area is a splendid monumental ensemble built by a succession of Mamluk sultans. The largest element is the Qalawun complex erected in 1284 for the Bahri Mamluk Sultan Qalawoan, who founded a dynasty that lasted almost a century. It includes a madrassah (residential college), a mausoleum, a mosque and the remains of a maristan (charitable hospital); a clinic still operates on the site.

Qalawoan is buried in the majestic **Mausoleum Qalawoan ㉓**. His son An Nasir Muhammad – who reigned longer than any other Mamluk – chose to be buried with him rather than in the next-door **Madrassah of An Nasir Muhammad ㉔** (1326), which was intended to be his mausoleum. The Gothic-looking doorway was taken from a crusader church at Acre; the Spanish stucco-work on the minaret was carved by Andalusian craftsmen, refugees from Christian persecution.

The third important building in the ensemble is the **Madrassah and Khanqat of Barquq ㉕**, the first of the Circassian Mamluk sultans. Barquq's son Farag built another and far grander mausoleum in the Northern Cemetery (where Barquq is actually buried).

Almost directly across the street is the **Bashtak Palace**, the five-storey edifice built by Amir Bashtak, a son-in-law of An Nasir, in 1339. The remains of a water-raising device that supplied running water to every floor are still in evidence. At a corner a few metres further on stands the charming little 18th-century **Sabil kuttub** (fountain-school) **of 'abd Arrahman Katkhudah**.

The Qasabah proceeds to the left here, leading past the badly restored Fatimid **Mosque of Al Aqmar**, "The Moonlit"

BELOW: coffee shop in the Old City.

(1125), which sits below street level a few metres further along. At No. 19 in the totally renovated Darb Al Asfar, the first large lane to the right beyond Al Aqmar, is **Bayt As Sehaimi** ㉖, a charming 17th-century townhouse, open to the public (daily 9am–5pm; charge).

Another 100 metres/yds up the Qasabah stands the great congregational **Mosque of Al Hakim** ㉗ (1010), the second Fatimid caliph, rebuilt in the early 1980s by a Shi'a sect from western India who claim descent from the Fatimids. The Al Hakim Mosque stands against a surviving section of the **North Wall** that connects the round-towered **Bab Al Futuh** ㉘ ("Gate of Conquest") with the square-towered **Bab An Nassr** ("Gate of Victory"). The wall and both towers are well worth exploring, and the views southwards take in countless domes and minarets. Northwards is the **Bab An Nassr Cemetery**, in continuous use since Fatimid times.

Burial grounds

Scarcity of housing and overcrowding in the capital has forced many to move into the "**Cities of the Dead**" – otherwise known as the Northern and Southern cemeteries. But this is not a new trend; tomb guardians have lived with their families since as far back as the 14th century.

Many tombs were built with spaces for overnight visitors and tables to eat from, so that families could visit their ancestors in comfort. Abandoned tombs have been taken over by families, and the area now has electricity, a post office, restaurants and cafés.

Principal monuments in the **Northern Cemetery** ㉙, northeast of the Citadel, include the **Khanqat of Farag Ibn Barquq** (daily 9am–5pm; charge), one of the most impressive buildings in Cairo, built in 1410, complete with minarets and domes that lie off a simple courtyard. Be sure to look at the dome ceilings painted in a geometric pattern of red and black. Two other huge complexes, built by Sultan Inal (1456) and Amir Qurqumas Al Kabir (1507), are part of long-term restoration projects.

A hundred metres/yds south of the Khanqat of Farag Ibn Barquq is the complex of **Sultan Al Ashraf Bersbay**

Statisticians say there are as many as 50,000 people living amongst the tombs. Unofficially, the figure is more like ten times that number.

BELOW: the cemeteries are inhabited by the living as well as the dead.

TIP

The best time to visit the cemeteries is on Friday, the traditional day when Cairenes pay their respects to the deceased. While the "cities" are populated by low-income earners, it is a safe place to go on these open days. Be sure to dress simply and keep valuables at home just in case.

(1432) and further down the same road is the **Mosque of Qayetbay** (1472), an architectural jewel that is depicted on the Egyptian one-pound note. With this building, the most exquisite of the Circassian Mamluk monuments, the art of stone-carving in Cairo reached its pinnacle. The dome exterior is carved with floral and star designs and is often considered the finest example of carving work in all of Egypt. Chambers are panelled in marble and shaded to provide comfort on even the hottest days. For an amazing view, climb the minaret to see all of Islamic Cairo below.

In the larger and older **Southern Cemetery** ㉚, to the south of the Citadel, is the **Mausoleum of Al Imam Ash shafi'I**, the founder of the Shafi'ite school of Islamic law, whose tomb was built by order of Salah Ad Din in 1180. Salah Ad Din's carved cenotaph for the saint still stands in the tomb chamber. Nearby is the **Hoash Al Basha**, built by Muhammad Ali in 1820 as a family tomb, though he himself is buried at the Citadel. Many Bahri Mamluk princes are buried here.

BELOW: the tea terrace of the Marriott Hotel.

Island retreats

Congestion and air pollution make touring modern Cairo either on foot or by car increasingly unpleasant. The islands in the Nile, however, offer great escapes from the dirt and bustle. On Roadah, for example, is the **Manyal Palace complex** ㉛ (daily 9am–5pm; charge), which can be visited in combination with Old Cairo and the Nilometer mentioned previously. Built by Prince Muhammad Ali, the younger brother of the *khedive* Abbas II Hilmi, first cousin of King Faruq and heir apparent until 1952, it contains a huge *salamlek* (reception palace), the two-storey *haramlek* that was the prince's residence, a model throne room, a museum with superb examples of furniture, calligraphy, glass, silver, textiles, costumes and porcelain and a hunting museum (to the right of the main entrance).

Gazirah

On the island of **Gazirah** the most important structure is the Japanese-funded **Opera House** ㉜ at the Gazirah Exhibition Grounds. Opened in 1988, it offers three stages, as well as exhibition halls and practice rooms, and has hosted troupes from all over the world. Also within the Exhibition Grounds are the **Museum of Modern Egyptian Art** ㉝ (Tue–Sun 10am–1pm, 5–9pm, Fri 10am–noon; charge), which houses an impressive collection of 20th- and 21st-century Egyptian art, and the **Hanager Art Centre**, devoted to contemporary art. Across the road is the **Mokhtar Museum** (Shari' Tahrir; Tue–Sun 10am–1pm, 5–9pm, Fri 9am–noon; charge), dedicated to the sculptor who created the sculpture of Saad Zaghlul on the nearby square.

The 187-metre (614ft) **Cairo Tower** ㉞ (daily 9am–1am; charge) offers magnificent views from its viewing platform and revolving restaurant (although if you are staying in one of central Cairo's high-rise hotels, you'll get the same view free). Nearby are the Gazirah Sporting Club (members only), which was laid out by the British army on land given by the *khedive* Tewfiq. The **Gazirah Palace**, built by the *khedive* Ismail between 1863 and 1868, forms part of the **Cairo Marriott Hotel**, which contains much of the furniture that the *khedive* brought back from the Paris Exposition of 1867. Next door, another small palace contains the **Gazirah Arts Centre** (Sat–Thur 9am–1pm; free), with a unique collection of Islamic ceramics.

Zamalik

The residential area of **Zamalik** occupies the northern half of Gazirah; it is here that most of the foreign embassies are located. The upper middle classes of Cairo live in these (relatively) leafy streets reminiscent of a faded Parisian neighbourhood. Here you will find designer boutiques, intimate eateries and residences catering to the moneyed elite. But the high rents are slowly taking effect, as the best shops move out to the new shopping malls in the suburbs, where air conditioning and modern construction mean owners need not battle the effects of pollution and subsidence. This is a shame, as Zamalik has character and atmosphere, unlike the suburbs on the Giza side of the Nile – Al Mohandessin, Al Aquzah, Ad Duqqi – which could be the suburbs of any city.

Zamalik is also home to the **Islamic Ceramics Museum** (Sat–Thur 9.30am–2pm, 5–9pm; charge), located in the former palace of Prince Amr Ibrahim. The collection dates back to the 7th century and includes examples of work from across the Islamic world – from Morocco to India. The art gallery in the basement level showcases modern Egyptian work and is free of charge.

French masters

On the west bank of the Nile, on Shari' Al Gizah, just south of the Cairo Sheraton, the **Muhammad Mahmud and Emilienne Luce Khalil Museum** (Tue–Sun 10am–5.30pm; charge; visitors must show ID) houses the **Khalil Collection.** This bequest to the nation contains primarily French 19th-century painting – Ingres, Delacroix, Corot, Courbet, Renoir, Sisley, Pissarro, Degas, Manet and Monet. The house, confiscated from the Muhammad Ali family, is worth visiting in its own right. ❑

Art for sale in Altabar Square.

BELOW: at Al Fishawy, a famous Cairene coffee house near the Khan Al Khalili Bazaar.

EGYPTIAN MUSEUM

This museum, one of Cairo's greatest attractions, contains a breathtaking display of objects, from jewellery to mosaics and, of course, mummies

The Egyptian Museum was first established in 1857 by a Frenchman, Auguste Mariette, founder of the Egyptian Antiquities Service. Mariette's tomb and a memorial to him can be seen outside this grand neoclassical building. It was Mariette who, in 1860, excavated the incredible black diorite statue of Pharaoh Khafra (Chephren), which is still one of the highlights of the collection. Originally located in the suburb of Bulaq, the museum relocated to Giza in 1891, and the present building was opened in 1902 to house the ever-expanding collection. There are so many objects within the storerooms that most have little opportunity of being seen by the public, and even the experts are left to rediscover important pieces that have been "lost" in the museum for years. But the very best examples of statues, carvings, paintings, funerary objects, mummies, jewellery and mosaics are on display here. A new museum is under construction at Giza, and the artefacts will be distributed between the two sites.

The most popular attractions are the amazing objects from the tomb of King Tutankhamun, but the small dark room containing his death mask often becomes uncomfortably crowded. If this is the case, take the opportunity to see the wonderful objects from the lesser-known Royal Tombs nearby, discovered unplundered at Tanis in the northern Delta in 1939. The golden objects are simply stunning, dating to the 21st and 22nd dynasties (around 1000 BC), when Tanis was the capital of kings who originated in Libya to the west. Coinciding with the outbreak of World War II, this discovery went almost unnoticed, and even today few people know about these gorgeous objects. Had they been discovered at any other time these finds would have been as famous as Tutankhamun's relics. Tanis has since gained notoriety as the fictional setting of the original *Indiana Jones* film, where the Ark of the Covenant was "rediscovered".

ABOVE: dwarfed by colossal limestone statues of Amenhotep III and his wife, Tiye, visitors to the museum stand in awe at the remarkable collection of antiquities within the Egyptian Museum. But it is rare to see the rooms so empty – usually they are thronged with visitors, many of whom, overwhelmed by the sheer size of the collection, concentrate on the Tutankhamun exhibits and the ever-popular Mummy Room.

RIGHT: original pieces of papyrus give Egyptologists additional information about inscriptions and tomb paintings. On the staircases of the museum are some wonderful examples, with colours that are still remarkably fresh. Upstairs in Room 29 are ornamental texts from the *Book of the Dead* and samples of the writing equipment used.

LEFT: the funerary death mask of King Tutankhamun was probably very lifelike and indicates that he was a young man. Above his face on the gold and blue striped headdress is the vulture and *uraeus* (a cobra signifying royalty), while a false beard has been attached to his chin.

THE TOMB OF KING TUTANKHAMUN

One of the great events of 20th-century archaeology was the discovery of the intact tomb of King Tutankhamun in 1922. Howard Carter was on the brink of giving up his long search in the Valley of the Kings, when a single step leading to the tomb's doorway was uncovered below the debris of another tomb. Over the following years, thousands of delicate objects were removed to the safety of the Egyptian Museum. Since the discovery there have been rumours of a "curse" upon those individuals who dared to enter the tomb, which perhaps began when the man who financed Carter's excavations, Lord Carnarvon, died soon afterwards at his Cairo hotel.

Tutankhamun's worldwide appeal is so great that his Egyptian motifs and designs are inspirations for fashion, jewellery, decoration and architecture, beginning with the 1930s Art Deco period. Highlights of the collection regularly tour the world and are exhibited in some of the greatest museums.

ABOVE: it was not only human bodies that were mummified; so, too, were animals that were considered sacred because of their association with important gods, such as the falcon-headed Horus or the cat-goddess Bastet. Room 53, on the upper floor, has a fascinating collection of mummified animals including cats, dogs, snakes, baboons and even a 6-metre (18ft) long crocodile. Animal mummies are usually popular with children, and the museum has initiated an adopt-an-animal-mummy project.

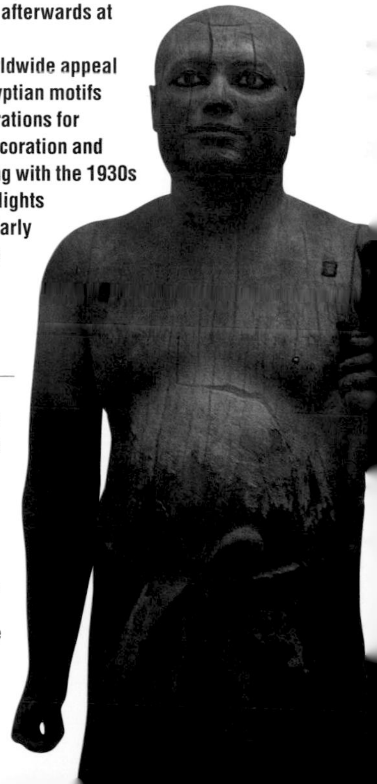

RIGHT: the wooden statue of dignitary Ka-Aper dates from 4,500 years ago, and is now known as Sheikh al-Balad or the "village mayor". When the statue was excavated, the workmen thought it looked remarkably like the headman of the village of Saqqarah.

THE DELTA

Crisscrossed by streams and canals, the fertile lands of the Delta are heavily populated and relatively undiscovered by tourists. After the capital, the Mediterranean breezes in Alexandria and along the coast are a welcome change

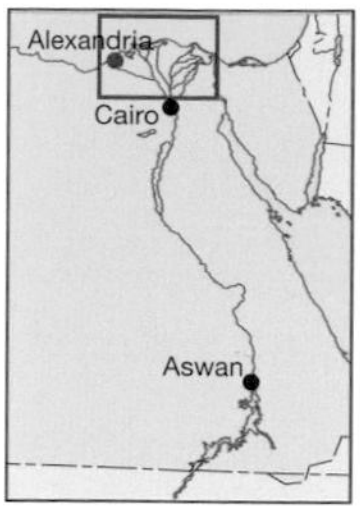

Main attractions
- AL QANATIR
- TANTA
- DAMIETTA
- BUBASTIS
- TANIS
- ROSETTA
- ALEXANDRIA

After the noise of Cairo, the River Nile is ready for the peace of the sea. In its hurry to get there it splits, first in two, then into the myriad canals and streams of the Delta. But in this densely populated region of Egypt, so named by the Greeks for its similarity on the map to their triangular letter D, the river has yet to endure its most intensive use by man.

Around 160km (100 miles) wide at its Mediterranean base and about the same length, the flat, rich Nile Delta contains more than half of Egypt's agricultural land and much of its industry. More than 16 million Egyptians live in its thousands of villages, cultivating extensive mango and citrus orchards, cotton, wheat and vegetables for the stomachs of the insatiable capital. Roads, railways, bridges and canals crisscross the land. To the east and west, the once impenetrable desert is giving way to mammoth land reclamation projects.

Building on the floodplain

The Delta was once part of the sea. Millennia of Nile alluvia washing down from Ethiopia created first swamps, then exceptionally fertile farmland. During the annual flood, river water turned the Delta into a vast lake. Consequently the ancient Egyptian inhabitants built their towns on hills and hummocks, which appeared like islands when the inundation was at its full height.

Even though the Delta has a massive – and growing – population, this area of Egypt is largely workaday, with few major sites on the "must-see" tourist map. This is largely due to the constant flooding that affected the region until the completion of the Aswan High Dam. Temples were built here, but the regular flooding washed the structures away during the rainy season. Even

PRECEDING PAGES: the Bibliotheca Alexandrina. **LEFT:** a sphinx near the Serapeum, Alexandria. **RIGHT:** along the Corniche.

The natural gas production facility at Idku.

with the dam, the region is not safe from being washed away as the Mediterranean coastline creeps ever inward each year *(see page 278)*.

Unsurprisingly, the people of the Delta are known chiefly for their industriousness, in contrast to the laid-back image of the Upper Egyptians. Despite a proximity to Cairo and Alexandria and a relatively prosperous economic base, patches of the Delta do not display much of this prosperity, as can be seen from the vintage taxis that chug along its byways.

A watery past

Early in Egyptian history the Delta was a relatively wild region and its people were distinct from their cousins in Upper Egypt. Some 5,000 years ago the first pharaohs joined Egypt's marshy north to the south in a united kingdom, symbolised in their headdress known as the double crown, which combined the red crown of Lower Egypt and the white, conical crown of Upper Egypt. In the course of time the Delta became much tamer, and by late antiquity its cities – Tanis, Sais, Naucratis, Bubastis – had largely overtaken Memphis, Thebes and other southern cities in importance.

Sadly for us, whereas Upper Egypt enjoyed an accessible supply of sturdy building stone, the Delta had to make do with mud-brick. As a result, little of the glory of its past has endured. Although many of the most precious individual objects in the Egyptian Museum were found in the Delta, its ancient sites are for the most part mounds of mud and shards intelligible only to the most patient of excavators. The greatest of them, Tanis in the Eastern Delta, is nothing but a desolate heap of dirt littered with chunks of masonry.

Because of their lack of standing structures, the Delta sites have until recently received little attention from archaeologists. But with the intensification of agriculture that followed the building of the High Dam at Aswan, waterlogging has become a serious worry to Egypt's Antiquities Organisation, which now actively promotes excavation in the Delta to save what they can before it's too late.

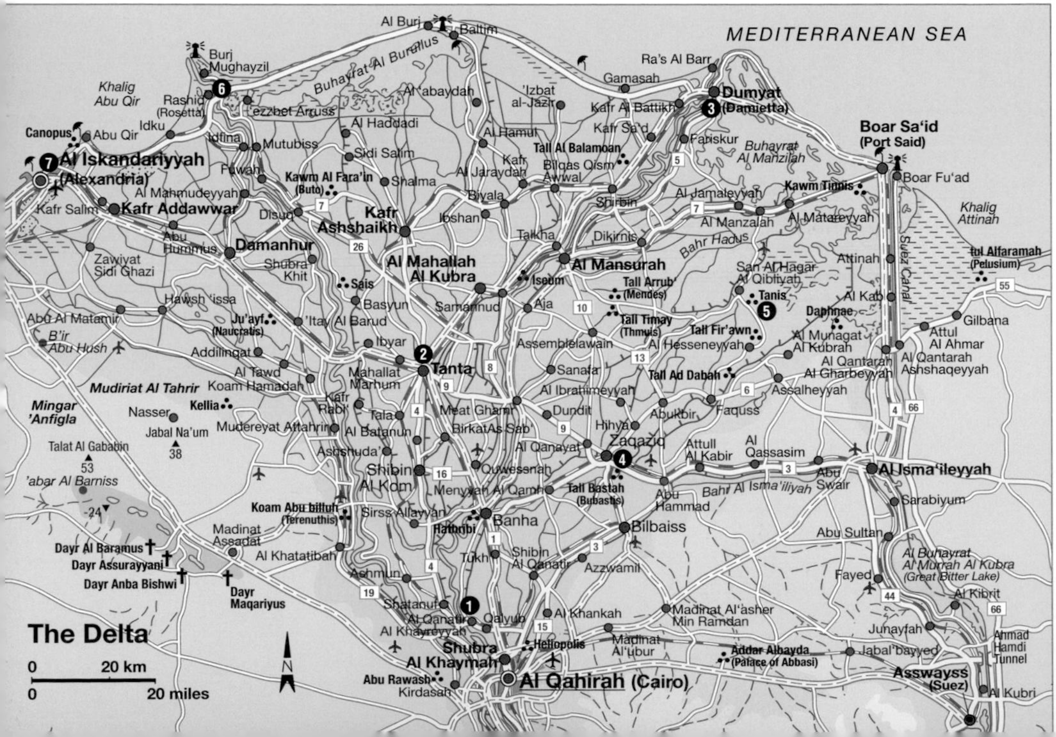

A Delta tour

The Delta begins in Cairo itself, where the first of its canals branches eastwards, heading ultimately to the Suez Canal at Al Isma'ileyyah along the route of the ancient seaway built by the Persians in the 6th century BC. But the great city's industrial suburbs do not end until the river itself divides. This spot is marked by the multiple arches and sluices of the barrages at **Al Qanatir** ❶, built in the 19th century to control the annual flood. Here extensive parks, now somewhat scruffy, are a favourite destination for summer outings.

Northwards the plain broadens continuously, dotted with tiny hamlets and the remnants of the huge estates that were divided up by the revolutionary government of the 1950s. Sadly, a loss of local pride seems to have accompanied the decline of the landed gentry that once built stylish villas and parks here. Provincial towns like Shibin Al Kom, Damanhur, Kafr Ashshaikh, Banha and Al Mansurah are overgrown and have little to offer.

The largest city of the Delta is **Tanta** ❷, a ramshackle place that marks the halfway point between Cairo and Alexandria. Every October its half-million inhabitants are swollen to four times their number during the Islamic saint's day of Ahmed Al Bedawi, a 13th-century mystic who founded Egypt's biggest Sufi brotherhood. This ancient, perhaps even pre-Islamic, *mawlid*, the biggest of the Egyptian calendar, is celebrated with the enthusiastic use of megaphones, strobe lights and riot police. By day, pilgrims flood to the grandiose tomb and mosque of the saint, which is ringed by the kind of commercial enterprises that usually surround an important tomb or pilgrimage centre – from circumcision booths to stalls selling nougat, dates, whistles and party hats. By night increasingly rowdy revellers throng the streets.

Other towns hold smaller festivals for their local saints, but these days Delta cities are better known for their industries. **Talkha** is dominated by its mammoth fertiliser plant, **Kafr Addawwar** and **Al Mahallah Al Kubra** are centres of the cotton industry. **Damietta** ❸ (Dumyat), an ancient seaport near the mouth of the river that bears its name, rivalled Alexandria in the Middle Ages. In modern times, it has grown prosperous as a centre for the production of lurid rococo-style furniture.

Ancient sites of the Delta

The town of **Zaqaziq** ❹, heavily polluted by the fumes from a soap factory, is the nearest town to the ancient site of **Bubastis** (daily 8.30am–4pm; charge), a thriving cult centre for the cat-goddess Bastet. Some 157km (97 miles) northeast of Zaqaziq is one of the oldest known sites in Egypt, the town of **Tanis** ❺, thought to have been the capital of the 21st Dynasty. In 1939 the French archaeologist Pierre Montet discovered the tombs of Osorkon II and Psusennes II filled with the so-called treasure of Tanis, now on display in the Egyptian Museum in Cairo. There are further remains of a large Ramessid temple devoted to Amun. Nearby is Tall Ad Dabah,

TIP

If you want to visit the barrages at Al Qanatir, on Friday special boats, packed with weekending Cairenes, leave from the Maspero dock opposite the television building in Cairo.

BELOW: an effective means of transport in the mud lanes of the Delta.

The Rosetta Stone

A simple stone discovered in Rosetta in 1799 was the key to unlocking the mystery of the ancient Egyptian hieroglyphs

Pierre Bouchard, a Frenchman working for Napoleon, was strengthening a fort at Rosetta when he turned up a slab about the size of a gravestone. Its implications were obvious even to an army engineer. He announced his discovery in the armed forces newspaper which Napoleon's printing presses were producing in Cairo: "a stone of very fine granite, black, with a close grain, and very hard... with three distinct inscriptions separated in three parallel bands."

Two of the bands were in the meaningless scripts to be seen on monuments all along the Nile. No one had been able to understand the hieroglyphs since the 4th century AD, and the few words which had passed into the Coptic language were no help.

The exciting part of Bouchard's discovery was the last of the parallel bands, which was in readable Greek. The stone identified itself as a proclamation by Ptolemy V in 196 BC and said that the other languages were Egyptian. One was the classic form of hieroglyphs, the other a more manageable demotic script derived from it. The stone was hurried to Cairo where Napoleon had casts made.

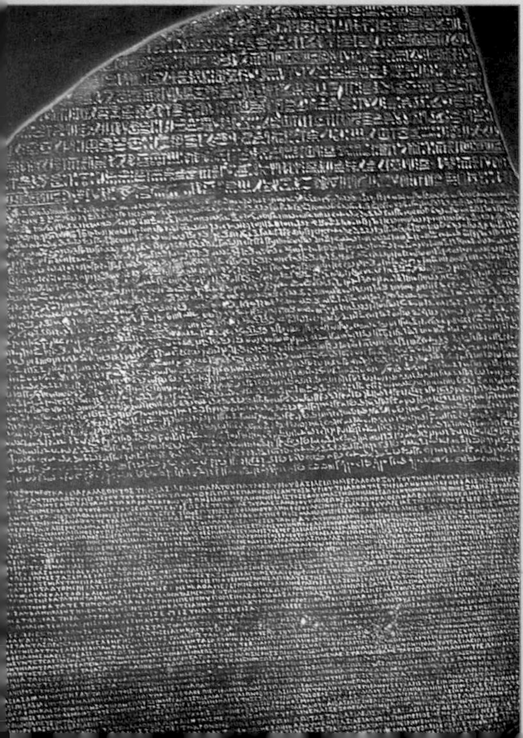

Napoleon later sneaked back to France, and in due course his army surrendered to the British. One of the terms of surrender was that Britain would take everything the *savants* had collected in Egypt. The French scholars were appalled and threatened to dump the whole lot.

Happily the British were willing to negotiate – over everything but the Rosetta Stone. On this point the British army officers were being strenuously lobbied by two civilians, one of them being William Hamilton, on whose advice Lord Elgin had carted off large chunks of the Parthenon in Athens, the still controversial "Elgin Marbles". Like the Marbles, the stone was taken to London's British Museum.

Deciphering the code

The decipherment of the Rosetta Stone became something of a race, albeit at a snail's pace. A Swede named Akerblad spotted that royal names in the Greek part had fairly obvious equivalents in the demotic. He also recognised three words: "his", "Greek" and "temple". In England the pioneering work was done by Thomas Young, who went on to become the *Encyclopaedia Britannica*'s authority on some 400 languages.

He made quick work of the demotic signs, establishing that the "rope-loops" now called cartouches were the names of kings. Recognising that all three versions had letters which spelt out p-t-o-l-e-m-y meant that hieroglyphs must have been a kind of alphabet and had a grammar.

Thomas Young forwarded his findings to a Professor Jean-François Champollion in France, who was still labouring under the idea that hieroglyphic symbols represented whole ideas when Young put him on the right track, a debt he never acknowledged.

Nonetheless, full credit is due to Champollion for the conclusive decipherment. Unluckily he died in 1832 at the age of 42 before the publication of his historic grammar, after which, instead of being mere decoration on walls and papyri, hieroglyphs sprang to life as the deeds, words and thoughts of people who had been muted for 1,500 years. ❑

LEFT: the Rosetta Stone, which now resides in the British Museum in London.

where discoveries have led archaeologists to believe that this was Avaris, the vanished Hyksos capital. In 1991 in a Hyksos palace, archaeologists discovered beautiful Minoan-style frescoes. One layer revealed the bodies of non-Egyptians, mainly of children under the age of two.

Alone among its sister towns, **Rosetta** ❻ (Rashid), where the famous stone was found *(see opposite)*, was a notable city in the Middle Ages. It still has charm; its neat, narrow lanes lined with brick houses characteristic of the Delta run down to a waterfront crammed with fishing vessels and boatyards. Eight kilometres (5 miles) downstream, the Rosetta branch of the Nile, much reduced by man's exploitation, slides quietly into the sea. To the west, the Damietta branch does the same, entering the Mediterranean at Ra's Al Barr. In between, the windswept coast is largely barren.

Along the shore lies a series of wide, marshy lakes: **Maryut**, **Idku**, **Burullus** and **Manzilah**. Accessible only by punts, these wetlands are a hideout for fugitives from justice. They also provide refuge for the migrating waterfowl.

The Bride of the Sea

Although it is not strictly of the Nile – the river is linked to it by a canal – no description of Egypt would be complete without mentioning its second city, **Alexandria** ❼ (Al Iskandariyyah), easily reached by train from Cairo's main railway station on Meadan Al Rameses. To Egyptians, this great and ancient port is known as the "Arousat Al Bahr" or the Bride of the Sea. The name may seem corny, but Alexandria's intimate relationship with the Mediterranean makes it strangely appropriate – it has always been Egypt's conduit to the Mediterranean world. The city of over 6 million inhabitants is slender, but it stretches along the shore from east to west for over 48km (30 miles), and almost anywhere in the city one is never far from the sound of surf or the smell of fresh fish. In summer millions of festive Egyptians descend upon its streets and its beaches, while in winter occasional sea storms bombard the buildings, rusting away the wrought-iron balconies on the Corniche. The sea lends a sense of freedom to Alexandria, which is refreshing after the confinement of the Nile Valley.

A wealth of history

Alexandria was named after its illustrious founder, Alexander the Great, who marked the city's boundaries around the small fishing village of Rhakotis in 331 BC, but never saw his great city as he left for Siwa shortly after and died a few years later in 325 BC. Ever since, emperors, monarchs, archaeologists and admirers of the great general have searched for his lost tomb, believed by some to lie beneath the city.

Under Alexander's successors, the Ptolemies, the city grew into the most illustrious centre of Hellenistic culture in the Mediterranean. The Ptolemies embellished their capital with fine buildings, including the Pharos (lighthouse), which was considered to be one of the Seven Wonders of

Montazah Park lighthouse. In ancient times the city's Pharos was one of the Seven Wonders of the Ancient World.

BELOW: the Cap d'Or bar, Alexandria.

> *...few cities have made so magnificent an entry into history as Alexandria.*
>
> E.M. Forster

the Ancient World. The city's famous Library and Mouseion carried the baton of Greek science and literature until the fall of the Roman empire. It was here that Eratosthenes declared that the earth was round, the Old Testament was translated, Euclid developed geometry, and medical science made more advances than in the ensuing 1,000 years. The last and probably most famous Ptolemy was Cleopatra VII (69–30 BC), the lover of first Julius Caesar and later Mark Antony.

Alexandria's decline

Alexandria's wealth and glory slowly disappeared after the Arabs conquered Egypt in AD 641. The discovery of the sea route towards India and the Orient around the Cape of Good Hope hit Alexandria hard. Up until then, Alexandria had been the entry point for transporting goods overland to the Red Sea and beyond. The sea route around Africa meant that land crossings were less viable, and Alexandria swiftly lost its importance along the trade routes. By the end of the 18th century, the population of the city had fallen to just 5,000 and houses were crumbling from disrepair.

The city regained some of its fame, wealth and splendour during the 19th century when Muhammad Ali

decided to make Egypt a maritime power and needed a suitable harbour. The Mahmudiyyah Canal linked the city to the Nile, and a large modern harbour was created; the city also became the centre of Egypt's prosperous trade in cotton. As European merchants settled in town it became the cosmopolitan city of many pleasures that is described by Lawrence Durrell in his four novels *Alexandria Quartet*.

In retaliation for the Orabi revolt against foreign influence in 1882, British warships bombed the city. Although this did not deter the foreign nationals in the city, when President Nasser nationalised foreign businesses after the Suez Crisis in 1956 most foreigners decided it was time to leave town.

The nationalist fervour sparked by the events of 1956, so important in forming a sense of pride in the Egyptian psyche, also served to decimate the international flavour of this city on the sea. Where once there were Christians and Jews, French and Turks living side by side, there are now just Egyptians – and a few remaining and rapidly ageing Greek residents who didn't have the heart (or means) to leave their beloved city.

Illusion or disillusion?

In spite of so much history, no other Egyptian city reveals so little of its past. At first sight modern Alexandria's buildings seem tired and dilapidated, and certainly nothing like the magical city that its name conjures up. Where are Cleopatra's Palace, the legendary Pharos or even the elegant city where Justine conducted passionate affairs in Durrell's *Alexandria Quartet*? And where are the sleazy brothels in which the poet Cavafy sought to relieve his loneliness? The answer is simple: in Alexandria the past is always underneath your feet.

The Graeco-Roman Museum

One of the best places to start exploring the city is at the **Graeco-Roman Museum** Ⓐ. This museum has been closed for restoration for many years – at the time of writing it was due to reopen in 2013. It contains Egypt's largest collection of Graeco-Roman

Head of Serapis, a composite of the Greek god Dionysos and the Egyptian Osiris, in the Graeco-Roman Museum, Alexandria.

BELOW LEFT: cutting it fine in a barber's shop.

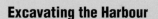

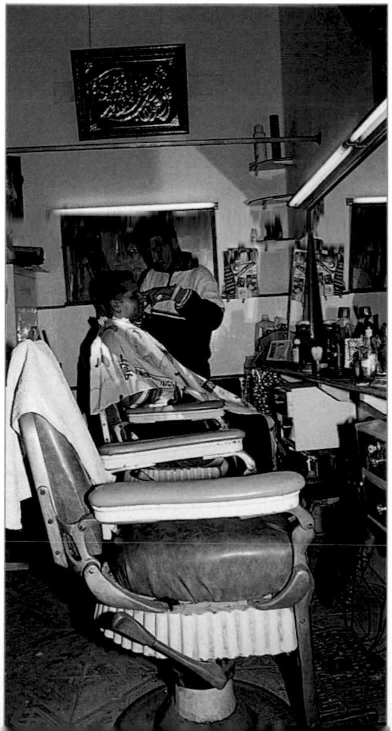

Excavating the Harbour

Alexandria has been continuously inhabited since antiquity, with each civilisation building on top of the previous one. Today, every construction site is studied by archaeologists before building can commence, and new areas and relics of the ancient city, including statues, sculptures and pottery, are continually being revealed. It has been known for holes to open up suddenly in a road, uncovering catacombs or other treasures.

But it is offshore that the most exciting finds have been uncovered. Two separate teams have recently been at work beneath the Eastern Harbour, raising thousands of fragments from Cleopatra's Palace and the Pharos, including large statues, obelisks and some 20 sphinxes. In the majority of cases, the sea has eroded the inscriptions, but under the barnacles covering one obelisk they found the title of the New Kingdom pharaoh Sety I (1291–1278 BC).

Some of the recovered treasures can be seen in the National Museum of Alexandria. It is hoped that visitors will eventually be able to see many of the remains in situ, and plans for an underwater museum are currently under way. In the meantime a small company, **Alexandria Dive** (tel: 03-483 2045; www.alexandra-dive.com), offers diving tours of all these underwater sites.

TIP

Alexandria's best beaches are found outside the city centre, specifically to the east near the Montazah Gardens. Other beaches can also be found at Ma'amoura or in the village of Abu Qir further east. Alternatively, go west to the resort towns of Agami, Hannoville or Sidi Krear.

artefacts (*c.*331 BC–AD 300) from sites in and around Alexandria. Exhibits are arranged chronologically, starting with a magnificent 2nd-century AD black-granite Apis bull and a Roman bust of the main god of Alexandria, Serapis, a hybrid of Dionysos and Osiris, which was an attempt by the Ptolemies to unite the Egyptian and Greek cults.

The **National Museum of Alexandria** Ⓑ (110 Tariq Al Hurriyyah; daily 9am–5pm; charge) provides a broader history of the city. It is laid out chronologically over three floors: the basement is devoted to the pharaonic period, the ground floor to the Graeco-Roman period, which includes sculptures found in the Eastern Harbour, and the top floor to Coptic, Muslim and modern Alexandria.

Interesting finds to look out for include a massive mosaic of Medusa's head discovered during construction on a local cinema, and a number of impressive statues found buried in the seabed off the coast *(see box, page 277)*, including a basalt statue of the goddess Isis.

Downtown Alexandria

Alexandria's modern centre still more or less follows the plan of the Ptolemaic city – the two main streets, Canopic and Soma Street, are now **Shari' Tariq Al Hurriyyah** and **Shari' An Nabi Danyal**. Some believe the tomb of Alexander lies underneath the **Nabi Danyal Mosque** Ⓒ, on Shari' An Nabi Danyal, which also houses the tombs of Danyal Al Maridi and Lukman the Wise.

In Shari' Sharm Al Sheikh, a small side street off Shari' An Nabi Danyal, the former flat of the Greek poet Constantine Cavafy (1863–1933) has become the **Cavafy Museum** Ⓓ (Tue–Sun 10am–3pm; charge), a place of pilgrimage for fans from all over the world. On display are collections of his work, his bed, desk and letters of correspondence.

Just off the shopping street Shari' Al Hurriyyah, near the Pastroudis patisserie (a favourite hangout for Durrell and Cavafy), is **Kom Ad Dekkah** Ⓔ ("Pile of Rubble"; daily 9am–4.30pm; charge), with a 2nd-century Roman Odeon, the only surviving theatre of the Graeco-Roman city; it has marble

The Delta's Fragile Environment

The Delta environment is the most threatened of any in the Nile basin. Overuse of irrigation has caused serious drainage problems, pushing salts to the surface and reducing the fertility of the soil – which is no longer replenished by the Nile's flood-borne silt. Pollution from untreated waste and agricultural chemicals has sharply reduced the fish catch, particularly in the northern lakes where fishing was once a major source of livelihood. Attempts to control some hazards have exacerbated others: government use of weed-killer on the water hyacinth, an attractive blue-flowered plant that clogs canals, was found to be decimating aquatic fauna.

Worst of all, the Mediterranean Sea is swelling with the melting of polar ice caps, and threatens to drown the low-lying Delta. Where the Nile flows into the sea at Damietta (Dumyat) and Rosetta (Rashid), gigantic concrete dykes have been built to prevent shore erosion. Already lighthouses built onshore have been swamped. In the resort of Ra's Al Barr, just north of Damietta, a whole row of beach houses has been swallowed up, and high tides now lap in the living rooms of the next row.

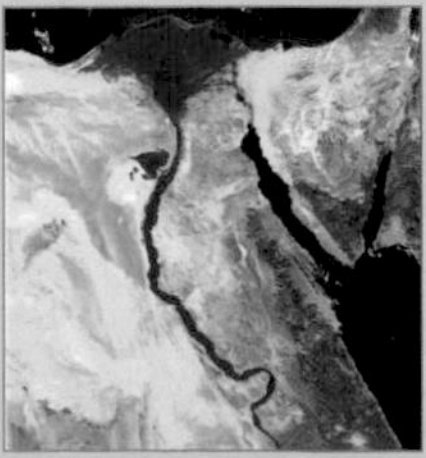

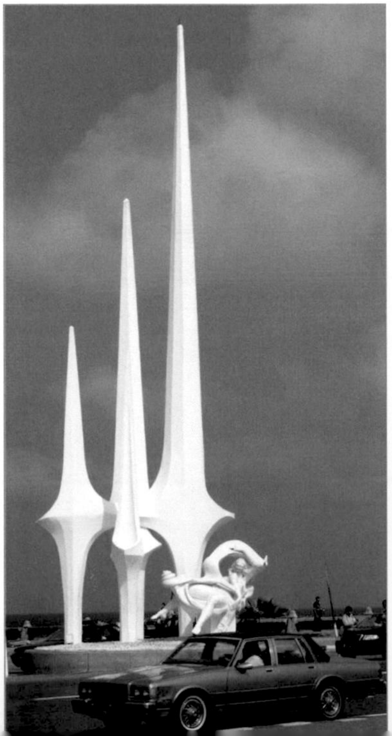

BELOW RIGHT: modern sculpture in Alexandria.

seating and a beautiful mosaic floor. The open-air museum in the gardens displays underwater finds from the Eastern Harbour, including a sphinx and the re-erected obelisk of Sety I.

The Corniche

A walk along the promenade will take you past turn-of-the-20th-century buildings slowly crumbling as they battle the effects of the sea air. This stroll is popular amongst couples and families, especially during the summer, when a refreshing breeze is a precious commodity.

The most famous location that speaks of Alexandria's cosmopolitan past is the **Grand Trianon** (Meadan Sa'd Zaghlul; daily 7am–midnight, patisserie closes at 8pm), an Art Nouveau masterpiece that houses a popular café, patisserie and restaurant. Since the day it opened in the 1920s, this is where Europeans conducted business deals, gossiped and dined. Today these expats have been replaced by upwardly mobile Egyptians who continue the traditions.

On the seafront is the once glamorous **Cecil Hotel** Ⓕ, whose rooms look out over the site of the Ptolemies' palaces and of the Caesareum, Cleopatra's monument to Mark Antony. Built in 1930, the hotel is an institution; former guests include Noel Coward, Somerset Maugham and Winston Churchill.

Liberation Square

Near the Cecil Hotel is **Meadan At tahrir** Ⓖ (Liberation Square), laid out by Muhammad Ali in 1830; his impressive equestrian statue stands at the centre. This was the heart of the European quarter during colonial times. The city's labyrinthine **Attarine souq** lies at the southwestern end of the square. As a wave of nationalism overtook Egypt post-independence, expat communities sold their family treasures to the antique sellers of the souq to raise funds. This became the place to go for authentic Greek, Roman, European and Egyptian items – all for a song. You're unlikely to find any such bargains now, but it's fun searching.

At tabhanah Ⓗ is one of the few remaining ancient mosques in the city. It was built in 1685, but has undergone numerous alterations since then. Two classical columns support the minaret,

The Corniche has been spruced up with new sights.

BELOW: fisherman at rest.

TIP

To the east of the city is the Royal Jewellery Museum (daily 9am–4pm), a dazzling testament to royal excess. Exhibiting jewels owned by the royal family from the rule of Pasha Muhammad Ali until the end of King Faruq's reign in 1952, highlights include a gold and diamond-studded chess set, the platinum, diamond and gold crown of Queen Safinaz, and a variety of beautifully inlayed and enamelled snuff boxes.

while other columns support a beautifully ornate ceiling.

The Citadel

Dominating the north of the bay is the 15th-century **Citadel of the Mamluk Sultan Qal'at Qayetbay** ❶ (daily 9am–2pm; charge), which stands on the site of the 125-metre (400ft) high Pharos built in 279 BC by Sostratus for Ptolemy II but destroyed by several earthquakes. It is believed that some of the stones from the ancient lighthouse may have been used in the original construction of the Citadel in the 1840s. A recent restoration has returned it to its former grandeur – the walls literally gleam. A wander around takes you through a small mosque, a naval museum showcasing artefacts taken from nearby wrecks, and various keeps and courtyards.

Alexandria's library

The splendid **Bibliotheca Alexandrina** ❶, at the other end of the Eastern Harbour (www.bibalex.org; Sat–Thur 11am–7pm, Fri 3–7pm; charge), is intended to become an international centre of knowledge like its ancient ancestor. The library is far from having the 8 million books it is designed to contain, but the building is spectacular and is one of Egypt's major cultural venues.

Opened to great fanfare in 2002, the library boasts the world's largest reading room, with enough space and light to accommodate 2,000. Guided tours of about 20 minutes' duration are offered throughout the day in multiple languages. Other highlights include the adjacent Manuscripts Museum, which has a copy of the only papyrus text to survive from the ancient library, and an interactive history "experience" called Culturama, which takes visitors on a walk through Egypt's past.

BELOW: Bibliotheca Alexandrina.

Temples and catacombs

In the southwest of central Alexandria is **Pompey's Pillar** ❶ (daily 9am–4pm; charge), a 27-metre (89ft) high pink granite column, built in around AD 295. Crusaders thought it supported a statue of Pompey, but it is more likely to have been one of Diocletian. This was the area of Rhakotis, where Alexander first marked out the city; nearby are the scant remains – two sphinxes and a few statues – of the **Serapeum**, which was destroyed by Christians in the 4th century. With its splendid Serapis temple and the Second Alexandrian Library containing Cleopatra's private collection of some 200,000 manuscripts, the Serapeum was for 400 years the most important intellectual and religious centre in the Mediterranean.

A donkey falling through the ground led to the discovery of Egypt's largest Roman burial site, the 2nd-century **Catacombs of Kom Ash Shuqafah** ❶ (daily 8.30am–4.30pm; charge). The impressive rooms of the catacombs, which are cut out of the rock to a depth of about 35 metres (115ft), are decorated in the distinctive Alexandrian blend of Egyptian, Greek and Roman motifs exemplified in the gods Anubis and Sobek dressed as Roman legionaries. ❑

The Suez Canal

Engineered by the French, built by the Egyptians and coveted by the British, the Suez Canal has been a troubled but lucrative waterway

Construction of the Suez Canal began in 1859. It took 10 years, with 25,000 labourers working three-month shifts, to cut the 160km (100-mile) channel. The total cost, including the building of the Sweetwater Canal for drinking water from the Nile, reached £25 million, of which Egypt put up more than two-thirds. Amid extravagant fanfare, the canal was opened to shipping in November of 1869, transforming trade and geopolitics as dramatically as the Portuguese and Spanish discoveries of the 15th century. At the same time, Cairo acquired an extravagant new opera house and a new palace (now the Marriott Hotel) to entertain and accommodate the important guests who attended the opening.

However, Egypt's mounting debts forced the sale of its stake to the British Government for a paltry sum of £4 million sterling. As London's *Economist* dryly commented in the year of its opening, the canal was "cut by French energy and Egyptian money for British advantage". The strategic importance of the canal to the British empire was one of the excuses for occupying Egypt in 1882.

The fortunes of five wars

Britain imposed draconian measures on Egypt while defending the canal in both world wars. For Egyptians, foreign possession of the canal came to represent the major reason for the anti-imperialist struggle. Not until 1954 did Nasser achieve the withdrawal of British troops occupying the Canal Zone.

In 1956, hard up and seeking to finance the High Dam, Nasser turned as a last resort – having been refused financing by the United States – to nationalising the canal, from which Egypt received only a tiny portion of the revenue. Unreconciled to the rapid decline of its empire, Britain responded by invading, with the collusion of Israel and France, in what became known as the Suez Crisis. Only the intervention of the US and the Soviet Union resolved the crisis, marking a turning point in international relations. Ten years later all that remained of Britain's empire were Gibraltar, Hong Kong and a few remote islands. Meanwhile Egypt had become dependent upon Russia.

In June 1967, the Israelis again attacked Egypt in the Six Day War, and held the Sinai Peninsula up to the edge of the canal. Heavy bombardment during the War of Attrition shattered the canal cities and made refugees of their 500,000 inhabitants. For six years, until the successful Egyptian counter-attack of the Yom Kippur War in 1973, the waterway was closed to traffic.

Today, the canal is the third-largest source of foreign currency after tourism and remittances from Egyptians working abroad. Almost 8 percent of all shipping traffic goes through the canal each year – more is expected as new construction is due to make the canal viable for supertankers within the next two to three years. ❑

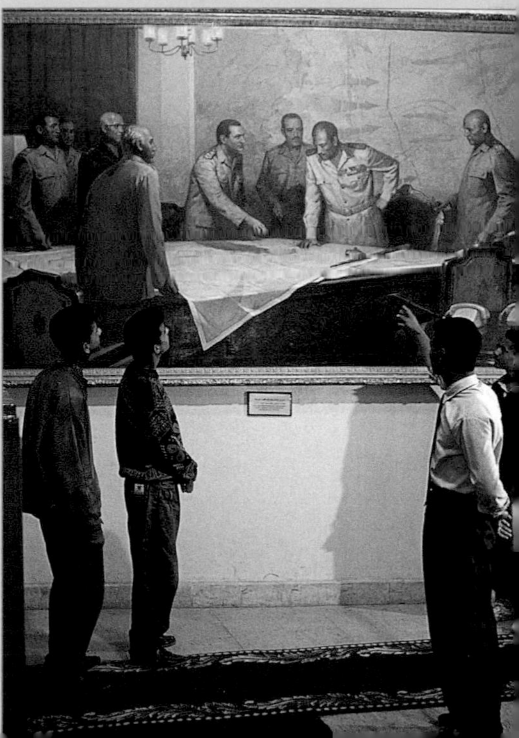

ABOVE: the grand opening of the canal in 1869.
RIGHT: visitors to the War Museum in Port Said.

INSIGHT GUIDES **TRAVEL TIPS**

THE NILE

Transport

Getting There 284
By Air 284
By Sea 285
By Land 285
Getting to Ethiopia, Sudan and Uganda 285
Getting Around 285
From the Airport 285
Public Transport 286
By Taxi 286
Private Transport 288
Orientation 286
Distances from Cairo 287
Getting Around Ethiopia, Sudan and Uganda 288

Accommodation

Booking Your Hotel 289
In Egypt 289
In Ethiopia 289
In Sudan 290
In Uganda 290
Price Categories 290
In Egypt
Nubia and Lake Nasser 290
Aswan 291
Luxor 292
Middle Egypt 293
Cairo and Environs 293
The Delta 296

Eating Out

Street Food 297
Middle Eastern Food 297
Drinking Notes 297
In Ethiopia 298
In Sudan 298
In Uganda 298
In Egypt
Aswan 299
Luxor 299
Cairo 300
The Delta: Alexandria 302

Activities

The Arts 304
Art Galleries 304
Ballet and Dance 304
Theatre 304
Casinos 305
Cinemas 305
Sound and Light Shows 305
Festivals and Events 306
Shopping 306
Shopping Tips 307
Antiquities/Antiques 306
Appliqué 306
Baskets 306
Books 306
Brass and Copper 307
Carpets and Rugs 307
Clothing 307
Crafts 307
Furniture/Woodwork/Textiles 307
Jewellery 307
Leather 308
Musical Instruments 308
Muski Glass 308
Papyrus 308
Perfume 308
Participant Sports 308
Balloon Rides 308
Cycling 308
Diving 308
Fishing 308
Fitness Centres 308
Gliding 308
Golf 308
Horse Riding 308
Yachting 309
Spectator Sports 309
Football 309
Horse Racing 309
Cruises 309
Nile Cruises 309
Cruising on Lake Nasser 309
A Felucca Cruise 310
Dahabiyyahs 310
Dining with your Captain 310

A – Z

Admission Charges 311
Age Restrictions 311
Budgeting for your Trip 311
Calendars 312
Children 312
Climate 312
Crime and Safety 313
Customs Regulations 313
Disabled Travellers 314
Electricity 314
Embassies/Consulates 314
Emergencies 315
Etiquette 315
Gay and Lesbian Travellers 316
Health and Medical Care 316
Internet 316
Left Luggage 316
Lost Property 316
Maps 316
Media 316
Money 317
Opening Hours 317
Photography 317
Postal Services 318
Public Holidays 318
Religious Services 318
Telephones 319
Time Zone 319
Toilets 319
Tourist Information 319
Tour Operators/Travel Agents 319
Visas and Passports 320
Weights and Measures 320
Women Travellers 320

Language

Egyptian Arabic 321
Transliteration 321
Vocabulary 321

Further Reading

The Nile 323
Ancient Egypt 323
Explorers 323
Culture and Society 323
Travellers 323
Fiction 323
Authors 323

TRANSPORT

Getting There and Getting Around

Getting There

By Air

Egypt is served by international airports at Alexandria, Cairo, Aswan, Luxor, Hurghada, Taba, Marsa Alam and Sharm Al Sheikh.

Return tickets may have to be confirmed before departure. Check with a travel agent in your hotel or contact the airline office in Cairo. Most major airlines have offices at the Cairo International Airport and in and around Meadan At tahrir in downtown Cairo.

Cairo International Airport is now a first-class facility. Despite the fact that it is located to the north of the city, most airlines from Europe approach the air field from the south. In daylight passengers have a magnificent view of Cairo, the Nile and the Giza Pyramids.

Alexandria Airport is served by a range of Middle Eastern scheduled carriers.

Luxor Airport now has direct flights from many European cities via Egyptair and several charter companies.

Hurghada Airport is serviced by easyJet, Austrian Airlines and a number of Eastern European budget carriers, while **Sharm Al Sheikh** Airport receives charter and scheduled flights from all over Europe, including British Airways and easyJet. Marsa Alam and Taba International Airports are strictly for charter flights and some seasonal scheduled services.

Other airports in Egypt are at Asyut, Aswan, Abu Simbel, Al Arish, St Catherine's and Al Khargah Oasis.

Above: Cairo International Airport is served by most major airlines.

Domestic Airlines

Egypt has two national carriers for internal flights, Egyptair and its subsidiary Egyptair Express. They both run multiple flights daily between Cairo, Alexandria, Luxor, Aswan, Asyut, Abu Simbel, Marsa Alam, Taba, Sharm Al Sheikh and Hurghada and twice a week to Al Khargah Oasis.

Egyptair Offices
www.egyptair.com.eg
Alexandria
19 Meadan Saad Zaghlul, tel: 03-486-5701
Aswan
1 Abtal Al tahrir, Corniche An nil, tel: 097-231-5000
Cairo
9 Talaat Harb Street, tel: 02-2392-7664
6 Adly Street, tel: 2390-0999
Zamalik Club Force, Shari' 26th of July, Al Mohandessin, tel: 3347-2027
Cairo Sheraton, tel: 3336-2020
Heliopolis
22 Ibrahim Al Lakany, tel: 2418-3722
Luxor
Winter Palace Arcade, tel: 095-2336-5409

Cairo Terminals
Terminal 1
International carriers including Air France and KLM
Terminal 2
International Airlines including many regional Middle Eastern carriers
Terminal 3
Domestic Egyptair flights and international flights including all Star Alliance and Egyptair departures

Porter Service

For a rental of E£2, baggage trolleys are available at Cairo International Airport. There are also porters with larger trolleys to service individuals and groups.

Terminal 4
International cargo. English-language information, tel: 291-4255/66/77.

By Sea

Alexandria and Port Said on the Mediterranean Sea, and Suez and Nuweibah on the Red Sea, are ports of entry. There are no longer any direct ferries from Europe to Egypt.

By Land

From Israel

Private vehicles are not permitted to enter Egypt from Israel; however, travellers may use public transport and enter Egypt via Rafah on the northern coast of Sinai or from Eilat on the Red Sea. Buses run regularly from Tel Aviv and Jerusalem to the border at Rafah, but check beforehand that the border is open. Passengers disembark from the Israeli vehicle, go through customs and take an Egyptian bus or taxi. There are no facilities for issuing visas at the border. You will be subject to pay the Israeli departure tax and the Egyptian entry tax. In Eilat, Israeli buses are permitted to enter Egypt and travel as far as Sharm Al Sheikh at the southern tip of Sinai.

From Sudan

There is a weekly ferry from Wadi Halfa up Lake Nasser to Aswan. A ferry leaves Aswan every Monday at 3pm and arrives the following morning in Wadi Halfa, returning on Wednesday. Tickets are available in 1st or 2nd class from the Nile Navigation Company in Aswan, tel: 097-203-3348, in the office located next to the Marhaba Hotel. Visas must be presented prior to purchasing a ticket in either direction.

You must have a transit or tourist visa to enter Sudan, and if you plan to pass through you must have a visa for your next destination. All arrangements to enter Sudan, including visas, must either be made before you leave your home country (from the Sudanese embassy) or in Cairo. You can only receive a visa a maximum of 30 days prior to entering the country, and it is only valid for 30 days. All visas are single-entry only. Be aware that it can take the Sudanese embassy up to a month to issue a visa (3 Ibrahim Street, Garden City, Cairo tel: 2794-9661).

A word of warning: customs officials in Sudan have been known to take as long as half a day to process passengers.

From Libya

The border with Libya is open, and buses and taxis make regular runs between Cairo and Alexandria and Benghazi or Tripoli. However, there are some travel restrictions for Westerners. Consult your nearest Libyan embassy for details.

Driving to Egypt

All private vehicles entering Egypt must have a triptyque or *carnet de passage en douane* from an automobile club in the country of registration or pay customs duty, which can be as high as 250 percent. Emergency triptyques are available at the port of entry via the Automobile and Touring Club of Egypt. This permits a car to enter Egypt for three months with one extension. The extension is available from the Automobile and Touring Club of Egypt, Qasr An Nil, Cairo. All persons travelling in the vehicle must have a valid passport. Drivers must have an International Driver's Licence. (*See Private Transport, page 288* for details on driving in Egypt.)

GETTING AROUND

From the Airport

All airports in Egypt have a taxi service to city centres, operated on a flat-fee basis (ask your airline). In Cairo, transport includes limousine, taxi, and bus. Kerbside limousine service is offered by Misr Limousine (tel: 02-259 9813).

Official Cairo taxis are predominantly black and white and Alexandria taxis are black and orange. There are also larger Peugeot taxis in a variety of colours, but they all have an emblem and number painted on the driver's door. Fees are the same as the limousine service. New blue and yellow taxis with air conditioning and working meters are a welcome addition to the transport scene, but are very hard to spot.

Getting to Ethiopia, Sudan and Uganda

Ethiopia

Ethiopia is serviced by a number of international airlines, including British Airways, Egyptair, Kenya Airways, Lufthansa and the flag carrier, Ethiopian Airlines. Addis Ababa's Bole International Airport is the only international airport in the country.

If travelling by road, Ethiopia's borders are all currently open, with the exception of its border with Eritrea. You will need to divert via Djibouti instead. Not all border crossings are open to foreigners at all times. Check with the embassy in advance to determine the current state-of-play. Visas are required in advance for most bordering countries as they are not (usually) available at the border and you will be turned back if you don't have one.

Sudan

Ferries leave Egypt once a week to reach Wadi Halfa in Sudan, departing from Aswan on Monday afternoons. Alternatively, you can fly to Khartoum. Land routes do sometimes open with Egypt, but this ruling often changes according to the state of current relations.

From Ethiopia, the only border crossing is at Metema/Gallabat, 180km (110 miles) west of Gondar. There are also land routes to Kenya, Uganda, Chad and the Central African Republic; however, they are often closed, and reaching them can be treacherous as they are close to locations of intense conflict. Travelling by land from these locations is extremely ill-advised.

Uganda

While the border with Sudan remains open, it is completely unstable and battles often break out north of the border between the government and rebels. As such, crossing into or out of Uganda via Sudan is not advised given the current political situation. Land borders with Tanzania and Kenya are frequently used, and there are numerous buses that make the overnight journey between Kampala and Nairobi or Dar es Salaam.

Entebbe International Airport is the destination for a number of carriers from Africa and Europe, including British Airways, Kenya Airways, KLM, Ethiopian Airways, Brussels Airlines and South African Airways. Emirates also offers services from the Middle East.

If arriving from Tanzania, consider taking the ferry across Lake Victoria to Kampala. Boats depart the town of Mwanza on a regular basis; however, schedules change often.

Orientation

The Nile flows through the country from south to north. Upper Egypt is therefore the south, Lower Egypt the Delta. Upstream is south, downstream north. Maps are available from good bookshops.

Book them in advance by calling 16516.

The Airport Bus Service (No. 356) operates from Terminal 1. The bus leaves when full and stops at Meadan At tahrir in downtown Cairo, behind the Egyptian Museum. More convenient is the new Airport Shuttle Bus that takes travellers directly to or from destinations throughout the city, including Giza, Heliopolis, Zamalik and downtown. A new highway links Giza with the airport. Completed in 2009, it now slashes the time required to travel to this formerly traffic-snarled suburb.

Public Transport

By Rail

The Egyptian State Railway is a government-owned system founded in 1851, which services the entire Nile Valley down to Aswan, the Red Sea cities of Suez and Port Said, the Delta and northern coast cities of Alexandria (two stops) and Marsa Mutrah. There are at least half a dozen through trains a day on major routes, but train travel for foreigners is restricted – check at stations.

Fares are inexpensive, but unless you are travelling with a tour, tickets must be purchased at the main train stations (in Cairo, the main one is Rameses Station at Meadan Rameses).

The privately owned Wagon-Lits train company runs three fast turbo-trains a day from Cairo to Alexandria (2½ hours). Booking should be done in advance at Rameses Station, Cairo, or at Alexandria station. Wagon-Lits also operate trains and sleepers between Cairo and Luxor (10 hours) and Aswan (15 hours).

An English-speaking tourist office attendant can be reached 24 hours a day by calling 02-2579 0767. Bring passports for everyone travelling.

By Bus

Air-conditioned buses link most parts of Egypt to Cairo and Alexandria. Seats may be reserved up to two days in advance. There is also a fleet of cheaper, non-air-conditioned buses, with very frequent departures.

Tickets for air-conditioned buses must always be booked in advance. Bus tickets can be booked at the central bus stations of each major city. Tourist offices can be of assistance with schedules, but actual tickets must be booked in person or through a designated agent.

The fastest buses to Alexandria (3 hours) are operated by the Superjet and West & Middle Delta companies. The principal carrier to Aswan and Luxor is Upper Egypt Travel. One bus departs each day to complete the run to Aswan, departing early evening and arriving early the next morning.

Air-conditioned Superjets to Luxor and Aswan are not recommended, as the services involve overnight travel with non-stop loud videos.

The East Delta Co. covers the Canal Zone and most of the Delta. Most buses leave from the Turgoman Bus Station (Mo'af Turgoman), in Bulaq, 1km (½ mile) northwest of Rameses Station near the crossing of Shari' 26th of July and Galaa. Services for Sinai can still also be picked up from the old Sinai Terminal in Abbaseya.

By Bus around Cairo

The main local bus station is at Meadan Abdel Moniem Riad, behind the Egyptian Museum. The large red-and-white and blue-and-white buses are usually so overcrowded they assault one's sense of private space. They also provide ample opportunity for petty theft and unwelcome sexual encounters. But here are a few routes for the adventurous tourist:

- Numbers 13 and 49 to Zamalik
- Number 337 to Al Mohandessin
- Number 400 and 346 from the airport to downtown
- Number 755 to the Citadel
- Numbers 900, 355, 357 to the Pyramids

More comfortable are the smaller orange-and-white minibuses, which do not permit standing. Here are a few major routes (from Abdel Moniem Riad):

- Number 27 to Rameses station, Abbassiyah and the airport
- Number 49 to Zamalik

By Metro and Tram

Both Alexandria and Cairo have tram or metro systems that run through at least part of the city. Trains run every few minutes from early morning (5.30am) to midnight, and fares are inexpensive.

By Taxi

For one of the experiences of your life, take an Egyptian taxi. Taxi drivers seem to take over the whole road, and sometimes the pavement too. All taxis have orange licence plates and are identified by a number on the driver's door; both licence and identity numbers should be displayed on the dashboard. In Cairo and Alexandria taxis ply the streets at all hours of the day or night and can be flagged down. There are also taxi ranks at all the major hotels and public squares. Sharing a taxi is not unusual.

Official or metered prices are unrealistic, and meters are seldom used except in the new fleet of pre-bookable orange-and-blue taxis now available in Cairo. The fare should be agreed beforehand in non-metered taxis. The majority of taxi drivers are honest, but some try to cheat unwary foreigners, especially between five-star hotels and such destinations as the Pyramids or Khan Al Khalili. Do not hesitate to ask for assistance from the tourist police. At your destination, pay the fare in exact change (no tip is expected) and walk away. Drivers will not have change so be sure to carry small bill denominations with you at all times.

Taxi drivers are friendly, many speak English, some are college graduates moonlighting to supplement their incomes, and most are very eager to be hired by the day. The fee is negotiable, something in the region of £27–35 (E£150–200) per day. Such an arrangement is ideal for shopping or for seeing several scattered monuments. Many hotels and travel agents offer tours of Memphis, Saqqarah and Giza, but it's easy to arrange things independently. You can hire a taxi for the day fairly inexpensively – if you prefer, you could take a taxi just for the morning, to drive you to Memphis and Saqqarah and then drop you off at the Pyramids around lunchtime; from there you can later hire another taxi or catch a bus to take you back to town.

Taxis in Luxor and Aswan are equally easy to find (they line up outside all the hotels), but for the distance travelled they work out more expensive than those in Cairo *(see also Long-Distance Taxis, page 287)*.

Distances from Cairo

Distances between Cairo and Other Cities

North to Alexandria
225km/140 miles (Delta road)
221km/138 miles (desert road)
to Damietta
191km/119 miles
to the Barrages
25km/15 miles

South to Al Menyyah
236km/151 miles
to Asyut 359km/224 miles
to Luxor 664km/415 miles
to Esna 719km/449 miles
to Edfu 775km/484 miles
to Kom Ombo 835km/521 miles
to Aswan 880km/550 miles

ABOVE: a popular alternative to walking around Luxor.

By Tram around Alexandria

Tram lines in Alexandria run only between Ramleh Station (called "Terminus") near the Cecil Hotel and destinations to the east of the city.

- Tram 1 (Bacos line), Ramleh Station to Sidi Bishr
- Tram 2 (El Nasr line), Ramleh Station to Sidi Bishr
- Tram 3, Ramleh Station to Sidi Gaber
- Tram 4, circular route: Sidi Gaber, Ramleh Station, Sidi Gaber
- Tram 5, Ramleh Station to San Stefano via Bacos
- Tram 6, Ramleh Station to Sidi Bishr via Glym

By Metro around Cairo

In Cairo, the metro system is identified by circular signs with a big red M. The metro is clean and efficient, and an easy way to get around. Note that the first carriage on every train is reserved for women, and if you are a woman travelling on your own you may prefer to use it. The system runs north–south from Al Marg to Helwan through the heart of the city. Another line runs from the northern suburb of Shubra Al Qheima to Giza and Al Mounib. A third line is currently under construction that will link the airport once complete.

BELOW: Cairo taxi.

Useful stations are:
Mubarak Station Rameses Square, with access to the main train station and bus stations to Upper Egypt and the Oases.
Urabi Station Shari' Gala'a. *Al Ahram* newspaper.
Nasser Station Meadan Tawfiqiyyah.
Sadat Station Meadan At tahrir, with 10 entrances and access to Egyptian Antiquities Museum, the American University in Cairo, all major airline offices and the Mugamma'a (central administrative building).
Mari Girgiss at Old Cairo, with access to the Coptic Museum, Coptic churches and Roman fortress.
Saad Zaghlul Station The National Assembly. Zaghlul monument.

By Tram around Heliopolis

Only a few lines now remain operational outside the northern suburbs around Heliopolis. The most useful line runs from north of Meadan Rameses, more or less in front of the post office, to Meadan Roxy on the south side of Heliopolis. From there it splits into three lines: Abd Al Aziz Fahmi (green line) to the Heliopolis Hospital and Shams Club, Nuzha (red line) to Meadan Al Higaz and Nuzha, and Mirghani to Meadan Triomphe and the Military College.

By Service Taxi

Collective service taxis are a faster alternative to the bus, and will get you just about everywhere in Egypt. The fare is about the same as for the bus, and on the main routes there are several departures daily. These taxis, often estate Peugeots (hence their pet name of "Beejoo") seat six or seven and leave as soon as they are full. Drivers are renowned for their speed, since the sooner they arrive the sooner they can load up again. The service station is usually beside the bus or train station.

Long-Distance Taxis

Booking a taxi for a long-distance journey is often the most convenient and cost-effective method – especially if you want to travel between two points on your own schedule and don't want to be subject to the delays Egyptian transport methods usually experience. Travelling between Aswan and Luxor is often undertaken by taxi as it is an easy trip along a paved highway. When taking a taxi between the two cities, be sure to negotiate hard and inform the driver how many stops you want to make along the way, keeping in mind that the taxi will not be able to pick up fares during the return journey. Count on spending approximately E£300 for the one-way trip including stops at Kom Ombo and Edfu if you haggle well.

If you don't like to haggle, budget about E£50–100 more for the trip depending on how much the driver thinks he can get away with. The key to effective haggling is to offer about half of what the initial offer is and go from there *(see also box on page 307).*

Private Transport

Car Rental

Driving in Egypt is very demanding and not recommended (*see Driving Conditions* below). The best alternative is to hire a driver and a car together, thus freeing yourself to enjoy the scenery.

Car rental agencies exist at most major hotels and international airports. Foreigners must have an International Driver's Licence and be at least 25. Some agencies offer four-wheel drive vehicles, with or without driver, for desert travel. You will need your passport, driver's licence, and a prepayment. Credit cards are accepted.

Rental Agencies

Avis
Entrance 1, Sadat Academy Street, Maadi
Tel: 2527-5400
www.avis.com

Budget
22 Al Mathaf Al Zeraee Street, Dokki
Tel: 2539-1501
www.budget.com

Europcar
6M, Meadan 1226, behind Florida Mall, downtown
Tel: 2267-2439
www.europcar.com
Also for four-wheel drive vehicles with or without experienced desert drivers. Branch office in Sharm Al Sheikh.

Hertz
195 Shari' 26th of July, Al Mohandessin
Tel: 3347 4142
www.hertz.com

Limousines

Limousines are available for those who want to travel in style or at a fixed price:

All Egypt Limousine
1 Muhammad Maxhar Street, Zamalik
Tel: 2737-4422
www.allegyptlimousine.com

Misr Travel Limousine
Misr Travel Tower, Meadan Abbassiya 13th Floor
Tel: 2682-7029, Downtown location, tel: 2393-0010

Smart Limousine
151 Corniche An nil, Maadi
Tel: 2524-3006
www.smartlimo.com

Driving Conditions

The roads that lead from Cairo to Upper Egypt are the most congested and most dangerous in Egypt.

It is not advisable to drive at night; vehicles stop dead in the road and turn out their lights; unlit donkey carts move at a snail's pace and are usually not seen until it is too late; and long-distance taxis and overloaded trucks travel too fast, often without lights.

There are petrol stations throughout the country. Fuel, inexpensive and sold by the litre, is available in 90 octane (*tisa'iin*), which is super, or 80 (*tamaniin*), regular. Super is the better fuel for most purposes.

Road signs are similar to those used throughout Europe. Driving is on the right-hand side of the road. Speed limits are posted on major highways and are enforced by radar.

Getting around Ethiopia, Sudan and Uganda

Ethiopia

First the good news. The bus network in Ethiopia is extensive and affordable. It goes pretty much everywhere in the country and services can be relied upon. Plus, there are strict rules against carrying passengers in the aisles while the bus is in motion, meaning you don't have to face hours of crowding as you do in other countries.

Now for the bad news. Because distances are so vast in Ethiopia, journeys can take days to complete. And while it is illegal to crowd the buses, they are still incredibly uncomfortable. For long domestic trips, flying may be the better option.

Sudan

Trains run between Wadi Halfa and Khartoum on a weekly basis, generally departing Wadi Halfa after the ferry arrives. This can be as little as an hour or two after the arrival of the ferry to as much as a day or two, depending on the state of the line. Take plenty of bottled water, as there will be none available once you board and the trip can take as long as three days. There are also trains between Khartoum and Port Sudan and from Nyala to Er Rafad in the west. Routes to and from Khartoum are safe but time-consuming. Avoid basing your itinerary on published schedules as the train will never depart or arrive on time. Petty theft is a possibility so keep your eye on personal belongings at all times.

It is possible to drive in Sudan, but you will need an International Driver's Licence (and a devil-may-care attitude). Driving can be chaotic and road quality is poor, especially outside major urban centres. Many highways are little more than dirt tracks making navigation a challenge after heavy rains.

Buses cover urban centres well, but the road quality between cities means they aren't practical for longer trips. Instead, locals rely on 4WD trucks that will sit on roads and at stations waiting to pick up passengers. Departure time is whenever thc truck gets full.

Flying may save time, but the only domestic carrier is Sudan Airways. Cancellations and schedule changes are frequent.

Upon arrival in Sudan, you need to register with the local police. If staying at a major hotel, the staff will take care of this for you on check-in.

If you have plans to travel outside the Arab north or the road to Ethiopia, you will need to register for a Permit to Travel. Permits cost US$15 to arrange through the police and can take as long as a day to process.

Uganda

In the cities, locals use *boda-bodas* to get around cheaply and rapidly. These are converted scooters or mopeds with cushions on the back for passengers to sit on. Be careful if you travel using this method as *boda-bodas* get into accidents frequently.

Kampala is the main hub for bus travel in Uganda. Buses run between all the major and minor population centres and are relatively efficient. Schedules are non-existent. The bus will leave once it's full – and by full, we do mean full. Even the aisles will be packed so you may have to stand and wait for a passenger to disembark before you can sit down.

Matatus are mini bus-style taxis that are cheaper and slower than buses. They make frequent stops and drive rapidly, often ending up in accidents. Additionally, conductors often try to take advantage of tourists by overcharging. Choose instead a private-hire taxi and negotiate prices before you drive off.

Uganda once had an extensive train system, but this is no longer the case. Two stretches of track remain between Kampala and Port Bell and from Kampala to the Kenyan border. Neither stretch offers passenger services.

ACCOMMODATION

BOOKING YOUR HOTEL

Accommodation in Egypt

Luxury Hotels

Egyptian hotels run the gamut from fleapit to pharaoh's glory and everything in between. The introduction of the Four Seasons chain to Alexandria and Cairo has done much to spark up a little competition. Prior to the arrival of the luxury chain, international hotel groups would arrive in Egypt, build a new five-star hotel and then run it into the ground, filling every room with package tourists and investing very little into upkeep. While the hotels faded in quality, they still retained their five-star status due to the amenities they offered (and the name). The result is that a five-star hotel built last year could vary hugely in quality and service from a five-star built 20 years ago.

In Cairo, renovations have now become a must, and the closure of the Nile Hilton is a sign that the big hotel players are finally paying attention.

The Breakfast Box

Realising that many of their visitors want to start sightseeing at the crack of dawn, hotels responded by offering breakfast boxes. On offer across the country, breakfast boxes are intended for early-morning temple-hoppers and explorers.

They can include gourmet sandwiches or basic rolls with pasteurised cheese spread, bottles of water or fruit juice. Ask your concierge or front desk staff 24 hours in advance to ensure you get one on your way out of the hotel.

ABOVE: pools at the Meridien Pyramids.

You'll find that if you book a five-star in the capital, you'll get the quality you expect. In Luxor and Aswan, however, it's a different matter.

Both cities still face the issue of the faded star status, so you may be in for a shock when booking what is sold as a luxury room in both of these locations.

Moderate and Budget Hotels

Those travelling on a more modest scale won't care much about the luxury wars – and they'll be in luck. The volume of hotels in the budget and moderate categories is high. You can get a clean, comfortable, spacious room in a decent hotel with a balcony or view for as little as US$30 per night. In off-season, it can be even less.

Be sure to look around on the internet before your arrival as there are usually good deals, especially in Luxor. Aswan, however, has fewer hotels to choose from and can fill up in high season.

Hotel Scams

Be wary of hotel scams when you arrive in any city by air or rail. Taxi drivers get kickbacks from many hoteliers. There have been stories of travellers giving the name of their hotel to the driver only to be told the property "just burned down", or "is closed". Ignore what they say and insist on going there to see for yourself. It's quite likely that, if you get a room from the hotel they are offering, you'll end up at an inferior property that requires more money per night from you.

How to Book

If you arrive in any city without a reservation, the tourist office is a great, impartial resource to consult. In most cities, the tourist office is located near the train station. There is no "one-stop-shop" accommodation booking service in Egypt. In this country, it's every hotelier for themselves. In fact, tour operators based in Egypt will often gouge you with high fees. Better to book your rooms in advance. Online prices are often much lower than the one you will be quoted on the phone or in person.

Accommodation in Ethiopia

Accommodation in the region near the Nile's source is surprisingly interesting. Many hotels around Lake Tana are located in historic homes or buildings and blend in nicely with the Unesco World Heritage-listed buildings. Five-star hotels aren't really an option. For that you need to go to Addis Ababa. Instead, it's all about intimate hotels and B&B-style guesthouses.

ABOVE: cool interior of the Hilton Pyramids Golf Resort.

There are modern, concrete hotels in some of the more industrial towns on the lake, such as Bahir Dar, but these usually offer at least a garden as a form of environmental respite from the drab exterior. There isn't a lot to choose from, so if you have plans to travel in high season, book well in advance to secure a room.

Accommodation in Sudan

Staying in Sudan is passable at best or an adventure at worst. In Khartoum, the oil industry has developed a network of decent business-class properties filled with all the mod cons an oil executive could ever need. Leave Khartoum and you're pretty much on your own. Tourism infrastructure is incredibly limited, especially if you go south. Your best bet is to book hotel nights through a Sudanese-based tour operator, who will book you into hotels of a minimum quality level. In most cities, there may only be one hotel of decent quality available, so you won't have much of a choice. As long as you go with an open mind and can roll with the punches (such as regular power losses, toilets that don't flush and peeling wallpaper), you'll be fine.

Accommodation in Uganda

Until the Amin regime, accommodation in Uganda was on a par with some of the more developed nations in Africa. Unfortunately, civil war and a lack of investment have done much to lower quality. The best hotels of an international standard can be found in the big cities of Kampala and Entebbe – but what is referred to as five-star here wouldn't be five-star back home.

What you do get by splurging on the stars is guaranteed hygiene, amenities, business facilities and access to power in the form of generators. You also get safes in your rooms and additional security – not something to think lightly of, as hotel-room burglaries are common in Uganda.

Outside the big cities, there are safari camps and resorts, once again of a basic nature. Investment is starting to return, and there are hopes that exclusive resorts catering to big-spending adventure tourists will arrive, but none have broken ground yet.

Price Cateogries

Prices given here are based on rack rates (the published rate). Discounts are common throughout the year as occupancy fluctuates; you may be able to get a room with a published rate of over £200 per night at a considerable discount. It's best to negotiate with the hotels directly.

ACCOMMODATION LISTINGS

NUBIA AND LAKE NASSER

Abu Simbel

Hotel Abbas
Abu Simbel Tourist Village, 2 km (1¼ miles) from temples
Tel: 097-340 0092
The cheapest spot in town – and the bathrooms definitely look it. Rooms are clean and comfortable but in dire need of renovation. Most have air conditioning and en suites. If you're really broke, you can negotiate with management to cut out the a/c and breakfast. But seeing as this property is already dirt cheap, you'd have to be pretty desperate to warrant the hassle. **£**

Eskaleh Eco-Lodge
Tel: 097-340 1288/012-368 0521
Email: fikrykachif@genevalink.com
The Nubian musician Fikry Kachif, who also works as a guide, recently opened this small but charming mu-brick hotel with just five rooms. The rooms are simple but comfortable, with very clean bathrooms and some have their own terrace overlooking the lake. The hotel also has a library with lots of books on Nubian culture, a roof terrace and a restaurant serving delicious food cooked with produce from their own organic garden. **££**

Nefertari Hotel
Tel: 097-340-0510
Basic rooms are uninspiring, but the swimming pool overlooking Lake Nasser and convenient location near the Temple of Rameses II makes up for the standard interiors. **£££**

Nobaleh Ramsis Hotel
Abu Simbel Tourist Village
Tel: 097-340 1118
Located 2km (1¼ miles) from the temples (near the bus station), this simple hotel isn't the best choice for visitors looking to get easy access to Abu Simbel, but it's a good choice for those on a tight budget. Rooms are very minimal, with TVs and mini-fridges. **££**

Seti Abu Simbel
Tel: 097-340 0720

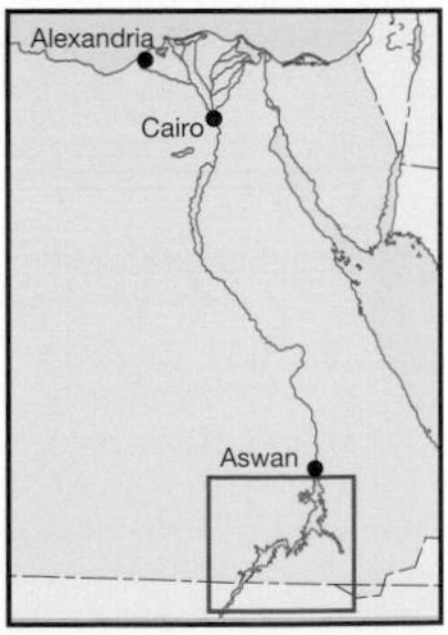

The first and only five-star hotel in Abu Simbel, with chalet-style rooms set in a garden overlooking the lake. All modern amenities, and very relaxing atmosphere. **££££**

ASWAN

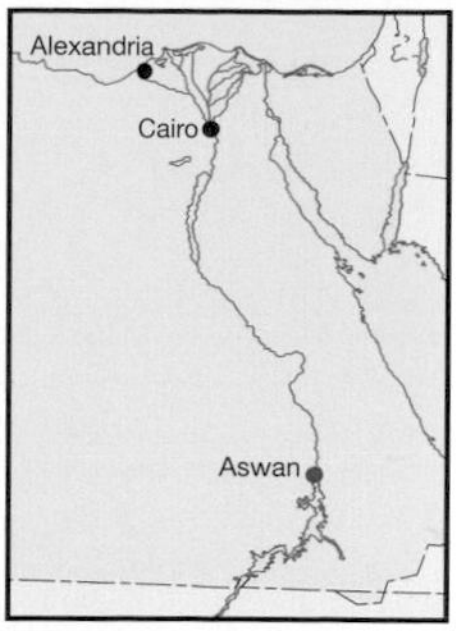

Basma
Shari' Abtal At tahrir
Tel: 097-231 0901
www.basmahotel.com
A full-blown resort hotel with all the modern conveniences you would expect, including a huge swimming pool. Most rooms have excellent views over the river. **££££**

Hotel Cleopatra
Shari' Saad Zaghlul
Tel: 097-231 4003
Clean rooms with phone and private bathroom, near the souq, with a small pool on the roof. **£££**

Isis Corniche
Corniche An nil
Tel: 097-232 4744
Built on the riverbank in the centre of town, this resort hotel could do with some renovation, but its location on the Nile and in the centre is excellent. The garden has a pool and several restaurants. **££££**

Keylany Hotel
25 Shari' Keylany
Tel: 097-231 7332
www.keylanyhotel.com
By far Aswan's best budget hotel, with simple but clean air-conditioned rooms, modern furniture and spotless bathrooms. The manager is extremely friendly and helpful, there is a great roof terrace for sunset drinks and an internet café. Highly recommended. **££**

Marhaba Palace Hotel
Corniche An nil
Tel: 097-233 0102
www.marhaba-aswan.com
Modern hotel overlooking the Nile which has spacious rooms with private bathroom, air con, satellite TV and internet access. The hotel has a good restaurant with views on the Nile and a heated swimming pool in the garden. **£££**

Memnon Hotel
Corniche An nil
Tel: 097-230 0483
www.memnonhotel-aswan.com
Solid budget property with clean rooms. Furnishings are a little rough around the edges. Some rooms have good views but you may have to deal with noise issues. **££**

Mövenpick Resort Aswan
Elephantine Island
Tel: 097-230 3455
www.moevenpick-hotels.com
Recently (for Aswan) renovated spa-hotel. The huge, ugly tower is still there but the spacious rooms are great, with wide views over the Nile. It is a peaceful resort with a pool set in the garden, and a spa specialising in sand treatments for rheumatism. A free ferry transports guests in and out of town. **£££££**

Nuba Nile Hotel
Shari' Abtal Al tahrir
Tel: 097-231 3267
Good budget hotel near the train station, with a variety of rooms. Make sure you have a window as a few rooms don't have one. Popular with backpackers who also hang out in the neighbouring *ahwa* (coffee house). **£**

Orchida St George
Shari' Muhammad Khalid
Tel: 097-231 5997
www.orchida-sg-hotel.com
Small modern hotel with a variety of rooms. We recommend you check the room before you take it, although all are clean. **£££**

Paradise Hotel
373 Shari' Saad Zaghlul
Tel: 097-232 9690
www.paradisehotel-aswan.com
If being in the middle of all the action is what you treasure most, then the Paradise is a good choice. Situated just 50 metres/yds from the train station on the pedestrianised road that leads to the souq entrance, the Paradise is perfect for budget travellers who want the Aswan experience without forking out the extra Egyptian pounds for Nile-side location. **££**

Pyramisa Isis Island Resort & Spa Aswan
Isis Island Aswan
Tel: 097-231 5100
Fax: 097-231 5500
www.pyramisaegypt.com
Huge resort hotel, owned by the Mubarak family, set on its own island upriver from Aswan. The property is very tired and in need of a renovation, but the location is the big plus, right on the river overlooking Elephantine. Complimentary boats sail regularly into Aswan town. **£££££**

Sara Hotel
Shari' Al Fanadak
Tel: 097-232 7234
www.sarahotel-aswan.com
Modern hotel with great views over the Nile and the Western Desert. The rooms don't have a lot of character, but are spotless and have satellite TV and air conditioning. There is also a pool and sun terrace for the days you want to take it easy. A shuttle bus runs into town every hour. **£££**

Sofitel Old Cataract
Shari' Abtal At tahrir
Tel: 097-231 6000
www.sofitel.com
Aswan's most famous property harks back to the days of colonial splendour. Currently being renovated, it will probably be closed until at least 2011. **£££££**

PRICE CATEGORIES

Price categories are based on the cost of one night in a double room in high season:
£ = under £20
££ = £20–50
£££ = £50–100
££££ = £100–200
£££££ = over £200

BELOW: Sofitel Old Cataract hotel, Aswan.

LUXOR

East Bank

Emilio Hotel
Shari' Youssef Hassan
Tel: 095-237 3570
This is a very good mid-range hotel with comfortable rooms that are equipped with all mod cons. There is a rooftop pool and sundeck. Book in advance in winter, as it is popular with tour groups. **£££**

Luxor Sheraton Resort
Shari' Al Awameya
Tel: 095-237 4544
www.sheraton.com
Faded luxury hotel that nevertheless offers spacious rooms overlooking the Nile or bungalows in a shaded garden. The Italian restaurant in the garden with pond inhabited by pelicans and flamingos is a popular choice in Luxor. **£££££**

Maritim Jolie Ville Luxor
Crocodile Island, 6km (4 miles) out of town
Tel: 095-227 4855
www.jolieville-hotels.com
The best hotel on this side of town occupies its own island. European-managed, with excellent service, good food and a relaxed atmosphere. The comfortable bungalow rooms are set in a splendid garden with a swimming pool. Most have views of this beautiful stretch of the Nile. **£££££**

Mercure Hotel
Corniche An nil
Tel: 095-237 4944
www.mercure.com
This hotel offers clean, modern rooms in a really central location. The shaded gardens offer a nice place in which to cool down and have a drink. **££££**

Mina Palace
Shari' Corniche An nil
Tel: 095-237 2074
Good-value and friendly hotel, on the Corniche, with slightly run-down air-conditioned rooms and private bathrooms. Some corner rooms have balconies overlooking the Nile and Luxor Temple. **££**

New Philippe
Shari' Dr Labib Habashy
Tel: 095-237 2284
Fax: 095-238 0050
Excellent three-star hotel offering spotless air-conditioned rooms, TV, fridge and some balconies. The pleasant roof terrace has a small pool and bar. Book ahead, especially in winter. **£££**

Saint Joseph
Shari' Khaled Ibn Al Wallid
Tel: 095-238 1707
Fax: 095-238 1727
Popular hotel with budget-minded Brits, this hotel offers great value, clean rooms and a great rooftop pool with views of the (slightly obscured) Nile. **££**

Sofitel Old Winter Palace
Shari' Corniche An nil
Tel: 095-238 0422
www.sofitel.com
Old-style hotel, refurbished to some of its former splendour. The rooms in the old building have more character than the new garden wing, but service can be slow at times. **£££££**

Sonesta St George
Shari' Corniche An nil
Tel: 095-238 2575
www.sonesta.com
One of the newer luxury options in Luxor, perhaps not the most handsome building, but offering good value for money, as well as good views over the Nile and all modern conveniences. **£££££**

BELOW: at the Sofitel Old Winter Palace.

West Bank

Al-Gezira Hotel
Al Gezira, near the ferry landing
Tel/fax: 095-231 0034
www.el-gezira.com
Very friendly budget hotel with views over the Nile and the east Bank, and perfectly clean rooms. **£**

Al-Moudira
Daba'iyya, 15km (9 miles) south of ticket office on the west bank
Tel: 012-325 1307
www.moudira.com
Palatial desert resort designed by French-Egyptian architect Olivier Sednaoui, who did a fabulous job. The vast rooms are sumptuously decorated with locally made furniture, Ottoman fabrics and antiques. Set on the edge of the desert, with a gorgeous garden and a great pool that overlooks the pink Theban hills. Very good food and friendly service, but not convenient for those who want a central location. **£££££**

Amoun Al Gazira
Geziret Al Bairat (near the ferry landing, left at the Mobil petrol station)
Tel: 095-231 0912
Pleasant family-run hotel in a standard modern building overlooking the Theban hills and fertile countryside. The rooms are simply furnished, but spotless and comfortable, some with private bathroom. From the roof terrace you can watch the stars. A gorgeous sunset, breakfast and tea are served in a pretty shaded garden. **£**

El Nakhil
Geziret Al Bairat (near the ferry landing, 200m/yds from village mosque)
Tel: 095-231 3922
Well-run establishment with a nice adjoining restaurant. Particularly good for mobility-challenged tourists. Property features ramps for wheelchairs and accessible bathrooms. **£**

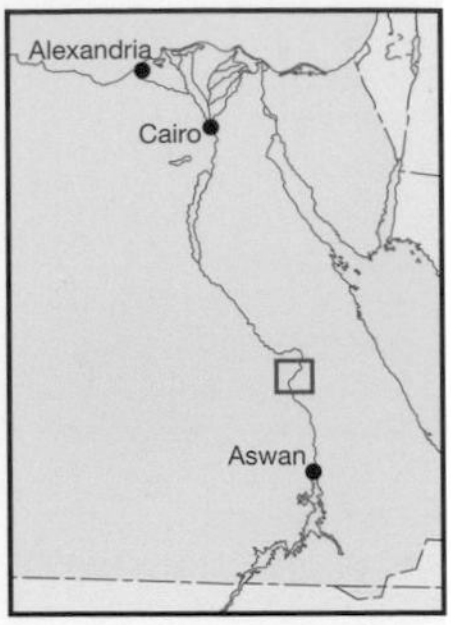

Marsam Hotel
also known as Sheikh Ali's Hotel, opposite the Tombs of the Nobles, west bank
Tel: 095-237 2403
Email: marsam@africamail.com
In 1881 the Abdul Rassoul family discovered the Dair Al Bahari cache of royal mummies, now on show in the Cairo Museum. The late Sheikh Ali's son now runs this simple hotel. The tranquil garden has views over green fields. **£**

Nour Al Gourna
Opposite the ticket office, Qurnah
Tel: 095-231 1430
Delightful small hotel run by a French woman, Eléonore, and her Egyptian partner, with large, simple but stylish rooms overlooking the sugar-cane fields or pretty palm-grove; all have fans and mosquito nets. There is now also a delightful mud-brick sister hotel, which is even quieter: the Nur Al Balad behind the Medinet Habu Temple (tel: 095-242 6111). Both are highly recommended. **£££**

Pharaoh's
near the ticket office on the west bank
Tel: 095-231 0702
Fax: 095-231 1205
This is the only mid-range hotel on this side of the Nile, with clean rooms, some with private bathrooms and a pleasant garden bar/restaurant. **££**

MIDDLE EGYPT

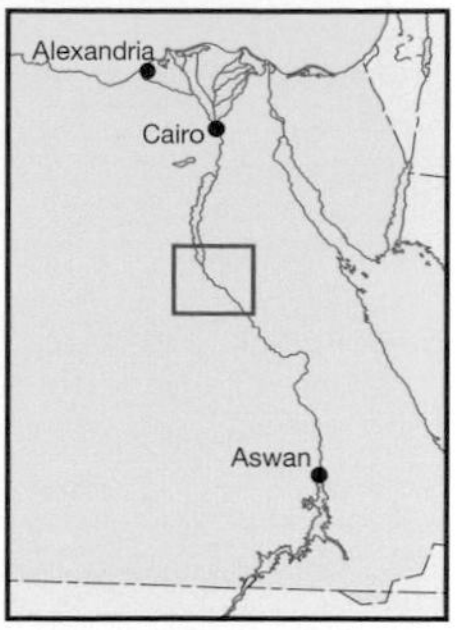

Al Menyyah

King Akhenaten Hotel
Shari' Corniche An nil
Tel: 086-236 5917
Good Nile views and free WiFi make this a popular location for both business and holiday travellers. Located about ten minutes by foot from the train station, it's a fairly central option for those looking for comfort and convenience. **££**

Lotus
1 Shari' Port Said
Tel: 086-236 4500
This is a reasonable budget option, with clean rooms with fans. The bar-restaurant serves good food and is frequented by beer-drinking locals, which adds to the colour of the place. **££**

Mercure Nefertiti/Aton
Shari' Corniche An nil
Tel: 086-233-1515
Most upmarket hotel in the area, with restaurant and bar, comfortable rooms - some facing the Nile - and a swimming pool in the garden. **££££**

The Palace
Meadan At tahrir
Tel: 086-236 4071
Small and simple hotel with colonial-style furniture and high ceilings. Some rooms have air conditioning and private baths. Enjoy the views over the Nile, and the character of the place. **£**

BELOW: donkey carts are still a common mode of transport.

Asyut

Al Nahr Hotel
41 Shari' Muhammad Ali Maqaram
Tel: 088-233 4175
Bargain hotel that's perfectly serviceable for the price. Rooms are clean and comfortable complete with air conditioning and private baths. Most also come with balconies from which you can watch the world go by. Budget travellers make it a popular choice, so try and book in advance during peak season. **£**

Assiutel Hotel
146 Shari' Nile
Tel: 088-232 9022
Two levels of room to choose from: the faded standard or the recently refurnished luxe. Standards have balconies and tired interiors. Luxe rooms are fresh and come complete with flatscreen TVs and new beds. Go for the luxe if you can afford to splurge. **£££**

Casa Blanca Hotel
Shari' Muh.Tawfik Khashaba
Tel: 088-233 7662
Basic three-star hotel with clean rooms, but very little atmosphere. It's not as nice as the Assiutel but it is in a better location. **£££**

CAIRO AND ENVIRONS

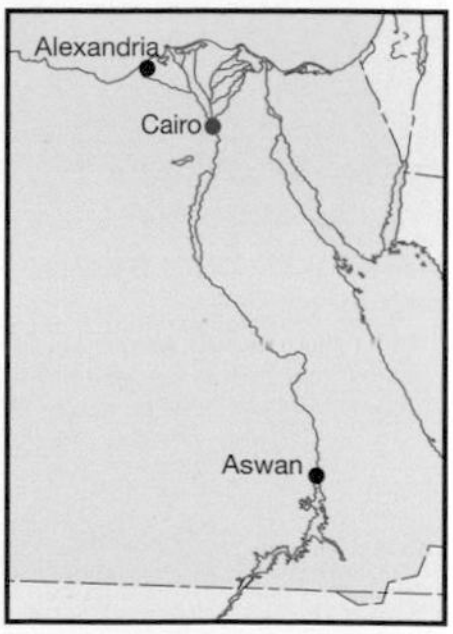

Berlin Hotel
2 Shari' Shawarby, downtown
Tel: 02-2395-7502
Email: Berlinhotelcairo@hotmail.com
Large double or triple rooms as well as dormitories in a quieter back street of downtown Cairo. The Art Deco rooms still retain many period features, including the furniture and bathrooms, but modernity has arrived in the form of internet access and a good sauna. **££**

PRICE CATEGORIES

Price categories are based on the cost of one night in a double room in high season:
£ = under £20
££ = £20–50
£££ = £50–100
££££ = £100–200
£££££ = over £200

Cairo Marriott
16 Shari' Saray Al Gazirah, Zamalik
Tel: 02-2728 3000
www.marriott.com
The Marriott Hotel has built this facility around the former palace of the *khedive* Ismail, built to commemorate the opening of the Suez Canal in 1869. Antique furniture graces the halls and public rooms. Eugénie's Lounge, an elegant cocktail bar in the former rooms of the Empress Eugénie, and the Garden Promenade, the open-air café in the *khedive* Ismail's garden, make this a good place to recover from Cairo's hustle and bustle. There are several other restaurants and the popular Harry's Pub. **£££££**

Carlton Hotel
21 Shari' 26th of July, downtown
Tel: 02-2575-5181
www.carltonhotelcairo.com
Near the Cinema Rivoli, the Carlton seems to be stuck in a time warp. The rooms have some 1950s detail but vary in size and comfort, so check them out first. Good value and central location. There is a nice rooftop café, but no alcohol is served. **££**

Concorde Cairo as-Salam Hotel
65 Shari' Abd Al Hamid Badawi, Heliopolis
Tel: 02-2622-4000
Fax: 02-2622-6037
www.concorde-hotels.com
Peaceful and elegant hotel set in a garden with swimming pool, offering large and airy rooms with all mod cons. Perfect for those who want to see some of the Art Deco architecture in Heliopolis. **£££££**

Conrad International
1191 Corniche An nil, Bulaq
Tel: 02-2580 8000
www.conradhotels1.hilton.com
The ideal business hotel in Cairo, located beside the World Trade Centre, and

certainly one of the most luxurious in town. It offers fantastic views over the Nile and excellent service. **£££££**

Cosmopolitan
1 Shari' Ibn Tahlab, downtown
Tel: 02-2392 3845
A grand Art Nouveau building offering spacious, comfortable rooms with all mod cons. Surprisingly quiet. **£££**

Dahab Hostel
7th floor, 26 Shari' Mahmoud Bassiouni, downtown
Tel: 02-2579-9104
www.dahabhostel.com
The small rooms on the rooftop of one of the buildings in the heart of Downtown tries to simulate the relaxed atmosphere of a Dahab beach camp. Great communal terrace, reggae music and laid-back ambience, but the rooms are rather poky. **£**

El Hussein
Meadan Al Hussain, Al Azhar
Tel: 02-591-8089
A noisy affair during religious festivals, this hotel is the place to stay if you want to get lost in Cairo's Old City. Clean, basic rooms. **££**

Four Seasons Cairo
35 Shari' Al Giza, Giza
Tel: 02-3573 1212
Fax: 02-3568 1616
www.fourseasons.com
One of Cairo's best and most sumptuous five-star hotels. The large, airy and elegant rooms command glorious views over the Pyramids and the Nile. The staff are attentive and the service is excellent. Spa, wellness centre, sophisticated exercise room and outdoor pool. The hotel is part of the First Residence Tower, which houses the prestigious First Mall shopping centre. **£££££**

Garden City House
23 Shari' Kamal Ad Din Saleh, Garden City
Tel: 02-2794-4969
www.gardencityhouse.com
Pleasant, dusty pension, popular with scholars and archaeologists, with large clean rooms. Half board is compulsory, but meal times provide a good opportunity to meet some interesting people. **£**

Golden Tulip Flamenco Hotel
2 Shari' Al Gezirah Al Wusta, Zamalik
Tel: 02-2735 0815
www.flamencohotels.com
Modern hotel in a quiet, tree-lined street in the residential part of Zamalik, with some rooms overlooking the Nile and even the Pyramids on a clear day. The Florencia restaurant serves excellent paella. **££££**

Hilton Pyramids Golf Resort
Dreamland, El Wahat Road, 6th of October City, Giza
Tel: 02-3855 3333
Email: pyramidsgolf@hilton.com
Plush rooms, all overlooking either the 27-hole championship golf course with the Giza Pyramids as a backdrop, or the outdoor pool. Offers WiFi, children's club, spa, and a host of bars and restaurants. **££££**

Horus House
21 Shari' Ismail Muhammad, Zamalik
Tel: 02-2735 3634
A home away from home, the Horus is often booked up by returning guests. The restaurant offers a good-value lunch, popular with older residents. Book well in advance. **£££**

Ismailia House
8th floor, 1 Meadan At tahrir
Tel: 02-2796 3122
Email: ismahouse@hotmail.com
Popular with backpackers on account of its clean white rooms, many communal bathrooms and most important of all its view over Cairo's main square. **£**

Lialy Hostel
3rd floor, 8 Meadan Talaat Harb, downtown
Tel: 02-2575-2802
Very clean and welcoming budget option on one of downtown's most picturesque squares. The rooms are large and very clean, albeit a bit noisy. Staff are very friendly, and there is a good internet café. **£**

Longchamps Hotel
21 Shari' Ismail Muhammad, Zamalik
Tel: 02-2735-2311
www.hotellongchamps.com
Longchamps is an old-time favourite for those who visit Cairo often. Managed by the very helpful Heba Bakri and her husband Chris, the hotel is like a home away from home. The rooms are spotless, and many have great shady balconies overlooking the leafy streets of Zamalik. There's also a small bar and restaurant. **££**

Lotus
7th floor, 12 Shari' Talaat Harb
Tel: 02-2575-0966
www.lotushotel.com
Good value and as central as it gets. Airy, clean rooms with balconies and air conditioning. **££**

Mayfair
9 Shari' Aziz Osman, Zamalik
Tel: 02-2735-7315
www.mayfaircairo.com
Tranquil hotel with tidy rooms overlooking a tree-lined street. Pleasant terrace for an afternoon drink. **£**

Mena House Oberoi
End of Shari' Al Haram, Pyramids Road, Giza
Tel: 02-3377 3222
Fax: 02-3376 7777
www.oberoihotels.com
An historic landmark refurbished by the Oberoi chain, the Mena House is the only hotel in Egypt with its own golf course. The rooms in the 19th-century *khedival* hunting lodge are particularly recommended, being tastefully decorated with antiques, but most rooms are in the less atmospheric modern garden wing. The elegant Moghul Room is the best Indian restaurant in town, with live music. The Rubayyat, the main dining room, serves Continental and Middle Eastern meals accompanied by live entertainment. Even if you are not a guest here, lunch by the pool is strongly recommended after a visit to the Giza Pyramids. **£££££**

Meramees Hotel
32 Shari' Sabry Abu Alam, downtown
Tel: 02-2396 2518
http://ierameeshotel.net/
A good comfortable hotel with spotless rooms, all with bathroom and a balcony. It is centrally located near Meadan Talaat Harb, but quiet, and the owner loves to share his knowledge and enthusiasm for Cairo. Guests have use of a kitchen and washing machine. **£**

Nile Plaza Four Seasons
1089 Corniche An nil, Garden City
Tel: 02-2791 7000
www.fourseasons.com
Cairo's most impressive hotel (at least until the Nile Hilton completes its renovation), the second Four Seasons Hotel does not fail to impress. The spacious rooms have fabulous views and are decorated in a contemporary style. The level of service is amazing, the staff very friendly and

BELOW: elegance at the Semiramis InterContinental.

ABOVE: there are great views of the Nile from the Sheraton Cairo Hotel.

there is a spa and wellness centre, as well as two swimming pools and five excellent restaurants. **£££££**

Odeon Palace
6 Shari' Abdel Hamid, Qasr An nil
Tel: 02-2576 7971
Perfectly located budget option in downtown Cairo, with modern, clean and airy rooms. The rooftop terrace is a popular meeting place at night serving cold Stella beers. **£££**

Pension Roma
169 Shari' Muhammad Farid, downtown
Tel: 02-2391-1088
This is a popular hotel with travellers. All rooms have shiny wooden floors and old-style furniture. Book ahead. **£**

Pension Zamalik
6 Shari' Salah Al Din, Zamalik
Tel: 02-2735-9318
Another homely hotel on a quiet Zamalik street, with spacious old-fashioned rooms that are spotless. The owner does not like giving a double room to unmarried couples. **££**

President
22 Shari' Dr Taha Hussein, Zamalik
Tel: 02-2735 0718
www.presidenthotelcairo.com
More like a four-star hotel, this efficient, friendly hotel with a good business centre is a well-kept secret in a quiet Zamalik street. The Cellar Bar, always crowded, serves good meze. **£££**

Radwan Hotel
83 Shari' Gawhar Al Qaid, Meadan Al Azhar
Tel: 02-590-1311
A popular option for budget travellers, with clean and comfortable rooms as well as a communal satellite TV lounge and internet access. Good base for exploring Islamic Cairo. **£**

Ramses Hilton
1115 Corniche An nil, downtown
Tel: 02-2577 7444
www.hilton.com
Until the Nile Hilton re-opens, the Ramses is the next best option. Located across the street from the Nile, the Ramses is currently the closest hotel to the Egyptian Museum. Unfortunately, you'll need a bit of bravery as you'll have to cross one of the busiest streets in Cairo to get there. Rooms are a nice size and all feature balconies. Splurge for their executive rooms, which offer access to the top-floor lounge boasting panoramic views over the city. **£££££**

Richmond Hotel
41 Shari' Sherif, downtown
Tel: 02-2393 9358
Basic but clean rooms in a grand downtown apartment block. The rooms are a little on the dark side, and all share bathrooms. Friendly management. **£**

Sakkara Palm Club
Saqqarah Road, Badrashein
Tel: 02-3819 1555
A small resort-type hotel near the Saqqarah Step Pyramid, in the middle of the Egyptian countryside. The rooms are set in gorgeous lush gardens with a large lagoon-style swimming pool. This is the perfect escape from the traffic jams and a good base from which to explore nearby Memphis, Saqqarah and Giza. **£££**

Semiramis InterContinental
Corniche An nil, Garden City
Tel: 02-2795 7171
www.ichotelsgroup.com
Five-star luxury and views over the Nile, together with comfortable rooms, make this a great choice for those who want a central location. The hotel also boasts some of the city's best restaurants: the Sabaya and The Bird Cage *(see Where to Eat)*. **£££££**

Sheraton Cairo Hotel, Towers and Casino
Shari' Madis Quaset Al Fhawrg, Gazirah
Tel: 02-3336 9800
www.sheraton.com
Located a short walk away from the Opera House and Egyptian Museum, the Sheraton is city in a city. The tower construction isn't all that inspiring, but the views of the Nile from almost every room certainly do make the heart pump a little faster. At night, a choice of restaurants and popular casino provide diversions. **£££££**

Talisman
39 Shari' Talaat Harb
Tel: 02-2393 9431
www.talisman-hotel.com
Cairo's first boutique hotel, in a lovely downtown apartment building. It has spacious and stylish rooms decorated in oriental style and an atmospheric breakfast room, as well as salons to relax in following an exhausting day's sightseeing. The owners Véronique and Yusuf are serious Cairophiles, and love to share their passion for the city with their guests. They can also organise tours and guides. **£££**

Tulip
3 Meadan Talaat Harb
Tel: 02-2392-3884
Opposite Groppi's patisserie, this long-established budget hotel is still going strong, offering large clean rooms to young travellers, with private or shared bathrooms. Some overlook the elegant square, which can be noisy at night – the ones at the back are quieter. **££**

Victoria
66 Shari' Al Gumhuriyya, Meadan Ramses
Tel: 02-2589 2290
www.victoria.com.eg
Another old-style hotel between Meadan Opera and Rameses Station, with faded spacious rooms furnished with dark-brown furniture. Young Egyptian couples use the shaded garden to discuss their married future over a cold drink. **£££**

Windsor
19 Shari' Alfi Bey, downtown
Tel: 02-2591 5277
www.windsorcairo.com
For nostalgic souls, this is a place to sniff a Cairo that is no more. Faded but clean rooms and friendly service. The bar, with its old waiters, sunken sofas and heavy air, is an institution. **£££**

PRICE CATEGORIES

Price categories are based on the cost of one night in a double room in high season:
£ = under £20
££ = £20–50
£££ = £50–100
££££ = £100–200
£££££ = over £200

THE DELTA

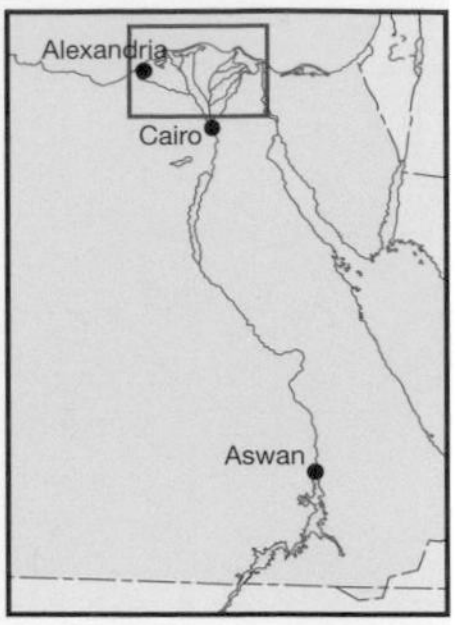

Alexandria

Acropole
27 Shari' Al Ghorfa Al Togariyya
Tel: 03-480 5980
No stars and rather run-down, but the rooms in this atmospheric, clean, Greek-owned pension enjoy the same views as the much more expensive Cecil Hotel. Book ahead in high season. **£**

El Salamlek Palace Hotel
Montazah Palace Gardens
Tel: 03-547 7999
www.sangiovanni.com
If you think this former royal guest house has an air of the Alps about it, you wouldn't be wrong. The property was built for the Austrian-educated *khedive* (and more specifically his Austrian mistress). For luxury with history, this is the place. **£££££**

Four Seasons
399 Shari' Al Gaish, San Stefano
Tel: 03-581 8000
www.fourseasons.com
Opened in 2007, this hotel still looks as if the wrappers have only just come off. The decision of the Four Seasons group to open a property in this city has brought hope that Alexandria is about to experience a new Renaissance. A private beach was constructed just for guests, including exclusive cabanas and a yacht marina for those who want to just sail right in. **£££££**

Green Plaza Hilton Alexandria
Green Plaza Shopping Mall, 14th of May Bridge, Smouha
Tel: 03-420 9120
www.hilton.com
International five-star that is heavy on amenities and light on style. Mainly oriented towards business travellers, the large rooms are equipped with all mod cons; the hotel has a good business centre and it is close to the Nozha Airport. The Green Plaza Mall has all the cinemas, shopping, eating and drinking facilities that you might need, but the hotel is quite a distance (a 20-minute taxi ride) from the city centre and historical monuments. **£££££**

Helnan Palestine Hotel
Montazah Palace Gardens
Tel: 03-547 3500
www.helnan.com
An Alexandrian institution, very popular with expat residents and local families, who come at weekends to enjoy the peaceful bay and to swim in a slightly cleaner sea. Rooms are worn, but the view makes it worthwhile. **£££££**

Metropole Hotel
52 Shari' Saad Zaghlul
Tel: 03-484 0910
www.paradiseinnegypt.com
Centrally located hotel with plenty of charm and atmosphere. Most of the high-ceilinged and spacious rooms overlook the square, and the front ones have a view over the bay. The service is good and the staff are extremely helpful. Recommended. **££££**

Nile Excelsior Hotel
16 Shari' Al Bursa Al Qadima
Tel: 03-480 0799
Very central hotel in the same street as the Spitfire Bar, which offers clean and comfortable rooms. **£**

Nobel Hotel
152 Shari' Al Gaish
Tel: 03-546 4845
Tidy rooms with private baths. The tiny balconies provide excellent views. Pay a surcharge for air conditioning if you need it. **££**

Radisson Hotel Blu
Mehawar Al Taameer, Northern Coast Road
Tel: 589-6000
www.radissonblu.com
The Radisson Blu is the newest addition to the Alexandria hotel scene. It's a fairly typical business-style hotel filled with glass and beige. Good if you value mod cons, cleanliness and efficiency. **££££**

Sofitel Alexandria Cecil Hotel
16 Meadan Saad Zaghlul
Tel: 03-487 7173
www.sofitel.com
The Cecil is haunted by the ghosts of Noel Coward, Somerset Maugham and others, including Lawrence Durrell who immortalised it in *The Alexandria Quartet*. The glamour has long gone, but the charm of the place and views over the bay still pull the romantics. The coffee shop is a popular rendezvous for a cup of tea. **££££**

Union Hotel
164 Shari' 26th July, Al Ramy Station
Tel: 03-480 7312
The cost of rooms varies depending on how good your view is – but if you book well enough in advance, you'll get a great vista to enjoy. Rooms are clean and well-sized for the price. **£££**

Windsor Palace Hotel
17 Shari' Al Shohada, on the Corniche
Tel: 03-480 8123
www.paradiseinnegypt.com
Built in 1907, the Windsor was bought by Paradise Inns in the late 1990s and given a total make-over. Most of the period details, including the grand lobby and ancient elevators have been kept in all their glory, but the rooms are comfortable and cosy. The more expensive ones have sweeping views over the Mediterranean. **££££**

BELOW: relax by the water at the Hilton Pyramids Golf Resort in Giza.

PRICE CATEGORIES

Price categories are based on the cost of one night in a double room in high season:
£ = under £20
££ = £20–50
£££ = £50–100
££££ = £100–200
£££££ = over £200

EATING OUT

RECOMMENDED RESTAURANTS, CAFÉS AND BARS

Cairo and Alexandria have a good selection of restaurants, but smaller towns have a rather limited choice. Set menus and buffets in hotels offer an international cuisine with the occasional Egyptian dish, but Egyptian food is definitely worth trying out. Apart from the regular fare, five-star hotels often fly in European chefs for week-long ethnic extravaganzas. Hotel restaurants will only be mentioned here if they are really notable.

In recent years prices have risen steeply in Egyptian restaurants, and a good meal can cost almost as much as in London or New York, although the more basic restaurants are still a bargain. Cheaper restaurants often don't serve alcohol, while more upmarket places may only serve expensive imported wines.

Street Food

Street food in Egypt is often delicious, but take care if your stomach is unacclimatised. *Koshary*, a mixture of rice, macaroni, fried onions, lentils and chickpeas, topped with a spicy tomato sauce, is popular, as are *fuul* and *tamiyah* *(see box below)*.

For vegetarians, street food is likely to be meat-free as meat is expensive. Be warned that Egyptians only consider a dish without beef as "vegetarian", so double-check your food before eating.

A wide variety of sandwiches are available, filled with *pasturma* (a local dried meat), white cheese, chopped liver, kidneys and *tamiyah*. Roast corn, chicken soup and baked sweet potatoes are popular street snacks in winter.

Middle Eastern Food

Egyptians, like the Turks and Greeks, enjoy eating meze whilst chatting around a table with family and friends. Meze are hors d'oeuvres, salads and dips, served as a starter with drinks or, in larger portions, as a meal. An endless variety of dishes, hot and cold, are brought to the table and eaten with the fingers or scooped up in pieces of flatbread. Some of the most common dishes are:

- *baba ghanough* is *tahinah* mixed with garlic and roasted aubergine (eggplant)
- *fuul mesdames* is a stew of fava beans, Egypt's national dish, served with egg, meat, yoghurt or cheese
- *hummus*, a paste of chickpeas, garlic, *tahinah* and lemon topped with parsley, and sometimes served topped with tiny bits of fried lamb, is nothing like the shop-bought varieties found in the UK
- *kibbah* is a fried ball of cracked wheat stuffed with ground beef
- *kibda* is fried chopped calf's or lamb's liver
- *kofta is* minced meat with added herbs and spices
- *salata baladi* is chopped lettuce, tomato and cucumber with lots of parsley and lemon
- *tahinah* is a sesame paste mixed with water, oil and lemon juice, served as a dip or a sauce
- *tamiyah* are deep-fried fava bean balls
- *torshi* are pickled vegetables
- *waraa eynab* stuffed vine leaves

ABOVE: a selection of meze.

Drinking Notes

Non-Alcoholic Drinks

The traditional hot and cold drinks served in coffee houses are delicious and thought to be health-giving; they include *yansun* (aniseed), *helba* (fenugreek) and *qarqadeh* (hibiscus). The usual idea of American coffee is instant Nescafé. If you want decaffeinated coffee, bring your own.

Internationally formulated drinks made and bottled locally under license include a range of Schweppes and Canada Dry mixers, Coca-Cola, 7-Up, Sport and Pepsi. If you need water, ensure it is bottled and that the seal is secure.

Fresh juices such as orange, mango, strawberry, pomegranate, lime and many others, depending on

Above: mural of ladies lunching.

the season, are available in juice bars everywhere *except* in major hotels.

Beer

The local beer is Stella, a lager that comes in two varieties: Stella Export and ordinary Stella, which is less sweet and therefore usually preferred. Other beers are brewed in Egypt. Luxor beer and Sakkara are particularly good. The adventurous may encounter a mild homebrew called *buzah*, which is recorded as having been made in the 3rd Dynasty.

Wine

The long-established vineyard Gianaclis in the Delta produces red, white and rosé wines that are drinkable. Obelisque is the other local wine – both red and white – made in Al Boura from a good-quality Italian grape concentrate. Reds include Omar Qhayyam, Pharaohs, and Château Gianaclis; there is one rosé, called Rubis d'Egypte.

Among the whites, Gianaclis Village is the driest and is preferred with fish or seafood. Caution is advised when dining out, however, since quality is apt to vary from bottle to bottle. If there is a risk of spoiling an evening, the worst should be sent back immediately. Good French or Italian wine is available in the major hotels, at prices roughly 10 times their maximum value in Europe.

Spirits

The legal drinking age is 18. Imported spirits are available, although they are fairly expensive. Local spirits are quite popular among Egyptians. They include several kinds of brandy and various versions of zibeeb or araq, the Arab world's heady and dangerous version of ouzo, but beware!

Eating Out in Ethiopia

Ethiopian meals are long affairs often involving multiple courses. A typical table will be covered with meat and vegetable dishes often prepared as a series of rich stews. The stew needs to be thick, as utensils are not used at the Ethiopian table. Instead, diners use a piece of *injure* (a kind of flatbread) and use their right hand to scoop the various dishes out of their plates and bowls.

The Ethiopian Orthodox Church has many unique food restrictions, including regular fasts that can last as long as 40 days. Pork is forbidden, along with shellfish, in a reflection of the importance of the Old Testament in modern worship.

Gondar has a few stylish eateries, while Addis Ababa has the widest selection. Most five-star restaurants are restricted to the capital and aren't five-star in quality, but they will feed you with the familiar if you're worried about trying local dishes.

Eating Out in Sudan

Finding a good restaurant in Sudan can be quite tricky. Economic hardship and civil war means there are few imports. The good news is that your food will therefore be very fresh because it will have been grown or slaughtered very close to where you are eating. The bad news is you won't have much in the way of variety.

The best meat to eat is lamb and it is (usually) considered quite safe to enjoy. Beef is also edible, with little fear of contamination. Unfortunately for vegetarians, vegetables aren't so lucky. All vegetables grown in Sudan have to be treated with bleach, so you'll probably notice a chemical aftertaste whenever you tuck into a salad.

If you are a guest at a major event or family meal, a lamb will most likely be roasted in your honour. Get your stomach ready as the eye is considered a delicacy and will be offered to you to enjoy. It is considered very bad form to refuse.

Sudanese street food is similar to Egyptian, with *fuul* considered a staple of the diet. Sudanese coffee, however, is quite unique and delicious. The Sudanese fry the beans in a pot over charcoal and then grind the beans together with a mixture of spices.

Alcohol is completely forbidden in Sudan. You will not be allowed into the country if you are carrying any and you will be expelled if you are caught with any in your possession. Fruit juices are the popular alternative – always freshly made using locally grown, in-season produce.

Eating Out in Uganda

Like Sudan, Ugandan cuisine relies heavily on local produce. Unlike Sudan, the country has had large populations of expats who brought the flavours of their communities to the nation to complement local dishes.

Before the days of Idi Amin, an extensive Indian population called Uganda home. The tastes of India survive as restaurants have since reopened with familiar Indian spices adding zing to local meals. The most popular contribution the Indians brought to Ugandan kitchens was the *samosa*, the crisp, triangular meat- or veggie-filled pastry now found on almost every street corner. And where you don't find them, you will find *nyama choma* instead, a form of barbecued meat on a stick.

Almost all meals are served with a starch of some kind: cassava, sweet potato or yam are the most common. If you're really daring (and visiting during the rainy season), try fried *ensenene*, a large winged insect. Wash it down with a cold beer and you just might enjoy it.

International dishes are the reserve of the five-star hotel restaurants in Kampala. And to be honest, they won't be all that stellar. They may be comfortable and guarantee hygiene standards, but they lack atmosphere and won't blow you away.

RESTAURANT LISTINGS

ASWAN

Al-Dokka
Island in front of Old Cataract Hotel
Tel: 231-8293
Call ahead to book a table at this Nubian restaurant located on an island surrounded by the cataracts. A small boat will pick you up so you can enjoy the live Nubian music and varied menu. **££**

Al Masry
Shari' Matar, off Shari' As Souq
Tel: 230-2576
This greasy spoon has been serving up Egyptian grilled meats with all the trimmings for over 50 years. Don't expect luxury – just quick meals served fast in a lively setting. No alcohol. **£**

Aswan Moon
Corniche An nil
Tel: 231-6108
Floating restaurant on the Nile which attracts many *fellucciyas*. Beer, fresh fruit juices and standard Egyptian fare in a relaxing atmosphere. **£**

Biti
Meadan near the train station
Tel: 230-0949
Waiting for the train or finishing a tough day haggling at the souq? This pizza place is open 24 hours and serves great *fattir*. **£**

Chef Khalil
Shari' As Souq, near the train station
Tel: 231-0142
Simple but very popular fish restaurant that serves fresh fish, by the weight, from Lake Nasser or the Red Sea. **£**

The Lotus
Basma Hotel, Shari' Abtal At tahrir
Tel: 231-0191
A nice option if you're starting to get tired of the usual grilled kebab and fish. The menu at this elegant eatery is generally European. An all-you-can-eat buffet choice is also on offer. **££**

Makka
Shari' Abtal At tahrir
Tel: 230-3232
The best kebab and kofta in town, sold by the kilo, and served in a totally Islamic kitsch decor. No alcohol. **£**

Nubian House Restaurant
About 1km (½ mile) south of the Nubian Museum, on the riverbank
Tel: 232-6226
With beautiful views over the First Cataract and the Nile, this is the place for afternoon tea, a *sheesha* (water pipe) or a dinner with live Nubian music. Friendly service. **££**

Nubian Restaurant
Essa Island south of Elephantine, free shuttle boat from the dock opposite the Egyptair office
Tel: 230-0307
The Nubian offers a three-course set menu with a folklore show of regional music and dance. The food usually includes grilled meats and Nubian spicy stews, but you will probably be surrounded by tour groups. **££**

LUXOR

Al Hussein
Savoy Market, Corniche An nil
Tel: 237-6166
If you are on a tight budget, head over to this cheap and cheerful eatery dishing up large portions of Egyptian street food. No alcohol. **£**

Al Kebabgy
New lower Corniche opposite the Old Winter Palace
Tel: 238-6521
Good Egyptian fare including *tagines*, grilled meats and duck, all served with salads and rice. The stuffed pigeon is a speciality, and so is the duck with orange. Slightly more expensive than most, but great to sit out on the river. **£££**

The Flamboyant
Mercure Luxor, Corniche An nil
Tel: 237-4944
A favourite with large groups and package tourists, this restaurant serves familiar Continental cuisine. Try to avoid at lunchtime when the place can feel over-run with crowds. **££**

King's Head Pub
Shari' Khalid Ibn Al Walid
Tel: 238-0489
On those days when the idea of another kebab or meze meal makes you go numb, fill up on Western faves at the laid-back King's Head. Great selection of lager and wide-screen TVs are perfect for sports fans. **£**

Miyako
Sonesta St. George, Corniche An nil
Tel: 238-2575
Luxor's one and only Japanese restaurant is pretty good considering the lack of competition. While the sushi and sashimi are tasty, it's the teppanyaki that stands out. **££**

Mövenpick restaurants
Crocodile Island
Tel: 237-4855
The pleasant terrace restaurant serves fresh pasta, salads and grills as well as excellent Mövenpick ice creams. Two indoor restaurants serve either a good buffet or expensive French à la carte. **££–£££**

Nur Al Qurna
Opposite the ticket office on the west bank
Tel: 231-1430
Peaceful restaurant where many local foreign residents hang out, set in a beautiful garden with long tables in the shade of palm trees. Good simple Egyptian fare. No alcohol. **£**

Oasis Café
Shari' Dr. Labib Al Habashi
Tel: 237-2914
In Luxor you have your choice of cheesy budget restaurant or overpriced hotel eatery. The Oasis bucks the trend and is pretty chic. A sleek and sophisticated place for a light bite or coffee. **£**

PRICE CATEGORIES

Price categories are for a three-course meal for one person, including soft drinks and taxes, but not alcohol or tips:
£ = under £10
££ = £10–30
£££ = over £30

Snack Time
Shari' Luxor Temple
Tel: 237-5407
A bit like an Egyptian McDonald's, this fast-food joint offers a varied menu of Egyptian street food and Westen burgers and fries where you can fill up cheaply. **£**

Sofra
90 Shari' Muhammad Farid
Tel: 235-9752
Classic versions of Egyptian favourites served in a beautifully restored 1930s home with open terraces. The menu offers great descriptions that are sure to inspire you to recreate each dish back home. **££**

Tutankhamun
At the public ferry landing on the west bank.
Tel: 231-0918
Simple but clean restaurant, serving very good food. Worth crossing the Nile for. **£**

CAIRO

Asian

L'Asiatique
Le Pacha 1901 Boat, Shari' Saray Al Gezira, Zamalik
Tel: 2735-6730
Superb dishes impeccably served in a relaxed and youthful atmosphere. Definitely the best (and most expensive) Asian cuisine in town. **£££**

The Bird Cage
Semiramis InterContinental, Corniche An nil Garden City
Tel: 2795-7171
Delightful Thai restaurant, one of the best in town, serving well prepared and beautifully presented Thai dishes, including excellent deep-fried prawns in *konafa* (angel hair) and delicious spicy curries. The decor is simple but elegant Asian, the service is swift and the ambience great. **££**

Kandahar
3 Shari' Gameat Al Dowal Al Arabiya, Al Mohandessin
Tel: 3303-0615
Considered the best Indian restaurant in town by many, Kandahar offers a wide range of dishes. Of particular value are the extensive and very filling set menus including everything from appetizers to desert. **£££**

Moghul Rooms
Mena House Oberoi, Pyramids Road, Giza
Tel: 3383-3222
This may be the most expensive place in town, but one look at the luxurious interiors and you'll know where your cash is going. The melt-in-your-mouth Indian food is also top quality and the entertainment is surprisingly sophisticated. **£££**

Peking
14 Shari' Saraya Al Ezbekiya, downtown
Tel: 2591-2381
Well-prepared Chinese food served in a pleasant decor. The strange house speciality is Irish coffee served with much drama and accompanied by taped birdsong. **££**

Cafés/Bars

After Eight
6 Shari' Qasr An nil, downtown
tel: 010-339 8000
Tucked away down an alley, this café is hard to find but worth seeking out, particularly at night when there are live jazz/salsa and Arabic music performances. The menu includes simple Western and Middle Eastern specialities. Very busy on Thursday and weekend nights. **££**

Al Fishawy
Khan Al Khalili, just off Meadan Al Hussain
Apparently open since 1773, this exotic café in the heart of the souq is a great place to hang out, have a cup of mint tea or smoke a *sheesha* (water pipe), at any time of the day or night. As it is close to the mosque of Al Hussain no alcohol is served. It's a great place to watch the world – or at least half of Cairo – go by *(see also page 261)*. **£**

La Bodega
157 Shari' 26th of July, Zamalik
Tel: 2735-0543
Cool bistro with Mediterranean dishes, from North African *tagines* and couscous to Italian pastas and a selection of Spanish tapas. The über-trendy (for Cairo at least) lounge bar serves good fusion food in a minimal Asian decor, to a Buddha Bar beat. **££**

Café Riche
17 Shari' Talaat Harb, downtown
Tel: 2392 9793
Founded in 1908, the legendary Café Riche is steeped in history. This is the place where the famous singer Umm Kulthum started her career, and where her contemporary, Gamal Abd An Nasser, planned his big revolution. Nowadays there are fewer

BELOW: baking bread for meze in a traditional oven.

leftist intellectuals, but it is still a good place to meet for a drink or a simple Egyptian lunch. **£**

Cairo Jazz Club
197 Shari' 26th of July, Al Aquzah, opposite the Balloon Theatre
Tel: 3345-9939
The best jazz club in Cairo, with regular live performances and good food. **£**

Cilantro
31 Shari' Muhammad Mahmoud, opp AUC, downtown (other branch on 157 Shari' 26th of July, Zamalik)
Tel: 2792-4571
Popular café that serves good coffee with fresh croissants for breakfast, healthy sandwiches and delicious fresh juices. **£**

Estoril
12 Shari' Talaat Harb, downtown
Tel: 2574-3102
One for Cairo's artists and poets, this bar serves cold beer and intellectual theory to a young and trendy crowd. The food is great if you're feeling peckish. **£**

Groppi
Meadan Talaat Harb, downtown
Tel: 2574-3244
Only vaguely reminiscent of its former grandeur, the tearoom now serves increasingly stale pastries, but the old waiters are still smiling. **£**

Marriott Garden
Cairo Marriott Hotel, Shari' Saray Al Gezirah, Zamalik
Tel: 2728-3000
The garden of this old palace is an oasis in the city. You can eat, drink, meet people or watch the continuous flow of well-heeled Egyptians and Arabs. Ice creams are served, as well as some good sandwiches, pizzas and excellent grilled Egyptian specialities. **££**

Naguib Mahfouz Coffee Shop and Khan Al Khalili Restaurant
5 Al Badestan alley in Khan Al Khalili
Tel: 2590-3788
The only "upmarket" place in the souq. Less character, but more hygienic (with decent toilets). The coffee shop serves traditional Egyptian hot drinks, fresh juices, water pipes and sweets in an Oriental decor. The restaurant serves meze and Egyptian cuisine. **£–££**

Simmonds Coffee Shop
112, Shari' 26th of July, Zamalik
Meeting place for locals, Ethiopian students and foreign correspondents. Serves nice snacks, good cappuccinos and fresh juices. **£**

Egyptian/Levantine

Abou al-Sid
157 Shari' 26th of July, Zamalik
Tel: 2735-9640
Atmospheric Egyptian restaurant, furnished with traditional Louis Farouk-style furniture and work by local artists on the wall. Abou Al Sid serves all the Egyptian traditional dishes with style, to a funky Egyptian beat, and waterpipes are available. Trendy place, and very busy at weekends, so do book ahead. **££**

Abou Shakra
69 Shari' Qasr Al Aini
Tel: 2531-6111
Known as "the King of the Kebab", this is one of the best places to eat kebabs, and prices are very reasonable. **£**

BELOW: fresh fruit, locally grown.

ABOVE: serving tea at a city viewpoint in Aswan.

Alfi Bey
3 Shari' Al Alfy, downtown
Tel: 577-1888
Cheap 1940s restaurant with wonderful decor, antiquated waiters and traditional Levantine fare. No alcohol. **£**

Al-Tazaj
13-14 Sour Nadi Al Zamalik, Al Mohandessin
Tel: 09018 (dialled in Egypt only)
Grilled chicken....and that's it. The garlic-packed tahini is incredibly moreish but you may want to avoid your neighbours for a while after eating it. **£**

Andrea's Chicken and Fish Restaurant
(on the left bank of the Mariyutiyah Canal at number 59 heading towards Kerdassa, Giza)
Tel: 3383-1133
Some of the best meze in town and certainly the best grilled chicken. Mostly outdoors, with simple wooden and bamboo furniture. **££**

Atatürk
20 Shari' Riyadh, Al Mohandessin
Tel: 3347-5135
Old-fashioned Levantine restaurant with kitsch Moorish interiors and surprisingly good food. Menu items are usually given a slight twist to make them a bit out-of-the-ordinary with great results. Dishes are filling, so pace yourself as you go along. **££**

Barry's
2 Shari' Abu Aziza, next to the AA stables, in the village near the Sphinx Nezlat Es Semaan
Tel: 3388-9540
Wonderful Egyptian restaurant, run by an American woman and her Egyptian husband. The food is traditional Egyptian with good meze, grills and *tagines* (stews), but the best thing is the cold beer and superb views over the three Giza pyramids. The best place to lunch in the area or watch the sunset. **££**

Felfella
15 Shari' Hoda Shaarawi
Tel: 239-2833
The original Felfella restaurant, which now has several branches. Started as a cheap vegetarian restaurant, it still serves plenty of cheap vegetable dishes and meze beside the traditional *kofta*, kebab and stuffed pigeon. The cafeteria around the corner serves good *fuul* and *tamiyah* sandwiches. **£**

Greek Club
3 Shari' Mahmoud Bassiouni, downtown
Tel: 2575-0822
A lot of faded grandeur, but the old Greek Club is still a great place, with age-old waiters, cool beers and tasty meze, as well as a lovely roof terrace for summer nights. **£–££**

PRICE CATEGORIES

Price categories are for a three-course meal for one person, including soft drinks and taxes, but not alcohol or tips:
£ = under £10
££ = £10–30
£££ = over £30

Hilltop Restaurant
At the Al Azhar Park, Shari' Salah Salem
Tel: 510-9151/50
In an impressive Fatimid-style building, overlooking the formal gardens and with a magnificent view over historic Cairo and the citadel, this is a perfect choice for a lunch, sunset tea or dinner. The setting is spectacular, the food is good and service marvellous. (For lunch or a drink, there is also the Lakeside Restaurant on the lower side of the park, with equally good views). **££**

Koshary Abu Tarek
40 Shari' Champollion
Tel: 2577-5935
Order Egypt's favourite fast food, *koshary* – a blend of lentils, chickpeas, macaroni and spices – at this over-the-top palace celebrating the dish. Bright lighting, bubbling fountains, screaming kids and blaring TVs combine to give you a slice of authentic Egyptian life. **£**

Sabaya
Semiramis InterContinental, Corniche An nil Garden City
Tel: 2795-7171
Excellent Lebanese restaurant serving all the traditional meze, the best *kibbeh nayyeh* (raw pounded lamb) in town and a wide selection of Lebanese specialities. Excellent wine list, including some good Lebanese wines. **£££**

ABOVE: meze make the perfect starter.

Fish and Seafood

Fish Market
Americana boat, 26 Shari' An nil, Giza
Tel: 3570 9693
The best fish restaurant in town, on the upper deck of a permanently moored boat. Choose from the catch of the day and it will be weighed and cooked to perfection. **££**

Rossini
66 Shari' Omar Ibn Al Khattab, Heliopolis
Tel: 2291-8282
Located in a renovated villa in one of Cairo's nicest neighbourhoods, Rossini offers seafood cooked with Mediterranean flair. **£££**

French

Justine
Four Corners, 4 Shari' Hassan Sabri, Zamalik
Tel: 2736-2961
Creative French cuisine and a cosy, luxurious atmosphere in the most upmarket of the Four Corners restaurants. **£££**

Steaks
Four Seasons Nile Plaza, Corniche An nil. Garden City
Tel: 2791-7000
If you want your meat cooked Western-style, then Steaks is the place to go. The best beef is shipped in from around the world, including Wagyu and US prime Black Angus. A favourite amongst expat executives and embassy staff. **£££**

Italian

Maison Thomas
157 Shari' 26 Yulyu, Zamalik
Tel: 2735-7057
The name may be French, but this place serves the best pizza in town according to Cairenes in the know. Also serves up sandwiches and lighter bites if you aren't looking for a full meal. Open 24 hours; alcohol is served for takeaway only. **£**

Villa d'Este
Conrad International Hotel, 1191 Corniche An nil, downtown
Tel: 2580-8000
One of the best Italian restaurants in town, Villa d'Este caters to the expense account crowd. If you're trying to watch your waistline, choose from the "healthy heart" options. **£££**

Vegetarian

Aubergine
Shari' Sayed Al Bakry, Zamalik
Tel: 2738-0080
Intimate and chic, this restaurant is one of the few places in Egypt where you aren't considered odd for avoiding meat. The pan-fried halloumi is distinctly moreish. **££**

THE DELTA: ALEXANDRIA

Asian

China House
Sofitel Cecil Hotel, 16 Meadan Saad Zaghlul
Tel: 487-7173, ext 782
Alexandria's only Chinese restaurant, the China House makes a pleasant change. Highlights on the menu include the chicken dumplings and the desserts. The views over the Eastern Harbour are wonderful. **££**

Cafés/Bars

Athinelos
21 Meadan Saad Zaghlul
Tel: 487-7173
A combination of an old-fashioned patisserie, nightclub and pleasant restaurant serving Levantine and Mediterranean fare. **£**

Cap d'Or
4 Shari' Adib, off Shari' Saad Zaghlul
Tel: 487-5177
Wonderful Art Nouveau bar serving the best squid stew in town and good fried fish. Difficult to find, but it attracts a loyal crowd of locals and expats who come to chat over a beer while listening to vintage French pop. **£**

Coffee Roastery
48 Shari' Fuad
Tel: 03-483 4363
Extremely popular Western-style café-restaurant with great coffees, milk shakes, fresh juices and a large sandwich, snack and lunch menu. The place is busy with trendy young things and families, who come and watch MTV on the large screen. No alcohol. **£**

Spitfire Bar
7 Shari' Al Bursa Al Qadima
Tel: 480-6503
Smoky and fun rock-and-roll bar with walls decorated with interesting memorabilia. Attracts a mixed crowd of local die-

hards, expats and a few American sailors if the fleet is in town. **££**

Trianon
Meadan Saad Zaghlul
Tel: 482-0986
Wood-panelled elegant restaurant with Mediterranean-Levantine food and, occasionally, live music. The next-door patisserie does a large, good-value breakfast. **££**

Egyptian/Levantine

Al Farouk
Al Salamlek Hotel, Montazah
Tel: 481-6597
Classy service in a classy place. Enjoy traditional Egyptian cuisine in a regal location. You'll be dazzled by the flavours and the interiors. **£££**

Gad
1 Al Rami Station
No phone
Cheap and cheerful versions of Egyptian favourites, including *fuul* and *tamiyah*. **£**

Hood Gondol Seafood
Corner of Omar Lofty and Muhammad Motwe
Tel: 476-1779
Located close to the Biblioteca, this restaurant is easily the one Alexandrians like most when they have a yen for seafood. There's no menu so be prepared to point and play a game of charades as you try and get your order taken. **£**

Mohamed Ahmed
17 Shari' Shaqour Pasha
Tel: 487-3576
By far the best *fuul* and *tamiyah* in town. No alcohol. **£**

Tikka Grill
Al Kashafa Al Baharia Club, No. 26 on the Corniche
Tel: 480-5119
Excellent fish kebabs and meat dishes. Good views over the bay. **££**

Fish and Seafood

Abu Ashraf
28 Shari' Safar Pasha, Bahari
Tel: 481 6597
A 24-hour fish restaurant, very simple but with excellent fresh fish and seafood, straight from the market and sold by weight. Sea bass stuffed with garlic and herbs is a speciality. **££**

Fish Market
Al Kashafa Al Baharia Club, No. 26 on the Corniche
Tel: 480-5114
More upmarket fish restaurant with a huge display of fresh fish cooked the way you want it. Good service, excellent salad bar and a perfect view of the harbour. **££**

Qadoura
33 Shari' Bairam At Tonsi Ahfushi
Tel: 480-0405
Pick your meal by pointing at the fish of your choice, plucked from the sea earlier that day. Your selection will then be grilled and served up to your table, and you will be charged by the weight. Great atmospheric setting too, with tables outside in the narrow street. **££**

Samakmak
42 Qasr Ras Al Tin, Anfushi
Tel: 481-1560
One of the best fish restaurants in town, serving a selection of the freshest fish or seafood. You choose from the display and then discuss how you want it cooked. All dishes are served with superb meze and rice or bread. Finish the meal like the locals do, by smoking a digestive sweet *sheesha* (waterpipe). **££**

Seagull
Al Maks, on the road to Agami
Tel: 445-5575
Famous fish restaurant in a mock medieval castle with a playground for children. Lobster and shrimps are a speciality. **££–£££**

Zaphyrion
Abu Qir
Tel: 562-1319
It's a 40-minute trip to reach this temple of seafood located east of Montazah – but locals have been making the trek for good reason since the place opened in 1929. Well worth the journey. **££**

Greek

Elite
43 Shari' Safia Zaghlul
Tel: 486-3592
Endless menu of Greek and Egyptian dishes and windows with a view on the world. **£**

White and Blue
Hellenic Nautical Club, Qayetbay
Tel: 480-2690
This Greek eatery is a celebration of all things Hellenic. Meat dishes are OK, but it's the fish options that really stand out. **££**

Italian

Chez Gabi
22 Shari' Al Horiyya
Tel: 487-4404
Quality Italian cuisine in a typical taverna-style eatery complete with red checked tablecloths and candles on the table. **££**

Kala
Four Seasons, 399 Shari' Al Geish
Tel: 581-8001
Buffest restaurant that offers up dishes from the world. Western and eastern options collide in an orgy of food. Go very hungry to make the most of it. **£££**

Taverna
1 Meadan Saad Zaghoul
Tel: 480 5114
Great for a quick and tasty bite, this pizza restaurant serves the best varieties in town. If you want something more substantial, seafood dishes are available. **£**

PRICE CATEGORIES

Price categories are for a three-course meal for one person, including soft drinks and taxes, but not alcohol or tips:
£ = under £10
££ = £10–30
£££ = over £30

BELOW: contrasting cultures.

ACTIVITIES

THE ARTS, CINEMAS, FESTIVALS, SHOPPING, SPORTS AND CRUISES

THE ARTS

Art Galleries

Al Sawy Cultural Centre
Shari' 26th of July, Zamalik, under the bridge to Al Aquzah
Tel: 2736-8881
www.culturewheel.com
Excellent gallery for local artists.
Hanager Arts Centre
Opera House Grounds, Gazirah
Tel: 2735-6861
Open daily 10am–9pm.
This is the experimental space inside the Opera House complex. Currently being renovated in stages, its schedule has slowed down – but if you want something a bit different, then this is the place to head to.
Khan al-Maghraby
18 Shari' Al Mansour Muhammad, Zamalik
Tel: 2735-3349
Mon–Sat noon–8pm.
Well-established and respected gallery in Zamalik offering the best of contemporary Egyptian work.
Mashrabia
8 Shari' Champollion, downtown
Tel: 2578-4494
Sat–Thur 11am–8pm.
Contemporary Egyptian artists.
Townhouse Gallery for Contemporary Art
10 Shari' Nabrawi, downtown
Tel: 2576-8086
www.thetownhousegallery.com
Sat–Thur 10am–2pm, 6–9pm, Fri 6–9pm
The best (and most active) contemporary art gallery in town, with an annexe for video installations and movies, and a wonderful art bookshop.
Zamalik Art Gallery
11 Shari' Brazil, Zamalik
Tel: 2735-1240
Sat–Thur 10.30am–9pm.
Bright contemporary art gallery with a focus on showcasing Egyptian work.

Ballet and Dance

Ballet

Egyptian ballet dancers are trained at the National Ballet Institute in the City of Art complex on the Pyramids Road. The Institute was founded with Russian help in 1960 and staffed with Russian experts.

The Cairo Ballet currently includes Russian and Italian dancers and performs in the new Opera House.

Traditional Dance Troupes

Folk dance is popular in Egypt, and there are over 150 troupes. The most prominent are the National Troupe and Reda Troupe, which perform in Cairo and Alexandria.

Al Tannoura Egyptian Heritage Dance Troupe gives whirling performances at the Citadel's Sarayat Al Gabal Theatre in Cairo on Shari' Salah Salem every Sat and Wed at 8.30pm (tickets are free). They perform a whirling ceremony, a form of ecstatic mystical dance, though here it is a cultural performance.

BELOW: whirling dervish.

Theatre

Theatre season in Cairo is from September to May. There is a summer season (May–Sept) in Alexandria. Curtain is at 9.30pm, or 10.30pm during Ramadan. Except at the American University or the British Council, all performances are in Arabic.

Opera

Cairo Opera Company
From 1869 to 1971 Cairo was regularly visited by foreign opera troupes, which performed in the old Opera House. A local company has performed in Arabic since 1961, and features fine individual singers. Performances are at the Cairo Opera House.

Venues

Cairo
Al Genena Theatre
In the Al Azhar Park, Shari' Salah Salem, Darassa
Tel: 2362-5057
Open-air theatre seating 300. Often hosts big-name Egyptian and touring Western performers.
Al Qawmi (National) Theatre
Meadan Ataba, downtown
Tel: 2591-7783
Popular Arabic plays.

Al Sawy Cultural Centre
Shari' 26th of July, Zamalik, under the bridge to Al Aquzah
Tel: 2736-8881
www.culturewheel.com
Excellent Arabic and jazz concerts, lectures, films and documentaries.
The American University in Cairo Theatre
113 Shari' Qasr Al Ayni, Garden City
Tel: 2794-2964
Performs in Wallace Theatre and Howard Theatre on the AUC campus.
Arab Music Institute
22 Shari' Ramses
Tel: 2574-3373
Twice-weekly centre for classical Arabic music performances.
Bayt Al Suhaymi
Darb Al Asfra, Al Hussain, Islamic Cairo
Tel: 2591-3391
Folk music performances every Sunday at 8pm. Special shows during Ramadan to break the fast.
Cairo Opera House
(The Egyptian Education and Culture Centre) Gazirah
Tel: 2739-0114
www.cairoopera.org
In 1971 the Cairo Opera House, an elegant wooden structure with perfect acoustics built to celebrate the opening of the Suez Canal in 1869, burned to the ground along with the scenery, costumes (including those of the first performance of *Aida*) and props dating back 100 years. A new opera house now stands at the Gazirah Exhibition Grounds, with three theatres, an art gallery and library.
Cairo Puppet Theatre
Azbakkiyah Gardens
Tel: 2591-0954
Dialogue is in Arabic, but the gestures and meanings are not too difficult to follow. Thur–Sat at 6.30pm, Fri and Sun at 11am.

Center for Art and Life
2 Shari' Al Malik Al Saleh, near the Nilometer, Manyal, Roadah Island
Tel: 2363-1537
Regular Arab music concerts.
Gomhouriya Theatre
12 Shari' Gomhouriya Theatre
Tel: 2739-0114
Now part of the Cairo Opera House, the **Gomhouriya Theatre** is still used as a venue for performing arts.

Alexandria
Bibliotheca Alexandrina
Corniche Al Bahr, Chatby
Tel: 483-9999
www.bibalex.org
This is the most important cultural venue in town, if not in the country, and hosts major music festivals, international concerts and plays.

Cultural Centres

Cultural centres tend to be very active in Egypt's main cities, putting on concerts, lectures, film, theatre and exhibitions. For non-Arabic-speakers they may be good places to soak up some Western culture. Check with the daily English-language *Egyptian Gazette*, or the *Al Ahram Weekly*.
Cairo
American Research Center in Egypt
2 Meadan Simon Bolivar, Garden City
Tel: 2794-8239
Excellent library for researchers, lectures, films.
British Council
192 Shari' An nil, Agouza
Tel: 3300-1666
French Cultural Centre
1 Shari' Madrasset Al Huquq Al Faransiya, Mounira
Tel: 2794-7679
Goethe Institut
5 Shari' Al Boustan, Downtown
Tel: 2575-9877
Good films and concerts.

Sound and Light Shows

The Pyramids

Every evening, two performances of a one-hour sound and light show are held on the Giza Plateau in front of the Sphinx. English-language shows are held every night apart from Sundays. Photography is permitted but no video cameras are allowed.

Luxor

The Karnak sound and light show is one of the best in Egypt. It is held three or four times a night, with a daily English-language performance, and lasts around 90 minutes. To get to Karnak in the evening, hire a taxi and the driver will wait for you.

Abu Simbel

Colourful images are projected onto a cliff face at this popular show.

The Temple of Isis

English-language shows are held every evening.

For further details contact the tourist office in Cairo, Luxor or Aswan, or tel: 02-338-52 880, www.soundandlight.com.eg. Information is also given in *Egypt Today*.

Casinos

Gambling is only available for foreigners, and only in five-star hotels. Most casinos are in Cairo, but there is one at the Hilton International, Luxor and another at Al Salamlek in Alexandria.

You must be over 21 and show some form of identity card.

Note that in Cairo, the word "casino" is used to describe a teahouse.

Netherlands Institute
1 Shari' Mahmoud Azmi, Zamalik
Tel: 2738-2522
Interesting lectures Thursday evenings (Sept–June) on Egyptian history or archaeology.

CINEMAS

Cairo

Cairo has many cinemas, often super screens in five-star hotels and shopping malls. Films are listed in the daily *Egyptian Gazette*, *Al Ahram Weekly* and the free magazine *The Croc*. All the cinemas below show films in English.
Cairo Sheraton Cinema
Shari' El Galaa, Giza
Tel: 2760-6081
French Cultural Centre
1 Shari' Madrasset Al Huquq Al Faransiyah, Mounira
Tel: 2794-7679.
Weekly selection of French film, sometimes with subtitles.
Karim I & II
15 Shari' Emad Al Din, downtown
Tel: 2592-4830
Odeon
4 Shari' Abdel Hamid Said, downtown, off Shari' Talaat Harb
Tel: 2576-5642
Ramses Hilton Annex Cinema
Shari' Corniche An nil, downtown
Tel: 2574-7435
Renaissance Nile City
Nile City Building, Corniche An nil, Bulaq
Tel: 2461-9101
Stars/Golden Stars
City Stars Mall, Shari' Omar Ibn Al Qhatab, Heliopolis
Tel: 2480-2012
Townhouse Gallery 10 Shari' Nabrawi, downtown
Tel: 2576-8086
Good selection of foreign and art-house titles, sometimes shown with English subtitles.

Festivals and Events

Most Muslim festivals are determined by the Islamic calendar, based on the lunar cycle. As lunar months are shorter than our solar months, the dates vary from year to year. The calendar starts at the Higra in AD 622, the year the Prophet Muhammad left Mecca for Medina.
Ramadan The main event in the Islamic calendar is Ramadan, the ninth month, when all Muslims fast between sunrise and sunset. A cannon shot announces the time for breaking the fast, and the night-long party begins. Aid El Fitr marks Ramadan's end, with celebrations, family visits and gifts.
Aid Al Adha (or Aid Al Kabir) marks the time of the *haj*, the pilgrimage to Mecca. The feast lasts three days, and those families who can afford it slaughter a sheep to commemorate the sacrifice of Abraham.
Moulid An Nabi celebrates the Prophet Muhammad's birthday, with street parties and Sufi gatherings near the main mosques.
Moulid of Abu Al Haggag An annual Sufi festival celebrates Luxor's saint's day two weeks before the beginning of Ramadan. During the festival, several feluccas are carried up from the river to the mosque, not unlike in ancient times during the Opet festival, when the Pharoah's sacred barge was carried up to the temple at Karnak. This is the largest festival in Upper Egypt; the town is bedecked with flowers during the celebrations, and dancing and clapping greets the procession.

Other festivals and events include:
7 January Coptic Christmas.
19 January Epiphany.
February Luxor Marathon where competitors race around the ancient sights; Nitaq Festival, a contemporary arts festival in downtown Cairo.
April–May Coptic Easter.
Sham An Nessim Spring Festival, held the Monday after Coptic Easter. For this big festival – the name means "sniffing the breeze" – Egyptians, Muslims and Christians all take part in festivities directly descended from Ancient Egypt to celebrate the resurrection of Osiris and the return of spring. Families traditionally have a picnic of *fasikh*, dried fish with eggs and onions.
25 April Sinai Liberation Day.
1 May Labour Day.
23 July Revolution Day, commemorating the 1952 revolution.
September Experimental Theatre Festival in Cairo.
October Pharaoh's Rally for 4x4s and motorbikes through the desert.
December Cairo International Film Festival.

Alexandria

Green Plaza Mall Cineplex
14th of May Bridge
Tel: 420-9155
Six screens.
Renaissance City Center
Carrefour City Center Mall, at the beginning of the Cairo Desert Road
Tel: 397-0156
Seven screens for Hollywood blockbusters.
Renaissance Zahran Mall
Zahran Mall
Tel: 424-5897
Multiplex addition to the Renaissance cinema chain that dominates Alexandria.

SHOPPING

Antiquities and Antiques

Pharaonic and Islamic antiquities can only be exported through a few shops. Each sale should be accompanied by a letter of authenticity and permission to export the item, which the merchant should arrange for you.

Street vendors selling "antiquities" are in fact selling fakes, worth purchasing for their own merit, but not as authentic articles. There are many antique shops in Cairo around Shari' 26th of July, Shari' Huda Shaarawi in Zamalik, and in Maadi. In Alexandria the Attarin district is popular with antique-hunters.

Appliqué

The Tentmakers' Bazaar (Souq Al Khayyaneyyah), the only covered bazaar left in Cairo, is the place to buy appliqué tenting. This wonderful craft, traceable to Ancient Egypt, when appliqué banners billowed from the tops of temple gates, comes in pharaonic and Islamic designs in the form of pillow cases, tablecloths and wall hangings.
Fatima, 157 Shari' 26 July, Zamalik, tel: 2736-9951. Offers the finest embroidered textiles and clothing from across the country. There is a good selection of appliqué work and hand-woven carpets from the Wissa Wasef school in Haraniyyah (tel: 3381 5746; www.wissawassef.com).

Baskets

Every region has its own distinct type of basket, and it's best to buy them in the village souqs. In Aswan, the flat Nubian baskets are popular. The oases' craft shops have an abundance of baskets.

Books

Cairo is the publishing capital of the Middle East and there are hundreds of bookshops. English-language books can be found in all major hotels. The following bookstores stock foreign-language publications:
Al Ahram
Outlets at: 165 Muhammad Farid; Cairo Sheraton; Cairo International Airport; Meridien Hotel; Semiramis InterContinental Hotel; Ramses Hilton Hotel Annex.
American University in Cairo Bookshop
Hill House, 113 Shari' Qasr Al Aini
Tel: 2797-5700
Excellent collection of English-language books on Egypt.
Anglo-Egyptian Bookstore
165 Shari' Muhammad Farid, downtown
Tel: 2391-4237
General English bookshop.
Diwan
159 Shari' 26th of July, Zamalik
Tel: 2736-2578
www.diwanegypt.com
Great bookshop with wide selection of Arabic and English books, Arabic CDs and DVDs and a good kids' section. You can browse their books while sipping a coffee and eating brownies in their in-house café.
Lehnert and Landrock Bookshop
44 Shari' Sherif
Tel: 392 7606
Good selection of books about Egypt, great old photographs of the Middle East and Egypt and lots of postcards.
l'Orientaliste
15 Shari' Qasr An nil, downtown
Tel: 2575-3418
Valuable antiquarian Oriental books, maps and prints.
Virgin Megastore
City Stars Mall, Heliopolis
Tel: 2480-2240
One of Cairo's biggest bookstores.

Brass and Copper

The Souq Al Nahhasiin on Shari' Muizz Al Din Allah near Khan Al Khalili is the best place in Egypt to buy brass and copper, both antique and modern.

Carpets and Rugs

For Egypt's best carpets, head over to Qirdassah on the western fringes of greater Cairo, where a large market offers native weaving and carpet varieties. Alternatively, on the approach to Saqqarah are a number of carpet-making schools in the village of Harraniyyah. If you are travelling in a taxi, your driver may stop at one so you can see the weavers in action (and he can get a percentage of any sale).

Traditionally, weavers in Egypt have stuck to producing simple kilims, but skill levels are increasing. Rugs produced in Harraniyah will use naturally dyed wools based on either modern or traditional design patterns. Qirdassah rugs will be much more tribal in pattern. Quality and price will depend on how well the seller feels you know your stuff and how good a bargainer you are.

Clothing

The world's finest cotton is Egypt's major export product, but it can be hard to find good-quality cotton inside the country. Imported designer wear and casual wear are now available in the cities. On Safari (branches in the major tourist resorts) sells good, locally produced cotton holiday wear. The malls at the Nile Plaza Four Seasons on the Corniche in Garden City, and the First Mall on Shari' An nil in Giza, both have a large selection of boutiques selling local and imported clothes. The largest shopping mall in Egypt is the City Stars Mall in Medinet Nasr.

For lounging around there is nothing like an Egyptian *gallabiyyah*. A good place to buy them, as well as cotton fabrics, is **Ouf** in the alley beside the Madrassah of Barsbay off Shari' Al Muizz, Islamic Cairo. Most popular are white *gallabiyyahs* from the north coast; the most difficult to find are green-and-orange diamond patterns from Sinai.

Designs can be made to order in a day. Those from northern Sinai are cross-stitched in reds, oranges and yellows, or blues and pinks. They can be bargained for in villages on the way to Al Arish, in Khan Al Khalili, or at Qirdassah, or bought in the more upmarket shops such as Nomad *(see page 308)*.

BELOW: aromatherapy oils for sale.

Crafts

Khan Misr Tuloan, opposite the Ibn Tuloan Mosque (tel: 2265-3337), and **Egypt Crafts** on 27 Shari' Yahiya Ibrahim, 1st floor Apt. 8, Zamalik (tel: 2736-5123), sell high-quality Egyptian crafts at fixed prices.

Nagada at 13 Shari' Refa'a In Dokki (tel: 3748-6663; www.nagada.net) sells stunning hand-woven fabrics and Fayoum pottery.

Umm al Dounia on the 1st floor at 3 Shari' Talaat Harb, downtown (tel: 2393-8273) has a great selection of Egyptian crafts at reasonable prices and includes a good bookshop.

Al Khatoun behind Al Azhar Mosque at 3 Shari' Muhammad Abduh in Islamic Cairo (tel: 2514-7164) sells work by local artisans, including cotton fabrics printed with images of famous belly dancers and movie stars, paintings, clothes and toys, all with a typical Egyptian sense of humour and colour.

Furniture, Woodwork and Textiles

Loft, 12 Shari' Sayyed Al Bakri, Zamalik (tel: 2736 6931; www.loftegypt.com), is an interesting store full of oriental-style furniture, textiles and gifts.

Mit Rehan, 13 Shari' Mara' ashly, Zamalik (tel: 2735-4578) takes old motifs and applies them to new designs to create something unique. Think pharaonic symbols carved onto modern sofas for an idea of what to expect.

Morgana, Road 9, Maadi (tel: 010-125 0441), has an incredible collection of authentic antiques and traditional furnishings. Everything from small porcelains to massive four-poster beds can be found.

Shopping Tips

- Haggling is a way of life in Egypt, whether you are taking a taxi or shopping at the market. Even in shops, you may find that the price is negotiable. If you don't like haggling, then look for a sign in the window that says "fixed-price shop"and you will know that the price tag shows what you have to pay.
- When it comes to haggling, the general rule of thumb is to offer half of what the seller initially quotes as the price and go from there. Really good bargainers will be prepared to walk away from any purchase in the hopes that a counter-offer will be made before you leave the shop (or sometimes even halfway down the street).
- For larger purchases (carpets, alabaster, etc), you may be offered tea or a soft drink. This is all part of the haggling procedure and can be part of the fun. If you're lucky, you'll be told stories and be given a chance to ask questions about your host and everyday Egyptian life.
- The souq in Luxor is known as one of the most aggressive in Egypt. Go if Luxor is your only destination, but if you want less hassle while you haggle, Aswan and Cairo may be better options.
- If you want to buy art and craft items, don't tell your taxi driver. Chances are he'll take you to a location where he gets a hefty kickback for having dropped you there – and your final price will be inflated heavily as a result.

Jewellery

From modern pharaonic cartouches to antique Turkish, Art Deco and Art Nouveau pieces, jewellery is one of the best buys in Egypt.

Gold is sold up to 21-carat for traditional jewellery, and 18-carat for modern jewellery of chains and charms. One of the best places to shop is the Souq Al Sagha in the Khan Al Khalili. Here you will find traditional designs coveted by farmers' wives in the form of necklaces, earrings and bracelets. Special shops sell 21-carat hand-tooled or stamped Nubian designs. Modern designs are found in jewellery stores throughout the city, particularly on Shari' Abdel Khalek Sarwat west of Opera Square in Cairo.

In Luxor the jewellery bazaar is just behind Luxor Temple to the north of the Luxor Hotel.

ABOVE: gold is sold by weight.

Although gold is the preferred metal today, silver traditionally dominated the market. Designs tend to be large and heavy, and are therefore too costly to be made in gold.

Nomad on the 1st floor at 14 Saraya Al Gezirah in Zamalik (tel: 2736-1917) and at the Four Seasons in Cairo, has amazing original designs in silver and gold. **Azza Fahmy** at 73 Shari' Hussain in Dokki (tel: 3338 1342) or the **First Mall** in Giza (tel: 3573-7687) sell jewellery in gold and silver with traditional Arabic calligraphy.

Leather

Everything from large and small pieces of luggage to clothing can be found in many designs. Leathers include buffalo, crocodile, serpent, lizard, cow, moose and goat.

Musical Instruments

Middle Eastern instruments of all qualities are made in Cairo on Shari' Muhammad Ali near the Citadel.

Muski Glass

Recycled glass products come in six main colours: blue, brown, turquoise, green, aqua and purple. The glass is hand-blown into pitchers, beakers, cups, vases, dishes, ornaments and amulets. It's inexpensive, but imperfections and bubbles make this glass fragile.

Papyrus

The cultivation of papyrus has been revived by the Dr Ragab Papyrus Institute. Shops all over Egypt now sell hand-painted papyrus sheets. Designs are stunning and many duplicate ancient wall paintings.

Perfume

Perfume shops, with their beautifully decorated bottles, are easy to spot. Egypt grows and exports jasmine, geranium, rose, violet, camomile and orange for the major perfumiers in France, from whom essence is then re-imported.

SPORTS

Participant

Balloon Rides

With good quality hot-air balloons and the best safety record, Hod-Hod Soliman (Omar Ali Street, Television Avenue, Luxor; tel: 095-227 1116; email: hodhodoffice@yahoo.co.uk) offers spectacular rides for around 50 minutes for US$150 in winter (US$120 in summer).

Cycling

The Cairo Cyclists (tel: 352-6310) have regular Friday and Saturday morning cycle rides in and outside the city, starting from outside the Cairo American College, Meadan Digla in Maadi, at 8am.

Diving

Egypt has some of the best diving in the world, in the Red Sea, and you can start in Cairo. The Cairo Divers Group (tel: 570-3242) organises regular excursions and also meets on the first Monday of each month at the Semiramis Intercontinental Hotel, Corniche An nil, Garden City (tel: 355 7171).

Fishing

Fishing safaris on Lake Nasser are very popular. It is a great place to find the massive Nile perch, the Tiger fish and Vundu catfish. Numerous boats compete for business, but with over 5,000 sq km (2,000 sq miles) of lake, there is plenty of room to accommodate them all *(see page 142)*.

The **African Angler in Aswan** (tel: 097 230-9748/233-0090; www.african-angler.co.uk) operates big-game freshwater fishing safaris, sometimes escorted by well-known anglers who share their expertise of the waters.

Lake Nasser Adventure (tel: 097-232 3636; www.lakenasseradventure.com) also organises fishing safaris.

Fitness Centres

Gyms and fitness centres are becoming very popular in Cairo, although not all are as sophisticated as their Western counterparts, so it is advisable to check facilities first. The majority can be found in the city's five-star hotels, and are usually open to non-residents.

There is a good gym and excellent pool at the **Nile Hilton**, Meadan At tahrir (currently closed for renovation), Splash, at the **Cairo Marriott**, Shari' Saray Al Gezirah (tel: 2728 3000), has rowing and cycling machines alongside pool, sauna and floodlit tennis facilities, and there is a Spa and Wellness Centre at the **Four Seasons Hotel**, First Mall in Giza (tel: 3573 1212).

Gold's Gym on the 8th/9th floors of the Maadi Palace Mall (tel: 2380-3601), has a mixed gym, women-only gym, Jacuzzi and sauna.

Gliding

For a spectacular view of the Pyramids and portions of the city of Cairo, gliding excursions are available on Thursday and Friday at the **Imbaba Airfield** to the west of Cairo. The Egyptian Gliding Institute and the Egyptian Aviation Society offer motorgliders and lessons.

Golf

There is a nine-hole golf course at the **Gazirah Club** (tel: 736-0434/735-6000) in Zamalik, as well as one at the **Mena House Oberoi Hotel** (tel: 3377-3322; www.oberoihotels.com), with the Pyramids as a backdrop. The **Katameya Heights Golf & Tennis Resort** (New Cairo City 5th District, Ring Road, West Heliopolis in Cairo; tel: 2758-0512; www.katameyaheights.com) has an 18-hole and a nine-hole golf course. There is an exceptional 18-hole course at **Dreamland Golf and Tennis Resort** (6th of October City Road, Dreamland City, south of Cairo; tel: 01-0177 3410; www.dreamlandgolf.com). The largest resort in Cairo is the **Pyramids Golf and Country Club** (tel: 049-600 953), with various courses and a total of 99 holes.

For detailed information, visit www.touregypt.net/pyramidsgolf.htm

Horse Riding

There is little to compare with a dawn or dusk gallop through the desert. The Bedu at the Giza Pyramids have been catering for eager riders for generations, and there are several good stables in the area. Horses and camels are on offer, but to avoid the hassle of discussing prices, only hire horses from one of the renowned stables. In the village near the Sphinx, Nazlet Al Semaan, the most reputed stables are **AA** (tel: 012-153 4142) and **MG** (tel: 385-1241). The favourite stable of the expat community, particularly for riding lessons, is the well-organised **International Equestrian Club** (on Saqqarah Road at the end of the Al Moneeb Ring Road, tel: 742-7654/385-5016). The **Saqqarah Country Club** (Saqqarah Road to Abu Al Nomros, tel: 384 6115) has good facilities and offers temporary membership.

On the west bank in Luxor, go for a ride through the field with horses from the **Pharaoh's Stables**, near the Mobil station (tel: 231 0015).

Yachting

Docking facilities exist at major ports in Egypt and along the Nile at major cities. Yachts may enter the country through the various ports if they have the proper documentation. The Egyptian Tourist Information Centres throughout the world have a booklet for yacht enthusiasts, entitled *Egypt for Yachtsmen*, giving entry information and maps. *(See Tourist Information, page 319.)*

Spectator

Football

Football is the Egyptian national sport, and a national obsession *(see also page 98)*. Important fixtures cause traffic jams as people dash home to watch the match, and the service in certain neighbourhood restaurants is noticeably slower.

There is a strong national side, mostly made up of players from the two rival Cairo teams, Al Ahly (tel: 735-2114; www.ahly.com) and Zamalik (tel: 735-5690; www.zamalek.com). These share the Cairo Stadium in Heliopolis (tel: 260-7863/65), playing on Friday, Saturday or Sunday from September to May, at 3pm.

Horse Riding

Horseracing takes place from October/November to May at the Heliopolis Hippodrome (tel: 241-7086/7134) and the Gezira Sporting Club (tel: 736-0434/735-6000) on Saturday and Sunday from 1.30pm. The *Egyptian Gazette* lists details of events.

There are many stud farms in Egypt, but only four major ones. The biggest, with 300 thoroughbred horses, is the government-owned Egyptian Agricultural Organisation (EAO), Al Zahraa Station, Shari' Ahmad Esmat, tel: 243-1733. This farm has only pure-bred bloodlines and is the home of the most famous Arabian stallion of the 20th century, Nazeer. Every important stud farm in the world has some of his offspring.

CRUISES

Nile Cruises

A cruise on the Nile still is one of the best ways both to visit the temples and ancient sites and sample the peaceful life along the river. Hundreds of ships now cruise along the Nile following more or less the same itinerary but offering a wide choice of accommodation, suitable for every budget. It is usually cheaper to buy them as part of a package. Most boats travel between Luxor and Aswan in 3–4 days, or sometimes for six days to include Abydos and Dandarah. Today, boats suitable for tourists never sail the whole way from Cairo to Aswan due to security restrictions.

More expensive boats tend to have fewer and larger cabins and will make the effort to prepare good food. All boats provide guides to accompany passengers to the sites and some have small libraries on Egyptian history and culture.

But there is no doubt that cruising is no longer as romantic as it used to be. Some 300 cruise boats now ply the waters, and there are often delays at Esna due to the large number of boats passing through the lock, forcing some companies to bus their passengers to a sister boat on the other side of the lock. For the same reason not all boats dock in the centre of Aswan or Luxor; cheaper boats are often moored further along the riverbank, or will be wedged between other boats and therefore without any Nile views from the inside. Your travel agent should know if you will have a Nile view.

As there are so many boats to choose from, we have just listed a few that stand out from the crowd, that have more character, atmosphere or history than most.

MS *Philae*
Mena House Oberoi Hotel, Shari' Al Ahram, Cairo
Tel: 3377-3222
www.oberoiphilae.com
The award-winning *Philae* is designed as an old-fashioned paddle-steamer. There are 54 comfortable wood-panelled rooms, all with their own bathroom and balcony, four deluxe suites and a great library, but the best thing about this boat is that it cannot moor alongside another cruiser, so the views are always assured.

Cruising on Lake Nasser

In 1993 the five-star MS *Eugénie*, built in the style of a turn-of-the-century Nile steamship, was the first boat to offer luxurious three- or four-day cruises on Lake Nasser, stopping for passengers to visit the salvaged temples on the shores of the lake, and allowing them to visit Abu Simbel at dawn before the crowds descend.

Since then, several other boats have joined the *Eugénie*, including the *Qasr Ibrim* (like the *Eugénie*, run by Belle Epoque Travel, tel: 02-516 9649, www.eugenie.com.eg/www.kasribrim.com.eg), the Mövenpick *Prince Abbas* (Mövenpick MS *Prince Abbas*, tel: 02-690 1797, www.moevenpick-hotels.com), the *Nubian Sea* (High Dam Cruises, tel: 02-240 5274; email: nubiansea@mist-net.net), the five-star *Queen Abu Simbel* (Naggar Travel, tel: 10-140 7753, www.naggartravel.com) and the four-star *Tania*, a smaller boat with only 28 cabins (Travcotels; tel: 02-3854 3222, www.travcotels.com).

Cruises generally start in Abu Simbel or near Aswan with a visit to the temples at dawn. Depending on the itinerary, further stops are made at the remote sites of Qasr Ibrim, Amadah,Addar, Wadi As Subu, Addakkah, Muharraqah and the Tomb of Pennut, as well as the temples of Kalabshah and Bayt Al Wali and Qertassi. The experience is quite different from a Nile cruise, but no less magical. The views over the lake are spectacular *(see also page 142)*.

MS *Senator*
Travco 19 Shari' Yehia Ibrahim, Zamalik, Cairo
Tel: 735-4890
www.mssenator.com
The *Senator* is the ultimate in Nile Cruise luxury, with just 17 large and luxurious suites, all with panoramic windows, international phone, satellite TV and en suite bathrooms.

MS *Star Goddess*
Sonesta Cruise Collection, 3 Al Tayaran Street, Nasr City, Cairo
Tel: 2262-8111
www.sonesta.com
Palatial all-suite cruise ship with just 33 cabins – named after famous composers. All of the suites feature private terraces in case you don't want to mix and mingle with the *hoi polloi*.

MS *Sudan*
Seti First Travel, 16 Shari' Ismail Muhammad, Zamalik, Cairo
Tel: 736-9820
www.setifirst.com
The only old-fashioned steamer on the Nile, a gift from Queen Victoria to King Fuad, and used as a set in the movie *Death on the Nile*. It has 23 suites with private balconies. No pool, but it oozes character.

MS *Sunboat IV*
Tel: 574-8334
www.abercrombiekent.com
Small cruise boat offering large, luxurious cabins, spacious sun decks with plunge pools, excellent food and very good mooring facilities at Luxor and Aswan in central locations. The boat has on-board Internet access, satellite TV and daily deliveries of international newspapers.

MS *Triton*
www.roadtoegypt.com
The most luxurious boat on the Nile, with only 20 suites, an indoor and an outdoor pool and a great restaurant. Book through upmarket travel agencies outside Egypt.

A Felucca Cruise

A felucca is a traditional sailboat with a triangular sail. The basic shape and construction have varied little since the days of the pharaohs, and continue to dot the landscape up and down the Nile. In Aswan or Luxor a felucca trip is a great way to get a feel for the Nile, either for a morning or an afternoon, or, security concerns in the region permitting, for a 2–4-day cruise between the two towns.

If you haven't prebooked your cruise, the Aswan tourist office has a list of official prices for different felucca trips, and walking along the Corniche you will meet the boat captains. It's best to avoid the touts and tour operators and deal directly with the cruise manager or captain.

When selecting your boat, you should check to make sure it looks seaworthy and that there are life preservers on board. Check the state of the sails and that there is plenty of shade on board. Be wary of paying ahead of time; that way, if you are given an alternative boat at the last minute, you can refuse to hand over your money.

Food is usually included in the price; however, if you haggle, the quality of your meals may go down – so it doesn't always pay to go with the cheapest option. Make sure to bring plenty of water with you in addition to toilet paper. A sleeping bag is also a must as nights can get cool, even in summer.

If there are just two of you, you will be sharing the felucca with other passengers. Try to meet them before you depart, so you're not stuck sharing cramped quarters with travellers you don't get on with.

If the wind is unreliable, you are advised to sail from Aswan to Luxor, so at least the current will carry you downstream.

Dining with your Captain

Don't be surprised if your captain offers you the opportunity to stop during your felucca journey in order to meet his family. It's a wonderful addition to any itinerary, giving you the chance to see real Egyptian village life up close while also giving the captain the chance to see his wife and children. The felucca trade keeps captains away from their families for long periods of time, so any opportunity to see relations is welcome and appreciated.

You may also be offered the chance of a home-cooked meal prepared by the wife, mother or other female relative. Payment will be required, but it is usually very reasonable, covering the cost of ingredients along with a small profit. The profit goes directly to the wife, giving her a valuable revenue source. It's also appreciated if you take sweets and pens to hand out to the children.

Dahabiyyahs

If you have the budget for it, and you want to get a feel for what cruising used to be like before the traffic jams on the Nile, take a *dahabiyyah* (Arabic for a golden boat). Nineteenth-century travellers such as Flaubert, Amelia Edwards, Pierre Loti and Florence Nightingale sailed the Nile on wooden boats with cabins, propelled by two lateen sails. Some of these boats have been restored, others are being built in the same style, but are all much smaller than the cruiseboats. They make the journey from Luxor to Aswan slowly, typically taking six or seven days, and stopping at sites such as Jabal Silsilla and Al Qab, where the bigger boats can't moor. A chef on board cooks fresh food bought daily from the markets and farmers along the river.

Assouan
Tel: 010-657 8322
www.nourelnil.com
Built in the style of the magnificent 19th-century vessels, with eight double cabins, each with a fully equipped en suite bathroom.

Dongola
Tel: 010-699-3889
www.nile-dongola.com
Dongola is one of the larger *dahabiyyas* on the Nile. The boat, once the private yacht of Sultan Hussain (who ruled from 1914 until 1917), has been carefully restored, with one suite and four cabins. Individual cruise trips where everything is arranged according to the customer's wishes.

Royal Cleopatra
5 Shari' Muhammad Ibrahim, Dokki
Tel: 012-717-8225
www.nilecruiseegypt.net
The *Royal Cleopatra* is a luxurious lateen-rigged Nile sailing vessel, with sleeping accommodation for one to seven people.

Sonesta Amirat
Sonesta Cruise Collection, 3 Al Tayaran Street, Nasr City, Cairo
Tel: 2262-8111
www.sonesta.com
The newest *dahabiyyah* to launch on the Nile, this exquisite boat has just six cabins and two suites plus an open-air Jacuzzi on deck.

Vivant Denon
Tel: (00 33) 06-1015 3789/(00 33) 01-48 46 40 98 (France)
http://membres.lycos.fr/Dahabeya
This boat is available for a few weeks a year between October and April; it may be available in summer, but it gets very hot without air conditioning. Two double and two single cabins.

A – Z

A Handy Summary of Practical Information, Arranged Alphabetically

A Admission Charges 311
Age Restrictions 311
B Budgeting for Your Trip 311
C Calendars 312
Children 312
Climate 312
Crime and Safety 313
Customs Regulations 313
D Disabled Travellers 314
E Electricity 314
Embassies and Consulates 314
Emergencies 315
Etiquette 315
G Gay and Lesbian Travellers 316
H Health and Medical Care 316
I Internet 316
L Left Luggage 316
Lost Property 316
M Maps 316
Media 316
Money 317
O Opening Hours 317
P Photography 317
Postal Services 318
Public Holidays 318
R Religious Services 318
T Telephones 319
Time Zone 319
Toilets 319
Tourist Information 319
Tour Operators and Travel Agents 319
V Visas and Passports 320
W Weights and Measures 320
Women Travellers 320

Admission Charges

The tourism industry is one of Egypt's most important sources of revenue. Combine this fact with the sheer cost of upkeep required by literally thousands of ancient ruins and the result is admission charges – and lots of them. Almost every site of importance, both major and minor, requires a fee payment of some sort. The most expensive charges are at the iconic locations: the Valley of the Kings, Karnak Temple, Abu Simbel, the Giza Plateau and the Egyptian Museum. Sometimes there may even be extra charges for rooms or tombs within the site, such as for the Royal Mummy Room in the Egyptian Museum or the Tomb of Tutankhamun in the Valley of the Kings. Prices can vary wildly, from a single Egyptian pound up to E£150 for a day at the Egyptian Museum including extra exhibits.

There are usually three admission prices to choose from: an unlisted price for Egyptian nationals, the standard admission charge and a reduced price for children and students. If you are a student, an ISIC card is mandatory and will be asked for at every ticket office. A standard college or university ID will not be accepted.

Below: tourist police can help you.

Age Restrictions

The age of consent in Egypt is 18. This is the same age for the legal purchase of alcohol and driving with a valid licence. However, most car rental firms have a minimum age requirement of 25.

Budgeting for Your Trip

Average costs:
Glass of beer: E£ 7
Bottle of house wine: E£ 45
Main course at a budget/ moderate/expensive restaurant: E£ 2–5/10–20/30–50
Double room in a budget/ moderate/de luxe hotel: E£ 125–175/300–500/1,000–3,000
Taxi journey from airport to downtown Cairo: E£ 40
Single bus ticket: E£ 0.50–2
Single metro ticket (Cairo): E£ 1

Egypt is a very affordable country to travel in. If you plan wisely, it is possible to enjoy a stay in a quality three-star hotel, feed yourself on three filling courses and embark on a bit of sightseeing, all for less than E£400 a day. Hostels and basic accommodation can reduce costs even more, but you will (obviously) have to give up a little in terms of quality. Luxor, with its traditionally high proportion of package tourists, is the bargain-basement destination in Egypt. Aswan is slightly more expensive due to the comparative lack of properties and competition. In Cairo and Alexandria, costs can vary widely from next to nothing to astronomically high, especially if you are booked into one of the five-star hotels.

Sightseeing will be the biggest variable in your budget, as the major sights can add as much as E£60 per person to your day. If you are a student, the ISIC card can slash costs considerably, so it is a wise idea to get one before arriving.

Calendars

The business and secular community in Egypt operates under the Western (Gregorian) calendar. But other calendars have official status in Egypt. The Islamic (Hegirah) calendar is used to fix religious observances, and is based on a lunar cycle of 12 months of 29 or 30 days. The Muslim year is thus 11 days shorter than the year in the Gregorian calendar, and months move forward accordingly.

In the Gregorian calendar, for example, April is in the spring, but in the Muslim calendar all months move through all seasons in a 33-year cycle.

The Coptic calendar is the Julian calendar, which was replaced in the West by the Gregorian calendar between 1582 and 1752, but the months carry their current Egyptian names. The Coptic year consists of 12 months of 30 days and one month of 5 days. Every four years a sixth day is added to the shorter month.

Muslim Calendar	*Coptic Calendar*
Muharram	Toot (begins Sept 11 or 12)
Safar	Baaba
Rabi' il-awal	Hatour
Rabi' it-tani	Qiyaaq
Gamadah-l-uula	Tuuba (mid-Jan)
Gamadah-l-ukhra	Amshir
Raghab	Baramhat
Sha'aban	Barmuda
Ramadan	Bashans
Shawal	Bauna
Dhu'l	Abiib
Dhu'l	Misra Nasi (5–6 days)

Children

Travelling with children in Egypt is relatively pain-free. Egyptians love kids and will be sure to make a fuss of yours wherever you go. Children usually pay a reduced entry price at all locations. If you plan on going tomb- or temple-exploring, budget your time wisely and be aware of where your kids are at all times.

Health and safety aren't a top priority at historic sights. Pits with sharp drops are often not roped off and perilous drops are common, so be sure to keep watch. This is true also in some of the budget and three-star hotels in the country, where standards of construction are less than rigorous.

Distances between many of the major sites are long and draining, especially during the summer when temperatures can reach crippling heights. Under these conditions, a day of five temples and tombs can turn swiftly into a nightmare when dealing with younger (and shorter) attention spans. Instead, cut your day down by a sight or two to ensure a good combination of exploration and enjoyment. Remember the sunscreen and water on your days out.

If you want a night off, babysitting services can usually be arranged through most international-quality hotels. Ask the front desk or concierge for assistance.

Climate

Summers are hot and dry in Upper Egypt, and humid in the Delta and along the Mediterranean coast. In recent years the humidity has spread to Cairo, and the city swelters in August. Winters are mild with some rain, but usually there are bright, sunny days and cold nights.

Spring and autumn are short, and during the 50 days *(qhamseen)* between the end of March and mid-May, dust storms can occur sporadically.

Average Year-Round Temperatures

	winter	summer
Alexandria		
Celsius	21/11	30/21
Fahrenheit	70/34	86/70
Cairo		
Celsius	21/11	36/20
Fahrenheit	70/52	97/68
Luxor		
Celsius	26/6	42/22
Fahrenheit	79/43	108/72
Aswan		
Celsius	26/9	42/25
Fahrenheit	79/48	108/77

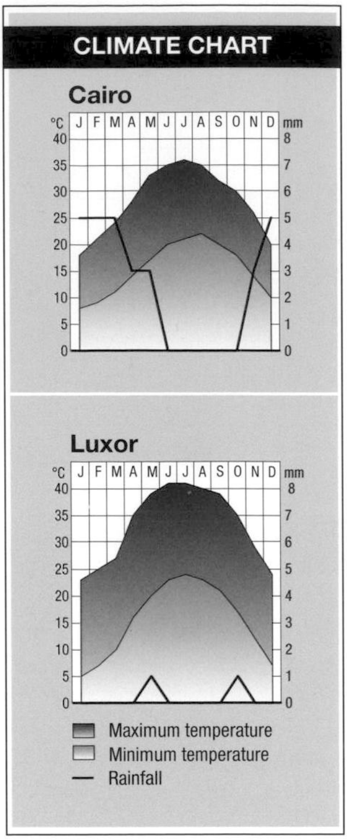

When to Visit

Peak season is from October to April, as this is when the heat cools off and temperatures are more bearable. Summer is slow season in terms of tourist numbers, and you can get really good deals as a result, but the sun makes temple-hopping treacherous, as the exposed locations and intense heat can sap even the most hardened traveller. If travelling during this time of year, make sure you bring bottled water wherever you go and keep hydrated at all times.

What to Bring

Almost everything is available in Cairo, but imported goods are expensive. If you have a favourite brand of protective sun cream, make-up, toothpaste or shampoo, bring it with you; it will almost certainly be cheaper to buy at home. A small supply of plasters, antibiotic ointments and anti-diarrhoea tablets may well come in handy.

What to Wear

Egypt is a conservative country. It is an affront to your hosts to appear in a mosque or even on the street in clothing that is considered immodest. Women should keep shoulders and upper arms covered. Neither men nor women should wear shorts except at holiday resorts or on the tennis court. No topless or nude bathing is permitted.

On the practical side, leave your synthetics at home as they will prove too hot in the summer and not warm enough in the winter. Cotton is suitable for all seasons, wool for winter and many summer nights.

Loose and flowing garments are extremely practical in a hot climate. Hats are vital to protect against heat-stroke, as are sunglasses, to defend the eyes against the glare.

Crime and Safety

Egypt

Like many other countries, such as the UK and the USA, Egypt has been troubled in the last decades by right-wing extremists and radical Islamic terrorists, and has also suffered from terrorist violence. In 1997, two attacks specifically targeting tourists – one outside the Egyptian Museum in Cairo and another at Hatshepsut's Temple, Luxor – significantly raised the overall death toll. In 2004, 34 people died when a bomb exploded in a hotel in Taba, northern Sinai, while a bomb in summer of 2005 killed over 80 people in Sharm Al Sheikh.

The most recent notable attack occurred in Khan Al Khalili in February 2009, which resulted in 24 wounded and the death of a French teenager. A heavy military response from the government designed to protect tourists and deter further terrorist activities cannot guarantee security and, many feel, may exacerbate the situation. However, tourists are statistically safer in Egypt than in many American cities, and Egyptian drivers present a greater threat than terrorists.

Visitors from abroad should nevertheless be warned that there are restrictions on travel along the Nile in Upper Egypt between Al Menyyah and Abydos. This region is beautiful but poverty-stricken, and historically given to violence, much of it directed against officialdom or formal authority. Travel restrictions also remain between Abu Simbel and Aswan where convoys run twice a day.

Elsewhere, common caution is advised. Social restrictions on women in Egypt can make foreign women seem particularly enticing to young Egyptian men, so care should be taken. Also, as Egypt's economic reforms have created great hardship, the incidence of petty theft has slightly increased, although you are still more likely to have a lost wallet returned intact than in many other countries.

If you do experience serious difficulties, you should report them immediately to the nearest tourist police post or police station. Egyptian police are usually found wearing an all-black uniform, while tourist police are clad in white.

Ethiopia

Most crime committed against foreigners are crimes of opportunity, such as pickpocketing or "snatch and grab" thefts. Be vigilant by crossing bags over your shoulder and keep wallets in your front pocket. There have been reports of car-jackings on the roads outside city centres, so you should limit driving to daylight hours if travelling independently.

Violence occasionally flares near the Eritrea border, and smugglers are active near Somalia. Check violence reports before undertaking travel to either region. Shopping in the Mercato at Addis Ababa can also be tricky sometimes. An explosion and drive-by shootings killed shoppers as recently as 2008.

Sudan

Crime is on the increase in Sudan, often resulting in death or injury, especially in the conflict zones of Darfur and the south. Anti-Western sentiment is common. Measures should be taken to respect Sudanese society as much as possible, as any perceived slight can spark violence.

Pickpocketing and theft are rife. Try not to check in luggage at airports as security cannot be guaranteed. Alcohol and anything thought of as military (camouflage, detailed maps) will be confiscated and can result in fines.

Violent crime, including car-jacking, sexual assault, murder and armed robbery, is prevalent in western and southern Sudan. Always travel in groups. And when leaving Khartoum, two cars are a must in case of breakdowns. Never camp alone.

Uganda

Pickpocketing and petty theft are common in Uganda. Leave all jewellery and large cash amounts in a hotel safe at all times. Locking your car or hotel room is not enough. Determined thieves will not let a locked door stop them. Robberies are getting increasingly violent, and do occur in public places and during daylight hours. Keep valuables out of sight at all times.

Do not drive alone after dark on Ugandan streets. If car-jacked, do not fight back, as injury rarely occurs if you don't cause any trouble.

Women should never travel alone on any form of transport apart from licensed taxis and buses. There have been reports of sexual assaults performed on expat women walking alone or using *boda-bodas*, especially after dark.

Never accept food or drink from strangers, and keep watch of your drink at all times as drugging is an increasing problem. Also, when using credit cards, tear carbons and keep your PIN code shielded at all times as fraud can be problematic.

Customs Regulations

A visitor is permitted to enter Egypt with 250 grammes of tobacco, 200 cigarettes or 25 cigars, one litre of alcohol and personal effects. Animals must have a veterinary certificate certifying good health and a valid rabies certificate.

Duty-free purchases of liquor (three bottles per person) may be made within a month of arrival twice a year at ports of entry or at the tax-free shops in Cairo and Luxor.

Persons travelling with expensive electronic equipment may be required

to list these items in their passports so that authorities can ensure that they will be exported upon departure.

On Departure

Although the traveller is free to buy and export reasonable quantities of Egyptian goods for personal use, the export of large quantities of items requires an export licence. Egyptian-made items over 20 years old are not permitted to leave the country, nor are foreign-made items deemed to have "historic value". Export of carpets is restricted. Travellers may be requested to show bank receipts as proof of payment for valuable items. Excess pounds may be changed back at the airport on showing valid bank receipts. Visitors can transport a maximum of E£1,000 into or out of the country at any single time.

Animal Quarantine

It is not wise to bring a pet to Egypt on holiday. Rabies is a problem in the country, and very few hotels have facilities for animals.

Disabled Travellers

Very few public or other buildings provide special facilities for the infirm or disabled in Egypt, but things are slowly changing. Before going, visit www.egyptforall.com, an excellent website dedicated to disabled travellers in Egypt. Egyptians are extremely friendly and will always be willing to give you a hand where they can. Most airports in Egypt are now equipped with ramps and lifts. Many five-star hotels have rooms equipped for the disabled, but smaller hotels usually don't. Some hotels, which are not specifically equipped for disabled guests, might still be a good option. The Mövenpick in Giza (tel: +202-3377 2555), Maritim Jolie Ville in Luxor (tel: +209-5227 4855), the four-star Basma hotel (tel: +209-7231 0901) in Aswan, and the four-star Mercure (tel: +209-5238 0944) in Luxor are all built on ground level, and the doorways are large enough to allow wheelchairs to pass through.

Amarco1 (tel: +202-3338 0444) is a new cruise managed by Optima hotels, which has four suites equipped for disabled guests. The entire boat is disabled-friendly, and all areas of the boat are accessible by wheelchair.

The Egyptian Museum in Cairo is now furnished with ramps and elevators, and medical care for the disabled. The Nubian Museum has been built with the disabled visitor in mind. The Giza Plateau is accessible by bus from which tourists can view the Pyramids and the Sphinx. The Citadel, the Papyrus Museum and Khan Al Khalili are all accessible by wheelchair. Disabled tourists can visit the High Dam, the granite quarries, and the Abu Simbel and Edfu temples in Aswan, but Philae Temple remains unreachable in a wheelchair. In Luxor, disabled tourists can enjoy visits to Al Karnak Temple, the Hatshepsut Temple and the Valley of the Kings, although some tombs are not accessible except by foot, and signs have been posted to mark them.

Electricity

Power supply in Egypt is 220 volts. Visitors from the UK and North America will need an adaptor. American items may also need a transformer.

ABOVE: armed police guard the main tourist sights.

Embassies and Consulates

Egypt

Embassies in Egypt

Australia
World Trade Center, 11th floor, 1191 Corniche An nil, Bulak
Tel: 02-2575 0444

Canada
26 Sharia Kamel Al Shenawy, Garden City
Tel: 02-2791 8700

Ireland
7th floor, 3 Shari' Abu Al Feda, Zamalik
Tel: 02-2735 8264

New Zealand
Level 8, North Tower, Nile City Towers, 2005c Corniche An nil, Ramlet Beaulac, Cairo
Tel: 02-2461 6000

South Africa
55 Road 18, 6th Floor, Maadi
Tel: 02-2359 4365

UK
7 Shari' Ahmed Ragheb, Garden City
Tel: 02-2794 6000
http://ukinegypt.fco.gov.uk/en

US
8 Kamal Al Din Salah Street, Garden City
Tel: 02-2797 3300
http://cairo.usembassy.gov/

Egyptian Embassies and Consulates Abroad

Australia
1 Darwin Avenue, Canberra
Tel: 612-6234 437

Canada
454 Laurier Avenue East, Ottawa
Tel: 613-234 4931

Ireland
12 Clyde Road, Dublin
Tel: 1-660-6566

South Africa
270 Bourke Street, Pretoria
Tel: 12-343 1590

UK
2 Lowndes Street, London SW1
Tel: 020 7235 9777
www.egyptianconsulate.co.uk

US
3521 International Court NW, Washington DC
Tel: 202-895 5400
1990 Post Oak Boulevard, Suite 2180, Houston
Tel: 713-961 4915
500 N Michigan Avenue, Suite 1900, Chicago
Tel: 312-828 9162/64
www.egyptianembassy.net

Ethiopia

Embassies in Ethiopia

Australia
Consular assistance provided by Canadian embassy

Canada
Old Airport Area,
Nefas Silk Lafto Sub City,
Kebele 4 ,House 122, Addis Ababa
Tel: +251 11 371 3022

Ireland
Kirkos Sub City, Kebele 6,
Sierra Leone Street, House 021,
Addis Ababa
Tel: +251 11 466 5050
New Zealand
Egyptian embassy handles all queries for Ethiopia
Level 8, North Tower,
Nile City Towers,
2005c Corniche An nil,
Ramlet Beaulac, Cairo
Tel: 02-2461 6000
South Africa
Old Airport Area, Nefas Silk Lafto Sub City, Kebele 3, Addis Ababa
Tel: +251 11 371 1002
UK
Comoros Street, Addis Ababa
Tel: +251 11 661 2354
US
Entoto Street, Addis Ababa
Tel: +251 11 517 4000

Ethiopian Embassies and Consulates Abroad
Australia
38 Johnston Street, Fitzroy, Victoria
Tel: 613-9417 3419
Canada
151 Slater Street, Suite 210, Ottawa
Tel: 613-235 6637
Ireland
26 Upper Fitzwilliam Street, Dublin
Tel: 1-678-7063
New Zealand
All queries should be directed to Consulate-General in Australia
South Africa
47 Charles Street, Pretoria
Tel: 12-346 3542
UK
17 Princes Gate, London SW7
Tel: 020 7838 3897
US
3506 International Drive NW, Washington DC
Tel: 202-364 1200

Sudan

Embassies in Sudan
Australia
Cairo embassy handles Sudan.
World Trade Center, 11th floor,
1191 Corniche An nil, Bulak
Tel: 02-2575 0444
Canada
29 Africa Road, Block 56, Khartoum
Tel: +249 156 550 500
Ireland
(Honorary Consul), DAL Food Division, No. 1/15, Block 4F, Industrial Area, Khartoum North
Tel: +249 1 5511 7886
New Zealand
Egyptian embassy handles all queries for Sudan.
Level 8, North Tower, Nile City Towers,

Emergency Numbers

Ambulance 123
Fire brigade 125
Police services 122
Tourist police 126

2005c Corniche An nil, Ramlet Beaulac, Cairo
Tel: 02-2461 6000
South Africa
Street 11, House 16, Block B9, Al Amarat, Khartoum
Tel: +249 183 585 301
UK
Off Sharia Al Baladia, Khartoum East
Tel: +249 183 777 105
US
Ali Abdul Latif Street, Khartoum,
Tel: +249 183 016 000

Sudanese Embassies and Consulates Abroad
Australia
There is currently no representation
Canada
354 Stewart Street, Ottawa
Tel: 613-235 4000
Ireland
Contact the embassy in London
New Zealand
There is currently no representation
South Africa
1203 Pretorius Street, Pretoria
Tel: 12-342 4538
UK
3 Cleveland Row, London SW1
Tel: 020 7839 8080
US
2210 Massachusetts Avenue, Washington DC
Tel: 202-338 8565

Uganda

Embassies in Uganda
Australia
Kenyan High Commission handles all queries for Uganda.
Riverside Drive, 400 metres/yds off Chiromo Road, Nairobi, Kenya
Tel: +254 20 4277 100
Canada
Kenyan High Commission handles all queries for Uganda.
Limuru Road, Gigiri, Nairobi, Kenya
Tel: +254 20 3663 000
Ireland
25 Yusuf Lule Road, Kampala
Tel: +256 41 771 3000
New Zealand
Egyptian Embassy handles all queries for Uganda.
Level 8, North Tower,
Nile City Towers,
2005c Corniche An nil, Ramlet Beaulac, Cairo
Tel: 02-2461 6000
South Africa
15A Nakasero Road, Kampala
Tel: +256 41 770 2100
UK
4 Windsor Loop, Kampala
Tel: +256 31 231 2000
US
1577 Ggaba Road, Addis Ababa
Tel: +256 41 425 9791

Ugandan Embassies, Consulates and High Commissions Abroad
Australia
7 Dunoon Street, Woden
Tel: 612-6286 1234
Canada
231 Cobourg Street, Ottawa
Tel: 613-789 7797
Ireland
All queries through High Commission in UK
New Zealand
All queries through High Commission in Australia
South Africa
882 Church Street, Pretoria
Tel: 12-342 6031
UK
Uganda House, 58–59 Trafalgar Square, London WC2
Tel: 020 7839 5783
US
5911 16th Street NW, Washington DC
Tel: 202-726 7100

Etiquette

Egypt is a modest country with traditional values. When exploring the city or countryside, you should remain covered up. Women should wear skirts or dresses that go below the knee and shirts that cover the shoulders and elbows. Low-plunging necklines are a no. Men should wear long trousers. Shoes need to be removed before entering mosques.

Close body contact with members of the opposite sex is considered wrong; however, you will often notice friends of the same sex kissing and hugging in greeting.

If you have the good fortune to be invited to a home for dinner, always use your right hand to eat. Do not show the soles of your feet to your host as it is considered rude. If you're full, placing your right hand over your heart symbolises thanks and humbleness.

Gay and Lesbian Travellers

Homosexuality isn't illegal in Egypt but it is highly frowned upon, as the practice is forbidden in the Qu'ran. Prosecutions are not unheard of and usually fall under vague laws concerning crimes against society or morality.

Despite this, eye contact with obvious sexual undertones is common along the Corniche in both Aswan and Luxor. Be aware that many who grab your attention are prostitutes and money boys.

Health and Medical Care

Evidence of yellow fever and cholera immunisation may be required from persons who have been in an infected area up to six days prior to arrival. No other inoculations are officially required, but it is always good to be up to date with polio, tetanus and cholera. Rabies is common, so if you are bitten by an animal it is wise to seek health advice immediately. Bilharzia, a tropical disease caused by parasitic worms, is common in the Nile region; avoid swimming in the river, especially where the current is slow.

Make sure you have comprehensive travel insurance.

Hospitals

There are good hospitals in Cairo and Alexandria. However, they require a cash deposit to cover the cost of treatment, and patients cannot use foreign medical insurance plans. Some hospitals are listed below:

Anglo-American Hospital Zohoreya
next to the Cairo Tower, Zamalik
Tel: 02-2735 6162

As Salam International Hospital
Corniche An nil, Maadi
Tel: 02-2524 0250

Cairo Medical Centre
4 Sharia Abou Obeida Al Bahr, Heliopolis
Tel: 02-2258 1003

Pharmacies

Pharmacies are usually open from 10am to 10pm. Medicines are inexpensive, and some products requiring prescriptions abroad are sold over the counter in Egypt.
24-hour pharmacies in Cairo include:

Ali and Ali
Outlets across Cairo, plus delivery service to all major hotels
Tel: 02-2760 4277

Talaat Harb Pharmacy
33 Shari' Talaat Harb, downtown
Tel: 02-2392 5341

Central Cairo

Isa'f Pharmacy
Sharia Ramses
(corner of 26th of July Street and Ramses Street)
Tel: 02-574 3369

Esam Pharmacy
101 Road 9
Tel: 02-358 4126

Zamalik

Zamalik Tower Pharmacy
134 Sharia 26th of July
Tel: 02-2736 1338

Internet

Internet cafés are easily found in the bigger towns and cities. Most hotels have at least one or two terminals available for guest use, and the charges are the same (or just a bit more expensive) than an internet café.

For travellers who use a smartphone or personal laptop, both budget and luxury hotels usually have WiFi.

Left Luggage

Left luggage facilities are available at Egypt's international airport. Lockers can be rented by the day at the train stations in Cairo and Luxor. Most hotels also have a left luggage room available for guests.

Below: the Egyptian pound is often abbreviated to LE in Egypt (livre égyptienne).

Lost property

Lost property offices are rare in Egypt. In the event you do lose track of your bags, inform the tourist police and register a report or check with staff at the airport and major train stations.

Maps

While tourist office staff and information is generally very good, maps distributed by these offices are usually poor. You can get around when you consult with them, but you'll find them lacking in detail.

Media

Radio

European Radio Cairo broadcasts on 557 AM and 95 FM, from 7am–midnight and plays European classical, pop and jazz. News is broadcast in English at 7.30am.
BBC World Service broadcasts to Egypt on 639kHz and 1323kHz. The higher-metre band gives better reception between sunrise and sunset. There are also shortwave alternatives. News is on the hour.
The **VOA** (Voice of America) broadcasts on a variety of wavelengths 3–10am daily, on 1290kHz.

Television

Satellite and cable TV have revolutionised viewing in Egypt. Most hotels offer satellite TV, and satellite dishes now top many of Cairo's apartment blocks. Local TV is rarely exciting and often packed with bad soap operas and action movies.

See the *Egyptian Gazette* for television schedules. These vary during Ramadan and in summer.

Newspapers

In Cairo all major English, French, German and Italian daily newspapers are available at larger hotels and at newsstands in Zamalik and Maadi, usually a day or more late.

The two most important local dailies are *Al Ahram* and *Al Akhbar*. *Al Ahram*, "The Pyramids", was established in 1875, making it the oldest newspaper in Egypt. Published daily, it also has a UK edition, a weekly English-language edition, *Al Ahram Weekly*, and a weekly French-language edition, *Al Ahram Hebdo*. Other English-language weeklies include the *Middle East Times* (www.metimes.com) and the *Arab Times*. *Al Akhbar Al Yaum*, "The News", established in 1952, offers a weekly edition in Arabic.

The Egyptian Gazette, established in 1880, is the oldest foreign-language daily newspaper still in operation in Egypt.

In French there are *Le Progrès Egyptien* and *Le Journal d'Egypte*; in Greek, *Phos*; and in Armenian, *Arev*.

Informal newsletters serve to keep foreign residents in Egypt in touch: the *British Community Association News* for the British community; *Helioscope*, serving the residents of Heliopolis; the *Maadi Messenger* for foreigners in Maadi, and *Papyrus* for the German community.

English-language magazines include *Arab Press Review*, a biweekly political magazine, *Business Monthly*, featuring business news, *Cairo's*, a monthly what's on, and *Egypt Today*, a monthly general-interest magazine. Free listings magazines for Cairo are available from trendy bars and restaurants.

Money

Egypt

Airport Exchange

There are banks at the airport offering currency exchange facilities. Egyptian money comes in the following denominations:

Pound notes (LE, EGP or E£): 200, 100, 50, 20, 10, 5, 1
Piaster notes (pt): 50, 25
Piaster coins (pt): 25, 20, 10

Credit cards are used in most major hotels, but not always in shops. Travellers' cheques are widely accepted. More and more cities now have ATM machines, which allow you to withdraw cash using Visa, MasterCard and so on. There is a lack of small-denomination bills across the country, and people rarely have change, especially taxi drivers. Keep small bills available for use whenever possible.

Tipping

Tipping – or *baksheesh* – is common in Egypt for even the smallest of services. Strangely, people who commonly receive tips in the UK and North America (such as waiters, taxi drivers and hairstylists) aren't given tips in Egypt. Rather, *baksheesh* is offered to people like bathroom attendants and security guards who point out a special location you may not have spotted before. Often the tip is given to help supplement a woefully small salary, and is relied upon just to make ends meet.

Requests for *baksheesh* can get very annoying, especially if asked for by someone who has done something seemingly irrelevant like holding an already open door. Politely smile and say a firm "no" if you want to avoid putting your hand in your pocket again.

Above: there are strict rules governing the taking of photos in many sights.

Ethiopia

Airport Exchange

There are banks at the airport offering currency exchange facilities. Ethiopian *birr* comes in the following denominations:

Birr notes: 100, 50, 10, 5, 1
Santim coins: 100, 50, 10, 5, 1

Credit cards are used only in major hotels or to pay for airline flights. Travellers' cheques are widely accepted, but ATMs do not accept foreign cards.

Sudan

Airport Exchange

Currency exchange facilities can be arranged at most banks, but foreign currency is preferred. Sudanese money comes in the following denominations:

Pound notes: 50, 20, 10, 5, 2, 1
Qirush coins: 50, 20, 10, 5, 1

Credit cards and travellers' cheques are not accepted widely (if at all) in Sudan. You will need to bring hard currency, preferably US dollars, to last throughout your stay.

Uganda

Airport Exchange

There are banks at the airport offering currency exchange facilities. Ugandan money comes in the following denominations:

Shilling notes: 50,000, 20,000, 10,000, 5,000, 1,000
Shilling coins: 500, 200, 100, 50

Credit cards are used widely in Uganda, with the exception of American Express. You will usually have to pay a 6–8 percent surcharge. Travellers' cheques are hard to redeem and may also be subject to service charges. Cash is the preferred method of payment, specifically US dollars. Some banks may not accept bills produced before 2003 due to forgery issues.

Opening Hours

Banks: 8.30am–1.30pm daily, closed Friday, Saturday and most holidays.
Businesses: Business hours throughout the week are flexible. Few businesses function before 8am; many are open until 5pm, but some close during the afternoon and then reopen at 5pm. Clinics usually open 5–8pm.
Government offices: 8am–2pm daily, closed Friday, Saturday, most holidays.
Shops: Shops keep hours according to demand. In central Cairo, many shops, including those owned by Muslims and Jews, are closed on Sunday.
Khan Al Khalili Bazaar: open 10am–7 or 8pm daily, and most shops close Sunday.

Photography

Egypt is a photographer's paradise. However, it is forbidden in security zones, often curiously defined, and a variety of rules pertain to pharaonic monuments.

No photography is allowed inside most museums, including the Egyptian Museum and Luxor Museum, and you can no longer buy photo permits. You are not allowed to take photos inside any of the tombs. In the Valley of the Kings, no photography is allowed anywhere, even outside. Cameras have to be handed in at the visitor centre, and you risk having your camera and/or phone confiscated if you use either to take photos. Restrictions may also apply in other areas, so check locally.

Photographing individual people requires a bit of consideration. The Egyptian people are constantly having cameras pushed in their faces, so be courteous and ask first.

Public Holidays

There are six official government holidays a year when banks, government offices, businesses and schools are closed. In addition there are Islamic and Coptic holidays spread throughout the year. Dates vary due to the nature of the Muslim calendar. *(See also page 306 for more on Festivals.)*

New Year's Day. Public holiday.

Coptic Christmas, 7 January. Copts observe the birth of Christ on the same date as all other Orthodox churches except the Armenian. Prior to the feast they abstain from eating meat and animal products for 43 days.

Feast of Breaking the Fast, Eid Al Fitr, celebrates the end of Ramadan, the month of fasting. Business hours are shortened during Ramadan and social life, centring on the meal eaten after sunset, called *iftar*, becomes nocturnal and intense. The Eid Al Fitr festivities usually last for three days.

Feast of the Sacrifice, Eid Al Adha, begins approximately 70 days after the end of Ramadan and commemorates Abraham's sacrifice of a sheep in place of his son, Isaac. Festivities last for four days.

Coptic Easter ends the Coptic Lenten season. Usually celebrated one week after Western Easter, Coptic businesses are closed.

Sham An Nissim, the Monday after Coptic Easter, is a holiday celebrated by all Egyptians regardless of their religion. Many businesses are closed.

Liberation of Sinai Day, 25 April. Public holiday.

Labour Day, 1 May. Public holiday.

Islamic New Year, Ras As Sana Al Higriyah. Public holiday.

Anniversary of the 1952 Revolution, 23 July. Businesses are closed.

Prophet's Birthday, Mawlid Al Nabi, is celebrated in honour of the Prophet Muhammad. A parade complete with drums and banners is held in the historic zone of Cairo. Public holiday.

Armed Forces Day, 6 October. Public holiday.

If a person does not want you to take his or her photo, do not take it. If he or she wants to be paid, pay. If you don't want to pay, don't take the picture.

Postal Services

Cairo's Central Post Office at Meadan Al Ataba is open Sat–Thur 7am–7pm, Friday and public holidays 7am–noon. All other post offices are open 8.30am–3pm daily, except Friday. Mailboxes on street corners and outside post offices are red for regular Egyptian mail, blue for overseas airmail letters and green for Cairo and express mail within Cairo. Allow seven days for airmail to Europe, 14 days to America. Mail sent from hotels seems to be quicker.

Express Mail Agencies

The major post offices, marked with the EMS sign, offer an Express Mail Service (EMS), which is more expensive but much faster (tel: 390-5874). In addition, there are various international courier services:

DHL
16 Sharia Lebanon, Al Mohandessin
Tel: 02-3302 9811

Federal Express
1079 Corniche An nil, Garden City
Tel: 02-2795 2803

Mail can be received at American Express offices (you don't need to be a cardholder). Letters can also be sent poste restante to most Egyptian cities or to 15 Shari' Qasr An nil, Cairo, A.R. Egypt. Bring along your passport when you pick up your mail. Some embassies may offer a mail holding service for their nationals.

Religious Services

Islam

Islam is the official religion of Egypt, but there is a large Coptic community and other Christian sects represented in the country. There is still a small Jewish community. The founder of Islam is Muhammad, a merchant who in about AD 609 was chosen as God's prophet.

Islam has five major principles, known as "pillars", which form the foundation of the religion. The first principle is the belief and statement that there is only one God and that Muhammad is the messenger of God. The second is ritual prayers, performed five times every day. Almsgiving is the third principle, and Muslims are encouraged to donate a percentage of their earnings to religious foundations. The fourth pillar is fasting during the holy month of Ramadan. The fifth pillar is pilgrimage to Mecca, *haj*, which all Muslims hope to perform at least once. The pilgrimage is performed during the month of Dhu'l-Higga, which begins 70 days after the end of the Ramadan fast.

Non-Muslims should not enter mosques while prayers are in progress and may be asked to take off their shoes and to cover up. Most mosques are free, although the guard may expect a tip. Some mosques listed as monuments and no longer in use may require an entrance fee.

Coptic Orthodox

The Copts, a minority in Egypt making up around 10 percent of the population, are a Christian sect that separated from the Byzantine and Latin churches in AD 451 over a disagreement in religious doctrine. Copts founded the world's first monasteries, and the monastic tradition is an important part of the Coptic faith. Visitors may attend any Coptic service.

Prior to independence, Egypt was a melting pot of cultures and largely tolerant of differing faiths. In fact, an important Jewish community once thrived and mingled with the Muslim majority quite freely. The emigration of Egypt's expats and multiple wars against the Israelis propelled the country towards the religious right, resulting in the upheavals in Middle Egypt that plagued the 1990s.

The tolerance is now a distant memory, as attacks by religious fanatics continue to occur, the most recent being a drive-by shooting of Copts worshipping north of Luxor in January 2010. The government is determined to continue the nation on a path of secularism and tries to ensure religious extremism is kept in check. However, anti-Western sentiment and soaring inflation do much to drive youth towards fanaticism.

Telephones

Most five-star hotels offer a direct-dial service, but they will charge highly for it. The Central Telephone and Telegraph offices (8 Shari' Adli, on Meadan At tahrir, 26 Shari' Ramses) are open 24 hours a day, as are many branch exchanges. Others are open from 7am–10pm daily.

Calls booked at telephone offices must be paid for in advance, with a three-minute minimum. Between 8pm and 8am the cost of phone calls is greatly reduced. In the cities there are international-call phone booths on almost every street corner, usually owned by Menatel. Cards are sold from many shops and kiosks bearing the Menatel sticker.

If you have an AT&T calling card it is possible to charge a call from Egypt to the United States to a US account; dial 02-510 0200.

Telephone Codes

Alexandria	03
Aswan	097
Asyut	088
Cairo	02
Hurghada	065
Luxor	095
Port Said	066
Sharm Al Sheikh	069
Suez	062
General Enquiries	140
International Dialling Code	+20

Time Zone

GMT plus 2 hours. When it's midday in Cairo, it's 10am in London and 5am in New York.

Toilets

Public toilets are at every major tourist sightseeing location, train and bus station. They are not usually found on the street – and where they do exist, they are definitely best avoided. Stick to the options in tourist-friendly locations such as hotels or restaurants. Asking permission with a smile on your face should be enough to allow you to use the facilities.

If you do use public loos, go prepared with pocket change to tip the attendant for their cleaning services; a single Egyptian pound is a generous tip. Some toilets may be squat in style, but most will be Western-style, with a hose attached to the wall for cleaning purposes. Egyptians prefer to clean themselves with water rather than toilet paper, which explains why the floors in public toilets are frequently covered in water. Bring a stash of toilet paper with you just in case.

Tourist Information

Egypt's international tourist offices are well-run and helpful. Before calling, check out the comprehensive website at www.egypt.travel, which has a wealth of practical information to help you plan your holiday. Inside Egypt, the tourist offices are less helpful. Staff will do what they can to assist, but levels of professionalism tend to

ABOVE: sign in Aswan.

vary from office to office. Literature is available and basic questions can be answered, although government-produced maps are poor at best.

Egyptian Tourist and Information Centres

Los Angeles
Suite 215, 8383 Wilshire Boulevard, Beverly Hills
Tel: 213-653 8815

London
3rd floor, Egyptian House, 170 Piccadilly, W1J 9EJ
Tel: 020 7493 5283

Montreal
2020 Rue University, #2260, H3A 2A5
Tel: 514-861 8071

New York
Suite 2305, 630 Fifth Avenue
Tel: 212-332 2570

Alexandria
23 East Port, Saad Zaghlul Square
Tel: 03-484 3380

Aswan
Railway Station Square
Tel: 097-231 2811

Cairo
5 Adly Street
Tel: 02-2391 3454

Luxor
Next to Railway Station
Tel: 095-237 3294

Websites

www.egypttoday.com
Online lifestyle magazine.

www.touregypt.net
Guide to historical sites and online comparative price guide.

www.drhawass.com
Website of the famous Egyptologist and Secretary-General of the Supreme Council of Antiquities, Dr Zawi Hawass.

www.horus.ics.org.eg
Fun website designed to help interest kids in Egyptian culture.

www.sis.gov.eg
Information portal run by the State Information Service.

www.yallabina.com
Youth-oriented information portal for Cairenes.

Tour Operators and Travel Agents

Cairo

Abercrombie & Kent
10th Floor, Bustan Commercial Centre, 18 Shari' Youssef Al Guindy
Tel: 02-2393 6255
www.abercrombiekent.com

American Express
City Stars Complex, Star Capital 8 Office 22, Heliopolis
Tel: 02-2480 1530
Also at 15 Shari' Qasr An nil
www.americanexpress.com

Cairo Dan Tours
13 Sabri Abou Alam Street, downtown
Tel: 02-2392 1336
www.cairodantours.com

Eastmar
13 Shari' Qasr An nil
Tel: 02-2574 5024
www.eastmar-travel.com

Egypt Panorama Tours
Opposite Maadi metro station
Tel: 02-2359 0200
www.eptours.com

Misr Travel
1 Shari' Talaat Harb, downtown
Tel: 02-2393 0010
www.misrtravel.net

Soliman Travel
95 Shari' Farid Semika, Meadan Higaz, Heliopolis
Tel: 02-2635 0350
www.solimantravel.com

Ethiopia

ENTTO
Hilton Hotel, Addis Ababa
Tel: +251 11 552 6622
www.ethiopiatourandtravel.com

Kibran Tours
PO Box 15475, Addis Ababa
Tel: +251 11 662 6214
www.kibrantours.com

Smiling Ethiopia Tours
PO Box 16618, Addis Ababa

Tel: +251 11 50 694
www.smilingethiopiatravel.com

Sudan

Happy Tours
Qasr Street, Aboulela New Building, Khartoum
Tel: +249 183 790 110
www.happytoursagency.com
Raidan Travel & Tours
Karary Street, Omdurman
Tel: +249 120 820 009
www.raidantravel.com

Uganda

AA Safaris and Tours
Suite F4, Sarah Mall, Old Kampala Road, Kampala
Tel: +256 39 288 3831
www.adventureugandasafari.com
Access Africa Safaris
Plot 4, Pilkington Road, Kampala
Tel: +256 31 226 5737
www.toursuganda.com
Churchill Safaris and Travel
Natete Wakaliga Road, Kampala
Tel: +256 41 434 1815
www.churchillsafaris.com

UK

Soliman Travel
113 Earls Court Road,
London SW5 9RL
Tel: 020 7244 6855
www.solimantravel.com

Visas and Passports

See pages 314–15 for embassy and consulate addresses.

Egypt

All travellers entering Egypt must have the appropriate travel documents: a passport with at least six months to run and a valid visa. Lost or stolen passports must be reported to the police immediately. New passports can be issued in a matter of hours at the consular office of your embassy in Egypt, but procedures will require a copy of your police report verifying loss. Tourist visas valid for one month are routinely issued at Cairo International Airport and other international airports, and the Port of Alexandria, but may also be acquired in advance of your visit at any Egyptian consulate.

Ethiopia

Visitors travelling to Ethiopia for tourism purposes require a visa, which can be obtained at your local embassy. Some travellers of select nations (Australia, Canada, Ireland, New Zealand, South Africa, UK and US) can also obtain their visa upon arrival at Addis Ababa International Airport. Single-entry visas are valid for 30 days, while multiple-entry visas are valid for anything from three months to one year. US citizens can only apply for a two-year, multiple-entry visa. Your passport must have at least six months' validity, and you will be asked for confirmation of return travel out of the country. You will also need a passport-size photograph. Visa fees vary per country. UK nationals pay £12 for a single-entry visa. Multiple-entry visas start from £18.

Sudan

All foreign citizens visiting Sudan require a visa. Visas are not available at the border and you will be turned away if you do not have one in your passport. The application process can be a nightmare so budget plenty of time. Australian and New Zealand citizens should apply at the embassy in Cairo upon arrival in the country if travelling via Egypt.

To get a tourist visa, you will need the sponsorship of a hotel or tour operator in Sudan, a completed application form, a passport with at least six months' validity and no Israeli passport stamps, and one passport photo. The fee is currently US$151 and must be paid in cash only. All visas are valid for a maximum of one month, but can be extended upon application at the Ministry of Foreign Affairs in Khartoum.

Uganda

Australian, Canadian, New Zealand, South African, British and American citizens need a visa to enter Uganda; this can be issued either from the Ugandan embassy in your home country prior to travelling or upon arrival at Entebbe International Airport. All visas must be paid in cash and are valid for a single entry of three months' duration. The cost of the visa is UD£50 per person. Irish citizens do not require a visa at the present time.

Weights and Measures

Egypt uses the metric system for all measurements.

Women travellers

Women will find Egypt a safe nation to travel through, but may find the hassle experienced from men overwhelming at times. If it ever gets too much, a hiss or warning cry should be enough to do the trick. Sexual touching is not unheard of in crowded locations. Avoid the bus and metro at busy times or choose to use the women-only carriage located at the front of each train on the metro system to stay comfortable.

When leaving your hotel or resort, cover your shoulders and wear modest clothing to avoid stares. Dresses and skirts should be below the knee and not tight-fitting.

Types of Visa

Single-entry visas obtained upon arrival at the airport are good for one entry into Egypt for a period of up to one month. If you require a longer stay than this, obtain your single-entry visa from an Egyptian embassy or consulate before departure. It will be valid for three months.
Multiple-entry visas should be requested from the Egyptian embassy or consulate before departure (valid for three months) if you plan to exit and re-enter Egypt during your visit.
Student visas for people studying in Egypt are valid for one year and are not issued until verification of registration at an Egyptian university.
Business visas are issued to those with business affiliations in Egypt.
Tourist residence visas are issued for extended visits. Holders are not permitted to work in Egypt and must be prepared to present evidence of having exchanged £180 a month for up to six months at a time. This type of visa is only issued in Egypt at the Passport Department of the Mugamma'a (Cairo's central administrative building on Meadan At tahrir). Persons holding a Tourist residence visa must apply for a re-entry visa whenever they plan to leave the country.
Extension of Stay
Visas can be renewed at the Mugamma'a, usually after a long wait. Visas are generally considered valid for 15 days after the expiry date, but if not renewed then a letter of apology from your embassy must be presented to the Mugamma'a or you will have to pay a fine.

LANGUAGE

UNDERSTANDING THE LANGUAGE

While Egypt is a nation that relies on tourism, very few locals speak or understand English unless they work in the tourist industry or come from the upper classes.

Hailing a taxi can be a hit or miss affair. Sometimes your driver will be completely fluent and engage you in witty conversation, enjoying a chance to practise his English. At other times you'll be frustrated as you find yourself being taken to the other side of town due to the driver's incomprehension at your pronunciation of a place name. This is especially true in Cairo, where thousands of migrants have turned to driving as a source of income yet are so new to the city that they still don't know where anything is. Try to get your concierge to instruct your driver where you are going, or have them write your destination on a piece of paper in Arabic.

Egyptian Arabic

Egyptian Arabic is the dialect spoken by most Cairenes – and subsequently the dialect most used in everyday life. This is the language spoken by broadcasters and entertainers. Despite this fact, Egyptian Arabic isn't recognised by the state. Rather, standard Arabic is the official language – a modernised version of the classical Arabic found in the Qur'an.

The use of Egyptian Arabic increased rapidly in the 19th century as the independence movement grew in stature; Egyptian Arabic became synonymous with national pride. Hoping to make Egypt the centre of a unified Arabic brotherhood, Nasser then enforced standard Arabic as the dialect of national use and attempted to erase traces of Egyptian Arabic from everyday vernacular. Following Nasser's death, Egyptian Arabic flourished once again; today there is ongoing discussion as to which language should be the one chosen for education and official government use.

Further south, residents speak Sa'idi Arabic – a dialect similar to Cairene Arabic yet adjusted slightly due to contact with Bedouins and southern Copts.

ABOVE: thankfully many tourist signs are in English as well as Arabic.

Transliteration

Converting Arabic into the Roman alphabet is notoriously difficult, and a standard system of transliteration has yet to be established. When you hear Arabic spoken, and see the language written down in a series of beautiful lines and squiggles, it becomes clear why the whole business of transliterating is fraught with pitfalls.

The French and English influence has only confused matters further, with different versions according to their own language. There is no single "correct" way of transliterating Arabic, and on your travels you will notice several different spellings of the same place. A word as common as *souq* (market), for example, is often seen as *souk*. The article *al* (the) is sometimes written as *il* or *el* and sometimes modified depending on the first consonant of the following noun (such as Jabal At tarif)

In this book we have endeavoured to standardise spellings of place names (although the sounds in spoken Arabic have not been represented, so we have omitted diacritical marks).

Where a place has become known by its English name (such as Luxor), we have favoured the commonly used version over the transliterated version (Al Uqsur). For the names of Egyptian gods, goddesses, pharaohs etc, we have taken the excellent *British Museum Dictionary of Ancient Egypt* as our guide.

Pronunciation

Vowels

ᶜ *cayn* or ' = glottal stop *(see box, page 322)*
a = a as in cat
aa = a as in standard English castle

or bath
e = e as in very
i = i as in if, stiff
ii = ee as in between
o = o as in boss
u = u as in put
uu = o as in fool

Consonants

(all emphatic consonants have been omitted):
All consonants are pronounced individually and as they normally are in English with these exceptions:
kh = ch as in Scottish loch.
sh = sh as in shut.
gh = Arabic *ghayn,* usually described as resembling a (guttural) Parisian r.
q = Arabic *qaf*, frequently pronounced in Cairo as a k or a glottal stop.

Sounds

Many sounds in spoken Arabic have not been represented by the transliteration used in this book. A particularly characteristic Arabic sound, however, is *cayn*, represented as ‘. All Arabic-speakers, native and otherwise, delight in producing the appropriate noise, described as a guttural hum or a voiced emphatic "h", which occurs in such common names as *‘Abbas, ‘Abdallah, Isma‘il* and *‘Ali.* Non-Arabic-speakers generally find pronouncing ‘ impossible without instruction and considerable practice; if it seems too difficult, it may be ignored. One will merely be marked as a non-Arabic-speaking foreigner.

Cairenes in the tourist industry speak English to some degree, though real ability to use languages other than Arabic is confined to the educated. A few words of colloquial Egyptian Arabic are therefore useful. The words and phrases listed below are not transliterated strictly, but spelt more or less phonetically following the Berlitz system. Take care over long and short vowel sounds, which may alter the meaning of a word substantially.

Vocabulary

airport *matár*
boat *mérkeb*
bridge *kubri*
car *arabiyya, sayára*
embassy *sefára*
hospital *mustáshfa*
hotel *fúnduq*
post office *bosta*
restaurant *matáam*
square *maydan/midáan*
street *shari‘*
right *yemiin*
left *shemáal*
and/or *wa/walla*
yes/no *aywa/laa’*
please/thank you *minfadlak/shukran*
big/little *kibiir/sughayyar*
good/bad *kwáyyis/mish kwáyyis*
possible *mumkin*
impossible *mish mumkin*
here/there *hena/henáak*
hot/cold *sukn/baarid*
many/few *kitiir/olayyel*
up/down *fo’* (*foq*)/*taht*
more/enough *kamáan/kefáya*
breakfast *íftar*
dinner *asha*
today *innahárda*
tomorrow *bokra*
yesterday *embáareh*
morning *is-sobh*
noon *id-dohr*
afternoon *b‘ad id-dohr*
at night *belayl*
next week *il esbuul-iggáy*
next time *il mara-iggáya*
last time *il-mara illi fáatit*
after a while *ba‘d shwayya*
I/you *ana/enta*
he/she *huwwa/hiyya*
they/we *humma/ehna*

Common Expressions

Hello, welcome *ahlan wa sahlan*
Good morning *sabáh-il-kheyr*
Response *sabaah in-nur*
Good evening *masaa-il-kheyr*
Response *masaa-in-nur*
Goodnight *tisbah* (m)/*tisbahi* (f) *ala kheyr*
Goodbye *ma‘a s-saláama*
What is your name?
(to a male) *íssmak ey?*
What is your name? (to a female) *íssmik ey?*
How are you?
(to a male) *izzáyak*
How are you?
(to a female) *izzáyik*
I am fine *kwayiss* (M), *kwayíssa* (F)
Thank God *il-hamdo li-lah* (standard reply). Often heard is "*insha’Allah*", which means "God willing".
Thank you *shukran*
Please *min fadlak* (m)/*min fadlik* (f)
You are welcome *‘afwan*
Sorry *aasif* (m)/*asifa* (f)
My name is *ismi...*
I don't understand *ana mish fahim* (m)/*fahma* (f)
Where is...? *feen....?*
Left/right/straight ahead *shimaal/yameen/ala tuul*
Nothing *walla haaga*
Not yet *lissa*
Never mind *maalesh*
Leave me alone *sibni li wahdi*
Go away *imshee*
I don't want *mish ayyiz* (m)/*ayyiza* (f)
How much is this? *bi-kam da?*
It's very expensive *da ghali awi*
That's OK *mashi*
How much is the bill? *bi-kam il-hisab?*

FURTHER READING

The Nile

The Nile, Robert Collins. This hefty tome covers the history and cultures of the Nile from source to mouth. You'll need to order the book online, but if you want a comprehensive account of the world's longest river, this is the book to get.
The Rape of the Nile, Brian Fagan. Fascinating account of how tomb robbers, European explorers and archaeologists have systematically ripped the treasures of the Nile out from their hiding places.

Ancient Egypt

British Museum Dictionary of Ancient Egypt, Ian Shaw and Paul Nicholson. Good one-stop shop chronicling the facts and figures related to over 4,000 years of Egyptian history. Drawings, photos and maps help illustrate the A–Z entries.
Chronicle of the Pharaohs, Peter Clayton. Reign-by-reign examination of each pharaoh and their contribution to ancient Egypt's legacy. Good reference source for those dipping their toe into the genre.
Cleopatra, Last Queen of Egypt, Joyce Tyldesley. Readable and accessible account of the famous queen whose relations with Rome (and its rulers) eventually resulted in the end of the Egyptian empire.
The Pyramids, Miroslav Verner. An interesting account of how the Pyramids were constructed and why. Verner combines history and science to tell the story of the ancient wonders.

Explorers

The Great Belzoni, Stanley Mayes. Biography of the circus strongman turned archaeologist who plundered more from Egypt's tombs than any other explorer of the 19th century.
Howard Carter, T.G.H. James. The life and times of the man who discovered Tutankhamun's tomb; the book covers a range of subjects, including his ambition, partnership with the Earl of Carnarvon and his lonely death.

Culture and Society

A Daughter of Isis, Nawal El Saadawi. The autobiography of Egypt's leading feminist writer, whose work is banned in Egypt. Fascinating insight into women and their place in Egyptian society.
The Voice of Egypt, Virginia Danielson. Egyptian society examined through its song. Special emphasis is placed on the role of Umm Kulthum and her growth from child star to national sensation.

Travellers

Flaubert in Egypt, Gustave Flaubert. Personal account of Flaubert's journey through 19th-century Egypt. Flaubert spares nothing and spends rather a lot of time chronicling his trips to brothels and bathhouses.
The Pharaoh's Shadow, Anthony Sattin. Modern-day tale of travelling through Egypt. Sattin explores how ancient and modern collide to make up contemporary Egyptian society.
A Thousand Miles up the Nile, Amelia Edwards. Edwards travelled the length of the Nile by *dahabbiyah*, sketching, measuring and writing along the way. Upon returning to the UK, she founded the first chair in Egyptology at University College London.
Travellers in Egypt, Paul and Janet Starkey. Collection of travellers' tales from the past and present. Works are drawn from across the spectrum, including accounts by artists, explorers, scientists and literary types.

Send Us Your Thoughts

We do our best to ensure the information in our books is as accurate and up-to-date as possible. The books are updated on a regular basis using local contacts, who painstakingly add, amend and correct as required. However, some details (such as telephone numbers and opening times) are liable to change, and we are ultimately reliant on our readers to put us in the picture.

We welcome your feedback, especially your experience of using the book "on the road". Maybe we recommended a hotel that you liked (or another that you didn't), or you came across a great bar or new attraction we missed.

We will acknowledge all contributions, and we'll offer an Insight Guide to the best letters received.

Please write to us at:
Insight Guides
PO Box 7910
London SE1 1WE
Or email us at:
insight@apaguide.co.uk

Fiction

The Alexandria Quartet, Lawrence Durrell. Four novels examining the lives and loves of a group of expats around the time of World War II. The books are set in a time when Alexandria's streets were filled with intrigue and grandeur.
Death on the Nile, Agatha Christie. Classic whodunit from the queen of the genre. Also made into a movie in the 1970s with a star-studded cast.
The Map of Love, Ahdaf Soueif. Sweeping family saga that takes the reader from contemporary New York to turn-of-the-20th-century Cairo. A tale of society and Egyptian nationalism through the decades.
The Mistress of Nothing, Kate Pullinger. Insightful historical fiction inspired by the life of Lady Duff Gordon, a Victorian writer who travelled to Luxor for her health.

Authors

Christian Jacq (born 1947). Popular French writer and Egyptologist who has written a number of fictional works inspired by Ancient Egypt. Some works favour the supernatural.
Naguib Mahfouz (1911–2006). Egypt's most celebrated novelist and winner of the Nobel Prize for literature in 1988. His works capture the flavour of Egyptian street life like no other. Best works to read include the Cairo Trilogy, *Children of Gebelawi* and *Midaq Alley*.

Art and Photo Credits

AFP Getty 3, 111
AKG London 63, 199
Art Archive 50, 62
Anthony Bannister/Gallo 117, 118, 169, 189T, 204T, 230
Bibliotheca Alexandrina 60
Bodo Bonzio 14T, 143, 241,
Chris Bradley APA 7ML, 100, 104R, 112R, 242/243, 244, 245, 294/T, 250, 251,/T, 252R/T, 253, 255, 260L/R, 261/T, 263T, 264, 265T
Corbis 23B, 25, 58, 64, 65L, 67R, 124, 220, 221, 223, 224L
Gerald Cubitt 75, 136, 120
David Dennis 112, 304
Jerry Dennis APA 213, 214, 217T
Nigel J. Dennis/Gallo 193
Jenn Dyer 144B
Egyptian Tourist Board/Bertrand Gardel 6TL, 36, 141, 142T, 158, 202R
Egyptian Tourist Board/Bertrand Reiger 152, 183, 191L, 208, 282, 291
Rudi van der Elst 165
Axel Kraus APA 2/3, 7BL, 9B, 125, 156/T, 157T, 195L, 198T, 212, 234, 235, 236t, 240T, 259/T, 273, 275/T, 277/T
Fotolibra 144T, 145, 278L
Dr A. Frankental 225
Glyn Genin APA 3B, 4B, 5B, 6MR/MT/TR, 7BR/ML/Mr/T, 8B/T, 9TL/TR, 10M/TR, 11B/T, 12/13, 14/15, 16/17, 18, 19B/T, 20, 21, 23T, 24, 26T, 28, 29, 39, 49L, 72, 73, 74B, 77, 85, 86B/T, 88, 92, 93, 94, 95, 96, 97, 99L/R, 101, 102R, 103, 104, 105, 121, 126/127, 128/129, 130/131, 132, 133B/T, 137, 142B, 146/147, 148, 149, 153T, 155, 157, 159L, 162/163, 164, 167, 168L/R, 170L/R, 171/T, 172, 173, 174, 175, 176, 177, 180/181, 182, 185, 186, 187/T, 189, 191R/T, 195R/T, 200, 202L, 203/T, 205, 218/219, 231, 232, 233, 234T, 236, 237, 239T, 240, 268/269, 270, 271, 272, 278R, 279/T, 280, 281/T, 284/T, 287/T, 289, 290, 292, 293, 294, 296, 297, 298, 301B/T, 302, 303, 304, 305, 306, 308, 309, 313, 314, 316, 317, 319, 321/T, 322
Getty Images 22, 59, 66
Dave Gilard 159R
Emad Hakim 227
Roger de la Harpe/Gallo 190T, 194, 216
Heiner Heine 239, 247, 248, 256
Hein von Horsten/Gallo 151B/T
Lanz von Horsten/Gallo 188,
Istockphoto 32, 160/T, 161/T, 177T
Kobal Collection 119
Jason Laure/Gallo 263
Chris Ledochowski 153
TJ Lemon 201, 262
Leonardo 297T, 299, 300B/T
Mary Evans 27L, 37, 38, 40, 41, 49R, 56, 82
Nature Picture Library 123
PA Photos 27R, 65R, 69, 98, 106
Robert Partridge 217B, 224
Pictures Colour Library 6BL, 138, 228/229
Gonsul Pillay 197
Rex Features 68, 76, 108L, 109R, 110
Sarah Louise Ramsay APA 102L, 206/207, 209, 210, 211, 212T, 225T, 252L, 257, 264,
Scala 30, 34, 35R, 47L/R, 51, 52, 54, 55L, 67L, 79
Spectrum 196, 215
The Star 89
Peter Steyn 74
Superstock 254
Susan Smart APA 48
John Thomas 113
TIPS Images 136, 140B/T
Topfoto 33,35L, 44, 45, 46, 78, 80B/T, 81, 84, 87, 256T
Starwood Hotels 10B, 289T, 295
Werner Forman 53, 55R, 57
Paul Wineberg/Southlight 26B
US Library of Congress 61, 70/71
Ed Yourdon 174T

Photo Features

42/43 All pictures Robert Partridge except: Glyn Genin APA 43TR
90/91
Egypt Tourist Board/Bertrand Reiger 90/91, 91BL, **Glyn Genin APA** 90BL/BR, 91BR/M/TR
114–115: Chris Bradley APA 114/115, 114BL/BR, **Istockphoto** 115B, **Mary Evans** 115TR, **Glyn Genin APA** 114M, 115M
178–179: Corbis 178/179, **Planet Earth Photos** 178BL, **Ancient Egypt Picture Library** 178BR, **Istockphoto** 179BR/M, **Glyn Genin APA** 179TR
266–267: Chris Bradley APA 266/267,267BR, **Corbis** 267M, **Art Archive** 266B, 267TR,

Map Production:
Mike Adams

Production: Linton Donaldson

INDEX

A

Abbas I, Pasha 40, 61
Abbas II Hilmi, Khedive 264
Abbas, Hisham 111
Abbasid caliphs **51–2**, 252
Abd Al Latif 87
Abd Arrahman Katkhudah fountain school (Cairo) 262
Abd Er Rassul, Muhammad 59
Abdel-Rahim, Shaaban 111
Abdelsalam, Shadi 108, 119
Abdin Palace (Cairo) 249
Abdou, Fifi 113
Abdullah, Yahya Taher 108
Abou Seif, Salah 109
Abraham 227
Abu Al Haggag 185–7
Abu Qir 278
Abu Qir, Battle of 56
Abu Qurqas 226
Abu Simbel **138–42**
- accommodation 290
- Rameses II 36
- rescue of 7, 137, 138
- sunrise 139–41
- sunset 9
- temples 7, **139–42**

Abu Sir 236
Abu'l-Dhahab 56
Abydos 8, 35, 209, **213–16**
accommodation 289–96
- Aswan 291
- Cairo 293–5
- The Delta 296
- Ethiopia 289–90
- Luxor 292
- Middle Egypt 293
- Nubia and Lake Nasser 290
- prices 311–12
- Sudan 290
- Uganda 290

Acre 53, 56
Actium, Battle of 39
activities 304–10
Adawiya, Ahmed 111
admission charges 311
Africa Cup of Nations 69, 98
afterlife 216
Aga Khan 149, 153, 156
Agami 278
age restrictions 311
Agiliqiyyah 76
agriculture
- ancient Egypt 30, **172**
- and Aswan Dam 76
- crops 125
- crops and livestock 173–4
- transformation of 61, **63**

Al Ahly football club 98
Ahmose I
- and Hyksos 34, 176
- mummy 192, 248
- and New Kingdom 34, 174, 176, 186

Ahmose (fan bearer) 224
Ahmose (son of Ebana) 174–5
Ahmose Pennekhbet 174–5
Aïd Al Adha 306, 318
air travel 284–5
Akef, Naima 113
Akerblad, Johann 274
Akhenaten
- Akhenaten Wall 192
- Amarna Letters 35
- and Amun-Ra 189
- and artistic realism 200
- Egyptian Museum (Cairo) 247
- revolution of **34–5**
- Tall Al Amarnah 186, **222–4**

Al Aqmar mosque (Cairo) 262–3
Al Arabah Al Mad Funah 213
Al Ashmunean 221, **226**
Al Attarin Souq (Cairo) 260
Al Azhar mosque (Cairo) 7, **260–1**
Al Azhar Park (Cairo) 10, **255–7**
Al Ballas 209–20
Al Banyana 213
Al Fayyum 236, 241
Al Fusat 249
Al Gawharah Palace (Cairo) 254–5
Al Genena Theatre (Cairo) 304
Al Ghuri mosque (Cairo) 260
Al Gumhureyyah (Cairo) 260
Al Hakim mosque (Cairo) 263
Al Harim Palace (Cairo) 255
Al Harireyyin Souq (Cairo) 260
Al Hawrah 241
Al Ismaìleyyah 273
Al Kab 174
Al Kamil 254
Al Khayyameyyah Souq (Cairo) **258**, 306
Al Lahun Pyramid 241
Al Lisht Pyramids 241
Al Mahallah Al Kubra 273
Al Manisterli Palace (Cairo) 252
Al Maridani mosque (Cairo) 258
Al Menyyah 221, 225, **227**
- accommodation 293

Al Qahirah 249, 257, 259–60
Al Qanatir 273
Al Qasr 213
Al Qatai 252–3
Al Qawmi (National) Theatre (Cairo) 304
Al Qurnah **203**, 204
- mystery of 59

Al Salih Talay mosque (Cairo) 259
Al Sawy Cultural Centre (Cairo) 304, 305
alabaster 11
alabaster sphinx (Memphis) 232
Albert, Lake 80, 161
alcohol 104, 297–8
Alexander, Bishop of Alexandria 48
Alexander the Great 32, **37–8**, 45
- Alexandria 275, 280
- Luxor 188

Alexandria **275–80**
- accommodation 296
- Christianity 46, 47, 48, 49
- eating out 302–3
- harbour excavations 277
- history 38, 45, 186, **275–7**
- transport 284, 286–7

Alexandria Airport 284
Alexandria Corniche 7
Ali Bey Al Kabir 56
Allenby, Lord 64–5
Amadah, Temple of (Lake Nasser) 142
Amarna Letters 35
Amenemhat I 34, 74
- Pyramids of Al Lisht 241

Amenemhat II 241
- Pyramid Complex (Al Hawrah) 241

Amenemhat III 34, 240
Amenemhat (governor) 227
Amenherchopeshef, Prince 199
Amenhotep I 248
Amenhotep II 143, 192
- tomb 196

Amenhotep III
- Colonnade of (Luxor) 287
- Court of (Luxor) 188
- mortuary temple (Luxor) 195
- statue (Cairo) 266
- statue (Luxor) 192
- Temple of Luxor 185

Amenhotep IV *see* **Akhenaten**
American Civil War 62
American Museum (Cairo) 204
American Research Centre in Egypt (Cairo) 305
American University (Cairo) 249, 305
Amin, Idi 161
Amir Aqasunqur mosque (Cairo) 258
Amir, Aziza 108
Amr Ibn Al 'Ass 51, 249
mosque (Cairo) 251
Amr Ibrahim, Prince 265
amulets 196
Amun/Amun-Ra 34, 37, 42
Karnak 188–91
Opet Festival 186, 187–8
Theban priests of 222
An Nahhasin Souq (Cairo) 262
animal quarantine 314
Anniversary of the 1952 Revolution 318
Anthony, St 47
antique shops 306
antiquities
fakes 306
theft of 59, 204
Antony, Mark 39, 276, 279
Anubis 42, 121, 179, 217
Aphrodite 211
Apis bull 236, 278
appliqué 306
Ar Rifa'i mosque (Cairo) 257
Arab invasions 249, 276
Arab League 280
Arab Music Institute (Cairo) 305
Arab Socialist Union 68
Arab-Israeli conflict 68, 281
Arabic 321–2
enforced use in Sudan 94
Arcadius, Emperor 48
Arians 48
Ark of the Covenant 144
Armant 177
Armed Forces Day 318
Arridisseyyah Bahari 170
arts
performing 108–11, 113, 304–5
visual 112–13, 304
Arya-Bhata 41
As Saghah Souq (Cairo) 262
Ashurbanipal, King 186
Assyrians 37, 186
Aswan **149–57**
accommodation 291
eating out 299
souq 7, 9, 150, **150**
Aswan Dams
Aswan High Dam 76, **157**
impact on Nubian people 24, 76, 137, 140
Old Aswan Dam 63, 75–6, **157**
saving the sediment 23, 76
Aswan to Luxor 165–77
Al Aswany, Alaa 108
Asyut 63, 293
Asyut barrage 63
At Tabbanah mosque (Alexandria) 279
Aten 222, 223, **224**
Athanasius 48
Atlas, Natacha 111
ATM machines 317
Al Atrash, Farid 109, 111
Attarine Souq (Alexandria) 9, 306
Auamutef 179
Augustus, Emperor 39, 45, 211
Avaris 275
Avenue of the Sphinxes (Luxor) 185
Aybek, Sultan 54
Ayn Jalut, Battle of 54
Ayyubid dynasty 53
Azzaqaziz 273

B

B Tombs (Saqqarah) 235
Bab Al Futuh (Cairo) 259, 263
Bab Al Quallah (Cairo) 254
Bab An Nassr (Cairo) 259, 263
Bab Zowaylah (Cairo) 259, 260
baboons, sacred 226, 227
Babylon 249, 250
Badr al-Jamali 53
Bahir Dar (Ethiopia) 145
Bahri Mamluks **54–5**, 254, 257, 264
Baker, Mrs 80
Baker, Samuel 79, 80
baksheesh 317
ballet 304
balloon trips (Luxor) 8, 308
banks 317
Al Banna, Hassan 66, 67
Barquq, Emir 55
barrages 63, 273
bars 297–303
Bashtak Palace (Cairo) 262
Basilica of St Pachomius (Faw Gibli) 212
basketware 306
Bastet 273
Baybars Al Bunduqdari, Sultan 54, 254
Bayn Al Qasrayn (Cairo) 262
Bayt Al Suhaymi (Cairo) 305
Bayt As Sehaimi (Cairo) 263
beaches 278
Bedad, Sheikh 247, 267
Al Bedawi, Ahmed 273
beer 104, 298
belly dancing 113
Belzoni, Giovanni 197
Ben Èzra Synagogue (Cairo) 251
Beni Hassan 221, **226–7**
"Bent" Pyramid of Dahshur 114, 115, **240–1**
Beta Israel 144
bibliography 323
Bibliotheca Alexandria 8, **280**, 305
Binoche, Juliette 119
birdlife **122–4**, **178**
Aswan 156
birdwatching 124
Lake Nasser 142
pied kingfishers 177
Birqash Camel Market 9
Birth House (Philae) 159
birth houses (Dandarah) 212
Bisharis 151
Black Pyramid (Dahshur) 240
Blessed Virgin Mary (Cairo) 250
Blue Nile 21–2, 23, 78, **144–5**
Blue Nile Falls 145
boats
cruise ships 86, 89, 90, 309–10
dahabiyyas 87, 88, 90, 165, 173, 174, 310
feluccas 6, 8, 10, 87, **91**, 154, 165, 310
history of 83–9
paddle-steamers 87, 89
book shops 306
Botanical Garden (Kitchener's Island) 154
Bouchard, Pierre 274
Brando, Marlon 117
brassware 262, 307
breakfast boxes 170, 289
Breasted, James 200
Britain
bombing of Alexandria 277
intervention and rule 56, 60, 62–4
Protectorate 64–5
and Suez 66, 67, 281
British Council (Cairo) 305
Brown, Gordon 119
Bruce, James 78
Brugsch, Emile 59
Bubastis 272, **273**
budgeting 311–12
bulls, sacred 236
Burji Mamluk dynasty 54, 55
burqas 94
Burton, Richard 117
Burton, Richard Francis 78, 79–80, 119
Burullus, Lake 275
bus travel 286
business hours 317
Bwindi Impenetrable Forest (Uganda) 161
Byzantium 48–9, 51

C

Cachette Court (Karnak) 191
Caesar, Julius 39, 153, 212, 276
Caesareum (Alexandria) 279
Caesarion 39, 212
cafés 297–303
Cairo 245–67
accommodation 293–5
distances from 287
eating out 300–2
history 52, 53, 56, **249**
population 96
transport 286–7
Cairo International Airport 284
Cairo Marriott Hotel 265
Cairo Opera House 111, 249, **264**, 304, **305**
Cairo Puppet Theatre 305
Cairo Tower 9, **264**
calèches (Luxor) 10
calendars 312
Caligula, Emperor 211
Cambyses, King of Persia 37
camels
camel rides (Giza) 10, 233
Daraw camel market 167
Camp, Maxime du 88
canoes 85
car rental 288
Caracalla, Emperor 168
caravan routes 166–7, 209
caravanserai 176
Carnarvon, Lord 58, 196–7, 198, 267
carpets 235, 307
Carriage Museum (Cairo) 255
Carter, Howard 58, 88, 201
Howard Carter's House (Luxor) 195, 202
and Tutankhamun 196–7, **198**, 248, 267
casinos 305
Catacombs of Kom Ash Shuqafa (Alexandria) 280
cataracts 24
cattle 95
Cavafy, C.P. 107, 277, 278
Cavafy Museum (Alexandria) 278
Cecil Hotel (Alexandria) 279, 296
cemeteries
see also **tombs**
Northern Cemetery (Cairo) 263
Southern Cemetery (Cairo) 264
visiting 264
Zouhreyyet Al Mayteen (Al Menyyah) 227
Centre for Art and Life (Cairo) 305
Chad, Lake 84
Chahine, Youssef 109
Champollion, Jean-François 274
Chapel of the Sacred Boat (Karnak) 191
Chapelle Rouge 192
Chephren *see* **Khafra**
children 312
best activities for 10
Choke Mountains 22
Christianity 46–9
Crusades 53
Ethiopia 95, 144
Hammadi codices 212–13
persecution 48, 227
Roman/Byzantine era 212–13
Christie, Agatha 88, 119, 152
churches
Basilica of St Pachomius (Faw Gibli) 212
Blessed Virgin Mary, "Hanging" (Cairo) 250
Roman Basilica (Dandarah) 212
St Barbara (Cairo) 251
St George Greek Orthodox (Cairo) 250
St Sergius (Cairo) 250
cinema 107, **108–10**
cinemas 305–6
the Nile in 116–19
Citadel (Cairo) 254
Citadel of the Mamluk Sultan Qal'at Qayetbay (Alexandria) 280
civil wars 99, 112, 161
Claudius, Emperor 211
Clement (Christian scholar) 46
Cleopatra VII 39, 45
Alexandria 276, 279, 280
in cinema 116–17
Cleopatra's Palace (Alexandria) 277
Dandarah 212
and Nubia 140
climate 312–13
climate change 69
clothing
etiquette 257
shops 307
what to bring/wear 312–13
coffee 6
Colbert, Claudette 117
Colonade of Amenhotep III (Luxor) 187
colonialism 62
Colossi of Memnon (Luxor) 194
Commodus, Emperor 177
community, sense of 97–8
Complex of Sultan Al Ashraf Bersbay (Cairo) 263–4
Congo River 19
conservation 204
Constantine the Great 48
Constantinople 48, 49
consulates 314–15
Convent of St George (Cairo) 251
convoy system 138, 139, 210, 213, 221
Cook, Thomas 83, 88, 89
copperware 262, 307
Coptic calendar 312
Coptic Christians 39, **49**, 93–4, 224
religious services 318
Coptic Christmas 318
Coptic Easter 318
Coptic Museum (Cairo) 213, **250**
Coptic script 38, 46, 49
Corniche (Alexandria) 279
Corniche (Luxor) 9, **193**
Council of Chalcedon 49
Council of Nicea 48
coup d'état (1952) 67
Court of Amenhotep III (Luxor) 188
Court of Offerings (Edfu) 171
Court of Rameses II (Luxor) 185, 187
crafts 307
credit cards 317
Crete 34, 60
crime 313
Crocodile Island (Luxor) 124
crocodiles 169, 178
Lake Nasser 142
Sobek 32, 121
Cromer, Lord 63, 64
cruises 90–1, **309–10**
Aswan to Luxor 165
behind the scenes 86
Cairo 9
dahabiyyah 174, 310
dinner cruises 10
dinner with your captain 310
felucca 310
history 83–9
Lake Nasser 90, 138, 142, 143, **309**
restrictions on 87, 90, 133, 210
ships 86, 87, **309–10**
Crusades 53
cultural centres 304, 305
currency 317
curses 58, 267
Curse of the Pharaohs 41
customs regulations 313–14
cycling 308

D

dahabiyyas
Aswan to Luxor 165, 173
cruises 90, 174, 310
history of cruising 87, 88

Dahshur 114, 115, 231, 238, **240–1**
Dair Al Bahari 248
Dair Al Madinah 197–9
Dakkah, Temple of (Lake Nasser) 143
Damietta (Dumyat) **273**, 278
dance 260, **304**
Dandarah 8, **210–12**
Daraw 166–7
Daraw camel market 167
Darb Al Ahmar 257
Darb Al Arba'in 167
Darfur 69
Darius 74
Davis, Bette 119
Dayr Mowass 222
de Mille, Cecil B. 116–17
Debod, Temple of (Madrid) 139
Decius, Emperor 47, 227
deference 95
The Delta 19, **271–81**
accommodation 296
eating out 302–3
environmental problems 24, 76, 272, **278**
formation 231, 271
history of 272
Delta Barrage 63
Derr, Temple of (Lake Nasser) 142
Diab, Amr 111
dinner cruises 10
Diocletian, Emperor 47–8, 227, 280
disabled travellers 314
distances from Cairo 287
diving 308
Djer 216
Djoser 114, 233–4
Dome of the Wind (Aswan) 154
Domitian, Emperor 168
donkey rides 10, 199
Dr Ragab's Papyrus Institute (Cairo) 179, **308**
drinks 104, 297–8
driving
in Egypt 288
to Egypt 285
drought 124
Durrell, Lawrence 277, 278
dynasties 32

E

Eady, Dorothy 216
East Bank (Luxor) **185–93**, 292
eating out 297–303
Aswan 299
Cairo 300–2
The Delta: Alexandria 302–3
Ethiopia 298
Luxor 299–300
prices 311–12
Sudan 298
Uganda 298
eco-tourism 161
economic issues 96
Edfu 8, **165**
Edict of Milan 48
education 96
Edwards, Amelia 89, 158, 159
Edwards, I.E.S. 114
egrets 122
Egyptian Empire 60
Egyptian Military Museum (Cairo) 255
Egyptian Museum (Cairo) 7, 9, 59, **247–8**, **266–7**
Egyptian people 93–4, 95–9
electricity 314
Elephantine Island (Aswan) 150–1, **152–4**
Elephantine Island Museum (Aswan) 152
Elgin, Lord 274
embalming 194, 256
embassies 314–15
emergency numbers 315
Entebbe (Uganda) 160
Eratosthenes 276
Eritrea 31
Esna 165, **175–7**
lock 175
Esna barrage 63
Ethiopia
accommodation 289–90
art and culture 112
crime and safety 313
eating out 298
embassies and consulates 315
flora 125
food 102
getting around 288
getting to 285
history 31
money 317
Nile in 21, 144–5
people and society 95, 99
tour operators 319–20
Ethiopian Highlands 145
Ethiopian Orthodox Church 21, 49
etiquette **315**
clothing 257
photography 317–18
Euclid 276
Euphrates, River 85
Ezana, King of Aksum 49

F

facila scarring 95
famine 53, 144
Farid, Samir 109
Faruq, King 66, 67, 152, 264
tomb 257–8
Fashoda 62
Fathy, Hassan 151, 203
Fatimid rule **52–3**, 249
Faw Gibli 212
Fayyum Portraits 248
Feast of Breaking the Fast 318
Feast of the Sacrifice 318
feluccas 6, 8, 10
Aswan 154, 165
chartering 87, **91**
cruises 310
Festival Hall of Thutmose III (Karnak) 191
festivals and events **306**
Aïd Al Adha 306
Anniversary of the 1952 Revolution 318
Armed Forces Day 318
Coptic Christmas 318
Coptic Easter 318
Feast of Breaking the Fast 318
Feast of the Sacrifice 318
food 103
Islamic New Year 318
Labour Day 318
Liberation of Sinai Day 318
Moulid of Abu Al Haggag 306
Moulid An Nabi 306
Prophet's Birthday 318
public holidays 318
Ramadan 93, 103, 104, 306
Sham An Nissim 318
Fiennes, Ralph 119
Fifth Cataract 31
film *see* **cinema**
First Cataract 24, 31, 74, 75, 150
First Intermediate Period 33
Fishawy's (Cairo) 10, **261**
fishing **308**
Lake Nasser 142
Lake Victoria 160
fitness centres 308
Flaubert, Gustave 87, 88, 176
flora 125
Foad, Mohammad 111
food and drink 101–4, 297
best dining 11
restaurants 297–303
football 69, 98, 309
foreign rule 36–8
Forster, E.M. 276
Fouad, Nagua 113
France
colonialism 62, 63
expedition to Egypt 56
Free Officers 66, 67
French Cultural Institute (Cairo) 305
Frescobaldi 85–7
Freund, Karl 118
Fuad, King 65–6, 257
Funj 55
Fur 55
furniture shops 307

G

Gamal, Samia 113
Gardner, Helen 116
gay and lesbian travellers 315–16
Gayer-Anderson Museum (Cairo) 8, **253**
Gazirah Arts Centre (Cairo) 265
Gazirah (Cairo) 245, **264–5**
Gazirah Palace (Cairo) 265
Geb 42, 167
El Geretly, Hassan 110
Geta, Emperor 168
Ghali, Waguih 108
Gielgud, John 117
Giza Plateau
  by moonlight on horseback 10
  camel rides 10
  mapping project 237
  Pyramids of Giza 6, 32–3, 231, **236–40**
  sunset 9
glassware 308
gliding 308
global warming 278
Gnostic movement 46
gods and goddesses
  ancient Egypt 42–3, 167
  animal 121, 178–9
  Nile 32
  Theban triad 188
Goethe Institut (Cairo) 305
Golding, William 87–8
goldsmiths 262, 308
golf 308
Gomhouriya Theatre (Cairo) 305
Gondar (Ethiopia) 144
Gondokoro 79, 80
Gordon, Lady Duff 149
gorillas 160–1
Gorst, Sir Eldon 63
Graeco-Roman Museum (Alexandria) 277–8
Grand Trianon (Alexandria) 279
Granger, Stewart 116
Grant, Captain James 78–9
grave goods 196
grave robbers 58, 199, 204
Great Court (Karnak) 190
Great Hypostyle Hall (Karnak) 190
Great Pyramid (Giza) 40, 85, 114, 157, **237–8**
Greaves, John 41
Greeks 37–8, 45, 46, 78
  Alexandria 275–6, 277
  Hermopolis 226
Groppi (Cairo) 249

H

Hadrian, Emperor 46
Hadrian's Gateway (Philae) 159
Hafez, Abdel Halim 111
haggling 11, 307
the *Haj* 204
Al Hakim, Caliph 52–3, 251
Al Hakim, Tawfiq 107
Hall of the Company of Nine Gods (Dandarah) 211
Hamama, Faten 109
Hamid, Marwan 108
Hamilton, William 274
Hammadi codices 212–13, 250
Hanager Art Centre (Cairo) 264, 304
Hannoville 278
Hapu 192
Hapy 42, 170
Harkhuf 155
Harrison, Rex 117
Hassan, Sultan 257
Hathor 210
  Temple of (Dandarah) 210–12
  Temple of Queen Nefertari (Abu Simbel) 141–2
Hatshepsut, Queen 31
  Chapelle Rouge (Luxor) 192
  obelisks (Luxor) 157, 190–1
  Temple of (Luxor) 200–1
Hawara 34
health 316
Heliopolis 240, 241
  transport 287
Hellenistic Period 37–8, 275–6
Herakleapolis Magna 33
Hermopolis 225, **226**
Herod, King of Judaea 45
Herodotus 33, 34, 74, 78
Heterpheres 241
Heyerdahl, Thor 83–4
hieroglyphics 226
  Rosetta Stone 274
  symbols from nature 121, 178
High Dam (Aswan) see **Aswan Dams**
Hikaptah 232
hippopotamus gods 32
history 26–69
Hittites 36, 141, 202
Hoash Al Basha (Cairo) 264
Honorius, Emperor 48
Horemheb 35, 186
  Temple of (Jabal As Silsilah) 170
horse racing 309
horse riding 233, **308–9**
Horus 43, 217
  Dandarah 211
  Festival of the Coronation 172
  Kom Ombo 168, 169
  Temple of (Edfu) 170–2
hospitality 102
hospitals 316
hotels 289–96
  historic 88
House of the Governor 143
House of the Morning (Edfu) 172
Howard Carter's House (Luxor) 195, 202
human rights 69
hunter gatherers 29–30
hunting 124
Hurghada Airport 284
Husayn Kamil, Sultan 257
Al Hussain ibn Ali 261
Hussein, Taha 107
Hyksos
  Avaris 275
  invasion by 32, 83
  war of liberation 34, 175, **176**, 186
Hypostyle Court (Esna) 176
Hypostyle Hall (Abu Simbel) 141
Hypostyle Hall (Abydos) 214
Hypostyle Hall (Dandarah) 210
Hypostyle Hall (Edfu) 171
Hypostyle Hall (Philae) 159

I

ibis 122
  worship of 225
Ibn al-Haytham 23
Ibn Tuglij, Muhammad 52
Ibn Tuloan, Ahmad 52, 252–3
  mosque (Cairo) 8, **253**
Ibrahim Bey 56
Ibrahim Pasha 60, 61
Ibrahim, Sonallah 107
Ibrim Palace (near Abu Simbel) 142
Id al-Kehir 103
Idku, Lake 275
Idris, Yusuf 107
Iman, Adel 108, 109, 110
Imhotep 42, 233–4
Imhotep Museum (Saqqarah) 233
Inal Amir Qurqumas al-Kabir, Sultan 263
independence 64–5
industries 61, 67
Inherkau, Tomb of (Luxor) 199
Intef 33
internet access 110–11, 316
Iran 54, 55
Iraq 54
irrigation 24, 61, 76, 173
Isis 42, 43, 167, 217
  Temple of (Philae) 158, 159

Islam 93–4
fundamentalism 68, 210
religious services 318
spread of 51–6
Islamic Art Museum (Cairo) 9, **259**
Islamic Ceramics Museum (Cairo) 265
Islamic Group 68
Islamic New Year 318
Ismail, Khedive 62–3
Cairo Opera House 111
Meadan At Tahrir (Cairo) 248
sugar cultivation 177
tomb 257
Israel
conflict with Arabs 68, 281
entering Egypt from 285
Israelites (Biblical) 275

J

Jabal As Silsilah 166, **169–70**
Jabal At Tarif 212
jackals 179
Jami *see* **mosques**
Janissaries 55–6
Jawhar, General 52
Jerome, St 212
Jerusalem 53
jewellery 11, 307–8
Jews 38, 45
Ethiopia 144
Jinja (Uganda) 22–3
Jones, Michael 204
Juba (Sudan) 161
July Revolution 67, 97
Justinian, Emperor 49

K

Ka-Aper 247, 267
Kafr Addawwar 273
Kafur 52
Kalabshah, Temple of (Lake Nasser) 142, **143**
Kamose 176, 186
Kampala (Uganda) 160
Karioka, Tahiya 109
Karnak 7, 183, **188–91**
kayaking 160
Kazazian, George 111
Al Khadem, Saad 112
Khafra 33
Pyramid of (Giza) 239
Sphinx (Giza) 239
statue 247, 266
Valley Temple (Giza) 239
Khalig canal (Cairo) 74, 75
Khalil Collection (Cairo) 265
Khan Al Khalili bazaar (Cairo) 9, **261**
Khan Al Maghraby (Cairo) 304
Khanqat Farg Ibn Barquq (Cairo) 263
Al Kharrat, Edward 108
Khartoum (Sudan)
Blue Nile 21, 22, 31
visiting **145**
White Nile 22, 23, 31
Khnum 226
Temple of (Esna) 176–7
Khonsu 187, 188
Khufu 33, 114
Great Pyramid (Giza) 237–8
Kibale Forest (Uganda) 161
Kitchener, Lord 62, 63
Kitchener's Island (Aswan) 150, **154**
Kléber, General 56
Kom Ad Dekkah (Alexandria) 278–9
open-air museum 279
Kom Al Ahmar 175
Kom Ombo 8, 165, **167–9**
Konya, Battle of 60
Kuchuk Hanem 88, 176
Kush/Kushites 31, 34, 37, 140
Kyoga, Lake (Uganda) 23

L

Labour Day 318
Lake *see by name*
language 321–2
Arabic 94, 321–2
Central Sudanic 95
Nilotic 95
leather 308
left luggage 316
Leigh, Vivien 116
Lesseps, Ferdinand de 61
Liberation of Sinai Day 318
Libya
entering Egypt from 285
history 34, 36, 37
lighthouses
Montazah Park Lighthouse (Alexandria) 275
Pharos of Alexandria 275, 276, 277, **280**
limousines 288
List of Kings (Abydos) 215
literature 107–8, 323
Livingstone, David 81
long-distance taxis 287
lost property 316
Louis IX of France 53–4
Lower Egypt 29, 30–1, 168, 216
Luxor 183–204
see also **Thebes**
accommodation 292
balloon trips 8, 308
eating out 299–300
history 186
massacre 165, 183, 210
night visits 10, 189
Temple of 183, **185–8**
Luxor Airport 284
Luxor Corniche 9, **193**
Luxor Museum 9, 188, **191–3**
Luxor to Abydos 209–16

M

Ma'amoura 278
Macrinus, Emperor 168
Madinat Habu (Luxor) 202
madrassahs
Madrassah An Nassir Muhammad (Cairo) 262
Madrassah and Khanqat Barquq (Cairo) 262
Mosque and Madrassah of Sultan Hassan (Cairo) 257
Magui, Effat 112
Mahfouz, Naguib 93, 107, 261
Mahmudiyyah Canal (Alexandria) 277
Al Mallakh, Kamal 85
Mallawi 225
Mamluks 53–5, 56, 60, 75
Mandulis, Temple of (Lake Nasser) 143
Manetho 31, 38
Mankiewicz, Joseph L. 117
Manuscripts Museum (Alexandria) 280
Manyal Palace complex (Cairo) 264
Manzilah, Lake 275
maps 316
Marchand, Jean-Baptiste 62
Mariette, Auguste
Egyptian Museum (Cairo) 247, 266
Serapeum (Saqqarah) 236
Temple of Horus (Edfu) 171
Temple of Khnum (Esna) 176
Marinus of Tyre 78
Maritim Jolie Ville (Luxor) 124, 292
Marj Dabiq, Battle of 55
Mark, St 46
markets and souqs 7, 9, 10
Aswan Souq 7, 9, **150**
Attarine Souq (Alexandria) 9, 306
Birqash Camel Market 9
Daraw Camel Market 167
Khan Al Khalili bazaar (Cairo) 9, **261**
Luxor Souq 7, 9, **185**
Souq Al Àttarin (Cairo) 260
Souq Al Harireyyin (Cairo) 260
Souq Al Khayyameyyah (Cairo) **258**, 306
Souq An Nahhasin (Cairo) 262
Souq As Saghah (Cairo) 262

marriage 97
Maryut, Lake 275
Mashrabia (Cairo) 304
Mastaba of Mereruka (Saqqarah) 235–6
Mastaba of Ti (Saqqarah) 235
mathematics 41
Matt 196
Mature, Victor 118
Mausoleum of the Aga Khan 153, **156**
Mausoleum Al Imam Ash Shafiì (Cairo) 264
Mausoleum Qalawoan (Cairo) 262
Maydum Pyramid 114, **241**
Meadan At Tahrir (Cairo) 248
Meadan Tal'at Harb (Cairo) 249
Meaden Al Operah (Cairo) 249
Meaden At Tahrir (Alexandria) 279
media 316–17
medical care 316
Meguid, Ibrahim Abdel 107
Mehit Weret 192
Mekhu 155
Memphis 8, **231–3**
  history 31, 186
  museum compound 232
Mena House Oberoi (Giza) 236, 237, 241, 294
Menelik I 144
Menes *see* **Narmer**
Menkaura 33, 115
  Pyramid of (Giza) 239
Mentuhotep 33
Merenptah 195
Merenra 155
Mereruka, Mastaba of (Saqqarah) 235–6
Meri-Re 224
Mesopotamia 34
metro systems 286–7
meze 102–3, 297
Middle Egypt 221–7
  accommodation 293
Middle Kingdom 32, **33–4**
migrations, bird 122
Min 209
Misr Al Qadimah 249–51
Misr Al-Fatat 66
Misr-Fustat 249
missionaries 49
Mit Rahinah 232
Modern Egyptian Art Museum (Cairo) 264
modernisation 61, 62
Mohammad Reza Shah Pahlavi 258
Mokhtar Museum (Cairo) 264
Monastery of St Palomon (Al Qasr) 213
Monastery of St Simeon (Aswan) 156
monasticism 47, 48
Monet, Pierre 273
money 317
Mongol invasions 53, 54
Monophysites 48
Montazah Park (Alexandria) 275, 278
Montazah Park Lighthouse (Alexandria) 275
mortuary temples *see* **temples**
Moses 83–4, 117
mosques
  Abu Al haggag (Luxor) 185–7
  Al Aqmar (Cairo) 262–3
  Al Azhar (Cairo) 7, **260–1**
  Al Ghuri (Cairo) 260
  Al Hakim (Cairo) 263
  Al Maridani (Cairo) 258
  Al Salih Talay (Cairo) 259
  Amir Aqasunqur (Cairo) 258
  Amr Ibn Al 'Ass (Cairo) 251
  An Nasir Muhammad (Cairo) 254
  Ar Rifa'i (Cairo) 257
  At Tabbanah (Alexandria) 279
  Ibn Tuloan (Cairo) 8, **253**
  Muhammad 'Ali (Cairo) 254
  Nabi Danyal (Alexandria) 278
  Qayetbay (Cairo) 264
  Qaymas Al Isshaqi (Cairo) 258
  Sayyedna Al Hussain (Cairo) 261
  Sultan Hassan (Cairo) 257
  Sultan Mu'ayyad Sheikh (Cairo) 260
  Umar Makram (Cairo) 248
Mougel Bey 75
Moulid of Abu Al Haggag 306
Moulid An Nabi 306
Mountains of the Moon 78, 79
Mubarak, Gamal 69
Mubarak, Hosni 68–9, 240
Mubarak Pumping Station 76
Mugamma'a (Cairo) 248
Muhammad Mahmud and Emilienne Luce Khalil Museum (Cairo) 265
Muhammad, the Prophet 51, 94, 112
Muhammad Ali Pasha 60–2, 75, 176, 264
  Alexandria 277, 279, 280
  Mosque (Cairo) 254
  statue (Cairo) 249
Muhammad Ali, Prince 264
Muharraqah, Temple of (Lake Nasser) 143
Al Mu'izz, Caliph 52
Mukhtar, Mahmoud 112
mummification 193, 194, 248, **256**
Mummification Museum (Luxor) 10, **193**
Murad Bey 56
Murchison Falls National Park (Uganda) 23, **161**
Murchison, Sir Roderick 79, 81
museums and galleries
  best 9
  American Museum (Cairo) 204
  Bibliotheca Alexandria 280
  Carriage Museum (Cairo) 255
  Cavafy Museum (Alexandria) 278
  Coptic Museum (Cairo) 213, **250**
  Egyptian Military Museum (Cairo) 255
  Egyptian Museum (Cairo) 7, 9, 59, **247–8**, **266–7**
  Elephantine Island museum (Aswan) 152
  Gayer-Anderson Museum (Cairo) 8, **253**
  Gazirah Arts Centre (Cairo) 265
  Graeco-Roman Museum (Alexandria) 277–8
  Hanager Art Centre (Cairo) 264
  Imhotep Museum (Saqqarah) 233
  Islamic Ceramics Museum (Cairo) 265
  Khalil Collection (Cairo) 265
  Kom Ad Dekkah open-air museum (Alexandria) 279
  Luxor Museum 9, 188, **191–3**
  Mallawi museum 225
  Manuscripts Museum (Alexandria) 280
  Memphis museum compound 232
  Mokhtar Museum (Cairo) 264
  Muhammad Mahmud and Emilienne Luce Khalil Museum (Cairo) 265
  Mummification Museum (Luxor) 10, **193**
  Museum of Islamic Art (Cairo) 9, **259**
  Museum of Modern Egyptian Art (Cairo) 264
  National Museum of Alexandria 9, **278**
  National Museum of Sudan (Khartoum) 145
  National Police Museum (Cairo) 255
  Nubia Museum (Aswan) 9, 137, **152**
  Open Air Museum (Karnak) 191
  Palace Museum (Khartoum) 145
  Royal Jewellery Museum (Alexandria) 280
  Solar Boat Museum (Giza) 238–9

Town House Gallery (Cairo) 113
Umm Kulthum Museum (Cairo) 252
music 111, 304–5
instruments 308
Nubian 138
shopping for 11, 308
Les Musicians du Nil 111
Muski glass 308
Muslim Brotherhood 66, 67
Muslim calendar 312
Muslims 93–4
see also **Islam**
Al Mustansir, Caliph 53
Mut 187, 188
Mutesa, King 79, 80

N

Nabi Danyal mosque (Alexandria) 278
Nag Hammadi 213
Nag Hammadi Codices 46
Nagui, Mohammad 112
Nakht, Tomb of (Luxor) 200
Nalubaale Hydroelectric Power Station 23
Napoleon
Egyptian expedition 56, 88
and Great Pyramid 41
Nile projects 75
and Rosetta Stone 274
savants of 40, 41, 58, 190
Narmer 31–2, 73
Memphis 231
Narmer Palette 175, 247
Thinis 216
An Nasir Muhammad 54–5, 262
mosque (Cairo) 254
Nassallah, Yousri 109
Nasser, Gamal Abdel 67–8, 76
Suez Crisis 66, 277, 281
Nasser, Lake
accommodation 290
activities 142
creation of 24, 76, 137
cruises 90, 138, 142, 143, **309**
National Museum of Alexandria 9, **278**
National Museum of Sudan (Khartoum) 145
national parks, Murchison Falls National Park (Uganda) 23, **161**
National Police Museum (Cairo) 255
nationalism 63, 64, 277
Naucratis 272
Navarino, Battle of 60
Nebhetepre Mentuhotep, Temple of (Luxor) 201
Nectanebo I 159
Nectanebo II 153
Neferhotep 215
Neferirkare Pyramid (Abu Sir) 236
Nefertari 138
Temple of (Abu Simbel) 141
tomb (Luxor) **199**, 202
Nefertiti 200, 223, **226**
Neguib, General 67
Nekhen 175
Neolithic era 31
Neoplatonism 47
Neos Dionysos *see* **Ptolemy XII**
Nephtys 42, 167
Nero, Emperor 78, 211
New Kingdom 32, **34–6**, 176, 186
Newell, Mike 118
newspapers 316–17
Nicene Creed 48
nightlife 10
Nile, River 21–4
cruising 83–91
delta 19, **24**, 76, 231, **271–81**
dependence on 29, 73
floods 19, 23, 29, 73
people 93–9
search for source 78–81
taming 73–6
wildlife 121–4, 178–9
Nile Hilton (Cairo) 248–9
Nilometers
Aswan 152–3
Cairo 74, **251–2**
Edfu 172
Nitiqret, Queen 73
Nobles, Tombs of the (Aswan) 154–5
Nobles, Tombs of the (Luxor) 179, **199–200**
Nofret 241
North Wall (Cairo) 263
Northern Cemetery (Cairo) 263
Nubia 137–43
accommodation 290
and Aswan High Dam 24, 76, 137, 140
history 23–4, 34, 51, 74, 140
people and culture 99, 137, **138**, 140
visiting villages/homes **151**, 167
Nubia Museum (Aswan) 9, 137, **152**
Nur ad-Din 53
Nut 42, 167

O

obelisks
Queen Hatshepsut (Karnak) 157, **190–1**
Sety I (Alexandria) 279
Temple of Luxor 185
unfinished obelisk (Aswan) 157
Octavian *see* **Augustus, Emperor**
oil (Sudan) 145
Old Aswan Dam *see* **Aswan Dams**
Old Kingdom 31–3
Ombos 167–8
Open Air Museum (Karnak) 191
opening hours 317
monuments 255
opera 111, 304
Opera House (Cairo) 111, 249, **264**, 304, 305
Opet Festival 187–8
Orabi revolt 277
orientation 286
Origen 46
Osirion (Abydos) 215–16
Osiris 42, 43, 158, 159, 167
Abydos 213–16
cult of **217**
Um Al Gab 216
Osiris Room (Philae) 159
Osorkon II 273
Ottoman Turks 55–6, 60, 64

P

Pachomius, St 48, 212
Palace Museum (Khartoum) 145
palaces
Al Gawharah Palace (Cairo) 254–5
Al Harim Palace (Cairo) 255
Al Manisterli Palace (Cairo) 252
Bashtak Palace (Cairo) 262
Cleopatra's Palace (Alexandria) 277
Gazirah Palace (Cairo) 265
Ibrim Palace (near Abu Simbel) 142
Manyal Palace complex (Cairo) 264
Palace Museum (Khartoum) 145
Palaearctic-African Bird Migration 122
Palaeolithic era 29–30
Palestine 34, 38, 53, 54, 55, 66
palm trees 125
Palomon, St 212, 213
Panehese 224
Pantanaeus 46
papyrus 11, **179**, 308
parks and gardens
Al Azhar Park (Cairo) 10, **255–7**
Botanical Garden (Kitchener's Island) 154

Montazah Park (Alexandria) 275, 278
Murchison Falls National Park (Uganda) 23, **161**
Pascal, Gabriel 116
passports 320
Paul, St 47
Pennut, Tomb of (Lake Nasser) 143
Pentu 224
people 93–9
Pepy I 155
Pepy II 155
perfumes 11, 308
Persians 37–8, 45, 51
Petosiris 225
Pettigrew, T.J. 256
pharaohs
chronology 215
festivals 203
funerary practices 195–6, 237
incarnations of Horus 172
New Year Festival 172
pharmacies 316
Pharos of Alexandria 275, 276, 277, **280**
Philae 158–9
rescue of temple 75–6, 137, 158
Philippe II of France 53
photography 317–18
Piankhy 37
piety 93–4
pilgrimages 213
plague 53
Pliny 84
Plutarch 217
political tensions 99
pollution 204, 278
polygamy 97
Pompey 39
Pompey's Pillar (Alexandria) 280
popular culture 107–13
population 96
Cairo 245
Porphyry 47
porter service 284
postal services 318
pottery, *ballas* 209–10
poverty 95, 96
Precinct of Amun-Ra (Karnak) 189
prices 311–12
pride 95, 97
private transport 288
Prophet's Birthday 318
Protectorate 64–5
Psamtek 37
Psusennes II 273
Ptah 42, 232
Ptolemaic dynasty 38–9, 45, 275–6
Ptolemy I 38
Ptolemy II 38, 280
Ptolemy V 168, 274
Ptolemy VIII 168
Ptolemy XII 39, 168, 171
Ptolemy, Claudius 78
public holidays 318
public transport 286–7
Punt 31
puppets 305
Pylons
Luxor 189
Philae 159
Pyramid Texts 234
pyramids
"Bent" Pyramid of Dahshur 114, 115, **240–1**
Black Pyramid (Dahshur) 240
buidling materials 115
building of 32–3, 73–4, 83, **114–15**
grave robbers and curses 58–9
Great Pyramid (Giza) 40, 85, 114, 157, **237–8**
Pyramid of Al Lahun 241
Pyramid Complex of Amenemhat II (Al Hawrah) 241
Pyramid of Khafra (Giza) 239
Pyramid of Khufu *see* Great Pyramid
Pyramid of Maydum 114, **241**
Pyramid of Menkaura (Giza) 115, 157, **239**
Pyramid of Neferirkare (Abu Sir) 236
Pyramid of Sahure (Abu Sir) 236
Pyramid of Unas (Saqqarah) 234–5
pyramidology and pyramidiocy 40–1
Pyramids of Al Lisht 241
Pyramids of Giza 6, 32–3, 231, **236–40**
Red Pyramid (Dahshur) 114, **240**
Step Pyramid of Zoser (Saqqarah) 8, 114, **233–4**
Unfinished Pyramid (Zawiyat Al Aryan) 236
visiting 233
Pyramids, Battle of the 56
Pythagoras 41

Q

Qadesh, Battle of 36, 141, 185
Qal'at Qayetbay, Sultan 280
mosque (Cairo) 264
Qalawun, Sultan 54, 262
Qansuh al-Ghuri, Sultan 260
Qarun, Lake 124
Qasabah (Cairo) 259
Qasr *see* **palaces**
Qaymas Al Isshaqi mosque (Cairo) 258
Qena 209, 210
Qerbah 216
Qift 209, 210
quarries 157
Qur'an 93, 94, 104

R

Ra 42, 114, 249
Ra I* and *Ra II 84
Ra-Horakhty 138
racial tensions 94
radio 107, 316
Rafelson, Bob 119
Rahotep, Prince 241, 247
rail travel 286
rainfall 29
Rains, Claude 116
Ramadan 93, 103, 104, 306
Rameses I 36, 186
mummy 192
Rameses II 36, 186
mummy 202, 248
and Nefertari 202
Ramesseum (Luxor) 185, **202**
sons of 195
statue (Memphis) 232
Temple of (Abu Simbel) 137, **141**
Temple of (Abydos) 215
Temple of Luxor 185
Rameses III 36, 185
Karnak 190
Madinat Habu (Luxor) 203
mummy 248
Rameses VI, tomb 196, 198
Rameses XI 186
Ramesseum (Luxor) 185, **202**
Ramose, Tomb of (Luxor) 200
Ra's Al Barr 275, 278
Red Pyramid (Dahshur) 114, **240**
Red Sea canals 74, 75
reincarnation 216
Rekhmire, Tomb of (Luxor) 199–200
religious services 318
religious tensions 94, 224
restaurants 101, 297–303
best 11
resurrection myth 30
Revolution of 1919 64
Richard the Lionheart 53
Ripon Falls 79, 81, 160
road travel 285
Roadah (Cairo) 245, 249, **251–3**, 264
Robson, Flora 116
Roman Basilica (Dandarah) 212
Romans 39, 45–8, 75, 78

Rosetta **275**, 278
Rosetta Stone 247, **274**
Rossellini, Roberto 119
Rostom, Hind 109
Royal Geographical Society 78, 79, 80, 81
Royal Jewellery Museum (Alexandria) 280
rugs 235, 307
running 309
Russia 60

S

Saad Wafd 66
sabil-kuttub 262
Sabni 155
Saccas, Ammonius 47
Sacred Lake (Karnak) 191
Al Sadat, Anwar 68, 138
safety 99, 313
  Sudan 145, 313
  Uganda 161, 313
Safinaz, Queen 280
Saheylle Island 154, **156**
Sahure Pyramid (Abu Sir) 236
Said I 61–2, 63
Said, Mahmoud 112
sails 83, 84
St Barbara Church (Cairo) 251
St George Greek Orthodox Church (Cairo) 250
St Sergius Church (Cairo) 250
Sais 272
Saite Period 37
Saladin (Salah Addin) 53, 254, 264
As Salih, Sultan 53–4
Salih, Talib 112
Salmawy, Mohammad 110
Saloga Island (Aswan) 124
Sanctuary (Edfu) 172
Saqqarah 8, 231, **233–6**
  first pyramids 33, **233**
Sarayat Al Gabal Theatre (Cairo) 260
Sasanians 51
Satet, Temple of (Yebu) 153
Sayhel Island 8
Sayyedna Al Hussain (Cairo) 261
scams, hotel 289
scarab beetles 178
Scaturro, Pasquale 119
School of Fine Arts (Cairo) 112
Scott, Walter 254
Scott-Moncrieff, Sir Colin 75
Scott Thomas, Kristin 119
Sea Peoples 199, 203
sea travel 285
sediment 23, 29, 76, 178
Sekhmet 42
Selim the Grim, Sultan 55
Seljuk Turks 53
Senmut 201
Sennar 55
Sennar Dam 22
Sennedjem, Tomb of (Luxor) 199
Senusret I 241
Senusret II 241
Senusret III 221
Seqenenra 186
Serapeum (Alexandria) 280
Serapeum (Saqqarah) 236
Serapis 277, 278, 280
service taxis 287
Seshat 214
Sesostris III 74
Seth 42, 43, 167, 168, 171, 217
Sety I 35, 36, 185, 186, 190
  mummy 248
  obelisk (Alexandria) 279
  Temple of (Abydos) 214–15
  Temple of (Luxor) 202
  tomb 196, **197**
Shaarawi, Hoda 97
Shagar Ad-Durr 54
Sham An Nissim 318
Shari' Ad Darb Al Ahmar (Cairo) 258, 259
Shari' Ahmad Mahir (Cairo) 259
Shari' Al Azhar (Cairo) 259–60
Shari' An Nabi Danyal (Alexandria) 278
Shari' As Salibah (Cairo) 254
Shari' Tariq Al Hurreyyah (Alexandria) 278
Sharif, Omar 109
Al Sharqawi, Abdel Rahman 107
Shaw, George Bernard 116
Shaykh Airport 284
Sheba, Queen of 144
sheesha 6, 11, 261
Shepheard's Hotel (Cairo) 88
Sheshonq 36
Shi'a Muslims 52
shopping **306–8**
  see also **markets and souqs**
  best buys 11
  opening hours 317
  tips 307
Shu 42, 167
Sidi Krear 278
Siemens, Sir W. 40
silk merchants 260
silverware 262, 308
Simmons, Jean 118
Siwah Oasis 37
Six Day War 281
Sixth Cataract 24, 31
Smenkhkara 35, 223
smuggling 59
Sneferu 33
Snofru 114, 240–1
Soane, Sir John 197
Sobek 32, 121, 170, 192
  Kom Ombo 168, 169
Sofitel Old Cataract Hotel (Aswan) 9, 88, **151–2**, 291
Sofitel Old Winter Palace Hotel (Luxor) 88, **193**, 292
Sokar 233
Solar Boat **84**, 85, **238–9**
Solar Boat Museum (Giza) 238–9
Solomon, King 144
Sostratus 280
Soueif, Ahdaf 107, 108
sound and light shows 10, **305**
  Abu Simbel 141
  Aswan 305
  Giza 240, 305
  Karnak 192, 305
  Philae 159
souqs *see* **markets and souqs**
Southern Cemetery (Cairo) 264
Speke, John Hanning 78–80, 81, 119
Sphinx (Giza) 6, **239–40**
sphinx, alabaster (Memphis) 232
Sphinx Theatre (Giza) 240
spices 11, 151
spirits 298
sport 308–9
Stack, Sir Lee 65
Stanley, Henry Morton **81**, 160
Stanwood, August 256
Stele of Apries (Memphis) 233
Step Pyramid of Zoser (Saqqarah) 8, 114, **233–4**
Stoker, Bram 118
storytellers 107
Strabo 41
street food 297
Sudan
  accommodation 290
  art and culture 112
  Civil War 161
  crime and safety 145, 313
  eating out 298
  embassies and consulates 315
  entering Egypt from 285
  flora and fauna 121, 125
  food 102
  getting around 288
  getting to 285
  history 64, 65, 69
  money 317
  Nile in 21–4, 144–5, 161
  people and society 94–5, 99
  tour operators 320
  visiting **161**
Sudd swamp (Sudan) 23
Suez Canal 63, **281**
  opening of 62, 81, 111
  proposals for 61, 75
Suez Crisis 66, 67, 281
Sufis 273

dance performances 10, 113, 260
sugar cultivation 177
Sultan Hassan mosque (Cairo) 257
Sultan Mu'ayyad Sheikh mosque (Cairo) 260
sun-god 224
Sunni Muslims 52, 53
sunsets 9
Sydney, Basil 116
Syria 34, 36, 53, 54, 60, 68
see also **Hyksos**

T

Tafa, Temple of (Leiden) 139
Al Tahawi, Miral 108
Taher, Bahaa 107, 108
Tal Al Muqattam 231
Talkha 273
Tall Ad-Dabah 273–5
Tall Al-Amarnah 34–5, 186, **222–4**
Tana, Lake 21–2, 84, **144–5**
Tanganyika, Lake 78, 81
Tanis 266, 272, **273–5**
Al Tannoura Egyptian Heritage Dance Troupe 260, 304
Tanta 273
Tawfiq 63
taxis 287, 288
Taylor, Elizabeth 117
Taylor, John 40
Tefnut 42
telephone services 318–19
television 107, **110**, 316
Tell al-Kabir, Battle of 63
temperatures 312
temples
Abu Simbel 7, **139–42**
Madinat Habu (Luxor) 203
Mortuary Temple of Thutmose III (Luxor) 201
Ramesseum (Luxor) 185, **202**
Temple of Amadah (Lake Nasser) 142
Temple of Amun-Ra (Karnak) 7, 183, **188–91**
Temple of Dakkah (Lake Nasser) 143
Temple of Debod (Madrid) 139
Temple of Derr (Lake Nasser) 142
Temple of Hathor (Dandarah) 209, **210–12**
Temple of Hatshepsut (Luxor) 8, 194, **200–1**
Temple of Horemheb (Jabal As Silsilah) 170
Temple of Horus (Edfu) 153, **170–2**
Temple of Isis (Philae) 8, 75–6, **158–9**
Temple of Kalabshah (Lake Nasser) 142, **143**
Temple of Khafra 157
Temple of Khnum (Esna) 176–7
Temple of Kom Ombo 167–9
Temple of Luxor 183, **185–8**
Temple of Mandulis (Lake Nasser) 143
Temple of Muharraqah (Lake Nasser) 143
Temple of Nebhetepre Mentuhotep (Luxor) 201
Temple of Queen Nefertari (Abu Simbel) 141–2
Temple of Rameses II (Abu Simbel) 141
Temple of Rameses II (Abydos) 215
Temple of Rameses III (Karnak) 190
Temple of Satet (Yebu) 153
Temple of Sety I (Abydos) 214–15
Temple of Sety I (Luxor) 202
Temple of Thoth (Hermopolis) 226
Temple of Wadi Abbad 174
Temples of Tafa (Leiden) 139
Valley Temple (Giza) 239
tentmakers 258, 306
terrorism 68, 165, 183, 210, 221, 261
textiles 11, 307
theatre 110, 304–5
theatres
Al Genena Theatre (Cairo) 304
Al Qawmi (National) Theatre (Cairo) 304
American University in Cairo Theatre 305
Cairo Puppet Theatre 305
Gomhouriya Theatre (Cairo) 305
Opera House (Cairo) 111, 249, **264**, 304, **305**
Thebes
see also **Luxor**
history 31, 33, 34, 177, **186**
mapping project 204
Theodora, Empress 49
Theodosius I, Emperor 48
Theophilus 48
Thinis 213, **216**
Thoth 121, 178, 225
Temple of (Hermopolis) 226
Thutmose I 174, 199, 201, 248
Thutmose II 201, 248
Thutmose III 34, 176, 183, 191
Mortuary Temple (Luxor) 201
mummy 248
tomb 197
Thutmose IV 200
Ti, Mastaba of (Saqqarah) 235
Tiberius, Emperor 168, 211
time zone 319
tipping 317
Tiye 266
toilets 319
tombs
Al Kab 174–5
B Tombs (Saqqarah) 235
Beni Hassan 226–7
Catacombs of Kom Ash Shuqafa (Alexandria) 280
grave goods 196
grave robbers and curses **58**, 204
Hoash Al Basha (Cairo) 264
living among 203, 263
Mastaba of Mereruka (Saqqarah) 235–6
Mastaba of Ti (Saqqarah) 235
Mausoleum of the Aga Khan 153, **156**
Mausoleum Al Imam Ash Shafiì (Cairo) 264
Mausoleum Qalawoan (Cairo) 262
ministers and viziers 115
noblemen's tombs (Saqqarah) 235
Serapeum (Saqqarah) 236
Tomb of Ahmose (Tall Al Armanah) 224
Tomb of Akhenaten (Tall Al Amarnah) 223–4
Tomb of Amenemhat (Beni Hassan) 227
Tomb of Inherkau (Luxor) 199
Tomb of Meri-Re (Tall Al Armanah) 224
Tomb of Nakht (Luxor) 200
Tomb of Nefertari (Luxor) 199
Tomb of Panehesi (Tall Al Armanah) 224
Tomb of Pennut (Lake Nasser) 143
Tomb of Pentu (Tall Al Armanah) 224
Tomb of Petosiris (Tunat Al Jabal) 225
Tomb of Prince Amenherchopeshef (Luxor) 199
Tomb of Ramose (Luxor) 200
Tomb of Rekhmire (Luxor) 199–200
Tomb of Sennedjem (Luxor) 199
Tomb of Sety I (Luxor) 197
Tomb of Thutmose III (Luxor) 197
Tomb of Tutankhamun (Luxor) 196–8
Tombs of the Nobles (Aswan) 154–5
Tombs of the Nobles (Luxor) 179, **199–200**

Um Al Gab 216
Valley of the Kings (Luxor) 6, 10, 183, **195–7**
Valley of the Queens (Luxor) 183, **199**
visiting 195
Toshka Project 76
tour operators 319–20
tourist information 319
Town House Gallery (Cairo) 113, 304
trade routes (ancient) 32
Trajan, Emperor 45, 153
Trajan Decius, Emperor 177
Trajan's Kiosk (Philae) 159
trams 286–7
transliteration 321
transport 284–8
travel agents 319–20
travel restrictions 87, 90, 133, **210**, 221–2
traveller's cheques 317
travellers' tips 11
tribal diversity 94, 95
Tunat Al Jabal 221, **225–6**
Turan Shah 54
Turkish slave armies 51–2, 53, **54**
Tutankhamun 35
curse of 58
Egyptian Museum (Cairo) 248, 266–7
tomb 192, **196–8**, 267

U

Uganda
accommodation 290
art and culture 112
crime and safety 161, 313
eating out 298
embassies and consulates 315
flora and fauna 121, 125
food 102
getting around 288
getting to 285, 288
money 317
Nile in 22–3, 160–1
people and society 95, 99
tour operators 320
Um Al Gab 216
Umar Makram mosque (Cairo) 248
Umm Kulthum 109, **110**, 111, **251**, 252
Umm Kulthum Museum (Cairo) 252
Umm Sety 216
Unas Pyramid (Saqqarah) 234–5
unfinished obelisk (Aswan) 157
Unfinished Pyramid (Zawiyat Al Aryan) 236
United Arab Republic 68
Upper Egypt 29, 30, 31, 168, 217, 221
Ustinov, Peter 119

V

Valley of the Kings (Luxor) 6, 183, **195–7**
donkey rides 10
Valley of the Lions (Lake Nasser) 142
Valley of the Queens (Luxor) 183, **199**
Valley Temple (Giza) 239
vegetarians 297
the veil 97
Verdi, Giuseppe, *Aida* 111, 185
Victoria, Lake (Uganda) 22, 79, 81
activities 160
village life 94, 95, 97
visas 320

W

Wadi Abbad, Temple of 174
Wadi Al Hammamat 209
Wadjyt 178
Wafd 64, 65–6, 67, 68
Wahab, Mohammad Abdel 111
water, drinking 104
weddings 96
weights and measures 320
Wepwawet 179
West Bank (Luxor) **193–204**, 292
Western Desert 177
whirling dervishes 10, 113, 260
White Nile 21, 22, 78, 145, **160–1**
white-water rafting 160
Wikala Al Ghouri (Cairo) 113, 260
wikalahs 259
wildlife 121–4, 178–9
see also **birdlife**
gorillas 160–1
Murchison Falls National Park 161
wine 104, 298
women
in Egypt 97
Nubian 152
in Sudan 94
travellers 320
in Uganda 95
wood carving 112, 307
World War II 66

Y

yachting 309
Yam 31
Yebu (Elephantine Island) 153
Yemen 68
Yom Kippur War 281
Young, Thomas 274
Yusuf Kamal, Prince 112

Z

Zaghul, Saad 64, 65–6
Zaghul, Safia 64
Zamalek Sporting Club 98
Zamalik Art Gallery (Cairo) 304
Zamalik (Cairo) 245, **265**
Zangids of Mosul 53
Zawiyat Al Aryan 236
Zoser *see* **Djoser**
Zouhreyyet Al Mayteen (Al Menyyah) 227

IMBABAH
Birqash Camel Market
Shubra Kiosk
Sh. Tur'at Ghaz. Badran
Sh. Masarrah
Massara
SHUBRA
Shari' Ibn Al Kurani
St Mark's Monastery
Shari' Shubra
Shari' Ahmad Badawi
Shari' Al Attar
Shari' Ahmad Hilmi
Sh. AL Imam
ASHSHARRABEYYAH
Shari' Al Khalig Al Masri
Shari' Sittah Octuber
Shari' Ahmad Lutfi As Sayyed
Shari' Ramssis
Ghamra
Abdo Pasda
AL ABBASSEYYAH
Shari' As Sakakini
Shari' Boar Sa'id
Shari' Al Abbasseyyah
AL ZAHIR
Meadan Al Geash
Al Geash
Sultan Baybars
GHAMRAH
Shari' Az Zahir
Shari' Ramssis
Rameses Railway Station
Railway Museum
Meadan Rameses
Mubarak
BAB ASH SHA'REYYAH
Shari' Kamil Sidqi Basha
Shari' Al Geash
AL HUSANEYYAH
page 258
Bab Al Futuh
Bab An Nassr Cemetery
Bab An Nassr
Al Hakim
Meadan Bab al-Shai'yyah
Bab Al Shai'yyah
Al Ahmar Massgid
AL MUSSKI
Shari' Al Geash
Madrasat wa Khanqat Sultan Barquq
Bayt As Shaimi
AL GAMALEYYAH
Madrasat An Nasir Muhammad
Madrasat wa mosoleyum Qalawoan
Sh. Al Mu'ez Li Dinillah
As Salih Najm Addin Mausoleum
KHAN AL KHALILI
Sayyedna Al Hussain
Shari' Al Musski
Shari' Al Azhar
Barsbay
Al Azhar Massgid & University
Sh.Goahar Al Qa'id
Museum of Islamic Art
AL GHUMHREYYAH
Sultan Mu'ayyad Shaykh
Bab Zowaylah
Meadan Ahmad Mahir
Shari' Al Mansu yyah
Shari' Salah Salim
Khangat Farg Ibn Barquq
Sultan Al Ashraf Bersbay
Qayetbay
Bab Al Wazir
AZ ZAMALIK
Shari' Ummu Kulthum
Shari' An nil
An nil (Nile)
Korneash (Corniche) An Nil
Sh.Abu al-Farag
AS SABTEYYAH
Shari' Assabteyyah
Gazirat Badran
Shari' Isma'il Muhammad
Shari' Sitt wa Shrin Yulyu
Sinan Pasha
Akhenaten Centre of the Arts
World Trade Centre
Shari' Bulaq Al Gadid
AL QULALI
Sh. Al Mansuri
Shari' Shanan
Meadan Al Qulali
BULAQ
Shari' Sitta wa 'eshrin Yulyu
Kubri sitta wa 'eshrin Yulyu
Gazirah Arts Centre & Museum of Islamic Ceramics
Marriott Hotel
FISH GARDEN
Sh. Hasan Sabri
Shari' Al Gazirah
AL GAZIRAH
British Council
Shari' Gamal 'bd An nassir
Shari' Hassan Pasha
Gazirah Sporting Club
AL 'AGUZAH
Shari' Al Mathaf Az Zera'i
Kubri Sittah October
Cairo Tower
Museum of Modern Egyptian Art
Opera
Shari' Al Gabalayah
Sh. Assad
Kubri At tahrir
Korneash (Corniche) An nil
Radio & TV Building
River Bus Terminus
Rameses Hilton Hotel
Egyptian Museum
Nile Hilton Hotel
Umar Makram
Ass Sadat
Meadan At tahrir
American
Shari' Al Gala
Shari' Sittah October
'Urabi
Shari' 'Urabi
Nasir
Shari' Sittah wa 'shrin Yulyu
Old Cathedral of St Mark
Shari' Clot Bey
AL AZBAKEYYAH
Synagogue
Attaba
Meadan Al Opera
Meadan Al'atabah
Shari' Ramssis
Law Courts
Tal'at Harb
Meadan Mustafa Kamil
Central Post Office
Shari' Al Gumhureyyah
Shari' 'bd Al 'aziz
Shari' Al Qal'ah
Meadan Tal'at Harb
Qasr An nil
Groppi's
St Joseph's
Bank Misr
Abdeen
Sh. Al Bosstan
Meadan Al Falaki
Shari' Hassan Al Akbar
Farid
Qasr 'bdin (Abdin Palace)
At tahrir